edited by **GAYL D NESS &**

PREM P TALWAR

ASIAN
URBANIZATION
IN THE NEW
MILLENNIUM

AUICK
Asian Urban Information Center of Kobe

mc **Marshall Cavendish**
Academic

© 2005 Marshall Cavendish International (Singapore) Private Limited

Published 2005 by Marshall Cavendish Academic
An imprint of Marshall Cavendish International (Singapore) Private Limited
A member of Times Publishing Limited

Times Centre, 1 New Industrial Road,
Singapore 536196
Tel: (65) 6213 9300
Fax: (65) 6284 9772
E-mail: mca@sg.marshallcavendish.com
Website: http://www.marshallcavendish.com/academic

First published 2005
Reprinted 2005

ISBN-13: 978-981-210-345-1
ISBN-10: 981-210-345-7

A CIP catalogue record for this book is available from the National Library Board of Singapore.

Printed by Times Graphics Pte Ltd, Singapore
on non-acidic paper

London • New York • Beijing • Bangkok • Kuala Lumpur • Singapore

Contents

CHAPTER 1

Asian Cities: From Past to Future

GAYL D. NESS AND PREM P. TALWAR[1]

THE LONG PAST AND DISTINCTIVE CHARACTERISTICS

Asian urbanization has a long past and is rapidly moving to a radically new future. The past is not only long, but in many ways distinctive. We must begin by reviewing briefly the long history to identify the distinctive and enduring characteristics of Asian urbanization. We can then turn to the radical changes now underway.

THE ANCIENT PAST

Modern human populations arose probably 100 to 200 thousand years ago, first as hunters and gatherers. About 10,000 years ago, an agricultural transition took place in different parts of the world. Following agriculture, came another slow but profound transition to urban societies. The world's first villages arose in the Middle East some 5,000 years ago. The next millennium saw the rise of the great historic civilizations. Large-scale political organizations that exercised control over a substantial population arose at roughly the same time in the valleys of the Tigris and Euphrates, the Nile, and Indus rivers (Basham 1954, 14). Much more is known about the Nile and Euphrates civilizations (Whitmore et al. 1990, 25–39) as these left extensive writings that have become the standard texts of ancient history. The Indus civilization is less well documented and has as yet no decoded written texts. Nonetheless, archeological evidence shows it to have had a rich agricultural, village and urban civilization. Balochistan, for example, which we now know as a barren desert, was then heavily forested and watered by many rivers. Here, and to the west in Sind, the Harappa culture arose, with its urban jewels in Moenjodaro (literally

1

"mound of the dead") and Chanu Daro (Basham 1954). It was followed by the Aryan invasions and the Rig-Veda civilization of India, with major urban centers in what is now northern India and the Ganges Valley. Rajasthan, like Balochistan, now a desert, was a well-watered country 4,000 years ago, and also knew major urban centers of the Rig Veda civilization.

Farther east in China, major civilizations with urban centers can be traced back 4,000 years (Eberhard 1960). The Yangtze and Huang Ho river valleys, like the Nile, Euphrates, and Indus, supported relatively high population densities and urban centers. Rich and well-watered soils supported a productive agriculture. In Asia, as in the Middle East, agriculture provided a base for the emerging urban civilizations.

What is distinctive, and would prove to be enduring, in these ancient Asian urban civilizations, was that they were supported by rich and productive agricultural hinterlands. They all knew trade, to be sure, but their wealth was derived primarily from the surrounding area. More important, this hinterland was organized to produce an agricultural surplus to support the urban centers. From this surplus, the urban civilizations produced major arts and crafts, often of staggering complexity and creativity.

Much has changed since these early urban civilizations. Ecological changes have turned once rich lands into deserts, as in Balochistan and Rajasthan. East and Southeast Asia, on the other hand, have known more ecological stability. Throughout Asia, however, cities and civilizations rose and declined under combined environmental and human social changes. Militant civilizations arose and conquered surrounding territories. They imposed new rules, religions and arts, only to be conquered in turn by other militant civilizations. Throughout the 4,000 to 5,000 years from the third millennium BC to the present, however, the major Asian urban civilizations continued to be built primarily on the surplus of the urban hinterland (Murphey 1989, 242).

THE PAST 1,000 YEARS

One thousand years ago, the world's total population was about 265 million, less than the current population of the United States (McEvedy and Jones 1978). More than half the world's population at that time, 185 million or about 70 per cent, lived in Asia. By that time, Asia was also the world's leading area of urbanization. This would remain the case until

2

the 19th century, as is clear when we examine the location of the world's 25 largest cities (Chandler and Fox 1974).

As early as 430 BC, 14 of the world's 25 largest cities were in Asia; six in India and eight in China. Around the turn of the millennium, the rise of the Roman Empire heralded a rapid urbanization in the Mediterranean basin. In 100 AD, 12 of the world's 25 largest cities were under the Roman Empire. Asia then had only six of the 25 largest; one in India, one in Sri Lanka and four in China. Two centuries later, Asia with 11 and Rome with 10 were in near balance. By 600 AD, Rome had declined and Asia again dominated with 14 of the 25 largest. In addition to India's six and China's five, Myanmar, Cambodia and Sri Lanka each had one on the list. For the next 1,200 years, Asia would have half or more of the 25 largest cities. The Middle East and Mediterranean basin made up the remainder.

European cities did not make the list until 800 AD when Cordova was among the 25 largest. For the next five centuries, Europe would contribute only one or two to the list. From 1400 to 1800, Europe had four to six cities on the list. Even when the urban industrial tide had risen to produce more and larger Western cities, Asia remained the center of the largest cities. In 1850, for example, when Europe had seven and the United States two of the 25 largest, there were still 11 in Asia. By 1900, the urban industrial revolution had radically shifted the distribution of the world's 25 largest cities. In that year, Europe had 10, the United States four, and Asia's number had fallen to only five.

The size of the large cities did not remain static over the last millennium, of course. Figures 1.1 and 1.2 show the rising size of the largest and the smallest cities of the top 25 from the years 1000 to 1900. In 1000 AD, Cordova, in Muslim Spain, was the world's largest city with some 425,000 people. For the next eight centuries an Asian city led the list, and the size grew gradually to about 700,000 in 1700, and then rose quickly to 1,100,000 in 1800, when Beijing was the world's largest. In the next century, we saw an exponential growth in city size. London was then the world's largest city with over six million inhabitants. This long history is quite remarkable for its long-term stability and recent exponential change. For two millennia the world's largest cities hovered around half a million, with occasional spurts to one million. After 1800, the size of the largest cities rose to five, then 10 and now over 20 million. Obviously, this modern period is highly distinctive.

3

FIGURE 1.1 Size of the the world's larglst cities 1000–1800 (showing population of the largest and smallest of the top 25)

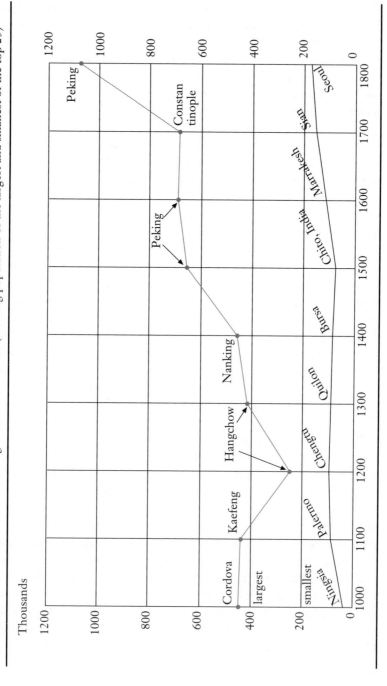

FIGURE 1.2   Size of the world's largest cities 1500–1900 (showing population of the largest and smallest of the top 25)

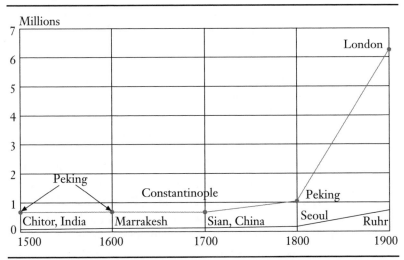

The size of the smallest of the 25 also grew, though more slowly until the 19th century. In 1000 AD, the smallest of the top 25 cities was Tangut City, Ninghsia with perhaps 50,000 inhabitants. By 1800, Seoul, Korea was the smallest of the top 25, and it had only 190,000 inhabitants. In 1900, the smallest of the 25 was Ruhr in Germany with 766,000 people, more than the largest city had had as late as 1700, when Constantinople was the largest with 700,000. The exponential growth of these largest cities was, of course, a mere symptom of a much broader change. The rise of a new urban-industrial society based on fossil fuels underlay the rapid growth of population that has brought us to over six billion today and still growing (Ness 1993).

CITIES AND TRADE: PERSISTANCE AND CHANGE

We noted above that traditionally Asian cities had been primarily administrative and cultural centers supported by a rich agricultural hinterland. This began to change with the rise of the west in the 15th century. Portuguese and Spanish seamen "discovered the seas" (Parry 1974) and tied the world together in one ecosystem. From the successful Portuguese attack on Ceuta in 1413, through the explorations around

5

Africa to Asia in 1498 and the Spanish crossing of the Atlantic in 1492, to Magellan's successful circumnavigation in 1521–22, the Iberian Peninsula created the beginnings of a new world order. In the 17th century, they were joined, then overtaken, by Great Britain, Holland, and France. At first slowly, but with increasing speed, all parts of the globe have been drawn into one universal community.

A distinctive aspect of this new community is trade. For most of the history of this new community, trade was carried by sea. This favored coastal cities, and gave rise to a new and rapidly growing group of port cities. This would radically change the world map of cities (Broeze 1989), especially in Asia.

Returning to the 25 largest cities of the world, it is striking how many were inland cities until recently. Along the ancient Silk Road we can see in 1000 AD, from west to east, Baghdad, Rayy, Isfahan, Nishapur, Bokhara, Ninghsia, Kaefeng, and Sian. In that year, of the 15 Asian cities among the top 25, only four—Tanjore (India), Soochow and Hangchow (China), and Sangdo (Korea)—were on the sea. The other 11 were inland cities. Asia's major cities remained inland political and cultural centers supported by a rich hinterland.

One part of Asia differs from this generalization, however, and anticipates what we shall see shortly when we look more closely at the differences within Asia. Southeast Asian cities were often port cities. Hanoi in Vietnam and Surabaya in Indonesia were major centers of power that repulsed Mongol invasions from China in the latter 13th century. Malacca was a major trading center in the 13th to 15th centuries. There were also Acheh, Pahang, Patani, and Banten. Unlike South and East Asian cities, these drew their sustenance from trade and imported food (Reid 1989). Of course, Southeast Asia has been for millennia a riverine and sea-based ecosystem. Its cities were small, usually only a few tens of thousands, though they often contained some 10 per cent of the country's population. When Southeast Asian cities did achieve very large size, however, as did Pagan and Angkor with populations greater than 100,000 in the 11th to 13th centuries, they were of the more common Asian types: inland political and cultural centers supported by a rich rice-growing hinterland.

But Western expansion was altering the urban scene radically. The change came slowly until the 19th century when many new small port cities were established as trading centers. As late as 1800, Asia still had 15 of the top 25 cities. Eight of these were inland cities. Change was

6

coming, however, as seven were newer port cities. By 1850, Asia had only 11 of the top 25, and seven of these were port cities. By 1900, Asian representation in the top 25 dropped to only five cities, and all but one of those, Beijing, was a newer port city. Bombay and Calcutta in India, Shanghai in China, and Tokyo and Osaka in Japan were all major seaports. The transformation was complete. It often entailed a rapid expansion of the new port cities. Indeed, many of the Asian port cities that grew to dominance in the 20th century were little more than small fishing villages as late as 1800. Kobe and Yokohama in Japan, Pusan in South Korea, Manila, Jakarta, Singapore and Rangoon in Southeast Asia, and Calcutta, Bombay and Karachi in South Asia, were scarcely on the map in 1800.

The growth of trade and port cities has not completely altered the basic character of Asian cities, however. There remains a strong undercurrent in the Asian urban political culture coming from its historic condition. Asian cities were and remain administrative and cultural centers supported by a densely settled and productive hinterland. To a certain extent, this gives a dual character to Asian urbanization. On the one hand are the new port cities reflecting Asian links to the new global market system (Reeves et al. 1989); on the other hand there remain more than vestiges of the older culture of the administrative center supported by a rich hinterland. Alongside the great port cities, there are older centers, sometimes reflecting more of Asian urban history and culture. In Japan, the political centers of Tokyo, Kyoto, and Osaka reign alongside the new port cities, Yokohama and Kobe, which were originally designed to keep the foreigners somewhat removed from the older political centers. In China, there is an array of port cities that were governed by foreigners in the 19th century, alongside Beijing that remains the cultural center of ancient China. In Indonesia, Jakarta and Yogyakarta provide the new-old symbolic centers. Colombo and Kandy do the same in Sri Lanka; Rangoon and Mandalay or Pagan in Burma; Bangkok and Ayuthia or Sukothai and Chiengmai in Thailand; Hanoi and Hue in Vietnam. In India, Calcutta and Mumbai (Bombay) are the new port centers, with Agra and Fatipur Sikri representing the most recent "old" culture, that of the Moghuls; Benares is older and there are many other urban centers that reflect even earlier Indian history.

The differences between the old and the new urban centers are now being eroded as all are drawn into the global economy. Consider, for example, the inland city, Bangalore, now known as the Silicon Valley

7

of India. But it is not only the new globalization that is transforming Asian cities. They are also being inundated by new people. From both natural increase and in-migration, the populations of all Asian cities are growing exponentially. Like Africa, Asia has lagged behind the West, Japan, and Latin America in the pace of urbanization. But it is now rapidly catching up. This has been the story of the past half-century, to which we must now turn.

THE RECENT PAST: 1950–2000

The second half of the last century saw the beginning of what we have called elsewhere (Ness and Low 2000), the second wave of world urbanization. The first began at the end of the 18th century, when Europe and North America experienced the great transformation from rural-agrarian to urban industrial society. By 1950, the world was divided into two major camps—the urban industrial "More Developed Regions" (MDRs) and the more rural agrarian "Less Developed Regions" (LDRs) of Africa, Asia, and Latin America. Table 1.1, below, shows this dichotomy in 1950, and how rapidly it has changed since then.

In 1950, more than half of the population in the MDRs lived in cities; that grew to 76 per cent by the end of the century. It is expected to continue growing slowly to over 80 per cent in the next quarter century. By contrast, the LDRs had less than a fifth of their populations in urban areas in 1950. That proportion more than doubled to 40 per cent in 2000, and is expected to continue to rise in the near future to well over 50 per cent.

The table also shows important differences between the world regions in this process of rapid urbanization. At mid-century, Africa and Asia were overwhelmingly rural. Latin America had already begun to change, with as much as 40 per cent of its population living in urban areas. In the next half-century, that region became overwhelmingly urban, reaching levels equal to the urban-industrial MDRs.

Even more striking is the great difference in the magnitudes of urban populations among the different regions. Even though Asia was only 17 per cent urban in 1950, its urban population was greater than that of North America and only slightly smaller than that of Europe. By 2000, the Asian urban population dwarfed all others. Almost half of all the world's urbanites were in Asia; by 2030 it is expected that Asia will have 58 per cent of the world's urban population.

8

TABLE 1.1   World urbanization 1950–2030: Urban population in **millions**, and percentage urban by region

Region	1950	2000	2030
World	750	2,845	4,889
	28%	47%	60%
More Developed Regions	446	903	1,010
	55%	76%	84%
Less Developed Regions	304	1,942	3,880
	18%	40%	56%
Africa	32	297	766
	15%	38%	55%
Asia	244	1,352	2,605
	17%	37%	53%
Europe	286	545	571
	52%	71%	80%
L. America & Caribbean	69	391	604
	41%	84%	83%
N. America	110	239	314
	64%	77%	84%
Oceania	8	21	31
	62%	70%	74%

SOURCE: UN 2001.

Africa is moving as rapidly as Asia in its urbanization, with proportions in the past, present and future basically the same as those we find in Asia. But the magnitudes are very different. Even with its rapid urbanization Africa had in 2000 less than a quarter of Asia's urban population (297 vs. 1,352 million).

Thus, this second wave of urbanization is much more rapid and involves immensely greater magnitudes of people than the first wave. This has led many to decry the rapid urbanization of Asia and the other LDRs. We shall take issue with this view shortly, especially as it refers to Asia, but first we must examine more closely the proportions and the magnitudes involved in the Asian urban transition. It is important to note here that the term "transition" is a description, not an explanation. We shall use the term at various critical points, where we wish to note that these major changes are always easier to describe than to explain.

THREE ASIAS: EAST, SOUTHEAST, AND SOUTH

The first point to make here is that, though we can and do speak of Asia as a single entity, it is also divided into at least three quite different regions. East Asia includes Japan, the Koreas, China (with Hong Kong), and Mongolia. Southeast Asia includes 11 nations from the Philippines to Myanmar and Vietnam to Indonesia.[2] South Asia, in our terms, includes Bangladesh, Sri Lanka, India, Nepal, and Pakistan. The United Nations regional economic and social commission, ESCAP, calls this South Central Asia and includes Afghanistan, Bhutan, Kazakhstan, Kyrgyzstan, Tajikistan, Turkmenistan, and Uzbekistan. We shall exclude these from our analysis. Further, the United Nations World Population and World Urbanization Prospects provide an additional sub-region, Western Asia, which includes 18 states from Armenia to Cyprus, including all of the oil rich Gulf States. These, too, will be excluded from our analysis.

More will be said about the differences among the three regions below, and will be seen clearly in the individual country chapters that follow. Here, we need merely note a major ecological difference. All three areas are well watered, but the sources and regularity of the waters are different. East Asia is watered by major rivers; Southeast Asia by rivers and monsoon rains; South Asia is dominated by the monsoon rains, except for Pakistan, which receives very little monsoon rainfall and is watered by the Himalayan snowmelt that flows through the massive Indus river basin. There is also a major difference between the regions in social organization, which is seen clearly in the dramatic difference in the status and autonomy of women and the consequent differences in child sex preference.

In South Asia, women have extremely low status and almost no autonomy. The preference for a male child is extremely strong, reinforced by the "Dowry System," which makes women even less valuable. In East Asia, the demand for male children is also very high, but the value of a woman is somewhat enhanced by the "Bride Price" system. In addition, a variety of historical circumstances have given women in East Asia substantially higher status than in South Asia. This is especially evident in rates of female literacy: very low in South Asia, very high in East Asia. By contrast, women in Southeast Asia stand out by their high level of autonomy. They are heavily involved in market activities, gaining thereby a substantial degree of economic power. In addition, male child preference in Southeast Asia is as low as it is anywhere in the world. More will be said of these major regional differences later, but this should be sufficient to establish the utility of the sub-regional break down we shall use.

SUB-REGIONS: THE PERCENTAGES

Figure 1.3 (p. 12), above, shows the sub-regional differences in the urbanization process, the changing percent urban from 1950 to 2000 and to the projected levels of 2030. In both East and South Asia, the total levels are heavily dominated by one country in each region: China and India. Both have about 10 times the population of the next largest country.[3] Southeast Asia is dominated by Indonesia, but its 212 million is only about three times the size of Vietnam or the Philippines.

Almost all countries in all regions have experienced a rapid increase in the proportion of population in urban areas. Only Hong Kong in China and independent Singapore in Southeast Asia were already urban states in 1950 and have remained so. Perhaps the single most rapid change among all countries is seen in the Republic of Korea, which went from 20 to 80 per cent urban in 50 years. In that same period, it was also transformed from an agrarian, high fertility society to an urban, industrial low fertility society. North Korea is moving in the same direction, but more slowly, and also with far more serious economic problems. Japan was already an urban industrial society by 1940, and merely completed the urban industrial transition in the few decades after the Second World War. China is now urbanizing rapidly, and will approach the level of the others by about mid-century.

Southeast Asia has achieved substantial transition as well. Malaysia and the Philippines have led in urbanization, both with now nearly 60 per cent of their population living in urban areas. Indonesia has also experienced much change, from about 10 to 40 per cent of its population living in urban areas in the past half-century. But the region also shows countries of very low urban proportions. Cambodia, Laos, Myanmar, Thailand, and Vietnam all remain predominantly rural. As we shall see, this list includes some interesting anomalies. Thailand remains highly rural, despite its rapid economic and social development. Until 2000, when urban redefinition raised the overall proportion to 30 per cent, Thailand remained about one-fifth urbanized for the past three decades.

This will raise a distinctive problem for us, which we shall see in many of the country chapters. We shall also deal with this issue in the comparative overview in the final chapter. Urbanization, as we are using

FIGURE 1.3   Changing urban percentages in Asia

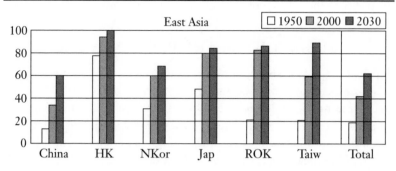

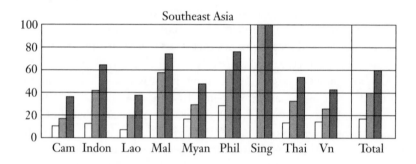

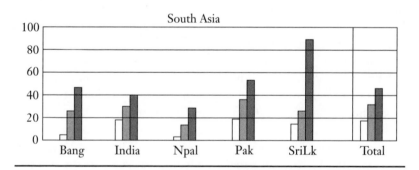

the term here, is defined by the percentage of people living in urban areas. But urbanization also implies major changes in living styles and behaviors. Urbanism is in fact a way of life, marked by changes in styles of life and patterns of consumption. Demographically it is marked by a dramatic shift from high to low fertility. The individual country chapters will deal with the urban-rural differences in styles and quality of life. Here, we need only note that Thailand's low proportion urban population is also associated with a sharp decline in urban-rural differences in both styles and quality of life. Though still largely rural, Thailand shows overall a distinctive urban life style.

South Asia appears far more homogeneous in urban transformation than the other regions. No country is yet above 40 per cent urban. And the lowest, Nepal, is only 20 percentage points below the overall regional total. All are marching in the same direction, however, and all, except Nepal, are expected to be at or near the 50 per cent mark by 2030 (UN 2001). South Asia also has, however, a country similar to Thailand in low urbanization and low urban-rural differences. Sri Lanka, like Thailand, is low in the urban percentage. Yet fertility, education, and health show remarkably low urban-rural differences there as they do in Thailand. Here is another apparently rural society with a distinctive urban life style.

SUB-REGIONS: THE NUMBERS

If the sub-regions and countries differ in their level of urbanization, they differ far more in the absolute sizes of their urban populations. Table 1, above, laid out the major changes in the world regions in the changing size of the urban population. Now we can look more closely at the size changes within Asia itself.

The numbers within Asia itself show the greatest of extremes. Alongside China's 410 million and India's 288 million urbanites in 2000, we have the three million in Singapore and the five million in Hong Kong. And those are thoroughly urbanized states or regions within other countries. Given these great disparities in absolute numbers, it is impossible to provide simple sub-regional graphs that can capture the numbers. Any graph that includes India or China reduces all other countries to mere scrapes along the bottom. But the differences between and within regions are still important for what they can tell us. Thus, in the next set of graphs, we begin by showing the five largest countries of Asia—China, India, Indonesia, Pakistan, and Japan. Following this we will show graphs of the three major sub-regions.

First, the largest five are seen in Figure 1.4. China now has over 400 million urbanites and India has 300 million. Indonesia and Pakistan have 88 and 58 million, respectively. Finally, there is the highly urbanized Japan with about 100 million, bringing this five-country total to about

FIGURE 1.4   Urban population growth in Asia's largest countries

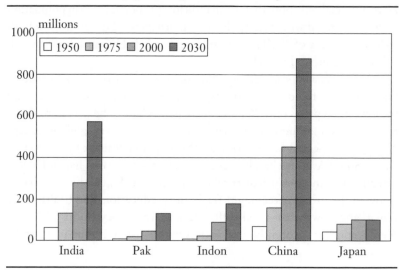

0.95 billion. This is a larger urban population than is found in all of Europe, the Americas and Oceania combined. When we add the roughly 150 million in all the "smaller" countries of Asia, we have a total of almost 1.1 billion Asian urbanites, just under half of the world's total urban population. As Table 2.2 (p. 16), shows, by the year 2030, the Asian urban populations of these largest countries will be massive, and they will continue to grow.

Figure 1.5 provides a graphic representation of the growth scenario in the three major sub-regions of Asia, excluding the countries over 100 million. They all show the same rapid growth in numbers, and, for the most part, they are all expected to continue growing rapidly.

The major exceptions are Hong Kong and Singapore. Already fully urbanized, and with relatively small populations of five and three million, respectively, they are not expected to grow much in the near future. Both have fertility rates below replacement levels, and are expected to show absolute declines in population in the near future. In both cases, highly controlled, and often temporary, in-migration will be a major feature of their populations. Otherwise, growth in absolute numbers of urbanites is both a condition of the recent past and is expected to continue only slowly for the next few decades.

FIGURE 1.5 Urban population growth in Asia

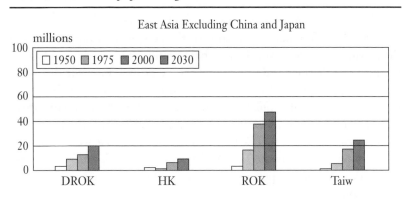

East Asia Excluding China and Japan

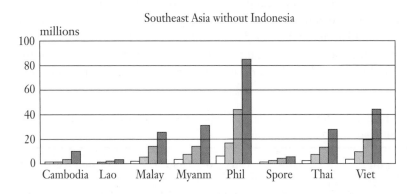

Southeast Asia without Indonesia

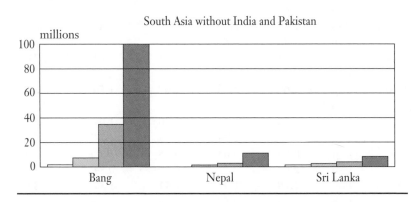

South Asia without India and Pakistan

URBAN AND TOTAL GROWTH RATES 1950–2030

Another way to depict the persistent and universal urbanization is to examine the differences between growth rates of total population and the urban population over the past half-century, and the projections for the next few decades. Table 1.2 shows these growth rates for the world and its major regions. To help make these differences more visible, we have shown the total population growth rates in bold type, and the urban growth rates in italics. The five-year period, 1950–55, is the beginning of our period of analysis. The five-year period, 1965–70, was the peak of world population growth. The final five–year period, 2025–30, marks the end of the current periodical United Nations projections for urban populations.

This table shows a number of interesting trends. First, throughout the world, urban populations have been growing more rapidly than the total population for the world as a whole and for all of its major regions for the past half-century; and this trend is projected to continue for the next three decades. Second, as the world becomes more and more

TABLE 1.2 Total population and urban average annual growth rates 1950–2030—world and major regions

Region		1950–55	1965–70	1980–85	1995–2000	2025–30
World	Pop	**1.79**	**2.04**	**1.71**	**1.35**	**0.82**
	Urb	*3.01*	*2.71*	*2.63*	*2.11*	*1.50*
Africa	Pop	**2.17**	**2.59**	**2.79**	**2.41**	**1.84**
	Urb	*4.48*	*4.64*	*4.37*	*3.97*	*2.58*
Asia	Pop	**1.93**	**2.42**	**1.88**	**1.41**	**0.71**
	Urb	*3.66*	*3.30*	*3.72*	*2.67*	*1.74*
L.Am.	Pop	**2.69**	**2.58**	**2.07**	**1.56**	**0.80**
	Urb	*4.48*	*4.64*	*3.03*	*3.97*	*2.58*
N.Am.	Pop	**1.70**	**1.10**	**0.98**	**1.04**	**0.65**
	Urb	*2.65*	*1.56*	*1.18*	*1.11*	*0.70*
Eur.	Pop	**0.99**	**0.68**	**0.38**	**-0.04**	**-0.39**
	Urb	*2.02*	*1.44*	*0.80*	*0.34*	*-0.03*
Ocean.	Pop	**2.18**	**1.92**	**1.51**	**1.37**	**0.84**
	Urb	*3.00*	*2.57*	*1.40*	*1.26*	*1.07*

SOURCE: UN 2001; total population in bold type; urban population in italics.

urbanized, the differences between urban and total growth rates diminish, as we would expect. Third, the largest differences in growth rates are in Africa, which began with the smallest urban populations. Finally, the differences are smallest, as we would expect, in the more developed regions, in Europe and North America. The power of urbanization remains, however. It is apparent especially where the European total populations are expected to decline in the next century. Even with total declines, European urban populations will remain near stable. Table 3 shows these same figures for Asia and its three sub-regions.

Like the rest of the LDRs, Asian urban population growth has outstripped total population growth by one to two (or more) percentage points for most of the last half-century. Urban growth will continue to be more rapid than total growth for the next few decades, though the differences diminish somewhat as the base of the urban population rises.

URBANIZATION AND ECONOMIC AND SOCIAL DEVELOPMENT

One final issue needs to be raised in this broad introduction. Urbanization has often been seen as a "problem" that requires attention. In one of the earliest United Nations conferences on Asian urbanization (UNESCO 1957), Philip Hauser laid out many of the problems as they were then seen. It was recognized that urbanization implies modernization,

TABLE 1.3　Total population and urban average annual growth rates 1950–2030—Asia

Region		1950–55	1965–70	1980–85	1995–2000	2025–30
Asia	Pop	1.93	2.42	1.88	1.41	0.71
	Urb	3.66	3.30	3.27	2.67	1.74
East	Pop	1.75	2.42	1.31	0.84	0.15
	Urb	3.93	2.72	3.41	2.02	1.22
Southeast	Pop	2.08	2.51	2.14	1.58	0.80
	Urb	3.72	3.97	3.87	3.57	1.78
South	Pop	2.04	2.35	2.30	1.81	1.00
	Urb	2.93	3.60	3.56	2.97	2.26

SOURCE: UN 2002 (population); UN 2001 (urban).

westernization, or economic development and the improvement of social welfare. But there was also a sense that Asia was more urbanized than it should be, given its levels of industrial development.[4] Finally, the rapid urbanization of Asia was thought to bring a host of social problems that Asian societies were not able to address.

This raises the question of the overall relationship between urbanization, economic development, and advances in social welfare or the quality of life. Though this will not be their major concern, the chapters in this book will provide some evidence to address this issue. Here, we need only lay out some aspects of the broad relationship.

Figures 1.6 and 1.7 show scattergrams of the relation between urbanization and economic development for the world as a whole and for a sub-set of 23 Asian countries. The data are cross-sectional, taken from the UNDP's World Development Report for 1995. We propose that the same relationship would be found with data for any year over the past half-century.

What is remarkable about these two distributions is their near equality. For both the world as a whole and for Asia, the patterns are quite alike, and the regression equations are almost identical. Urbanization is closely associated with economic development, or per capita wealth of a country. This is true for the world as a whole, and for Asia as a region of the world.

The distributions are presented as though urbanization (on the X axis) is the major cause of wealth, or the driving force that produces economic development (on the Y axis). We do not wish to pursue this argument in a simple form. Economic development is too complex a process to be driven by one simple change, the proportion of the people living in urban areas. We could easily reverse the graph, proposing that development drives urbanization. Neither simplistic argument is intended here. We recognize that many conditions—historical, political, economic, and geographic—affect both economic development and urbanization. These graphs are merely intended to show the similarity of patterns between Asia and the world as a whole. Economic development and urbanization are closely associated across the countries of the world today. Richer countries are more urbanized; poorer countries are less urbanized. This is true for the world as a whole and for Asia as a sub-region.

The graphs do show us another interesting phenomenon, however. Some countries are more wealthy than would be expected given their level of urbanization; or they are less urbanized than expected given their

FIGURE 1.6 Urbanization and wealth—World

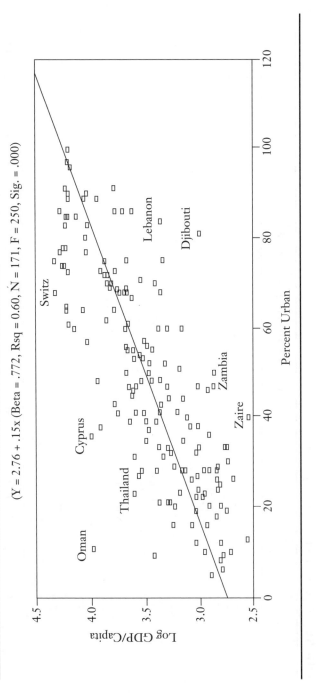

(Y = 2.76 + .15x (Beta = .772, Rsq = 0.60, N = 171, F = 250, Sig. = .000)

FIGURE 1.7 Urbanization and wealth—Asia

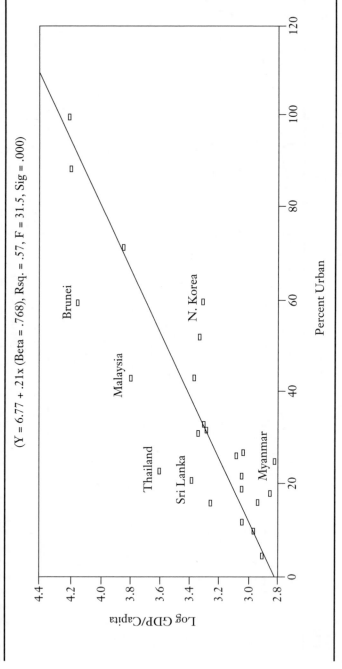

(Y = 6.77 + .21x (Beta = .768), Rsq. = .57, F = 31.5, Sig = .000)

level of per capita income. They can be said to be "underurbanized." For the world as a whole, this includes such countries as Switzerland, Cyprus, Oman, and Thailand. Others can be said to be "overurbanized," or to be more urbanized than expected given their per capita income. For the world as a whole, this includes Lebanon, Djibouti, Zambia, and Zaire. For Asia, the "underurbanized" countries are largely Southeast Asian: Thailand, Malaysia, and Brunei, but Sri Lanka in South Asia is also included. The "overurbanized" include Myanmar (because of its very low level of development), Mongolia, and North Korea. This is another way of approaching the differences between urbanization as percent urban and urbanization as a way of life.

We can also examine the overall statistical relationship between levels of urbanization and both per capita income and welfare. These can be seen in Table 1.4. Here we use the log of gross domestic product (GDP) per capita to indicate wealth. Human welfare is indicated by the Infant Mortality Rate (IMR), which is usually seen as the single most sensitive measure of a society's level of welfare, and Life Expectancy at Birth (E.o). These show an overall close relationship among all countries of the world as a whole and for the countries within Asia. Coefficients for the world (N=172) are shown in bold type in the upper right; those for Asia (N=25) are shown in the lower left in italics.

These data indicate that urbanization, national income, and welfare are closely associated. But what we have shown above in patterns of growth probably speaks more dramatically to this issue. Urbanization is a powerful force. Urban populations are growing more rapidly than total populations everywhere in the world, and especially in Asia. Much of this growth comes from in-migration. In some cases, people are being forced off the land by population growth and by highly unequal patterns of wealth

TABLE 1.4 Pearsonian Correlation Coefficients of urbanization, wealth and welfare (upper right: World; lower left: Asia)

	%Urb	GDP/Cap	IMR	E.o
% Urb	XX	.77	-.70	.68
GDP/Cap	.87	XX	-.87	.86
IMR	-.72	-.81	XX	-.97
E.o	.79	.84	-.95	XX

distribution and land holding. They are also being drawn to the cities by a range of positive forces. Cities offer opportunities for jobs, education, and a wide array of other enticements. All over the world, and in Asia, people are voting with their feet for cities, and sometimes for an urban way of life as well.

Here we must make another historical observation, which we included in the earlier AUICK book, *Five Cities* (Ness and Low 2000). The earlier urbanization of Europe was driven very much by heavy rural to urban migration. On the whole, cities in the early industrializing world were very unhealthy places, with death and sickness rates substantially above those in the rural areas. That changed as the modern epidemiological transition took place after 1945 and new investments were made in public health, especially in waste treatment and water purification. In Asia and in the other LDRs, over the past half-century, cities have been healthier than the rural areas. Both medical and public health infrastructures have been more developed in urban than in rural areas. This is something the following chapters will show in detail.

That rapid urban growth poses serious problems, especially in the need for public infrastructure—for housing, power, water, sewage, and refuse management—is quite clear. But cities offer more than problems. They also offer some hope for the future for many people.

It is these complex conditions and forces that we shall try to illuminate in this volume. Social scientists and administrators from the 14 countries covered here are examining the latest round of census findings to show us the urban conditions of the major countries of Asia at this critical juncture.

PLAN OF THE BOOK

We have divided the country chapters into three main sections. They follow regional divisions: South, Southeast and East Asia. Here we move generally from less to more urbanized areas, and roughly from West to East in each region. We have included in Southeast Asia, four small countries in one chapter prepared by the editors: Nepal, Myanmar, Laos and Cambodia. We also provide an explanation for including these four in one brief chapter. Finally, we provide a summary and overview of the country chapters, ending with a focus on scientific and policy problems that loom in the future.

In each country chapter, we have asked the authors to follow a general outline, so that the same topics and tables can be found in the same place in most chapters. We also invited individual authors to spell out what they considered to be the major historical trends and the major problems in their countries. This has sometimes caused a dilemma. It has not always been possible to maintain strict adherence to the outline, of course, since different authors choose to emphasize different themes and conditions. Still, we hope there is sufficient convergence to make this a useful reference at a crucial point in history. We are now at the threshold of a new style of human life in Asia. We are well into the fundamental transition from rural-agrarian to urban-industrial society. To date, this has meant an immense improvement in human welfare. The next generation will tell us whether that improvement is sustainable, or merely a bright spot in an otherwise dim history.

We hope that this compilation of data and analyses will be of use to both scholars and administrators; the people trying to understand or to deal with the major changes in human life that are going on in the process of urbanization.

ENDNOTES

1 Special appreciation is given to Dr. Arshad Zaman for helpful comments on an earlier draft of this chapter.

2 The 11 from east to west include: the Philippines, Vietnam, Cambodia, Laos, East Timor, Indonesia, Brunei, Singapore, Malaysia, Thailand, and Myanmar.

3 China with 1.28 billion is followed by Japan with 127 million. India with 1.01 billion is followed by Pakistan with 156 million.

4 This was a part of the received wisdom of the time. It was also wrong, as Ness showed in a paper in 1962 (Ness 1962).

CHAPTER 2

Urbanization
in Bangladesh

UBAIDUR ROB, M. KABIR, AND
M. MUTAHARA

The People's Republic of Bangladesh has a democratic parliamentary government headed by a Prime Minister, with a President as head of state. Bangladesh has a land area of 147,000 square kilometers and is divided into six divisions, 64 districts and 474 sub-districts. According to the 2001 census, the total population in Bangladesh was 129 million, of which approximately 90 per cent is Muslim. The population density of 836 persons per square kilometer is one of the highest in the world. More than 70 per cent of the population is rural. The economy of Bangladesh is primarily agricultural and traditionally dependent on the export of agricultural products such as jute, sugarcane, and tea. Approximately two-thirds of the labor force is engaged in agriculture, which accounts for half of the gross domestic product (GDP). Bangladesh's per capita income in 2000 was estimated to be US$360, growing at an estimated 5 per cent per year.

Since becoming independent in 1971, Bangladesh has made significant progress in reducing fertility and population growth. This has contributed to reductions in infant and child mortality. The contraceptive prevalence rate (CPR) has increased from 8 per cent in 1975 to 54 per cent in 2000. The total fertility rate (TFR) has declined from 6.3 births to 3.3 births, which is still well above the replacement level of fertility. Maternal mortality is currently estimated at 3.7 per thousand births, while over 90 per cent of women give birth at home, often with assistance from untrained birth attendants.

Although there were few urban centers in this part of the Indian sub-continent, significant urban centers were established during the Mughal rule (1450–1757). At that time, several rural areas were gradually transformed into urban centers for trade, commerce and administrative purposes. They were generally established on riverbanks to facilitate transportation of agricultural products to other parts of the country and to maintain the naval presence. During the British rule (1757–1947), more urban centers were established for the collection of exportable surplus and setting up administrative units.

Large-scale urbanization did not take place prior to the First World War. One of the major transformations occurring after the First World War was the rapid growth of urban centers and their population increase. Movements between rural and urban areas gained momentum as industrial units were set up in different locations and road communication become more developed. Still, during the first half of the 20th century, less than 4 per cent of the population lived in the urban areas. The partition of British India into two independent countries initiated large-scale migration between India and Pakistan. The impact of large-scale migration was most visible in the urban areas where many of the migrants settled. The liberation war in 1971 and subsequent political changes also influenced the urbanization process in Bangladesh.

Urbanization in Bangladesh has taken place without planned intervention. The urban population grew at an annual rate of less than 2 per cent until 1951, with the exception of the 1931–41 period when the annual growth rate was approximately 4 per cent. This high growth rate figure was believed to be politically motivated reporting in the 1941 census as a result of the eminent partition of British India. Since 1951, Bangladesh has experienced a rapid rate of urban population growth, at 5 per cent per year. With rapid urbanization, the number of people living in the urban area has increased from two million in 1951 to 13.2 million in 1974. Between 1981 and 2001, the urban population doubled from 13.2 million to 28.8 million.

URBAN GROWTH IN BANGLADESH

Definition of Urban in the Census

The censuses conducted between 1951 and 1974, included the municipality, civil lines, cantonment, and any continuous collection of houses inhabited by not less than 5,000 people as urban areas. Areas administered by town committees and places having concentrations of non-agricultural labor, high literacy rates, and where communities maintain public utilities, such as roads, water supply, and streetlights, were also considered to be urban areas.

Since the 1981 census, all Upazila (sub-district) headquarters have been considered as urban regardless of their size or population. In addition, places where amenities like roads, electricity, community centers, water supply, sanitation, and sewage systems exist, and which are densely populated, have also been considered urban areas. The concept of the statistical metropolitan area (SMA) was introduced in the 1981 census to separate the administrative divisional headquarters (Dhaka, Chittagong, Khulna, and Rajshahi) from the other large urban centers.

The 1991 census reclassified urban areas into four categories by the size of their populations: these are towns, municipalities, statistical metropolitan areas (SMA), and mega cities.

Mega city: A metropolitan area having a population of more than five million is termed a "mega city." Dhaka SMA is the only mega city in Bangladesh.

Statistical metropolitan area: A city corporation, together with its adjacent areas having urban characteristics, has been defined as an SMA. Besides Dhaka, there are three other SMAs in Bangladesh: Chittagong, Khulna, and Rajshahi.

Municipality: The areas covered by the 1977 Pourashavas Ordinance are considered to be municipalities. According to the 2001 census, there are 223 municipalities in the country.

Town or other urban area: The Upazila headquarters and non-municipal towns, which conform more or less to urban characteristics, are also

27

considered to be urban areas. There were 522 such urban areas identified in 1991.

PERCENTAGE OF URBAN POPULATION: 1951–2001

The factors that determine urban growth are natural population increase, rural to urban migration, territorial extension of the existing urban areas, and changes in the definition of urban areas. The natural increase is defined as the excess of births over deaths. Net migration can be described as a process characterized by the excess of in-migration over out-migration. Reclassification of geographic areas refers to changes in the urban boundaries by the addition of new areas, declassification of the existing urban areas, and alteration in the territorial jurisdiction of urban areas.

Among these factors, the extension in the definition of urban areas and the large influx of rural population to urban centers rapidly increased the urban population in Bangladesh between 1951 and 2001. Migration played the dominant role contributing to approximately 50 per cent of the increase in the urban population. Both rural "push" and urban "pull" factors caused large-scale migration from the rural areas to the cities. The persistence of rural poverty and landlessness brought about by natural calamities, such as riverbank erosion and flooding, acted as major influencing factors.

The distribution of the total and urban population of Bangladesh during 1951–2001 is shown in Table 2.1 and Figures 2.1 and 2.2[1]. The total population increased from 44 million in 1951 to 129 million in 2001. The annual growth rate was over 2 per cent in the intercensal period of 1951–91. Findings suggest that Bangladesh experienced the most rapid urban growth during 1974–81. The number of people living in urban areas increased from 6.27 million in 1974 to 13.23 million in 1981. In 2001, approximately 29 million people were living in urban areas.

The proportion of urban population increased from 4.1 per cent in 1951 to over 22.3 per cent in 2001. The growth of Bangladesh's urban population between 1961–74 was 138 per cent. The exponential growth rate was 6.7 per cent during 1961–74 as compared to a lower 3.7 per cent between 1951–61. The largest increase in the urban population occurred between 1974 and 1981. The population living in the urban areas doubled in seven years from 6.27 million in 1974 to 13.23 million in 1981. This

TABLE 2.1 Distribution of total and urban population, Bangladesh 1951–2001

Year	Total population (million)	Urban population (million)	Percent Urban	Inter census change in Urban population (percent)	Annual Growth Rate of Urban population (percent)	Annual growth rate of total population (percent)
1951	44.17	1.82	4.1	-	-	-
1961	55.22	2.64	4.8	45.1	3.7	2.3
1974	76.40	6.27	8.2	137.6	6.7	2.5
1981	89.91	13.23	14.7	110.7	10.7	2.4
1991	111.46	20.87	18.7	57.8	4.6	2.2
2001	129.15	28.81	22.3	38.0	3.2	1.5

SOURCE: BBS 1994 and BBS 2001b.

high growth rate of the urban population can be partly attributed to the extended definition of urban areas in the 1981 census. The inclusion of Upazila headquarters and small bazaars with electricity increased the number of people living in urban areas. It is estimated that approximately four million people living in areas that were not previously defined as urban areas were considered as urban in the 1981 census. In the following 20 years (1981–2001), the size of the urban population doubled from 13.23 million in 1981 to 28.81 million in 2001.

Table 2.1, above, also illustrates the annual growth rate of the population living in urban areas. The annual growth rate in these areas was more than double the natural increase of the total population during 1951–2001. For example, the annual growth rate of the urban population was more than 10 per cent during 1974–81 and declined to 4.6 per cent during 1981–91. The rate of growth in urban areas further declined to 3.2 per cent during 1991–2001, yet remained double that of the country as a whole.

As mentioned earlier, Bangladesh is divided into six administrative divisions (the Sylhet division was created in 1996). These divisions were created taking into consideration geographic proximity to the divisional headquarters and the homogenous nature of the population living in a particular division with respect to their social and cultural characteristics.

FIGURE 2.1 Total, urban and rural population growth in Bangladesh, 1951–2030

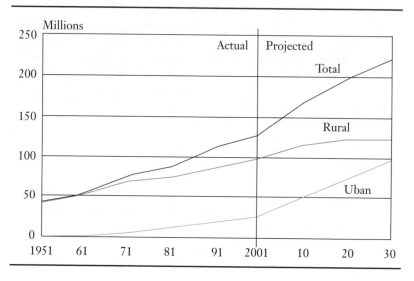

FIGURE 2.2 Percentage urban and urban and rural population growth rates in Bangladesh, 1951–2030

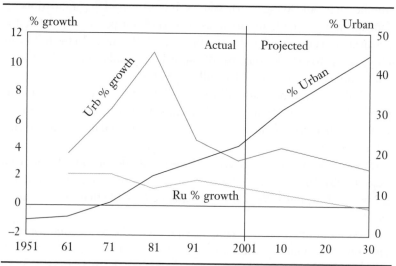

At the divisional level, variations in the level of urbanization can be seen. The information presented in Table 2.2 suggests that the Dhaka division has experienced a higher level of urbanization than the national average. Khulna and Chittagong were at the same level, slightly lower than the national average, while the Barisal division was the least urbanized division. Though the least urbanized, Barisal has experienced an exceptionally rapid urban growth in the past decade due to the reclassification of the urban areas.

The trend in percent urban population in the four administrative divisions is shown in Table 2.3. Considering 1961 as the base year, the change in urbanization has been calculated for these geographic areas. It is observed that the proportion of urban population increased approximately four times in the Dhaka and Chittagong divisions during the last four decades.

CHARACTERISTICS OF MIGRANTS

Migration is generally found to be a highly selective process which results in differences in the characteristics of migrants and non-migrants. Each of these characteristics, such as age, sex, education, marital status, and occupation, has a profound impact on the urbanization process. It is mainly rural to urban migration which leads to urban growth. Although national level information is lacking in Bangladesh, several small studies have reported on the characteristics of migrant populations. Migrants are generally young adults and the majority of them are poor. The aggregate data from several studies indicate that the majority of migrants moved to urban areas due to various economic reasons such as poverty, unemployment, and landlessness. Table 2.4 presents characteristics of migrants from a small study. It is observed that both highly educated and illiterate people migrated to urban areas in equal proportion.

THE NATIONAL SYSTEM OF CITIES

Distribution of Urban Population by Size Class

To analyze the distribution of population by size, the urban areas have been classified according to their population characteristics. The findings presented in Table 2.5 suggest that the number of urban centers increased from 64 in 1951 to 112 in 1974. However, due to the reclassification of

31

TABLE 2.2 Percentage distribution of total and urban population by administrative divisions, 1961–91

Division	1961			1974			1981			1991		
	Total (million)	Urban (million)	Percent urban	Total (million)	Urban (million)	Percent urban	Total (million)	Urban (million)	Percent urban	Total (million)	Urban (million)	Percent urban
Barisal	4.26	-	-	5.43	-	-	6.51	-	-	7.46	0.94	12.5
Chittagong	13.63	0.64	4.7	18.64	1.41	7.5	22.60	3.39	15.0	27.29	4.93	18.1
Dhaka	15.29	1.07	7.0	21.31	2.89	13.6	26.23	5.25	20.0	32.67	9.13	28.0
Khulna	5.81	0.43	7.3	8.77	1.05	12.0	10.64	2.46	23.1	12.69	2.32	18.3
Rajshahi	11.85	0.50	4.2	17.33	0.92	5.3	21.14	2.13	10.1	26.21	3.55	13.5
Total	50.84	2.64	5.2	71.48	6.27	8.8	87.12	13.23	15.2	106.31	20.87	19.6

SOURCE: BBS 1994.

TABLE 2.3 Index of urban population percent by administrative divisions (% urban shown in parentheses)

Division	1961	1974	1981	1991
Chittagong	100 (4.7)	160	324	385 (18.1)
Dhaka	100 (7.0)	194	285	400 (28.0)
Khulna	100 (7.3)	164	316	250 (18.3)
Rajshahi	100 (4.2)	126	240	321 (13.5)

TABLE 2.4 Characteristics of migrants

Category	Percent
Reasons for Migration	
Employment	53.5
Job Transfer	14.1
Education	19.9
River Erosion	1.3
Dependents	8.8
Others	2.4
Total	100.0
Education Level	
Illiterate	24.7
Primary	13.6
Less than Secondary	13.3
Secondary / Higher Secondary	21.9
Graduation	26.5
Total	100.0
N	594

SOURCE: Afsar, 2000.

33

the urban areas, the number of urban centers increased to 500 in 1981. The change in the size of the urban population between 1951 and 1991 was enormous. For example, in 1951, there were only 25 urban areas with populations of less than 10,000; by 1991, that figure jumped to 399. Similarly, 37 urban centers had populations between 10,000–100,000 in 1951 and the number increased to 105 in 1991. Table 2.5 shows that only three urban centers attained the "million-city" status in 1991 and this remained the same in 2001. The distribution of people living in different size urban centers has changed over time. The majority of the urban population live in the larger urban centers; however, the proportion living in the smaller urban centers (with populations of less than 10,000) increased, while that in towns of 10,000–100,000 declined.

Statistical Metropolitan Area

The disparity of urbanization is evident from the concentration of the urban population in a few urban centers. Among these centers, the four largest cities—Dhaka, Chittagong, Khulna, and Rajshahi—contained 51 per cent of the urban population of the country in 2001. The data presented in Table 2.6 indicate that from 1951 onwards these four cities had more than 40 per cent of the total urban population. The slight decrease in the urban population share of the cities in 1981 was due to a reclassification of the urban areas in the 1981 census. It should be mentioned that the extended definition of urban areas (i.e., the inclusion of Upazila headquarters as urban areas) accounted for one-third of the total increase in the urban population during 1974–81. The population size of Chittagong exceeded one million during 1974—81, as did Khulna between 1981–91. The Census Commission designated Dhaka a "mega city" after the 1991 census. It can be observed that the Dhaka SMA alone had 27 per cent of the urban population in 1981, which increased to 34 per cent in 2001. This is clearly a case of both single city primacy (Dhaka) and four-city primacy (Dhaka, Chittagong, Khulna, and Rajshahi) in the urban structure of Bangladesh.

Dhaka is the capital city and the largest urban agglomeration in Bangladesh. Table 2.6 shows the spectacular increase of Dhaka city's population since 1951. The population increased from less than half a million in 1951 to 9.91 million in 2001. Dhaka's portion of the total urban population increased from 27 per cent in 1961 to 34 per cent in 2001. The primacy of Dhaka is even stronger functionally than in terms

TABLE 2.5 Number of urban centers and proportion of population by population size, 1951–1991 (Percentages of total urban population shown in parentheses)

Population size	1951	1961	1974	1981	1991
Less than 10,000	25	30	16	297	399
	(8.5)	(7.8)	(3.2)	(21.6)	(17.5)
10,000–100,000	37	46	90	190	105
	(53.0)	(46.4)	(42.8)	(26.4)	(20.6)
100,000–500,000	2	3	4	10	14
	(38.5)	(18.5)	(8.1)	(10.6)	(11.1)
500,000–1million	-	1	1	1	1
		(27.3)	(12.9)	(4.9)	(2.6)
1million–5 million	-	-	1	2	2
			(33.0)	(36.5)	(14.9)
5 million+					1
					(33.3)
Total	64	80	112	500	522
	(100.0)	(100.0)	(100.0)	(100.0)	(100.0)

SOURCE: BBS 1994.

TABLE 2.6 Population (millions) distribution in SMAs 1951–2001

Name of the SMA	1951	1961	1974	1981	1991	2001
Dhaka	0.41	0.72	2.07	3.44	6.95	9.91
Chittagong	0.29	0.36	0.81	1.39	2.08	3.20
Khulna	0.04	0.13	0.47	0.65	1.02	1.23
Rajshahi	0.04	0.06	0.13	0.25	0.55	0.65
Total	0.79	1.27	3.48	5.74	10.60	14.99
Total Urban Population	1.82	2.64	6.27	13.23	20.87	28.81
SMAs % of Urban Population	43.3	48.2	55.5	43.4	50.8	52.0

SOURCE: BBS 1997, BBS 2001.

35

of its population. Administrative functions and civil employment, financial and banking services, international commerce, and trade activities are all highly concentrated in Dhaka. In addition, significant industrial and public sector investment has been made in Dhaka. More than 80 per cent of export-oriented garment factories are located in Dhaka. The dominance of Dhaka is even greater in the production of rubber products, books, furniture, footwear, leather, and electrical goods. The best educational, health, cultural, and sports facilities are also located in Dhaka.

It is estimated that about 65 per cent of all employment in Dhaka is in the informal sector. The most noticeable is the transportation sector. There are more than 400,000 tri-cycle rickshaws in Dhaka city providing employment to approximately one million people. The rickshaw industry, including renting, operating, repairing, and production involves more than 1.5 million people. During the 1990s, export-oriented garment factories located in Dhaka employed more than one million female workers. The high growth of population and comparatively limited scope of physical expansion of Dhaka city made it one of the most densely populated cities in the world. The analysis of data suggests that the "absolute poor"[2] and "hard-core poor"[3] account for 55 and 32 per cent of the total city population respectively (GOB-ADB 1998).

Table 2.7 shows the inter census population change and the annual growth rate of the four SMAs. Among the SMAs, Chittagong and Khulna are the two major industrial and port cities. They both experienced a rapid increase in urban population during 1951–2001. Rajshahi, being a

TABLE 2.7 Inter-census change and annual growth rate of SMAs, 1951–2001

Region	1951–1961		1961–1974		1974–1981		1981–1991		1991–2001	
	Percent change	Annual growth rate	Percent change	Annual growth rate	Percent change	Annual growth rate	Percent change	Annual growth rate	Percent change	Annual growth rate
Dhaka	74.9	5.7	187.6	8.5	66.3	7.5	102.0	6.6	42.6	3.5
Chittagong	23.8	2.2	123.6	6.2	70.9	7.6	49.5	4.1	54.0	4.3
Khulna	204.8	11.7	265.6	10.5	39.3	4.9	55.8	3.5	20.8	1.9
Rajshahi	57.5	4.6	111.1	5.9	91.0	9.7	116.1	7.2	17.9	1.6

SOURCE: BBS 1997, BBS 2001.

divisional headquarters and the largest urban center in the northern part of the country, has traditionally attracted the rural population. Note that all cities have seen a substantial decline in their growth rates in the past decade. This is in part a result of the overall decline in the national growth rate, but it also suggests some reduction in the pace of urbanization.

POPULATION CHANGE IN THE TEN NEXT LARGEST CITIES

The population of the 10 next most populated urban centers, after the SMAs, is presented in Table 2.8. These cities accounted for only 6.6 per cent of the urban population in 2001. Moreover, the share of these cities

TABLE 2.8 Growth of next ten major urban centers, after the SMAs 1974–2001

District	Population (000)				Inter census growth rate (percent)		
	1974	1981	1991	2001	1974–1981	1981–1991	1991–2001
Barisal	98	142	170	202	44.9	19.7	18.8
B' Baria	62	88	109	131	41.9	23.9	20.2
Bogra	47	69	120	150	46.8	73.9	25.0
Comilla	86	128	135	168	48.8	5.5	24.4
Dinajpur	62	89	128	157	43.5	43.8	22.7
Jessore	76	115	140	178	51.3	21.7	27.1
Mymensing	76	99	189	226	30.3	90.9	19.6
Nawabgonj	46	57	131	153	23.9	129.8	16.0
Rangpur	73	122	191	252	67.1	56.6	31.9
Sylhet	59	101	117	285	71.2	15.8	143.6
Total	685	1010	1430	1902	–	–	–
Total Urban Population	6274	13228	20872	28809	–	–	–
Percent of Urban Population	10.9	7.6	6.9	6.6	–	–	–

SOURCE: BBS 1997, BBS 2001.

has declined over time. The sharp increase in the urban population of many of these cities was primarily due to the expansion of the city limits. For example, the urban population in Sylhet increased from 117,000 in 1991 to 285,000 in 2001 primarily due to the inclusion of near-by areas as the town was given city corporation status in 1996. Like the SMAs, these smaller cities (with the exception of Sylhet) have also shown a substantial decline in their growth rates in the past decade.

FUTURE PROJECTION

Table 2.9 presents the projected total and urban population of Bangladesh for the next 50 years. Using the enumerated population in the 2001 census as the base population, and assuming that replacement level fertility will be reached in 2015, the Bangladesh Planning Commission projected the total population to be 170 million people in 2050. This projected figure is considerably lower than the earlier estimate, which was as high as 220 million. Using a linear function and assuming that the urban growth rate will decline from 3.2 per cent in 2007 to 2 per cent in 2037, we have also projected the urban population. Data presented in Table 2.9 indicate that the urban population might reach 60 million in 2027, amounting to 36 per cent of the total population. The gradual increase in the number of people

TABLE 2.9 Total and urban population projection 2001–2050

Year	Total population (million)	Urban population (million)	Percent urban
2001	129.15	28.81	22.3
2007	143.99	34.95	24.3
2012	153.49	41.06	26.8
2017	159.96	46.99	29.4
2022	164.85	53.78	32.6
2027	168.74	60.94	36.1
2032	171.59	69.06	40.2
2037	172.95	76.32	44.1
2042	172.69	84.35	48.8
2047	170.81	93.22	54.6
2050	169.03	98.98	58.6

living in urban areas will continue over the coming years, however. Approximately 60 per cent of the people may be living in the urban areas in 2050.

URBAN-RURAL DIFFERENCES

Age and Sex Composition

The average age structure of the population in Bangladesh is young. The 1991 census found that approximately 42 per cent of the urban population is under the age of 15. Little variation is observed between the age structures by sex but significant variation is observed by urban-rural residence. Table 2.10 presents the age and sex composition of urban and rural populations. As expected, the proportion of both males and females in the youngest age group is lower in urban areas than rural areas. This may be attributed to the sharp decline in fertility in urban areas. In general, urban women's better education and employment opportunities, access to public health and family planning facilities, better living standard, and inducement to late marriage affect their child bearing and rearing behavior.

The proportion of people in the economically-active age group is greater in urban than rural areas, indicating that people are migrating to urban areas in search of job opportunities. Table 2.10 also shows the sex selective migration to urban areas. It is observed that between the ages of 15 and 44 years, the percentage of males is higher in the urban areas than in the rural areas.

MARITAL STATUS

Table 2.11 presents the distribution of females between 15 to 54 years by marital status and residence. It is evident that the proportion of those who have never married has decreased over time. Approximately 98 per cent of females living in rural areas and 96 per cent in urban areas were married before reaching 30. We also see a trend towards a rise in the age of marriage in both urban and rural areas, especially in the in urban areas. For instance, in 1981, approximately 86 per cent of females aged 20–24 were married. This declined to 64 per cent in 1996, dropping just over 20 percentage points. In the rural areas, 83 per cent of females aged 20–24 were married in 1996, a drop of just under 10 percentage points from

TABLE 2.10 Age distribution of the population according to sex and residence, 1974–2001

Age group	1974 Census				1981 Census				1991 Census				2001 MMS			
	Urban		Rural		Urban		Rural		Urban		Rural		Urban		Rural	
	M	F	M	F	M	F	M	F	M	F	M	F	M	F	M	F
0–4	12.8	16.3	16.6	17.7	13.0	16.0	17.3	17.6	12.7	14.5	17.0	17.3	11.7	11.6	13.4	12.6
5–9	13.7	17.5	18.2	19.1	12.7	15.4	16.6	16.6	13.5	15.0	17.4	16.9	12.0	11.3	13.7	13.1
10–14	12.6	14.8	13.5	12.0	12.8	14.5	14.1	12.6	12.0	13.1	12.8	11.3	12.8	13.1	13.7	13.5
15–19	9.8	10.2	8.4	7.8	10.1	10.6	9.0	9.3	9.2	10.1	8.1	8.1	10.6	13.3	10.2	12.3
20–24	10.0	8.4	6.2	7.1	10.1	9.6	6.7	8.2	9.9	10.8	6.9	8.8	8.1	10.7	6.9	9.3
25–29	9.2	7.5	6.1	7.3	9.6	8.1	6.7	7.4	9.8	10.1	7.4	9.0	7.8	8.3	6.6	7.5
30–34	7.0	5.8	5.3	5.9	7.2	5.9	5.2	5.9	7.6	6.7	5.8	6.1	7.5	7.5	6.2	6.7
35–39	6.4	4.8	5.4	5.2	6.1	4.6	5.1	5.0	7.1	5.3	5.7	5.3	7.1	6.2	6.3	5.5
40–44	5.3	4.0	4.6	4.4	4.8	3.0	4.2	4.3	5.3	3.9	4.3	4.3	5.9	4.9	5.2	4.5
45–49	3.8	2.7	3.7	3.2	3.5	2.7	3.5	3.1	3.7	2.7	3.5	3.3	4.7	3.4	4.2	3.3
50–54	3.4	2.6	3.5	3.3	3.2	3.0	3.2	3.0	2.9	2.5	3.0	2.9	3.4	2.3	3.2	2.7
55–59	1.7	1.2	2.1	1.7	1.8	1.3	2.1	1.7	1.7	1.3	2.1	1.7	2.2	2.2	2.2	2.7
60–64	1.9	1.7	2.5	2.3	2.1	1.8	2.4	2.2	1.9	1.7	2.3	2.1	2.0	2.0	2.5	2.4
65–69	0.8	0.9	1.3	0.9	0.8	0.7	1.2	0.9	0.9	0.7	1.2	0.9	1.3	1.1	1.6	1.3
70+	1.6	1.6	2.6	2.1	2.2	1.9	2.7	2.1	1.8	1.6	2.6	2.0	2.8	2.2	4.1	2.5

SOURCE: BBS 1994; NIPORT and ORC Mac.

TABLE 2.11 Percentage distribution of women according to marital status, 1981–1996

Urban

Age	1981			1991			1996		
	Never married	Currently married	Widow/ Divorced/ Separated	Never married	Currently married	Widow/ Divorced/ Separated	Never married	Currently married	Widow/ Divorced/ Separated
15–19	45.1	52.7	1.7	60.9	37.9	1.2	79.6	18.0	2.4
20–24	10.9	85.7	3.4	18.0	79.4	2.7	33.5	64.0	2.5
25–29	2.6	93.0	4.4	4.2	92.2	3.6	10.8	86.7	2.6
30–34	1.7	91.8	6.5	1.5	93.2	5.2	5.1	89.7	5.2
35–39	0.7	89.5	9.8	0.8	91.8	7.4	3.0	89.0	8.0
40–44	1.5	81.3	17.2	0.8	86.3	13.0	2.2	85.9	11.9
45–49	0.7	74.9	24.4	0.6	81.5	79.3	2.6	78.1	19.3
50–54	4.8	63.7	31.5	0.8	70.4	28.9	1.9	70.8	27.3

Rural

Age	1981			1991			1996		
	Never married	Currently married	Widow/ Divorced/ Separated	Never married	Currently married	Widow/ Divorced/ Separated	Never married	Currently married	Widow/ Divorced/ Separated
15–19	28.7	67.8	3.5	45.3	52.9	1.8	63.1	34.6	2.3
20–24	4.0	91.8	4.2	8.4	88.6	3.0	13.9	83.0	3.1
25–29	1.1	94.6	4.3	1.96	94.4	3.6	4.8	92.2	3.0
30–34	0.9	93.0	6.1	0.96	94.0	5.1	2.5	93.1	4.4
35–39	0.4	89.8	9.8	0.5	99.2	7.3	1.7	91.4	6.9
40–44	0.6	81.9	17.5	0.5	87.1	12.4	2.1	87.3	10.6
45–49	0.3	74.4	25.3	0.4	81.8	17.9	1.9	80.9	17.3
50–54	0.8	62.2	37	0.5	70.6	28.9	1.6	73.1	25.3

SOURCE: BBS 1994, BBS 2001.

1981. Findings suggest a rise in the age of marriage in both rural and urban areas. In the rural areas, the females aged 15–19 who had never been married numbered only 64 per cent of their urban counterparts in 1981; this figure rose to 79 per cent in 1996. Even more striking is the rise in the number of females aged 20–24 who had never been married from 11 to 34 per cent in urban areas and from 4 to 14 per cent in rural areas. For the 15–19-year-olds, the urban-rural gap has remained roughly stable at about 16 percentage points. For the 20–24-year-old group, however, the gap is widening from 7 to 20 percentage points. This probably reflects the far greater opportunities for female employment in the urban areas.

LITERACY RATE

Although the literacy rate in Bangladesh is one of the lowest in the region, we have seen a dramatic change over the past decade. This is closely related to the expansion of school enrollments. Of the eligible children of school-going age in the 1991 census, 84 per cent of the boys and 74 per cent of the girls were enrolled in primary school. Among them, approximately 30 per cent completed the primary grade. Table 2.12 shows the urban-rural literacy rate of the population from 1974 to 1998. The national literacy rate of 51.3 per cent in 1998 is considered relatively low. Women are particularly disadvantaged. Nearly 60 per cent lack the functional ability to read, write or understand numbers, compared to 40 per cent for males. The 1998 literacy rate for rural and urban

TABLE 2.12   Literacy rate by sex and residence, 1974–1998

	Urban			Rural			National		
Years	Male	Female	Total	Male	Female	Total	Male	Female	Total
1974	62.5	33.1	48.1	34.6	12.1	23.4	37.2	13.2	25.8
1981	58.0	34.1	48.1	35.4	15.3	25.4	39.7	18.0	29.2
1991	62.6	44.0	54.4	38.7	21.5	30.1	44.3	25.8	35.3
1998	77.1	60.0	68.3	57.3	37.8	46.4	59.4	42.5	51.3

SOURCE: BBS 1994, BBS 2000 (for population 15 years and older).

populations is 46.4 per cent and 68.3 per cent respectively, showing a substantial urban advantage. However, examination of census data revealed that the proportion of literate people in urban areas remained unchanged for many years until the 1990s. The literacy rate among men living in urban areas did not increase during 1974–91; in 1974 approximately 62.5 per cent of urban males were literate, which remained the same till 1991. The reason for this particular trend in the literacy rate in urban areas is the migration of illiterate rural people to the urban areas. It has been reported that the average literacy rate among the urban poor is even lower than in the rural areas. Rural females, on the other hand, have seen steady progress since 1974, though their proportions have remained low.

Table 2.13 examines the literacy differences between males and females and between urban and rural areas. The male-female gap has declined steadily in both areas, though the decline has been greater in the urban areas. The male urban-rural gap has also declined steadily. The female urban-rural gap has, however, increased. This suggests a substantial out-migration of (probably younger) educated women from the rural areas, leaving behind the older and thus less educated women.

EMPLOYMENT IN THE URBAN SECTOR

Over half the country's labor force is employed in agriculture, accounting for approximately half of the GDP. Industry employs 19 per cent of the labor force, and the service sector accounts for an additional 26 per cent. In recent years, the export-oriented textile

TABLE 2.13 Literacy differentials (urban minus rural percentages)

	Gender		Urban – Rural	
	M – F Urban	**M – F Rural**	**Male U – R**	**Female U – R**
1974	29.4	22.5	27.9	21.0
1981	23.9	20.1	22.6	18.8
1991	18.6	17.2	23.9	22.5
1998	17.1	19.5	19.8	22.2

sector has played a major role in export earnings and has employed more than one million women. There are few reliable estimates of unemployment, but the widely cited figure of 25 per cent is considered a minimal estimate.

The total labor force of the country in 1995–96 was about 56 million. The urban sector provides employment to 10 million people, or 18 per cent of the total labor force. The rural sector contains more than 45.8 million people, representing 82 per cent of the total labor force. The contribution of the urban sector has been steadily increasing. In 1961, urban areas employed only 6 per cent. By 1974, this had increased to 10 per cent, and in 1985–86, to 15 per cent. Although absolute contribution of the urban sector to labor absorption increased in 1989 (5.7 million), its relative contribution declined to 11 per cent. It is interesting to note that the total labor force's rise from 16.9 million in 1961 to 51.2 million in the early 1990s is largely attributable to the entry of female workers in both urban and rural job markets.

The findings presented in Table 2.14, below, show that, in 1985–86, the total number of rural women engaged in the labor force was only 2.6 million. This increased dramatically to 19.5 million in 1989. The

TABLE 2.14 Number of persons engaged in labor force by sex and residence (million)

Year	National	Urban			Rural		
		Male	Female	Total	Male	Female	Total
1961	16.9	0.9	0.1	1.0	15.1	0.8	15.9
1974	21.9	2.0	0.1	2.1	19.0	0.8	19.8
1981	25.9	3.1	0.2	3.3	21.3	1.3	22.6
1983–84	28.5	3.4	0.5	3.9	22.5	2.1	24.6
1984–85	29.5	3.6	0.5	4.1	23.2	2.2	25.4
1985–86	30.9	4.1	0.6	4.7	23.6	2.6	26.2
1989	50.7	4.2	1.5	5.7	25.6	19.5	45.1
1990–91	51.2	6.6	2.1	8.7	24.4	18.1	42.5
1995–96	56.0	7.4	2.8	10.2	27.3	18.5	45.8

SOURCE: BBS 2001a, BBS 1992.

increase is due to definitional changes in economic activities, which included activities such as caring for domestic animals and poultry, threshing, boiling, drying and husking crops, and processing and preserving food. Thus, it was not a real change in the work carried out by the females, merely an official recognition of that work.

Table 2.15 shows rural-urban differences in some selected indicators. As expected urban residents have higher access to modern facilities such as electricity, piped water, and hygienic sanitation. Approximately 80 per cent of the households in urban areas have electricity connection compared to only 21 per cent in rural areas. The median age for marriage is lower in rural areas and rural women want slightly more children than their urban counterparts. Access to health care facilities is higher in urban areas and the residents also utilized the available services by a higher percentage as indicated by the proportion of women who received antenatal care (ANC) and Tetanus Toxoid (TT) services. Urban women are more aware of HIV/ AIDS than their rural counterparts.

TABLE 2.15   Urban and rural differential in selected indicators BDHS, 1999–2000

Indicator	Urban %	Rural %
Households with electricity	81.2	20.5
Households with piped water	30.6	0.4
Households with modern septic tank	35.1	4.3
Female median age at marriage	16.2	14.7
Mean ideal number of children	2.3	2.6
Pregnant women received ante-natal care	62.2	31.6
Pregnant women received Tetanus Toxoid	88.4	79.7
Deliveries in institutions	25.1	4.6
Infants immunized	69.7	58.5
Unmet need for family planning	12.4	16.0
Women heard about HIV/AIDS	64.3	22.6
Female median age at marriage (yrs)	16.2	14.7
Mean ideal number of children (no.)	2.3	2.6

CURRENT FERTILITY AND CONTRACEPTIVE USE

Current fertility levels derived from the demographic and health surveys and census are presented in Table 2.16. The most widely used measure of current fertility is the TFR. This shows a decline in fertility in both rural and urban areas, though urban areas consistently show lower fertility. The rise in urban TFR in 1999–200 is primarily due to the inclusion of some areas which were considered as rural in the earlier surveys.

The components of TFR, age specific fertility rates, show a number of interesting patterns. Fertility of the very young is declining substantially in urban areas, but not in rural areas. Fertility in the mid-reproductive ages (20–34) is declining in both urban and rural areas, but remains higher in the latter, as would be expected. Finally, fertility among older women is also declining in both urban and rural areas.

The Bangladesh National Family Planning Program is considered a success story in a setting where the expected improvements in socio-economic and health conditions required for rapid fertility decline have not been achieved. Relying on a vast network of field workers who provide health-related services, both at fixed locations and to the doorstep, the

TABLE 2.16 Age specific fertility rates among urban and rural women 1982–2000

Age Group	1981 Census Urban	1981 Census Rural	1989 BFS Urban	1989 BFS Rural	1993–94 BDHS Urban	1993–94 BDHS Rural	1996–97 BDHS Urban	1996–97 BDHS Rural	1999–2000 BDHS Urban	1999–2000 BDHS Rural
15–19	110	150	139	187	81	148	88	155	101	155
20–24	205	253	208	265	178	198	140	200	142	201
25–29	201	229	177	230	134	161	99	158	140	172
30–34	159	200	120	174	82	108	53	102	78	104
35–39	97	127	68	117	41	58	28	46	23	50
40–44	40	60	34	57	4	21	12	19	6	21
45–49	23	32	8	18	17	14	0	7	0	3
TFR	4.19	5.26	3.84	5.30	2.69	3.54	2.10	3.43	2.50	3.54

SOURCE: BBS 1999, NIPORT, Mitra and Associates and ORC Macro 2001, Mitra et al. 1997, Mitra et al. 1994, Huq and Cleland 1990.

FIGURE 2.3   Bangladesh TFR and CPR, 1975–2000

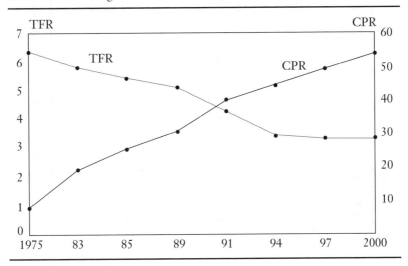

program has reached almost every eligible woman in the rural areas. The knowledge of modern contraceptive methods is universal. As mentioned earlier, CPR has increased from 8 per cent in 1975 to 54 per cent in 1999–2000. Consequently, TFR declined from 6.3 in 1975 to 3.3 in 1999–2000. Figure 3 shows the national level TFR and CPR during 1975–2000.

Table 2.17 presents contraceptive use rates by method in rural and urban areas. The CPR has increased dramatically, and the urban-rural gap has been significantly reduced, which is the mark of a successful program. In 1983, the contraceptive use rate was 35.7 per cent in the urban area, which increased to to 60 per cent in 1999–2000. Moreover, in 1983, the rural CPR was only half of the urban CPR; by 2000, the rural CPR was almost 90 per cent of the urban level. For any modern method, the progress was even greater, from 42 per cent in 1983 to 87 per cent in 2000. This, again, is the mark of a very successful national family planning program.

The oral pill is the most popular contraceptive method in Bangladesh; for this method, rural use amounted to only 25 per cent of the urban levels in 1983, but rose to 92 per cent in 2000. Many women begin and end their contraceptive use as oral pill users, even when other methods might be more appropriate. The 1999–2000

TABLE 2.17 Contraceptive use rates among currently married women by residence, 1983–2000

Method	1983 CPS		1989 CPS		1993–94 BDHS		1996–97 BDHS		1999–2000 BDHS	
	Urban	Rural	Urban	Rural	Urban	Rural	Urban	Rural	Urban	Rural
Any method	35.7	17.3	44.8	29.1	54.4	43.3	62.1	47.6	60.0	52.3
Any modern method	28.8	12.1	36.8	22.3	44.6	35.1	52.6	40.1	48.7	42.2
Pill	10.4	2.6	16.3	7.9	20.9	16.9	22.2	20.6	24.6	22.6
IUD	1.8	0.9	3.0	1.5	3.7	2.0	2.8	1.7	1.4	1.2
Indictable	0.7	0.2	1.4	1.0	4.4	4.5	5.7	6.3	5.7	7.6
Condom	5.2	1.1	6.1	1.2	8.3	2.3	13.2	2.7	9.8	2.9
Female sterilization	9.3	5.8	8.9	9.0	6.4	8.3	7.9	7.6	6.3	6.8
Male sterilization	0.7	1.3	0.7	1.6	0.7	1.1	0.7	1.2	0.4	0.6
Norplant	–	–	–	–	–	–	0.0	0.1	0.4	0.5
Any traditional method	6.9	5.2	8.0	6.8	9.8	8.2	9.5	7.4	11.3	10.1
Periodic abstinence	3.6	2.3	4.5	3.7	5.5	4.8	5.0	5.0	5.5	5.4
Withdrawal	1.3	1.3	1.8	1.1	3.8	2.3	3.5	1.7	5.2	3.8
Other traditional methods	1.0	1.7	1.6	2.0	0.5	1.1	1.0	0.7	0.6	0.9
Number of women	2,167	6,911	2,536	7,953	1,013	7,967	968	7,482	1,893	7,827

SOURCE: NIPORT, Mitra and Associates, and ORC Macro 2001, Mitra et al. 1997; Mitra et al. 1994; Huq and Cleland 1990; Mitra and Kamal 1985.

Bangladesh Demographic and Health Survey (BDHS) suggests that the condom is more widely used in urban than in rural areas. The use pattern of other contraceptive methods is more or less the same in both rural and urban areas.

There has been a constant decline in the crude death rate (CDR) in Bangladesh over the last two decades. The CDR decreased from 30 in the 1940s to less than 10 in 2001. The low CDR reflects the improvements in health, as well as the relatively young age, of the population, and the lower risk of dying associated with young age. Mortality rates cannot be reliably estimated due to the absence of a complete vital registration system in Bangladesh. Best estimates are, however, derived from surveys and data collected by the Bangladesh Bureau of Statistics (BBS). It is estimated that infant mortality was between 130 to 160 deaths per thousand live births until the early 1970s. A rapid decline has been observed in the last two decades in both rural and urban areas; it is now estimated to be 75 and 81, respectively. The rural-urban difference is observed in other indicators of mortality, such as child mortality and under-five mortality rates. Both child mortality and under-five mortality rates are lower in urban than rural areas.

TABLE 2.18   Indicators of mortality rate by residence, 1991–2000

Types of Mortality	1991 CPS		1993–94 BDHS		1996–97 BDHS		1999–2000 BDHS	
	Urban	Rural	Urban	Rural	Urban	Rural	Urban	Rural
Infant Mortality	69	84	81	103	73	91	75	81
Child Mortality	30	34	36	56	25	44	24	35
Under five Mortality	97	115	114	153	96	131	97	113

SOURCE: NIPORT, Mitra and Associates, and ORC Macro 2001; Mitra et al. 1997; Mitra et al. 1994; Mitra, Lerman and Islam, 1993.

IMPLICATIONS

Highlights of the Urban Conditions

In Bangladesh, the state of physical infrastructure is poor. It is unable to properly accommodate and facilitate a growing urban population. One of the reasons is that cities do not generate enough surpluses to invest in their own basic urban services. It is argued that rapid urbanization in Bangladesh has had serious implications for the level of productivity, the state of urban infrastructure, and environmental conditions. The argument follows that the cities are simply growing faster than the capacity of the economy to support them. In general, the rapid growth of the urban population is likely to increase the absolute number of under-served groups, therefore having serious implications on the people living in urban areas.

Poverty is highly prevalent among the urban population, thereby directly and indirectly affecting a majority of the people living in urban areas. The socio-economic conditions of the urban poor are often worse than the people living in rural areas due to dense urban living conditions. Rapid urbanization is likely to generate increased demands for facilities, services, and resources, which will continue to outstrip the ability of the local government to provide them. With an increase in the urban population, it is difficult to find waste disposal sites within easy access. This will likely delay the collection time and increase transportation costs.

Generally, people move to cities with the expectation of improving their economic condition and quality of life. It is apparent that many cities in Bangladesh have reached the point where the delivery of basic services is inadequate. In many urban centers, large numbers of people live in slums in extreme poverty. Squatter settlements of the poor are common in the large cities. These often-illegal settlements reflect the inability of the government to keep pace with the rapidly rising demand for housing and related services. As a consequence of rising urban poverty, it is not surprising that slum dwellers have inadequate access to health services.

Urban development depends heavily on the transportation system. Unfortunately, such essential infrastructure is poorly developed in Bangladesh. While small towns have managed with manual transport (like the cycle rickshaw for passenger movement or the cycle van for goods movement), the larger cities face a shortage of motorized vehicles. The public transport system available in the bigger cities is inadequate and poorly managed.

There has always been a conspicuous case of urban bias in the public sector investments. Although urban areas contain less than one-fourth of the national population in Bangladesh, the sector has received more than its fair share in resource allocation. The large cities generally make a disproportionate contribution to GDP as they enjoy economies of scale and consequently have a higher national income and productivity per capita than the rest of the nation.

Major Benefits

Despite many problems, migration to the cities generates opportunities for many. Migration to urban areas not only offers better opportunities for improving material conditions, but also opens up a wide scope of choices for children's education. Money remitted by migrants also directly contributes to the rural economy. Urban growth gives rise to economies of scale. Industries benefit from concentrations of suppliers and consumers, which allows for savings in communications and transportation expenditure. Large cities also provide differentiated labor markets and assist with the rapid pace of technological innovation. People benefit from improved education and health services with the expansion of urbanization.

The urban informal sector in Bangladesh is an important component of the urban sector. It provides employment and generates income for a large proportion of people. It is well recognized that the urban informal sector that comprises a number of small and micro enterprises and embodies a wide range of activities (e.g., hawking, street vending, knife sharpening, garbage and waste collecting, and rickshaw pulling) is no less important than the formal sector, even if it is far less taken into account in official statistics. The urban sector provides employment, shelter and extends the scope for income generation activities, education, and health care. Every year, a larger number of rural people move into the urban areas in search of jobs, better health care, higher education, and improved housing facilities. Some of these in-migrants to the urban areas might have either remained as surplus labor in the rural areas or stayed as disguisedly unemployed.

Major Problems

In Bangladesh, the central government manages urban development activities rather than the locally elected bodies. Several ministries are involved in the development of these urban areas. The involvement of multiple organizations created uncoordinated and overlapping service delivery systems, which resulted in duplication of efforts and sub-division of responsibilities.

Environmental conditions, especially water pollution problems arising from inadequate treatment of sewage, poor drainage, and inappropriate disposal of solid waste, are one of the major problems faced by the urban dwellers. The quality of the urban environment depends a great deal on the availability of the essential utility services like sanitation, sewerage, drainage, drinking water supply, garbage disposal, electricity, and gas or fuel for cooking. With rapid urban growth and expansion of geographic areas, the provision of essential services remains unsatisfactory and highly inadequate. Due to unplanned urban growth, many of the urban centers in Bangladesh now suffer from problems of drainage and stagnation of rainwater.

Problems of garbage collection and poor drainage are acute in all urban areas, particularly in the larger cities. Furthermore, waste generated from industries, such as textile, chemical, rubber, and plastics, is discharged into nearby water bodies. As slum dwellers and squatters often live near waste disposal dumps, they have a higher likelihood of being affected by the deteriorating urban environment. Subsequently, the incidence of morbidity is found to be higher among slum-dwellers.

The urban poor have little access to water and environmental sanitation. Particularly, access to these facilities is extremely limited in squatter populations. In some cases, the urban poor are worse off than their rural counterparts that are provided with low cost alternatives. In major cities, the rapidly growing slum populations live with little or no basic health services. Most of the programs and policies regarding water supply and sanitation do not include people living in slum areas as part of the target population. Plans for proper and hygienic collection and disposal of garbage are either non-existent or insufficient.

The proportion of urban population with access to tap water is small. A majority of the urban population, especially in the medium-sized and small towns, depend on tube wells for drinking water. Only the SMAs and a few other large towns are served by central water supply systems. According to the 1991 census, only 26 per cent of the urban population was served by piped water and only 11 per cent had access to adequate excreta disposal facilities. In urban poor settlements, only about one-third of the population has access to safe drinking water. The major sources of water in such settlements are private hand tube wells or other sources as opposed to municipal piped water. Moreover, supply of water has been rarely sufficient to meet the increasing demand and need.

Government's Overall Plan

Although the government of Bangladesh has long been aware of the rapid pace of urbanization and the associated physical, economic, and social problems, it does not have a defined policy on urbanization. There have been several specific policy measures, which indirectly affect the trend and characteristics of urbanization and urban growth. A number of planning documents, particularly Five-Year Development Plans, have identified several urban issues and allocated resources to solve these issues. Institutional arrangements for policy-making, planning, and providing services to the urban population lack coordination. For example, several government, semi-government, and local government organizations engage in providing services and they lack coordination among themselves.

The National Report on Human Settlement prepared by the government of Bangladesh for the 1976 UN Habitat 1 Conference identified the issues relating to human settlement and urbanization, and recommended specific measures to resolve them. In particular, it recommended the designation of various planning regions and identification of one medium-sized town as the focal point in each region. The Second Five-Year Plan (1980–85) suggested extending infrastructure and service facilities from 100 urban centers to 1,200 growth centers distributed all over the country. The primary objective of the policy was to prevent city-based polarized growth and to promote more balanced growth throughout the country.

In 1982, the government upgraded all Thana headquarters into Upazilas to promote a policy of decentralized administration and local level development. The Third (1985–90) and Fourth (1990–95) Five-Year Plans included several policy initiatives for balanced development. However, none of these plans was actually implemented. The Upazila system was abolished in 1991, which resulted in lowered importance of the Upazila headquarters as urban growth centers.

The National Housing Policy (1993), the Bangladesh Urban and Shelter Sector Review (1993), the Bangladesh Urban Sector National Programme Document (1994), and the Bangladesh National Habitat II Report (1996) have suggested policy issues and action plans for achieving a balanced development process. In addition, these documents also mentioned the issues related to spatial aspects of urbanization and urban poverty. Unfortunately, none of these policies have yet been implemented.

CONCLUSIONS

Rapid urbanization has created an inter-regional imbalance in Bangladesh's development process. Consequently, development activities have been concentrated in a few large cities. Large scale rural to urban migration has created a massive urban poor sector. Reducing the rate of growth of the large cities, particularly the SMAs, requires a concerted effort. The growth of these urban centers could be reduced by the decentralization of the administrative structures. To facilitate a more regionally balanced development, medium-sized cities should be given more support by allocating incentives for setting up industries in the less economically active regions. Moreover, rapid urbanization has serious implications for the level of productivity, the state of urban infrastructure, and environmental conditions. Since cities are growing faster than the capacity of the economy to support the extra labor force, social unrest is likely to remain a major factor in the coming years.

ENDNOTES

1   We have combined Bangladesh official data with UN projections to produce Figures 1 and 2. This will be done throughout the volume to provide a standard set of figures showing the period 1950 through 2030. Eds.

2   "Absolute poor" refers to the inability of an individual to meet the minimum requirements of life. In other words, an individual having an income which is inadequate for providing his minimum requirements of life is recognized as absolute poor.

3   A person having a monthly income below Taka 2500 (US$42) is defined as "hard core poor."

CHAPTER 3

Urban Scenario in India in the New Millennium

PREM P. TALWAR

India's urban scenario is similar to that of most of the developing countries. The second most populous country of the world, with both an ancient culture and sectors of high modernization, India is still overwhelmingly rural; only about a quarter (exactly 27.8 per cent in 2001) of its population is living in urban areas. It is less urbanized than any of the other major countries of Asia (except Thailand and Sri Lanka); its level of urbanization is in fact more akin to Africa than to the rest of Asia.

Though only a small percentage of the population lives in urban areas, that urban population is concentrated in a few large cities, which has made life difficult there. Living conditions in most of the urban slums where migrants settle down initially are often worse than the areas from where they moved. The physical environment, the mode of life, and economic and political conditions in urban areas are usually distinctly different from those in rural areas. There is, therefore, a need to study these urban population groups separately, in order to plan to meet their needs and enhance their quality of life. This chapter attempts to examine the urban scenario in India, including that in small towns, medium-sized cities, metropolitan areas, and mega cities. The emphasis will be on understanding the trends, structure and processes of urbanization, its advantages, problems, and issues so that its negative impact can be minimized and positive impact maximized.

URBAN GROWTH IN INDIA

Definition of Urban Areas

Definitions of urbanization differ around the world. For the most part, however, the concept is generally based on the following four considerations:

(1) size and/or density of habitation;
(2) predominant economic activity of the area;
(3) socio-economic characteristics; and even
(4) consideration of local administration.

In the case of India, the demographic data are presented separately for rural and urban areas. The unit of classification is "town" for urban areas and "village" for the rural. In the 2001 census, the definition of urban area (towns) is:

(a) All places with a municipality, corporation, cantonment Board or Notified Town Area Committee, etc.

(b) Places that satisfy the following criteria:
    (i) A minimum population of 5000.
    (ii) At least 75 per cent of male working population engaged in non-agricultural pursuits.
    (iii) A density of population of at least 400 persons per sq. km.

(c) Besides, some places having distinct urban characteristics were considered as urban even if they did not satisfy all the criteria mentioned under (b) above. Such cases include major project colonies, areas of intensive industrial development, railway colonies, important tourist centres, etc.

The census recognizes five different classes of urban areas.
Towns in India are divided into six population size categories:

100,000+	Size class I
50,000–99,000	II
20,000–49,000	III
10,000–19,999	IV
5,000–9,999	V
<5000	VI

56

Urban agglomerations (UA) are defined as clusters of towns where at least one of its constituent towns should satisfy the criterion given above and the total population of all the constituents should not be less than 20,000 (in 1991 census).

Cities are defined as towns with populations of 100,000 and above.

Metropolitan cities/urban agglomerations are defined as those with populations of one million and over.

Mega cities are defined as those with populations of five million and over.

India's Urban Population

All India

India is one of the least urbanized countries of the world. The growth in the urban population in India since 1951 is shown in Table 3.1. The level of urbanization has increased by only 11 percentage points in the last 50 years, from 17 to 28 per cent. The size of the urban population has increased from about 62 million in 1951 to 285 in 2001. This increase is almost five times in a period of five decades, though percent urban has gone up only 1.5 times in this period. Therefore, the significance of urbanization for India is more in terms of population size in urban areas than its level or proportion. The number of towns/urban agglomerations in which this population resides and the rate of growth of the urban population is also shown. The rate of urban population growth has started

TABLE 3.1   India's urbanization, 1951–2001

Census year	No. of towns and urban agglomerations	Total pop. (million)	Exponential Growth Rate	Urban pop. (million)	Percentage urban	Urban Exponential Growth rate
1951	2843	361.1	1.24	62.4	17.3	3.47
1961	2365	439.2	1.96	78.9	18.0	2.34
1971	2590	548.2	2.22	109.1	19.9	3.21
1981	3378	683.3	2.20	159.5	23.3	3.83
1991	3768	844.3	2.12	217.2	25.7	3.09
2001	4368	1,027.0	1.96	285.4	27.8	2.71

showing a decline after a peak of 3.83 in the decade 1971–81. Three observations are important here:

(1)   the number of towns/urban agglomerations is increasing rapidly;
(2)   there is a decline in the growth rate of both total and urban populations;
(3)   the pace of urbanization in India is slowing down, perhaps because the overall growth rate has declined. The urban growth rate is still greater than the total population growth rate by almost one percentage point.

This urban growth must be set in the larger context of India's population growth. Overall population growth rates in India increased from about 1.2 per cent to about 2.2 per cent in the first two decades after independence, due to a rapid decline in mortality that accompanied the spread of new medical and public health technology. After 1981, fertility began to decline as well, bringing down the overall growth rates from their peak of about 2.2 per cent to the level of about 2.0 per cent in the last decade of 1991–2001. Since 1999, it has come down to the level of 1.7 per cent.

The States
The total population of India in the 2001 census was 1,027 million, of which 285 million, or 27.8 per cent, live in urban areas. This population is spread over 35 administrative units—28 states and seven Union Territories. Only 19 administrative units (16 states and three municipal areas) were larger than 10 million in 2001 and they accounted for 97 per cent of the total population. This study of urban structure and conditions will, for the most part, limit itself to these 19 units with populations of more than 10 million each. The study of trends over the past half-century, however, will focus on only 16 major states, as three states were newly constituted in 2000.

The level of urbanization of different states in the country is shown in Table 3.2, below (first and last columns, figures in parenthesis). Though only about 28 per cent of the country's population lived in urban areas in 2001, the proportion ranges from a high of 44 per cent in Tamil Nadu (except Delhi, the capital town where 93 per cent of the population is urban) to 10.5 per cent in Bihar. Most of the states are urbanized to the extent of about 20–30 per cent.

58

The trend in the percent urban in India and its states in the last five decades is also shown in Table 3.2. In the first year (1951) and the last year (2001), the levels of urbanization have been shown; for the intervening periods the change in urbanization has been shown by index numbers, starting from 100 in the base year of 1951. The year 1951 represents not only the first decade of the last 50 years of the 20th century but also the first census of the Independent India.

The level of urbanization in India at the first independent census (1951) was quite low—only about 17 per cent, varying between 4 and 29 per cent in different states. There were only six states where the levels were in the twenties; the remaining had levels in tens or even lower. The levels were still low in the 2001 census, 28 per cent for the country as a whole and varying from 10 to 44 per cent. Two states, Orissa and Assam, where levels were very low, 4.1 and 4.3 per cent respectively in 1951, showed relatively sharp increases in urban population, their 2001 index numbers being 266 and 195 per cent, respectively. In contrast, Bihar, where the level of urbanization was also very low in 1951, comparable to

TABLE 3.2 Index of urban population percentages for large states, 1951–2001 (percentages shown in parentheses)

State/Region	% Index of Population Urban					
	1951	1961	1971	1981	1991	2001
India	100 (17.3)	104	115	135	149	161 (27.8)
Andhra Pradesh	100 (17.4)	100	111	134	155	156 (27.1)
Assam	100 (4.3)	167	205	230	258	295 (12.7)
Bihar	100 (6.8)	124	147	184	193 (10.5)	154
Gujarat	100 (27.2)	95	103	110	127	137 (37.3)

59

Haryana	100 (17.1)	101	104	128	144	170 (29.0)
Jammu & Kashmir	100 (14.1)	118	132	150	167	177 (24.9)
Karnataka	100 (23.0)	97	106	126	134	148 (34.0)
Kerala	100 (13.5)	112	120	139	196	193 (26.0)
Madhya Pradesh	100 (12.0)	119	136	169	193	223 (26.7)
Maharashtra	100 (28.8)	98	108	122	134	148 (42.4)
Orissa	100 (4.1)	154	205	288	327	366 (15.0)
Punjab	100 (21.7)	106	109	128	136	156 (33.9)
Rajasthan	100 (18.5)	88	95	114	124	126 (23.4)
Tamil Nadu	100 (24.3)	110	125	135	141	181 (43.9)
Uttar Pradesh	100 (13.6)	95	103	132	146	153 (20.8)
West Bengal	100 (23.4)	103	104	111	115	117 (28.0)

NOTE: The figures in parenthesis indicate the percent of the population in urban areas in 1951 and 2001. For the intervening periods, figures are given in index numbers with 1951 level as 100. This table gives information for only 16 states because two states, Chattisgarh and Jharkhand, have been newly formed, only around the year 2000. Delhi will be included in the study of metropolitan towns.

Orissa and Assam, showed only 54 per cent increases in the urban proportion in the last five decades.

Another interesting feature of increase in urbanization in the country is that most of the states have shown 50 to 60 per cent increases in the levels of urbanization in the last 50 years. Four states, however, Gujarat (in west), Karnataka (in the south), Rajasthan (in the north) and West Bengal (in the east) have shown much lower rates of increase in urbanization. West Bengal has been at the lowest rung with an increase in urbanization of only 17 per cent in the last 50 years. That is, urbanization is moving at very different rates in different states, which might in the future lead to a radical difference between states: some more wealthy and advanced, and others more backward.

Urban Population Growth and Its Composition

Three sources of growth of urban population, in the absence of changes in the definition of urban areas, are:

(1) natural increase (excess of births over deaths) in the population;
(2) migration of rural population to urban areas; and
(3) changes in the administrative boundaries from rural to urban—an annexation of some rural areas to urban agglomerations or rural areas becoming urban areas or *vice versa*.

Limited information is available on the third component. We know that the number of towns/cities/urban agglomerations in 2001 reached 4,368 from 3,768 in 1991. That is, 600 new towns/urban agglomerations have been added in the decade of 1991–2000. It is obvious that the expansion of urban localities through transformation of rural settlements into cities has contributed to the increase in the urban population, though its exact contribution cannot be estimated.

Information on the first two components, natural increase and rural-to-urban migration is more complete. Table 3.3 shows the natural growth rates and actual total growth rates of both rural and urban populations. The differences can be taken as estimates of out- or in-migration levels.

Care must be exercised in interpreting this table. First, the data for natural increase and total population growth rates come from two different sources. The comparison may thus be affected by the inaccuracies of data in these sources. In this connection, it may especially

61

TABLE 3.3 Rates of natural increase and total growth for rural and urban areas in the states of India

State/region	Rural Pop. Growth rate (%)		Urban Pop. Growth rate (%)	
	NI (1991–2000)	GR (1991–2001)	NI (1991–2000)	GR (1991–2001)
India	1.96	1.65	1.59	2.71
Andhra Pradesh	1.46	1.27	1.60	1.37
Assam	1.96	1.54	1.47	3.09
Bihar	2.22	2.37	1.78	2.56
Gujarat	1.89	1.58	1.70	2.83
Haryana	2.27	1.88	1.81	4.11
Karnataka	1.63	1.14	1.59	2.53
Kerala	1.17	0.96	1.18	0.74
Madhya Pradesh	2.22	1.81	1.68	2.79
Maharashtra	1.65	1.41	1.62	2.95
Orissa	1.58	1.29	1.43	2.61
Punjab	1.77	1.16	1.51	3.19
Rajasthan	2.48	2.43	1.97	2.71
Tamil Nadu	1.11	-0.53	1.23	3.56
Uttar Pradesh	2.42	2.12	2.04	2.84
West Bengal	1.82	1.56	0.98	1.84

NOTE: NI stands for natural increase in population defined as birth rate minus death rate for the period. GR stands for population growth rate and is defined as exponential growth rate obtained from two censuses 1991 and 2001. The source of data for the former is the Sample Registration System, recording births and deaths in a sample of areal units on a regular basis. The latter is obtained from two censuses. The data for Jammu and Kashmir have not been included as no census was taken in 1991.

be pointed out that the Sample Registration System data of Bihar are particularly suspect; it is difficult to say anything about their reliability.

Two observations from this table tell much of the story of the increasing urbanization in India:

(1)   the natural rate of population growth in rural areas is almost always higher than total rural population growth, implying that there is out-migration from the rural areas; and

(2) the total population growth rate in urban areas is almost always higher than the natural rate of population growth, implying in-migration in the urban areas.

That is, there is apparent out-migration from the rural areas in all the states of the country except Bihar (whose data are suspect). In the urban areas, on the other hand, total growth rates are higher than natural increase in all states except Andhra Pradesh and Kerala. (The latter has a high out-migration to all other states in India, and to the Middle East.) For all the other states, in-migration appears to be contributing substantially, about one percentage point, to urban population growth.

It will be of interest to compare the contribution of natural increase and migration to urban areas over time. Examining the difference between the rate of natural increase and the total growth rate for rural and urban areas in all India for the past three decades can do this. The data are shown in Table 3.4.

As overall growth rates decline, there is a decline in the apparent in-migration component of urban growth. Whereas in-migration added almost 2 percentage points to urban growth in 1971–81, that level has been reduced to just over 1 percentage point in the past decade. Apparently, rural out-migration has been more stable at about one-quarter to one-third of the rural population growth.

TABLE 3.4 Rate of natural increase and total increase for urban and rural areas in India, 1971–2001

Decade	Rate of natural increase (RNI)		Total Increase		Diff (Tot – RNI)	
	Urb	Rur	Urb	Rur	Urb	Rur
1971–81	1.93	2.00	3.83	1.78	+1.90	–.22
1981–91	1.96	2.14	3.09	1.80	+1.13	–.34
1991–2001	1.59	1.96	2.71	1.65	+1.11	–.29

Characteristics of Rural-to-Urban and Urban-to-Rural Migrant Populations

This section examines the background characteristics of rural-to-urban and urban-to-rural migrants.

Despite the need to know the characteristics of the migrants for both theoretical and policy considerations, little data are available on this aspect. The reason is that such a study requires a large sample and careful planning; it cannot be undertaken as a by-product of some other study on migration.

Fortunately, the National Sample Survey Organization of the Government of India conducted one study on migrants in India during the period July 1999–2000.[1] It took a large sample to collect data on different streams of migrants— rural-to-rural, rural-to-urban, urban-to-rural and urban-to-urban—and their particulars to give a profile of the migrants.[2] This section attempts to summarize those findings, particularly in relation to the stream of rural-to-urban and urban-to-rural migration, directly of interest to this chapter. The study brought out five major findings.

(1)   The total number of migrants in the study, considering all periods of migration, was found to be 245 million. This represents about 27 per cent of the total population. That is, just over one-quarter of the population was classed as migrants in the country in 1999–2000, though the time of their migration was not stipulated.

(2)   This number was split into various streams of migrants; their distribution is shown below:

Rural-to-rural	62%
Rural-to-urban	19%
Urban-to-rural	6%
Urban-to-urban	13%

The great majority of migration is rural to rural. When the urban-to-urban migrants are added, the total is 75 per cent. In other words, only about 25 per cent of all the migrants or about 7 per cent of the population changed their residence from rural to urban or urban to rural in India. This number comes to 61.3 million.

TABLE 3.5   Percentage distribution of migrants

Stream of movement	Within state		Between states	Total
	Same district	Different district		
Rural to rural	75	20	5	100
Rural to urban	44	36	20	100
Urban to rural	47	33	20	100
Urban to urban	37	43	20	100

(3)   This overall migration could be within a district, among districts within a state, or among states. This distribution is shown in Table 3.5. Rural-to-rural migration is short-distance movement, for the most part within one district, and there is very little between states. The rural-urban and inter-urban streams, however, involve a substantially longer movement, with as much as a fifth moving between states. We do not know, however, the actual distances involved. They may be very small if the migration occurs from border villages to border towns.

(4)   Migration is much higher among females than males; it is particularly so in rural areas.

	Females	Males
Migration rates per 1,000 persons: Rural	426	69
Urban	418	257

Just over 40 per cent of females move from rural and urban areas (to rural or urban); the percentage for males is 7 and 26 respectively.

(5)   The major reason for migration is strongly determined by gender. Males move for employment, studies, and other reasons; females move for family (marriage etc.) reasons. Table 3.6 provides the details.

65

TABLE 3.6 Distribution of migrants (per 1000) by reason for migration for each of the migration streams

Reason for migration	Male				Female			
	R to R	R to U	U to R	U to U	R to R	R to U	U to R	U to U
In search of employment	68	50	235	89	2	8	8	3
In search of better employment	118	82	195	99	4	8	11	3
To take up employment	68	69	86	94	1	6	4	5
Transfer of service or contract	49	88	44	163	2	5	5	15
Proximity to place of work	11	10	9	12	0	3	1	1
Employment	**314**	**300**	**570**	**448**	**9**	**30**	**28**	**28**
Marriage	121	23	17	14	906	642	614	550
Movement of parents/ earning member	268	225	244	315	51	315	292	337
Social	**389**	**248**	**261**	**329**	**957**	**858**	**906**	**887**
Studies	69	20	80	44	4	6	16	10
Other reasons	228	432	90	179	31	106	50	75
Miscellaneous	**297**	**452**	**170**	**223**	**35**	**112**	**66**	**85**

TABLE 3.7   Percentage migration by income

Stream by sex	Household monthly per capita expenditure class			
	< Rs. 340	340–525	525-950	950+
Male R-U	25.0	32.5	29.7	12.7
Female R-U	19.1	27.8	34.1	19.0
	Household monthly per capita expenditure class			
	<500	500–915	915–1500	1500+
Male U-R	40.9	34.7	14.9	9.5
Female U-R	42.4	34.7	13.5	9.4

NOTE: Rs. is Indian currency. US$1 is equal to about Rs.48.

(6) Migration in very much an economic or class matter. Table 3.7 shows that movement from rural to urban, for both males and females, comes primarily from middle class income categories. Almost 60 per cent of the urban in-migrants are in the category of Rs 340 or more. Those who migrate back from urban to rural are generally of lower income categories. Almost half of these migrants are in the lowest income category (< 500 Rs).

Distribution of Urban Population by City-Size Categories

Distribution of Towns/Cities in Different City-size Categories

The distribution of the total number of towns, cities, and urban agglomerations in different city-size categories is shown in Table 3.8. The percentage of towns and cities in the largest three categories (I, II, and III) has been increasing over time at the cost of towns in categories IV, V and VI.

The urban settlement pattern seems to have completely changed recently. This shows a clear reduction in the percentage of the population living in the smaller sized cities, under 50,000, and a sharp increase in the population living in large cities. The percentage of the population living in city-size 50,000 to 99,999 category II, has remained roughly constant. In other words, cities of 50,000 or less are losing urban population to cities of 100,000 and over. It may be noted that more than

TABLE 3.8 Number of towns, cities, and urban agglomerations in different size categories and their percentage distribution, 1951–2001

Year	No. of towns	Percentage distribution of urban agglomerations/ towns by size category					
		I	II	III	IV	V	VI
1951	2843	2.7	3.3	11.7	21.8	40.2	20.4
1961	2365	4.5	5.7	19.3	31.7	31.3	7.6
1971	2590	6.0	7.0	22.5	33.4	25.2	5.9
1981	3378	6.7	8.3	22.7	32.5	22.8	7.1
1991	3768	8.2	9.5	25.7	31.5	21.0	5.1
2001	4368	9.0	9.2	26.4	30.7	20.3	4.4

Town size categories
Class I: 100,000+
Class II: 50,000–99,999
Class III: 20,000–49,999
Class IV: 10,000–19,999
Class V: 5,000–9,999
Class VI: <5,000

TABLE 3.9 Percentage distribution of urban population in different city-size categories, 1951–2001

Year	Percentage urban population by city size					
	I	II	III	IV	V	VI
1951	44.6	10.0	15.7	13.6	13.0	3.1
1961	51.4	11.2	16.9	12.8	6.9	0.8
1971	57.2	10.9	16.0	10.9	4.5	0.4
1981	60.4	11.6	14.3	9.5	3.6	0.5
1991	65.2	10.9	13.2	7.8	2.6	0.3
2001	68.7	9.7	12.2	6.8	2.4	0.2

two-thirds of the urban population are settled in cities of 100,000 and over. The dual implications of (1) problems in large-sized cities, and (2) neglect of small-sized cities, are relevant to the overall social and economic development of the country. There is need to assess the infrastructural development policies in the light of this pattern of urban settlement.

The rapid increase in the population in large cities has resulted in the growth of what are called "slums" and "squatter settlements" where living conditions are often seen as pathetic. In India, 20–5 per cent of the urban population lives in slums and squatter settlements due to non-availability of affordable housing in formal settlements. This is very high, to the extent of even 50 per cent in the mega cities.

Settlement Pattern in Large Urban Agglomerations and Metropolitan Areas

There were 393 urban agglomerations in India with a population size of 100,000 and more in 2001; the number increased from 300 in 1991. Their distribution by size is shown in Table 3.10, together with the proportion of the category I cities and the sex ratios

TABLE 3.10   Distribution of Class I (>100,000) cities and urban agglomerations by population size, 1991 and 2001

Size Category	1991			2001		
	No. U.A.s	% Urb Pop	Sex Ratio*	No. U.A.s	% Urb Pop	Sex Ratio*
<200,000	167	16.4	1095	219	15.2	1087
200,000–299,999	40	6.9	1106	57	7.1	1088
300,000–499,999	40	11.1	1104	44	8.8	1085
500,000–999,999	30	15.0	1135	38	12.8	1110
> 1 mil	**23**	**50.6**	**1157**	**35**	**55.1**	**1148**
1mil–1,999,999	14	12.4	1134	22	14.0	1128
2mil-499,999	5	11.6	1115	7	10.5	1148
>5 mil	4	26.6	1188	6	30.6	1158
Total	300	100%		393	100	

NOTE: Sex ratio is males per 1000 females.

TABLE 3.11   Urban agglomerations, 1951–2001

Census Year	Pop. of million plus urban agglomerations as % of urban population and total population in India		
	No. of units	% of Urban Pop.	% of Total Pop.
1951	5	18.8	3.3
1961	7	22.9	4.1
1971	9	25.5	5.1
1981	12	26.4	6.2
1991	23	32.5	8.4
2001	35	37.8	10.5

The population in city-size one million and over increased by 5 percentage points in the decade 1991–2001. The overall sex ratio for all India is about 1,072 (males per 1,000 females). The cities all show higher sex ratios than the country as a whole. It is men who migrate to the cities, while women remain behind in the rural areas. There is also a tendency for the sex ratio to increase with city size.

Settlement Patterns in Metropolitan cities/Urban Agglomerations
Thirty-five cities in India had populations of one million or more in 2001 (defined as metropolitan urban agglomerations); this number was 23 in 1991 and only five in 1951. That is, India added 18 cities with populations of one million each in a matter of 40 years (1951–91); the addition in the last decade 1991–2001 alone was 12. These cities are dominating the pattern of urbanization in India as almost 50 per cent of the urban population of the large cities (population size of 100,000 and over) in 1991 were living in the metropolitan areas; the percentage increased to 55 in 2001.

Almost two-fifths of the total urban population in India lived in the cities with populations of one million and more in 2001, while 10 per cent of the total population of the country lived in these cities. It is therefore obvious that those living in these cities greatly affect the quality of life in the urban areas. Their problems become the problems of urban India. The state-wise location of these cities is shown below:

Uttar Pradesh	6
Maharashtra	4
Gujarat	4
Bihar	4
Andhra Pradesh	3
Madhya Pradesh	3
Tamil Nadu	3
Punjab	2

West Bengal, Karnataka, Rajasthan, Kerala, Haryana and Delhi have one each.

Settlement Pattern in Mega Cities

India had four cities with populations of five million and over in 1991: Mumbai, Kolkata, Delhi, and Chennai; this number increased to six in 2001 with the addition of Bangalore and Hyderabad. These six mega cities have:

- 5.8 per cent of the total population of the country
- 21 per cent of the total urban population
- 30.6 per cent of the population of cities of 100,000 and more
- 55.6 per cent of the population of metropolitan urban agglomerations (of one million and over)

The corresponding percentages in 1991 were 4.4, 17.1, 26.6, and 52.7 respectively.

The trend in population size of these six mega cities is shown in Table 3.12. The actual numbers (in millions) are shown in parentheses for the first (1951) and the last years (2001) and index number values for the intervening years.

The largest mega city in India is Mumbai with a population of 16.4 million. The fastest growing mega city is Delhi, which has grown by a factor of nine since Independence. Next in growth rates come Mumbai (8 times), Bangalore (7 times), Hyderabad (4.9 times), Chennai (4.3 times), and Kolkata (2.8 times). Kolkata was the largest city in India at the time of Independence but population growth there has remained very slow, in part because of economic and industrial stagnation. Another noteworthy fact is that Chennai has been a large city since Independence but its population growth remained slower than the other two southern mega cities of Bangalore and Hyderabad. Bangalore has been growing very rapidly, particularly after 1981.

71

TABLE 3.12   Index numbers of population size of India's six mega cities, 1951–2001

Mega City	Year					
	1951	**1961**	**1971**	**1981**	**1991**	**2001**
Mumbai (Pop Mil)	100 (2.0)	140	201	278	424	818 (16.4)
Kolkata (Pop Mil)	100 (4.7)	128	159	197	234	281 (13.2)
Delhi (Pop Mil)	100 (1.4)	164	254	399	583	914 (12.8)
Chennai (Pop Mil)	100 (1.5)	126	206	278	348	428 (6.4)
Bangalore (Pop Mil)	100 (0.786)	153	212	372	515	723 (5.7)
Hyderabad (Pop Mil)	100 (1.14)	110	160	230	383	487 (5.5)

Another important feature of the profile of these six mega cities is the discrepancy in the sex composition of the population. The sex ratios (males per 1,000 females) in 1991 and 2001 in these mega cities are shown below:

The following observations emerge:

1.   (1) The two fastest growing cities have higher sex ratios; the sex ratios of Mumbai and Delhi have further increased in 2001 over the level of 1991. It is a reflection on the pattern of migration: males are migrating alone to the cities; women are staying behind.

2.   (2) The sex ratio of Kolkata is moving back towards a balancing of male and female populations in the city.

72

TABLE 3.13   Sex ratios in the six mega cities, 1991 and 2001

Mega city	Growth Index 1951–2001	1991	2001
Mumbai	818	1206	1215
Kolkata	281	1209	1151
Delhi	914	1203	1217
Chennai	428	1079	1052
Bangalore	723	1108	1104
Hyderabad	487	1076	1066

3.   (3) The sex ratios in Chennai and Hyderabad do not show more sex selective migration than the total country where the sex ratio was 1,072 in 2001.

4.   (4) The city of Bangalore shows a relatively more balanced sex ratio despite its very rapid rate of growth; it lies between the fastest growing cities of Delhi and Mumbai and their sister cities of Hyderabad and Chennai.

Projections of Urban Growth

The Indian government makes periodic projections of population growth. In 1996, projections of urban proportions were made for three periods, 2006, 2011, and 2016. India's current 28 per cent urban is expected to rise to almost 34 per cent in the next 15 years. States are expected to vary from a low of 14 per cent in Assam to a high of 48 per cent in Maharashtra. There is a tendency for the southern states to be more urbanized than the northern states. The data are shown in Table 3.14.

RURAL-URBAN DIFFERENCES

Rural-Urban Differences in Population Growth

Population Growth Rates

Some characteristics of urban and rural populations for 2001 are given in Table 3.15. The growth rates in the urban areas of all the states are higher than in the rural areas. We saw in Tables 3.3 and 3,4, above, that

TABLE 3.14 Projected percentage urban population for India and its states, 2006–2016

State/Year	2006	2011	2016
All India	30.4	32.0	33.7
Andhra Pradesh	32.2	34.8	36.9
Assam	12.9	13.5	14.2
Bihar	16.3	17.4	18.6
Gujarat	39.3	41.0	42.7
Haryana	29.1	30.6	32.2
Karnataka	35.8	37.6	39.3
Kerala	33.7	36.4	39.1
Madhya Pradesh	28.9	30.9	33.1
Maharashtra	44.4	46.8	48.4
Orissa	18.9	21.1	23.1
Punjab	33.2	34.4	35.7
Rajasthan	26.8	28.2	29.7
Tamil Nadu	38.2	39.6	41.1
Uttar Pradesh	24.3	25.9	27.6
West Bengal	29.1	29.6	30.2

SOURCE: Registrar General of India, New Delhi. Population Projections for India and States, 1996–2001 (projected in 1996 before 2001 census of India).

urban areas have lower rates of natural increase than do rural areas, but that apparent in-migration has kept urban growth rates higher than rural growth rates. This typical phenomenon does not hold true for Kerala where the total urban population growth (0.74 per cent) is lower than the rural (0.96 per cent). This unique feature of the urban profile of Kerala was examined based on its natural rate of population increase for the decade 1991–2001. The figures are shown below:

	Rural	Urban
Exponential population growth rate (1991–2001)	0.96%	0.74%
Natural population growth rate (1990–2000)	1.17%	1.18%

The equality of natural increase in rural and urban areas suggests that demographic transition in the state has come to its final stages. Birth and death rates in both rural and urban areas have reached their lowest levels, though the population is still growing by its momentum. The reduction in the total population growth rates in both rural and urban areas suggests a good deal of out-migration from the state; both within India and out of India to the Middle East countries. Obviously, out-migration is substantially higher from the urban areas. Moreover, the same levels of rural and urban sex ratios in Kerala, which we see in Table 3.15, also suggest that there is no sex preferential movement. One may

TABLE 3.15 Selected characteristics of urban and rural areas for 19 large states in India, 2001

State/Region	Population ('000)	% Urban	% Growth Rates (1991–2001)			Sex Ratio (M/1000F)		
			R	U	U-R	R	U	U-R
India	1,027,015	2708	1.65	2.71	1.06	1057	1110	53
Andhra Pradesh	75,728	2701	1.27	1.37	0.10	1018	1036	18
Assam	26,638	12.7	1.54	3.09	1.55	1064	1139	75
Bihar	82,879	10.5	2.37	2.56	0.19	1079	1150	71
Chattisgarh	20,796	20.0	1.81	2.71	0.90	995	1073	78
Gujarat	50,597	37.3	1.58	2.83	1.25	1057	1137	80
Haryana	21,083	29.0	1.88	4.11	2.23	1153	1180	27
Jammu & Kashmir	10,070	24.9	2.52	3.09	0.57	1079	1216	137
Jharkhand	26,909	22.2	2.31	2.56	0.25	1039	1149	110
Karnataka	52,734	34.0	1.14	2.53	1.39	1025	1064	39
Kerala	31,839	26.0	0.96	0.74	-0.22	945	945	0
Madhya Pradesh	60,385	26.7	1.81	2.79	0.98	1078	1113	35
Maharashtra	96,752	42.4	1.41	2.95	1.54	1042	1144	102
Orissa	36,707	15.0	1.29	2.61	1.32	1014	1117	103
Punjab	24,289	33.9	1.16	3.19	2.03	1127	1180	53
Rajasthan	56,473	23.4	2.43	2.71	0.28	1073	1124	51
Tamil Nadu	62,111	43.9	-0.53	3.56	4.09	1009	1021	12
Uttar Pradesh	166,053	20.8	2.12	2.84	0.72	1107	1138	31
West Bengal	80,221	28.0	1.56	1.84	0.28	1053	1120	67
Delhi	13,783	93.0	0.15	4.14	3.99	1240	1217	–23

NOTE: Though India has 35 Administrative Units, this table gives information for only 19 large Administrative Units, which constitute 97 per cent of the population of the country.

75

also note that the sex ratio of females is more favorable here than in any other state in the country.

Another important point in the growth of the urban population is that the states of Haryana, Punjab, Tamil Nadu, and Delhi have large differences in the rates of population growth between rural and urban areas. While it may be easy to explain such phenomenon in the states of Haryana, Punjab, and Delhi, the reason may be different and difficult to explain for Tamil Nadu. Higher agricultural productivity, more pressure on land in Haryana and Punjab, and relatively better industrial development of these states may explain higher migration of the population from rural to urban areas. Delhi, on the other hand, is the national capital and attracts people not only from neighboring towns and rural areas but also from all parts of the country. In the case of Tamil Nadu, the natural rate of population growth of the rural areas was found to be lower than the urban (because of very low levels of fertility in the state). Further reduction in the rural rate of population growth because of migration to urban areas, created a large difference in the rates of population growth between rural and urban areas there.

Population Sex Ratio

Another feature of the urban population growth in India is an uneven sex distribution of the population, which we have already seen above in Tables 3.10 and 3.15. The overall sex ratio (males per 1,000 females) is 1,072 for the country as a whole, 1,057 for the rural areas, and 1,110 for urban areas. This difference and the direction in the difference suggest that male migrants to urban areas greatly outnumber the female migrants. This is true for all the states except (1) Kerala, where the rural and urban sex ratios are equal, and (2) Delhi, where the urban sex ratio is lower than the rural (though both are high relative to India).

Share of Urban Population in the Total Population Growth

The higher rate of population growth in urban areas is adding relatively larger numbers to the total population of the country though both rural and urban areas have been growing steadily. Even the relatively lower rate of population growth in the rural areas could add large numbers to the population size because of the larger base population. In order to examine the comparative contribution of rural and urban population growth to the total population growth, Table 3.16 shows the share of

TABLE 3.16   Increments in total, urban and rural populations, 1951–2001

Decade	Increment in Population size ('000)			Increment in Percentage	
	Total	Rural	Urban	Rural	Urban
1951–61	781467	616538	164929	78.9	21.1
1961–71	1089249	787475	301774	72.3	27.7
1971–81	1351721	848209	503512	62.8	37.2
1981–91	1629709	1048251	581458	64.3	35.7
1991–2001	1807125	1129686	677439	62.5	37.5

rural and urban population growth to the total population growth in India in the decades since 1951.

In 1951–61, urban growth contributed roughly 20 per cent to the total population growth. By 1991–2001, this had increased to over 37 per cent. Note that the share of urban to total growth appears to have reached a plateau in 1971. Since then, urban growth has contributed just over a third to the total population growth.

Urban and Rural Demographic and Socio-Economic Differences

Urbanization has always meant a change in social organization and life styles. Urbanization draws people into a larger, often global, network of communications and interactions. Urbanization changes the value of children and typically leads to different reproductive strategies. Urbanization usually implies higher levels of literacy, greater population densities, and, thus, interactions with more diverse peoples. It also implies a change in occupations and work habits— from self regulated agricultural pursuits to "other-regulated" precise hours of industrial and service work. Typically, urban residents have higher incomes than do rural peoples, though this does not always mean a higher standard of living. Urban peoples usually have higher quality and more extensive physical infrastructure, such as clean water, sanitation, and electric power. Finally, urban peoples have typically made the transition to low mortality and low fertility, completing the

TABLE 3.17 Selected urban-rural demographic differentials

Condition	% Urban	% Rural
1. Age Distribution		
< 15 years	34.1	38.3
15-59	60.3	54.6
60 +	5.6	7.1
2. Dependency Ratio (15–59/, <15+ 60+)	66	83
3. Sex Ratio (M / 1000 F) Total	1119	1065
Age <15	1074	1071
Age 15–59	1155	1058
Age 60 +	1026	1096
4. Female median age at marriage	18.3 years	16.0 years
5. % Females married below age 18 yrs. (minimum legal age at marriage)	41.3	61.1
6. Crude Death Rate	6.3	9.4
7. Infant Mortality Rate	44	75
8. Child (1–4 years) Mortality	17.0	34.6
9. Under 5 Mortality	61.0	109.6
10. Crude Birth Rate	20.8	27.6
11. Total Fertility Rate	2.3	3.5
12. Mean closed birth interval (mo)	30.9	30.8
13. Mean household size	5.2	5.5
14. Mean ideal number of children	2.3	2.8
Males	1.1	1.5
Females	0.8	1.0
No Preference	0.4	0.3

SOURCE: Census of India, 1991 and 2001; Sample Registration System; National Family Health Survey II, 1998–99.

TABLE 3.18 Selected urban-rural socio-economic and health differentials

Conditions	Urban %	Rural %
Socio-economic Conditions		
1. % Literate: Males	75.7	59.4
Females	63.8	38.9
Total	70.1	49.4
2. Per capita income, 1993–94 (Current Price)	13525	5383
3. % Households with electricity	91.3	48.1
4. % households with piped water	74.5	25.0
5. % households with flush toilet	63.9	8.8
6. Regularly exposed to media	87	50
Reproductive and Health Care Coverage		
1. % pregnant women with ante-natal svc.	69.9	37.4
2. % Pregnant women with Tetanus Toxoid	81.9	62.5
3. % deliveries in institutions	65.1	24.6
4. % infants immunized	60.5	36.6
5. Contraceptive prevalence rate	51.2	39.9
Terminal methods	37.8	35.4
Spacing methods	13.4	4.5
6. Unmet need for family planning	13.5	16.7
7. % women heard about HIV/AIDS	70.3	29.7

SOURCE: Census of India 2001; National Family Health Survey II, 1998–99.

modern demographic transition, earlier than have rural populations. These are some of the urban-rural differences we can observe in India in the recent past.

Tables 3.17 and 3.18, above, tell a common story about urban-rural differences throughout the less developed regions of the world. Demographically, rural populations have higher proportions of young people and women. Working aged men migrate to urban areas, affecting both the age structure and the sex ratio. The age of marriage for women is lower in rural areas. All mortality indices are higher for rural than for urban areas. Both crude birth rates and total fertility rates are lower in urban than in rural areas. Household size is smaller in urban areas and the desire for children is lower. There is a slight increase in urban areas for no sex preference in children. In effect, urban areas show higher levels of all indices of what have come to be called modern reproductive norms.

Exposure to media increases a person's knowledge. Research shows that such media exposure results in greater contribution towards productivity, leading to an overall improvement in economic status and a better quality of life. Table 3.19 shows that urban women are relatively well connected through the media, while rural women tend to be isolated.

A few important observations on the differential profile of urban-rural populations are given below:

(1) The level of literacy in rural areas is very low, particularly for females.
(2) Basic household facilities in rural areas are very poor when compared with urban areas.
(3) The levels of reproductive health program indicators in rural areas are very low; they are particularly poor for three ante-natal check ups of pregnant women, deliveries conducted in institutions, and coverage of infants by all vaccinations (BCG, three DPT, three Polio, and Measles).
(4) The dependency ratio in rural areas is quite high relative to urban areas.
(5) Males heavily inhabit urban areas during their young and productive years—obviously young men move to urban areas for employment purposes. This is evident from the slanted sex ratio in the younger age group (ages 15–59). In the older age group, males have a tendency to move back to the rural areas. That is, males tend to

TABLE 3.19   Percentage of urban and rural women exposed to different types of media

Media	Urban	Rural
Reads a newspaper at least once a week	43.4	12.8
Watches a TV at least once a week	80.6	33.4
Listens to radio at least once a week	46.3	33.0
Visits a cinema at least once a month	18. 1	7.9
Not regularly exposed to any media	12.9	50.1

SOURCE: National Family Health Survey II, 1998–99.

migrate to urban areas during their economically productive years and then migrate back to rural areas after the age of 60.

(6) The levels of mortality in rural areas are very high compared to urban areas; this is particularly so for infant, child, and under-five mortality.

(7) Use of spacing methods in rural areas is very low even though their use in urban areas is also low.

(8) The ideal family size for the rural population is reported to be about half-a-child more than in urban areas—2.8 vis-à-vis 2.3. This is in great part due to a greater preference for male children in rural areas.

(9) Urban women are much better connected through the media; rural women, in contrast, tend to be isolated.

IMPLICATIONS

Summary Scenario of Urban Areas in India

(1) India is one of the least urbanized countries of the world. But the size of its urban population in 2001 is greater than even the total population of the United States, the third largest country of the world. It is, therefore, important that the quality of life of this large group should be improved

(2) About 28 per cent of the population of the country live in urban areas. The pace of urbanization in India seems to have slowed down,

along with the pace of overall population growth. The contribution of the urban population to the total growth of India's population also seems to have reached a plateau. If it is because development of the rural infrastructure has reduced the push factor of rural-to-urban migration, then it is a good sign. If, on the other hand, pull factors of urban areas have reduced due to deteriorating urban conditions, then it is a matter of concern.

(3)   Though the decline in the pace of urbanization is good under the present circumstances (inadequate infrastructure, limited resources, and poor planning), it may still be too high in view of the declining quality of life in urban areas and increasing slum settlements.

(4)   The number of large cities has been increasing over time. Besides, the percentage of the urban population living in city-size categories of 100,000 and over is as large as 69; this percentage is 38 in the city-size category of one million and over, and 21 in the city-size category of five million and over. When these percentages are converted to the base of total population, then 10 per cent of the country's population live in the city-size category of one million and over and 6 per cent in the city-size category of five million and over. This pattern of settlement has problems both for large cities and small towns; the former are over-burdened and the latter are neglected.

(5)   The movement of population from rural to urban is not only towards large cities, it is also male-oriented. The sex ratio (males per 1,000 females) for populations living in different city-size categories is as follows:

100,000+	1,123
1 million+	1,148
5 million+	1,158

These ratios are quite large when compared with India's sex ratio of 1,072 and 1,057 for the total population and for the rural areas respectively. Delhi and Mumbai, the most rapidly growing mega cities, have sex ratios of 1,217 and 1,215, respectively. Though male-oriented movement may be a common phenomenon in rural-to-urban migration, such an imbalance in sex composition in urban areas has its own problems.

(6)   Delhi, closely followed by Mumbai and Bangalore, not only has a large urban population, but is also growing very rapidly. These mega cities need special programs to ensure that they are able to cater to the rapidly growing needs of their populations. In this context, it is worth noting that rural-to-urban migration of males is mainly for employment or studies, while for females, it is marriage or family. This suggests the need for job opportunities and houses for married couples to settle down in urban areas.

(7)   Though the condition of the overall urban population is very much better on socio-economic and demographic indicators, studies also show that life in the urban slums is much worse than even in some rural areas. It means that there are two clear-cut groups that live in urban areas; the latter having very low levels of quality of life indicators.

Implications for Program on Urban Development

Urbanization is generally associated with national economic growth and modernization. It enhances economies of scale in production and consumption, and nurtures a new breed of talent that a modern economy requires. Yet, urbanization has become something of a burden on the quality of life in India. The problem of rapid, uncontrolled growth of the cities, especially when their infrastructure development lags behind, has created the following situations:

(1)   Rapid growth of metropolitan areas, inhabited by imbalanced sex composition—the males outnumbering the females.

(2)   Massive increase in squatters and the proliferation of slums, particularly in metropolitan cities.

(3)   Stagnation and, in many cases, decline in small towns

Urban areas, therefore, are becoming problematic and difficult to manage and control. They are deprived of basic amenities, livable houses, useable transportation, fresh and healthy water and air, and are beset with law and order problems. Unfortunately, urban planners have not been able to respond to the call for urban renewal; the same untidy and unacceptable urban growth continues. The view is gaining ground that cities with a large number of inhabitants may not be sustainable in the long run; it is important and urgent to review and reconsider urban planning strategies. There is need for a two-pronged strategy—immediate measures to make living in mega cities reasonable as they will keep growing in the near future and long-term measures to reduce the burden on metropolitan areas by developing rural areas and small/medium-sized towns through agro-based industries and food processing industries etc. There is also a need to think in terms of integrated rural-urban policies that are required for sustainable development.

Efforts of the Government of India

The government of India has been very much concerned with the problem of rapid urbanization. It has helped the states to initiate several steps in the form of projects (with additional funding) to avoid deterioration in the quality of life in urban areas. The Constitution of India gives responsibility for urban development to the states. The role of the central government is limited to formulating a broad policy framework, issuing guidelines, sanctioning funds, implementing a number of centrally sponsored schemes, processing and monitoring assistance from international and bilateral institutions, and providing technical support and advice for orderly urbanization. Currently, the central government is in the process of formulating a national urban policy to provide long-term broad guidelines. In addition, the central government has sponsored the following schemes for which it provides total or partial funding:

(1) *Integrated Development of Small and Medium Towns.* The objectives of the scheme are: (a) improving infrastructural facilities and helping in the creation of durable public assets in small and medium-sized towns; (b) decentralizing economic growth and employment opportunities, and promoting dispersed urbanization; (c) increasing the availability of service sites for housing, commercial, and industrial use; and (d) promoting resource generating schemes for urban local bodies to improve their overall financial position.

(2) *Infrastructure Development in Mega Cities.* The primary objective of this scheme is to undertake infrastructure development projects of citywide and regional significance covering a wide range of components such as water supply and sewerage, roads and bridges, city transport, and solid waste management. The scheme also

envisages that a Mega City Nodal Agency will be set up with a revolving fund for infrastructure development on a sustainable basis with appropriate direct and indirect cost recovery measures. This scheme is applicable to Mumbai, Kolkata, Chennai, Bangalore, and Hyderabad (Delhi is being handled separately as it is the capital and seat of the central government).

(3) *Prime Minister's Award for Excellence in Urban Planning and Design.* Two national awards have been instituted to encourage innovations and special efforts in urban development. The first is for urban planning and design projects of the built environment of exceptional quality. The second is for innovative ideas, concepts, and plans in urban planning and design where the projects are still in the pipeline or at an early implementation stage.

(4) *Healthy City Program.* The objectives of this program is capacity building for integrating environmental health into all major urban policies and programs, including mega cities, and to take up pilot projects to demonstrate the advantages of the healthy cities program in the five mega cities.

In addition, the central government has also processed the international funding for the states for some of their important projects. These include:

(1) *Tamil Nadu Urban Development Project II.* The project objective is to improve urban infrastructure services in the state in a sustainable manner.

(2) *West Bengal Municipal Development Project.* The objectives of the project is to assist selected Urban Local Bodies (ULBs) in the state in developing strategies and comprehensive plans for environmental, economic, and social management, and to strengthen the capacity of the ULBs to deliver the objectives.

(3) *Karnataka Municipal Development and Urban Infrastructure Project.* The objective of the project is to develop urban infrastructure in the cities and towns in Karnataka.

(4) *Karnataka Urban Infrastructure Development Project.* The objective of this project is to decongest Bangalore city by developing the four neighboring cities of Mysore, Tumkur, Chennapatnam, and Ramnagram, and to build up the capacity of the urban local government to help to ensure the sustainability of the investment.

(5) *Rajasthan Urban Infrastructure Development Project.* The objective of the project is the development of the six large cities of Rajasthan: Ajmer, Bikaner, Kota, Jaipur, Jodhpur, and Udaipur. The project components include capacity building and community participation, water supply, rehabilitation, and expansion and improvement of urban transportation.

(6) *Loan for Urban and Environmental Management and Urban Development.* Three financial institutions have received loans from the Asian Development Bank for providing loans to Urban Local Bodies in the country for taking up various urban infrastructure projects.

Urban transportation has received special attention from the central government because of its potential contribution to the "working efficiency" of the cities. One project for a Delhi Metro Rail Transport System is already in progress. Two more are in the pipeline, one for Bangalore and the other for Hyderabad.

It may, therefore, be noted that India is very much concerned with the problems of urbanization development. Several steps have been undertaken to improve the situation. However, unfortunately, their progress is limited; it requires much more effort and a much faster pace.

Three more steps are urgently needed:

(a) (1) appointing efficient officers as urban administrators;

(2) imparting the necessary skills to enable them to be more effective managers; and.

(3) building a good management information system so as to be able to monitor progress on regular basis.

Learning from the successful practices of other countries of the region may be a very useful exercise for the urban administrators. The problem is huge, and the resources available limited. The "mantra" should be efficiency and speed. Such multi-level efforts seem to be the only solution to the huge problem of urbanization in India.

ENDNOTES

1   National Sample Survey Organization. Government of India, Ministry of Statistics and Programme Implementation. Migration in India 1999–2000. NSS 55th Round, Report No. 470 (55/10/8). September 2001.

2   A migrant has been defined as a person who has stayed continuously for at least six months in a place (village/town) other than the village/town where he/she was enumerated. The village/town where a person has stayed continuously for at least six months before moving to the place of enumeration was referred to as the "last usual place of residence" of the migrated person; it could be rural or urban. Similarly, the current place of stay could be rural or urban.

Urbanization
in Pakistan

IFFAT ARA AND ARSHAD ZAMAN[1]

"...Cities are the dynamic force of modern economies.
They generate wealth and prosperity that no rural idyll
could hope to match..."

The European, 6–12 June 1996

Although Pakistan emerged from colonial
British India in 1947 and her present
geographical boundaries date from 1971
when East Pakistan seceded to become
Bangladesh, the Indus valley is the third
most ancient area of permanent human
settlement in the world. Pakistan is
located along the north-west coast of the
Arabian Sea. It is surrounded by India on
the east and south-east, by China on the
north and north-east, by Afghanistan on
the north and north-west, and by Iran on the west. The total area of
Pakistan is 796,096 square kilometers. Its gross national product (GNP)
is estimated at US$57,589 million in 2000–01 and per capita income
amounts to US$414.

With almost 2.3 per cent of the world's population, Pakistan is the
seventh most populous country of the world. According to the 1998
population census, the population of Pakistan was 132.4 million with an
intercensal population growth rate of 2.6 per cent per annum. According

to official estimates, the population is estimated at 146 million in 2002. Over three million people are added to the population every year. If this rate of increment continues, Pakistan's population would reach 222 million by the year 2020, and by 2035 it will be the second largest contributor to the global population growth (after India; surpassing China) (Government of Pakistan Economic Survey 2000–1).

As elsewhere, the urban population has grown at a faster rate than the total population (about 3.5 per cent per annum, during 1981–98, vs. 2.6 per cent). It was estimated at 43 million in the 1998 population census and at 48.9 million in 2002. It amounts to 32.5 per cent of the total population. Although the urban population has not increased to the extent it was projected, the 1998 population census reveals that a large number of earlier rural communities are now being characterized as urban, and have several urban characteristics.

Cities (or urban areas) tie-up immense energies and have the potential to generate great creativity. Thus they provide impetus to economic and social development. But the beginning of the new millennium describes the cities of the developing world as cities with development of informal and unauthorized settlements, poorly serviced and designed residential areas, inadequate infrastructure, poor drainage and impassable roads, and problems such as improper sanitation facilities, inadequate access to safe drinking water, over-crowding, pollution, and other social problems. These problems lead to loss of productivity and reduced living standards. This happens as a result of lack of development planning/priorities favoring urban sector at national/local government level in correspondence with the rising population pressure. And always, the worst impact of unplanned urban expansion is borne by the poorest groups living in the cities.

Administrative Set-up

For administrative purposes, Pakistan consists of four provinces: Balochistan, the North-West Frontier Province (NWFP), Punjab, and Sindh; the capital city of Islamabad; Federally Administered Tribal Areas (FATA); Northern Areas; and Azad Jammu and Kashmir. Each province consists of divisions and districts. Within each district, rural areas comprise of tehsils, union councils, and villages; and urban areas, of metropolitan or municipal corporations, municipal committees, town committees, and cantonments. In Islamabad, there is a Capital

TABLE 4.1   Administrative setup and settlements by province, 1 July 1999

	Punjab	Sindh	NWFP	Balochistan	Islamabad	Pakistan
Divisions	8	5	7	6	-	26
Districts	34	21	24	26	1	105
Tehsils/Taluka	118	90	47	...	-	255+
Union Councils	2,870	...	122	...	12	2,992+
Villages/Dehs	25,875	5,871	3,644	...	132	35,390+
Metropolitan/Municipal Corporations	8	8	1	1	-	18
Municipal Committees	79	30	30	13	-	152
Town Committees	143	117	13	29	-	302
Military Cantonments	18	8	11	3	-	40

SOURCE: Government of Pakistan, Socio-Economic Indicators at District Level Sindh, Federal Bureau of Statistics, 2001; Government of Pakistan, Socio-Economic Indicators at District Level Punjab, Federal Bureau of Statistics, 2001; Government of Pakistan, 1998 Provincial Census Report of NWFP, Population Census Organization; Government of Pakistan, 1998 Provincial Report of Balochistan, Population Census Organization.
NOTE: "..." implies "not available", "-" implies "does not exist".

Development Authority (CDA) which is created for the development of the capital city. In the new local government plan (2000), the administrative divisions have been abolished and provinces are now comprised of tehsils and union councils (depending on the size of their population).[2] The data given in Table 4.1 provide information on the old administrative set-up, since data on the new set-up is presently not available. In FATA, the Ministry of States and Frontier Regions (SAFRON) is the coordinating ministry at the federal level while the Home and Tribal Affairs Department, NWFP works as the administrative department at the provincial level. Table 4.1 provides this information in detail.[3]

URBAN GROWTH IN PAKISTAN

Census Definition of "Urban"

The definition of urban used in the different census reports of Pakistan are given in Box 1.

Box 1: Census definition of "Urban" as reported in different census reports of Pakistan

Census Report 1951

A city or town is regarded as urban if it has a minimum of 5,000 inhabitants. All incorporated municipalities have, however, been treated as urban for census purposes even if they have fewer than 5,000 inhabitants.

Census Report 1961

Urban areas include municipalities, civil stations, cantonments and any other collection of houses inhabited by not less than 5,000 persons. This definition was made applicable even to some places having less than 5,000 inhabitants but having distinct urban characteristics conforming to certain criteria.

Census Report 1972

Urban areas include municipal corporations, municipal committees, cantonment boards and town committees. Other places having a concentration of population of at least 5,000 persons in a continuous collection of houses, where the community sense was well developed and the community maintained public utilities such as roads, street lighting, water supply, sanitary arrangements, etc. were also treated as urban areas. These places were generally centers of trade and commerce, with a population of mostly non-agriculturists and having comparatively higher literacy rates. As a special case, a few areas having the above urban characteristics but populations of less than 5,000 persons were also treated as urban.

Census Report 1981

All localities which were either metropolitan corporations, municipal corporations, municipal committees, town committees or cantonments at the time of census were treated as urban.

Box 1 (cont'd)

Census Report 1998

All localities which were either metropolitan corporation, municipal corporation, municipal committee, town committee or cantonment at the time of census were treated as urban.

Source: Government of Pakistan, Population Census Organization.

Data on Urban Population, 1959–2000: Regional Differences

The distribution of the population by provinces and by urban/rural areas of Pakistan, along with the proportion of urban population, for the year 2001, is given in Table 2. The total population of Pakistan is more than 143 million of which 33 per cent is urban. During the period 1951–98, when the overall population of Pakistan increased by almost four times, the urban population rose by slightly more than seven times.

The population of Pakistan is distributed unevenly among the four provinces. Punjab is the most populous province, accounting for more than 50 per cent of the total population of Pakistan. Moreover, its population (over 79 million) is more than twice that of the next most populous province, Sindh (over 33 million). Then comes NWFP (over 19 million) followed by Balochistan (over six million), which has only 5 per cent of the total population of Pakistan.

Sindh is the most urbanized province of Pakistan, mainly because of the population of the metropolis Karachi, which accounts for 33 per cent of the total population of the province. At present, almost 50 per cent of the population of Sindh resides in the urban areas. Although, in Punjab, the urban population is highest in terms of number, this constitutes only 32 per cent of the entire population of Punjab. In the provinces of NWFP and Balochistan, the share of the urban population is only 17 per cent and 25 per cent, respectively. In FATA, the proportion of urban population is about 3 per cent while Islamabad, being a capital city, accounts for nearly up to 67 per cent of the urban population.

The shares of each province in the total urban population of Pakistan are also provided in Table 4.2 (column 6), above. Of the total urban

TABLE 4.2 Population of urban and rural areas by province, and percentage share of urban, 2000/2001 (in numbers)

Region	Urban Population	Rural Population	Total Population	Urban % in Provinces	% share of urban in total urban population
Pakistan	47,708,128	95,422,698	143,130,826	33.3	100.0
Punjab	25,447,700	54,066,648	79,514,349	32.0	53.3
Sindh	16,462,760	16,606,347	33,069,107	49.8	34.5
N.W.F.P.	3,320,557	15,952,900	19,273,456	17.2	7.0
Balochistan	1,748,340	5,247,275	6,995,615	25.0	3.7
FATA	103,845	3,237,225	3,340,710	3.1	0.2
Islamabad	624,926	312,304	937,230	66.7	1.3

SOURCE: Government of Pakistan, 1998 Provincial Census Reports, Pakistan Census Organization, Islamabad; Government of Pakistan, 1998 District Census Report of Islamabad, Pakistan Census Organization, Islamabad; Government of Pakistan, Pakistan Statistical Yearbook, Federal Bureau of Statistics, 2001.

NOTES: These figures are computed by using the population figures of 1998 and, average annual, intercensal growth rates for the period 1981–98.

population of Pakistan, over 53 per cent live in Punjab, over 34 per cent in Sindh, 7 per cent in NWFP, nearly 4 per cent in Balochistan, 0.2 per cent in FATA, and slightly above 1 per cent in the capital city of Islamabad.

Table 4.3 portrays the changing proportion of population residing in the urban areas in all Pakistan and in the provinces (the level of urbanization) while Table 4.4 provides the rate of growth of total, urban, and rural population in Pakistan and its provinces, for the period 1951–2001. Two findings are apparent from these tables. First, the proportion of urban population has increased in Pakistan and in all the four provinces in the past 50 years. Second, despite this increase, the rate of urban growth, in overall terms, has declined in the last two intercensal periods. The same is true for Punjab and Sindh, while in NWFP it remained unchanged during 1972–81 and declined during 1981–98.[4]

In overall terms, the proportion of population residing in urban areas has increased from almost 18 per cent in 1951 to above 32 per cent in 1998.[5] The rate of growth of the urban population, during the intercensal periods 1951–61 and 1961–72, was relatively rapid, increasing

TABLE 4.3   Population residing in urban Aareas in Pakistan and provinces (in percentage)

Regions	1951	1961	1972	1981	1998
Pakistan	17.8	22.5	25.4	28.3	32.5
Punjab	17.5	21.5	24.4	27.6	31.3
Sindh	29.2	37.9	40.5	43.3	48.8
NWFP	11.0	13.2	14.2	15.1	16.9
Balochistan	12.2	16.9	16.4	15.6	23.3
FATA	...	1.3	0.5	...	2.6
Islamabad	-	-	32.6	60.0	65.7

SOURCE: Government of Pakistan, 1998 Provincial Census Reports, Population Census Organization, Islamabad (see Table 2.3); Government of Pakistan, Handbook of Population Census Data, Population Census Organization, December 1985, Islamabad.
NOTES: "..." "implies not available", "-" implies "does not exist".

on average by 4.8 and 5.1 per cent per year respectively. In the following intercensal periods 1972–81 and 1981–98, the urban population grew more slowly, by 4.1 per cent and 3.5 per cent per annum, respectively. The slowdown in the urban population growth could be because of a decline in the flow of migration from Bangladesh and India as well as possible slowdown of migration from the rural areas (Rukanuddin and Farooqui 1988). It is feared that some communities adjacent to cities that were treated as urban in the 1981 census were counted as rural in the 1998 census. This might have reduced the rate of urban growth in the period 1981–98 (Arif and Ibrahim 1998).

In Punjab, the urban proportion of population has increased from 17.5 per cent in 1951 to 31.2 per cent in 1998. This is mainly due to the emergence of new urban localities, city extensions, and rural-urban migration (1998 provincial census report of Punjab). The urban population grew at an average annual rate of 3.4 per cent during 1981–98, while it grew at a rate of 4.5 per cent and 4.2 per cent during 1961–72 and 1972–81, respectively. The urban population of Sindh that was 29.2 per cent of its total population in 1951 climbed to 48.8 per cent in 1998. The average annual growth rate of the urban population, however, has declined from 5.2 per cent during 1961–72 to 4.1 per cent during 1972–81 and to 3.5 per cent during 1981–98. The urban population of

TABLE 4.4 Rate of urbanization in Pakistan and provinces: Intercensal growth rates of urban population along with total and rural population growth rates (average annual)

Region	Total				Rural				Urban			
	1951–61	1961–72	1972–81	1981–98	1951–61	1961–72	1972–81	1981–98	1951–61	1961–72	1972–81	1981–98
Pakistan	2.4	3.7	3.1	2.7	3.5	3.5	2.6	2.2	4.8	5.1	4.1	3.5
Punjab	2.2	3.4	2.7	2.6	3.4	3.2	2.3	2.2	4.3	4.5	4.2	3.4
Sindh	3.3	4.6	3.6	2.8	3.5	4.5	3.0	2.1	6.0	5.2	4.4	3.5
NWFP	2.3	3.3	3.3	2.8	3.5	3.4	3.3	2.6	4.2	4.0	4.0	3.5
Balochistan	1.6	5.0	7.1	2.4	4.9	5.3	7.3	1.8	4.9	3.4	8.0	4.9
FATA	3.3	2.8	-1.5	2.1	7.8	2.8	-1.4	2.0	...	-5.4	...	...
Islamabad	...	...	4.4	5.2	...	...	-1.8	4.2	...	...	11.4	5.8

SOURCE: Government of Pakistan, 1998 Provincial Census Reports, Population Census Organization, Islamabad, (see Table 2.3); Government of Pakistan, Handbook of Population Census Data, Population Census Organization, December 1985, Islamabad.

NOTES: Rural population growth rates are computed using rural population figures from Government of Pakistan, Population Census Organization, Islamabad, Census reports for respective year.

"..." implies "not available".

NWFP rose up to 17 per cent in 1998, from 11 per cent in 1951. The rate of urbanization, which was 3.5 per cent per annum, during 1981–98, had decreased from 4 per cent, on average, during 1961–72 and 1972–81. In Balochistan also, a substantial increase in urban population has been observed during the period 1981–98. An interesting finding from Tables 4.3 and 4.4, above, is that, in spite of the fact that the level of urbanization in Balochistan has increased substantially, the rate of urbanization has declined by almost 3 percentage points. This is due to the fact that the urban population, on average, grew at a rate (4.9 per cent) that was double that of the total population (2.4 per cent). Also, in FATA, the proportion of the population living in urban areas has increased from 0.5 per cent in 1972 to 2.6 per cent in 1998.

These statistics indicate that urbanization in Pakistan has proceeded at a moderate pace in comparison to the Latin American, East Asian, and OECD countries. In these countries, urbanization levels averaged 70–5 per cent during the same periods (United Nations 2002). At the same time, the urban growth rates are higher than the total population growth rates for Pakistan as a whole, and for the provinces in every period (except for 1961–72 in Balochistan). This implies that urbanization is nevertheless increasing in Pakistan.[6]

Sources of Growth: Natural Increase, Migration, Changes in Administrative Boundaries

Urbanization is ascribed to three factors: when the rate of natural increase in population in the urban areas is higher than that in the rural areas; when population moves from rural areas to urban areas (or rural-urban migration); and sometimes when urban administrative boundaries are enlarged. Moreover, it also occurs as a result of external immigrants settling in the urban areas. Of these, the rural-urban migration is the major contributing factor. Thus, the discussion on urbanization is "fundamentally the discussion on net rural to urban migration, and an analysis of migration stimulating effects of various demographic, economic and social forces which are at work" (Cherunilam 1984, 21).

Two points are worth mentioning here. First, there are two elements in the computation of expansion of urban administrative boundaries or net reclassification: one is the annexation of a town into an urban area and another is the transformation of a formerly rural area into an urban area. The figures for reclassification are computed by using only the data of transformation of rural areas into urban areas. Data regarding the annexation of urban areas was not available. Second, as far as international migration is concerned, it is an important factor of urban growth in Pakistan because of both settlement patterns of Afghan refugees and the influx of illegal immigrants to large urban centers, particularly Karachi. But data are not available to segregate the effect of this component on urban growth (Arif and Ibrahim 1998, 515–6).

Table 4.5 provides estimates of the contribution made by each of the components mentioned above to the urban growth in Pakistan, for the period 1951–98. Although the results reported in this table are from two different sources, the information they impart is nevertheless similar in nature. In Pakistan, the growth of the urban population is largely a result of natural increase, followed by internal migration[7] and reclassification. A sharp rise in the contribution of natural increase is seen in the 1960s and the 1970s. The decline observed during the last two decades may be due to a decline in urban marital fertility rate, which declined from 8.1 per woman of reproductive age in the mid-1970s, to 5.7 in the early 1990s (Kiyani and Siyal 1991). The role of migration was large during 1951–61, as compared to the subsequent periods where it is almost similar. The share of reclassification in urban growth depicts a declining trend during the first three intercensal periods but afterwards, in the 1980s and 1990s, it shows a sizeable increase.

Table 4.5 also provides the contribution of the components of urban growth in each of the provinces (and the capital city, Islamabad) for the intercensal period 1981–98. In each of the provinces too, the share of natural increase in urban growth is higher than that of internal migration and reclassification. The role of internal migration is prominent in Balochistan, followed by Sindh, Punjab, and NWFP, respectively. In Islamabad, the urban population grew mainly as a result of internal migration.

Migration in Pakistan

The discussion on migration in Pakistan can be divided into two parts: catastrophic migration (in response to one-time historical events) and normal migration from rural to urban areas.

97

TABLE 4.5 Sources of urban growth (in percentage)

Period	Region	Natural Increase	Reclassification	Internal Migration	Total Increase
1951–61	Pakistan	44.8	15.1	40.1	100.0
1961–72	Pakistan	72.4	8.1	19.5	100.0
1972–81	Pakistan	78.4	2.6	19.1	100.0
1981–98	Pakistan	70.3	9.7	20.1	100.0
—	Punjab	74.2	11.3	14.5	100.0
—	Sindh	70.6	4.5	24.8	100.0
—	NWFP	70.0	20.9	9.1	100.0
—	Balochistan	43.7	18.4	37.9	100.0
—	Islamabad	35.1	-	64.9	100.0

SOURCE: Arif and Ibrahim (1998) for periods 1972–81 and 1981–98; Khan and Rahman (99/2000) for periods 1951–61 and 1961–72.

NOTE: The share of reclassification in urban growth is computed by considering only those formerly rural areas that were transformed into urban in corresponding next population census. Information about annexation of urban areas, that can affect share of reclassification, is not available.

Catastrophic Migration

In the recent history of Pakistan, there have been three occasions when large-scale extraordinary movements of population have taken place. First, in 1947, when modern India and Pakistan emerged from colonial British India, there was a large-scale movement of population. According to the 1951 census of Pakistan, 6.5 million refugees migrated to Pakistan from India. Similarly, as reported in the 1951 census of India, 4.7 million people were expatriated from Pakistan to India. Thus, as a result of partition, Pakistan had a net gain of 1.8 million migrants from India (Rukanuddin and Farooqui 1988, 21).

Almost 89 per cent of these displaced people came from the North West Zone of what is now India (Punjab, Delhi, Rajputana, Occupied Kashmir). "Of the total 6.5 million displaced persons ... 81 per cent settled in the Punjab and 18 per cent in Sindh. The impact of refugee migration was most prominent in Karachi, Hyderabad, Sukkur, Lahore, Faisalabad, Gujranwala, Multan, Rawalpindi, Peshawar, and Quetta. These cities were the major migration targets basically because they were

98

larger in size and were located on the main railway and road links. There is evidence to the effect that a considerable number of refugees who settled in the urban areas came from the rural areas of India." (Rukanuddin and Farooqui 1988). A significant proportion of the population also migrated from the North East Zone of India (mainly from Bihar, and the United Provinces), mainly to East Pakistan. In the 1950s and 1960s, a sizeable proportion of these migrants moved from the East to the West Wing of Pakistan, but no reliable numbers on these flows are available.

The next such incidence was the war with India in 1971, which ended in the secession of East Pakistan (now Bangladesh).[8] Although estimates are not available, it is thought that population movement was inhibited by geographical distance and political constraints. Nevertheless, it is known that a large proportion of the population that had migrated from the North East Zone of India to East Pakistan in 1947 (popularly referred to as "Biharis"), once again migrated now to West Pakistan, of which a highly visible proportion settled in Orangi Town, and other areas of Karachi (Rukanuddin and Farooqui 1988, 21).[9]

Finally, in 1979, when the Soviet Union invaded Afghanistan, an influx of Afghan refugees into Pakistan started, and peaked at 3.7 million in 1990. Due to geographical proximity, most were concentrated in Peshawar and Quetta, but a significant proportion also settled in Karachi. With the American invasion of Afghanistan in 2001, some repatriation of Afghan refugees has begun, but Pakistan still hosts around 2.2 million Afghan refugees (Government of Pakistan Economic Survey 2000–1).

Migration towards the Urban Areas of Pakistan
The 1998 census asked questions about migration status. The results are shown in Table 4.6. There were 6.9 million persons (16.1 per cent of the urban population) who migrated domestically and internationally into the *urban areas* of Pakistan. There is little difference in the proportions among the different regions, except for Islamabad. Of the migrants (among the 6 million persons who provided information on their previous residence), 4.5 million (10.5 per cent of the urban population) were internal migrants who moved either within the province (rural-urban) or between provinces (from rural and urban areas of one province to the urban areas of other provinces), while 1.5 million (3.6 per cent of the urban population) migrated from other countries into the urban areas of the provinces.[10]

TABLE 4.6 Migrants status of population in the urban areas of Pakistan and provinces, 1981–98 (in thousands)

Movements of Immigrants	Total	Punjab	Sindh	NWFP	Balochistan	Islamabad
Total urban population	42,898	23,019	14,840	2,994	1516	529
	(100.0)	(100.0)	(100.0)	(100.0)	(100.0)	(100.0)
Non-Migrants	35,990	19,520	12,288	2,612	1353	217
	(83.9)	(84.8)	(82.8)	(87.2)	(89.2)	(40.9)
Total Migrants	6,909	3,499	2,552	382	163	313
	(16.1)	(15.2)	(17.2)	(12.8)	(10.8)	(59.1)
Migrants within Pakistan	4,496	2,217	1,603	285	141	250
	(10.5)	(9.6)	(10.8)	(9.5)	(9.3)	(47.3)
Migrants within the province	2,456	1747	459	192	58	–
	(5.7)	(7.6)	(3.1)	(6.4)	(3.8)	
Migrants from other provinces	1,869	365	1,099	90	78	237
	(4.4)	(1.6)	(7.4)	(3.0)	(5.1)	(44.8)
Migrants from AJK and NA	172	105	45	3	5	13
	(0.4)	(0.5)	(0.3)	(0.1)	(0.4)	(2.5)
Migrants from Other Countries	1,530	798	661	20	7	44
	(3.6)	(3.5)	(4.5)	(0.7)	(0.4)	(8.4)
Migrants who did not report	882	484	288	77	16	18
	(2.1)	(2.1)	(1.9)	(2.6)	(1.1)	(3.4)

SOURCE: Government of Pakistan, 1998 Provincial Census Reports, Population Census Organization, Islamabad; Government of Pakistan, 1998 District Census Report of Islamabad, Population Census Organization, Islamabad.

NOTE: AJK and NA imply Azad Jammu & shmir and Northern Areas, respectively. Figures in parenthesis are the proportions of the respective populations.

Of the 4.5 million internal migrants, 2.5 million (5.7 per cent of the urban population) migrated within the province, whereas 1.9 million (4.4 per cent of the urban population) migrated between provinces. In terms of provinces, in Punjab and NWFP, the inflow of migrants has been predominantly higher from within the province, while migration from other provinces is prominent in Sindh. Of the total urban population, population movement within the province is 7.6 per cent in Punjab, followed by 6.4 per cent in NWFP, 3.8 per cent in Balochistan, and 3.1 per cent in Sindh. As far as movement of the population as a percentage of the urban population between the provinces is concerned, it is highest in Sindh (7.4 per cent) followed by Balochistan (5.1 per cent), NWFP (3 per cent), and Punjab (1.6 per cent). Moreover, Sindh also leads in absorbing immigrants from other countries. Their proportion in the urban population of Sindh is 4.5 per cent; of Punjab is 3.5 per cent while very minimal in the urban population of NWFP and Balochistan. The direction of migration from other provinces towards Sindh occurs due to the city of Karachi, which is one of the main centers of economic activity and accounts for 32 per cent of the total major industrial establishment of Pakistan.

Characteristics of Incoming and Outgoing Populations

The early literature provides the view that rural-urban migration is primarily motivated by the wage differential between the rural areas (agriculture sector) and the urban areas (industrial sector) (Yap 1977). The Todaro model of labor migration explains that the potential risk-neutral migrant compares the expected urban wage with the present rural wage before making a decision to migrate (Todaro 1969). Later literature points towards two principal hypotheses regarding the forces affecting migration and urbanization. The "pull" of apparent economic opportunity and facilities in urban areas, and the "push" of population growth pressing on limited farm acreage, famine, and natural disasters, all encourage migration to urban areas. It is interesting to note that most economists favor the former, while most demographers favor the latter explanation (Williamson 1988). In addition, the presence of a large urban informal sector also supports the migration into urban areas (Todaro 1997 and Williamson 1988). A number of specific studies have examined migration in different periods and can provide a partial picture of the process

(Barkley 1991, Parveen 1993, and Irfan 1989). These findings are summarized in the next three paragraphs.

Migration levels and rates are low in Pakistan relative to other developing countries in Asia (United Nations 1988, 50 as mentioned in Barkley 1991). During the 1970s, in terms of inter-provincial migration, the highest in-migration in males occurs in the age groups 10–14 years and 20–29 years, particularly in Sindh, and with the exception of Punjab. Punjab shows out-migration in these age groups while in-migration in the age group 50–54 and 65 and above. This indicates that young males largely from Punjab migrate to all the three provinces and return to their homes as they get older or after their retirement. Females migrate mainly as a result of marriage. A large proportion of female migration takes place in the age group 15–29. Only a small proportion of them moves for education and job opportunities (Parveen 1993).[11]

In terms of inter-district migration, future migration is more likely to occur to places where migration has occurred in the past. This is so because family ties and other linkages between the areas of origin and destination reduce both the financial and psychological costs of migration. Moreover, there is a positive association between migration and urbanization (industrial sector), which indicates that the modern (industrial) sector grows relatively faster than the rural (agriculture) sector. Higher levels of education (literacy) also facilitate migration between two districts because higher levels of education are linked with economic development. The development of local infrastructure also induces migration towards another district. Population density, however, has a negative impact on the inflow of migrants into an area (Barkley 1991).[12]

During the same period (i.e., the 1970s), 42 per cent of the migrants moved within a district, 39 per cent between districts but remained within the same province, while only 19 per cent crossed their provincial boundaries. Around 20 per cent of the migration flow was between rural areas, nearly 30 per cent from rural to urban areas, while the rest was equally shared by inter-city and urban to rural migration. Furthermore, people with higher education have a higher propensity to migrate. This propensity is higher in rural areas (33 per cent) than in urban areas (10 per cent). In rural areas, a majority (83 per cent) of this group move from rural areas to urban areas, while in urban areas, 80 per cent choose to move to another urban destination. On the other hand, in the case of illiterates, only 5 per cent moved from rural areas, while the majority moved to another rural area. In contrast, only 4 per cent of illiterates shifted from urban areas, of which more than half moved to another urban area (Irfan 1989).[13]

The reasons for the migration during the period 1981–98 were recorded in the 1998 census and are shown in Table 4.7. This migration includes those who moved from both rural and urban areas of one province to the urban areas of other province. It indicates that in all provinces (and in the capital city of Islamabad) the highest proportion of migrants, both males and females, moved with the head of the household, of which the proportion of females is very significant. This is so because adult females (due to cultural norms) and dependents (females and children) tend to migrate with the head of the household. In addition, the incidence of migration of males in rural areas increases after marriage as it enhances their financial responsibilities. Moreover, in many rural areas, education facilities are not available, therefore married couples move to urban areas for better education of their children.

Excluding this component, Table 4.7 shows that employment (or transfer) and business are the two main reasons for males migrating to urban areas. In females, a notable proportion also moves as a result of marriage. The other purposes of migration are study, returning home, and health. The lack of availability of disaggregated data, however, did not allow us to study the behavior of internal (rural-urban and urban-urban) and external immigrants separately.

As far as the proportion of in-migrant population by educational attainment in the urban areas during 1981–98 is concerned, the proportion of migrants who are formally literate is higher in all the provinces and Islamabad. The proportion of literate male in-migrants is higher in every province, in comparison with the female literate migrant and with the male illiterate migrant. On the other hand, the comparison of illiterate and literate female in-migrants indicates that in Punjab their proportion is the same, in Sindh the proportion of illiterate in-migrants is higher, while in NWFP and Islamabad literate in-migrant are in the majority (1998 provincial census reports).

The above synthesis implies that in Pakistan migration is age sensitive and occurs at places where job opportunities and other facilities are available. People move to urban areas primarily because of the pull factors, i.e., the pull of economic forces (particularly employment prospects for the educated), better opportunities for education, and other urban amenities, which are not available in rural areas. The coincidence of individuals' age of marriage and of entry into the labor force makes

103

TABLE: 4.7 Distribution of in-migrants by reasons of migration, 1981–98 (in percentage)

Region	Total Migrants Number	%	Moved with Head	Employment/ Transfer	Marriage	Business	Study	Returning Home	Health	Others
Punjab										
Both Sexes	3,498,632	100.0	41.4	14.7	17.4	8.0	1.3	1.2	0.1	15.8
Male	1,782,773	100.0	33.7	27.9	1.2	14.8	1.8	1.5	0.1	19.1
Female	1,715,859	100.0	49.5	1.1	34.3	1.0	0.8	0.8	0.1	12.5
Sindh										
Both Sexes	2,552,100	100.0	48.1	16.7	8.8	8.9	1.0	1.1	0.1	15.3
Male	1,469,231	100.0	36.4	27.7	0.8	14.0	1.5	1.4	0.1	18.1
Female	1,082,869	100.0	64.0	1.7	19.8	2.1	0.2	0.7	0.1	11.4
NWFP										
Both Sexes	382,090	100.0	54.5	24.5	8.4	5.0	2.4	0.7	0.0	4.4
Male	227,905	100.0	43.3	38.9	0.3	7.9	3.7	0.7	0.0	5.1
Female	154,185	100.0	71.1	3.3	20.3	0.7	0.5	0.8	0.0	3.3
Balochistan										
Both Sexes	163373	100.0	47.4	24.8	5.7	9.7	1.6	0.8	0.0	10.0
Male	101770	100.0	33.6	38.0	0.4	13.8	2.3	0.8	0.1	11.0
Female	61603	100.0	70.2	2.8	14.6	2.8	0.6	0.7	0.0	8.2
Islamabad										
Both Sexes	312640	100.0	53.0	25.0	4.4	5.8	3.2	1.1	0.1	7.4
Male	178623	100.0	35.2	41.2	0.3	9.8		1.3	0.1	7.9
Female	134017	100.0	76.7	3.5	9.9	0.4	1.9	0.8	0.1	6.8

SOURCE: Government of Pakistan, 1998 Provincial Census Reports, Population Census Organization, Islamabad; Government of Pakistan, 1998 District Census Report of Islamabad, Population Census Organization, Islamabad.

the migration higher in the age group 15–24. Highly qualified males move to urban areas in search of better jobs as these have national labor markets and are advertised in national newspapers. Higher per capita monthly income also induces migration to urban areas. Furthermore, people who move for economic reasons build their houses at their place of origin and come back there after retirement, particularly in Punjab.

National System of Cities

The classification of cities according to size of population is given in Table 8 for the period 1951–98. The table shows that during this period, the cities not only grew in numbers but also in size. The number of cities in Pakistan has more than doubled, from 198 to 472. However, over this period, a substantial decrease has been observed in the number of cities with populations of less than 10,000, while the number of cities with populations of more than 10,000 has increased.

In reviewing the data presented in Table 4.8, two points need to be made. First, as mentioned above, urban localities are comprised of metropolitan or municipal corporations, municipal committees, town committees, and cantonments. There were some urban localities whose boundaries were adjacent to one another. To treat such localities as cities these boundaries are added together according to the criterion established by the Population Census Organization. Second, the definitions of urban, illustrated in Box 1, above, used in the different census reports have greatly influenced the number as well as the size of the urban population. The definitions applied in the census reports of 1951, 1961, and 1972 were almost the same, where the city size was specified with a minimum of 5,000 inhabitants. However, in some cases, where the areas possessed urban characteristics, this was relaxed. Later, in the census reports of 1981 and 1998, this criterion was weakened with the introduction of administrative criterion.

The fact that Sindh is the most urbanized province of Pakistan, as we have seen above, is again apparent here. A significant increase in the number of cities in Sindh, almost five times during the same period, indicates a very rapid urbanization in this province, particularly of cities with populations of less than 100,000. Karachi, Hyderabad, and Sukkur are the cities that dominate Sindh. These cities constitute 72.6 per cent of the total urban population of the province. Unlike other provinces, Sindh has seen an increase in the smaller towns (with populations of

TABLE 4.8 Cities of different sizes (numbers)

Region	\	\	Size of Cities	\	\	\	\
	Under 10,000	10,000– 100,000	100,000– 500,000	500,000– 1 million	1 million– 5 million	Over 5 million	Total
Pakistan							
1951	107	82	7	1	1	-	198
1961	150	114	10	0	2	-	276
1972	114	195	15	3	2	-	329
1981	96	259	21	5	2	1	384
1998	64	356	42	3	5	2	472
Punjab							
1951	70	57	5	1	-	-	133
1961	78	74	6	-	1	-	159
1972	38	125	11	2	1	-	177
1981	28	153	15	3	2	-	201
1998	6	193	28	1	4	1	233
Sindh							
1951	15	14	1	-	1	-	31
1961	40	21	2	-	1	-	64
1972	53	39	1	1	1	-	95
1981	50	62	4	1	-	1	118
1998	44	94	10	-	1	1	150
NWFP							
1951	11	9	1	-	-	-	21
1961	14	17	1	-	-	-	32
1972	9	22	2	-	-	-	33
1981	5	29	1	1	-	-	36
1998	4	35	4	1	-	-	44
Balochistan							
1951	11	2	-	-	-	-	13
1961	18	2	1	-	-	-	21
1972	14	9	1	-	-	-	24
1981	13	15	1	-	-	-	29
1998	10	34	-	1	-	-	45

SOURCE: Federal Bureau of Statistics, 50 Years of Pakistan in Statistics, Vol. II, (1947–1997); Government of Pakistan, 1998 Provincial Census Reports, Population Census Organization, Islamabad.

NOTE: Islamabad is included in Punjab. Urban localities whose boundaries are adjacent to each other are added to consider them as a city.

under 10,000). This can be thought of as the growth of satellite towns around a number of major urban centers.

Although Punjab is the most populous province of Pakistan, it shows only a modest rate of urbanization, as the number of cities only doubled during the period 1951–98. However, over the period, a notable shift has occurred towards the emergence of cities with populations in the range of 10,000–100,000, rather than cities with populations of less than 10,000. Lahore, Faisalabad, Gujranwala, Multan, Rawalpindi, and Islamabad dominate this province. They jointly account for 49 per cent of its urban population. In NWFP, the number of cities in 1998 increased to more than double in comparison with that in 1951. The largest city is Peshawar, followed by Mardan and Kohat. If these three cities are added up together, their total population is 45.3 per cent of the total urban population of NWFP. Balochistan increased from 13 cities in 1951 to 45 in 1998. Quetta, Khuzdar, and Turbat, constituting 47.6 per cent of its total urban population, dominate Balochistan.

Table 4.9 gives the proportion of the urban population in cities of different sizes for the period 1951–98. The last row of the table shows that in 1951 there were nine big cities (with populations of 100,000 and over) containing 53 per cent of urban population. By 1998, the number of these cities increased to 52, accommodating over 72 per cent of the total urban population. The proportion of the urban population living in small cities (with populations under 10,000) declined notably from 11.6 per cent in 1951 to 1.1 per cent in 1998. In the medium-sized cities (with populations of 10,000–100,000), the proportion of the urban population also declined from 35 per cent to almost 27 per cent, though their number has increased from 82 to 259.

In 1951, Karachi and Lahore were the major cities of Pakistan, holding almost 17 per cent and 14 per cent of the total urban population of Pakistan, respectively. There were seven cities in the range 100,000–500,000 with a 21 per cent combined share in the total urban population. Some 35 per cent of the urban population were residing in the medium-sized cities (10,000–100,000) while nearly 12 per cent were in the small cities. Over time, the number of big cities increased significantly while that of small cities declined slightly. At present, Karachi and Lahore have become cities with populations of over five million. They jointly have more than 33 per cent of the total urban population of Pakistan. Faisalabad, Rawalpindi, Multan, Hyderabad, and Gujranwala are now cities whose urban populations lie in the range of one to five million.

TABLE 4.9 Trends in proportion of urban population in cities of different size

Size of Cities	1951		1961		1972		1981		1998	
	No. of cities	% Share	No. of cities	% Share	No. of cities	% Share	No. of cities	% Share	No. of cities	% Share
Under 10,000	107	11.6	150	10.3	114	5.3	96	3.1	64	1.1
10,000–100,000	82	35.2	114	31.5	195	31.1	259	29.2	356	26.4
100,000–500,000	7	21.4	10	25.0	14	13.6	21	14.4	42	18.3
500,000–1 million	1	14.1	-	-	4	15.7	5	14.5	3	4.8
1–5 million	1	17.7	2	33.2	2	34.3	2	17.0	5	16.1
Over 5 million	-	-	-	-	-	-	1	21.8	2	33.3
Total 100,000 & Over	9	53.2	12	58.2	20	63.6	29	67.7	52	72.5

SOURCE: Computed using Federal Bureau of Statistics, Pakistan Statistical Yearbook, ,2001, (table 2.11); Federal Bureau of Statistics, 50 Years of Pakistan in Statistics, Vol. II, (1947–1997); and–Khan and Rahman (1999/2000).

TABLE 4.10   Primate cities of Pakistan

Year	% Share in Urban Population of Pakistan		Index of Primacy	
	Karachi	Lahore	Karachi	Lahore
1951	17.7	14.1	2.11	1.17
1961	19.8	13.4	1.98	1.12
1972	21.2	13.1	1.78	1.10
1981	21.6	12.4	1.70	1.15
1998	21.8	12.0	1.76	1.40

SOURCE: Government of Pakistan, Pakistan Statistical Yearbook, 2001, Federal Bureau of Statistics, Islamabad.

NOTE: Index of primacy is the ratio of population of the largest city to the cumulated population of the next three largest cities. These figures are computed using population data from the above-mentioned source. The three next largest cities for Karachi are Lahore, Faisalabad and Rawalpindi and for Lahore are Faisalabad, Rawalpindi and Multan.

They together constitute above 16 per cent of the total urban population. Three cities—Peshawar, Islamabad, and Quetta—lie in the range of 500,000 to one million, with a combined share in the total urban population of slightly less than 5 per cent. Another 42 cities, with urban populations in the range of 100,000–500,000, together account for above 18 per cent of the total urban population. Medium-sized cities account for above 26 per cent while small cities only account for 1 per cent of the total urban population.

It can be seen that Karachi dominates the urban scene and is the primate city of Pakistan as shown in Table 4.10.[14] This table also indicates that though the share of Karachi in the urban population of Pakistan has been increasing over the period, its index of primacy is decreasing. On the other hand, this is reversed in the case of Lahore. After showing a decline in the first three census years, it is increasing in the last two census years.

Table 4.11 presents the population of capital cities of each of the provinces of Pakistan and their share in the provincial and state population, for the period 1951–2001. Karachi, the capital of Sindh, is the largest city of Pakistan. Its population, at present, is above 10.9 million,

TABLE 4.11   Population of capital cities and its share in provincial and total population (in thousands)

Capital Cities	1951	1961	1972	1981	1998	2001
Lahore						
Population	1,125	1,605	2,545	3,488	6,141	6,809
As % of Punjab population	5.5	6.3	6.8	7.4	8.3	8.6
As % of Pakistan population	3.3	3.7	3.9	4.1	4.6	4.8
Karachi						
Population	1,138	2,049	3,607	5,438	9,856	10,943
As % of Sindh population	18.8	24.5	25.5	28.6	32.4	33.1
As % of Pakistan population	3.4	4.8	5.5	6.5	7.5	7.6
Peshawar						
Population	386	516	784	1,084	2,039	2,265
As % of N.W.F.P. population	8.4	9.0	9.3	9.8	11.5	11.8
As % of Pakistan population	1.1	1.2	1.2	1.3	1.5	1.6
Quetta						
Population	209	140	249	382	743	839
As % of Balochistan population	17.6	10.1	10.3	8.8	11.4	12.0
As % of Pakistan population	0.6	0.3	0.4	0.5	0.6	0.6

SOURCE: Government of Sindh, Development Statistics of Sindh (1998), Government of Punjab, Punjab Development Statistics (1998), Government of NWFP, NWFP Development Statistics (1998), Government of Balochistan, Development Statistics of Balochistan (1998).Government of Pakistan, 1998 Provincial Census Reports, Population Census Organization, Islamabad.

which constitutes 33 per cent of the population of Sindh and almost 8 per cent of the population of Pakistan. The next largest city is Lahore, the capital of Punjab, which has a population of over 7 million. This is 8.6 per cent of the population of Punjab and around 5 per cent of the population of Pakistan. The capital of NWFP is Peshawar which has a population of 2.3 million. This makes its share up to 12 per cent of the provincial population and 1.6 per cent of the country's population. Quetta, the capital of Balochistan, has a population of 0.84 million, which constitutes 12 per cent and 0.6 per cent of the provincial and country's population, respectively.

TABLE 4.12 Urban population and its proportion living in capital cities (in thousands)

Capital Cities	1951	1961	1972	1981	1998	2001
Province of Punjab						
Lahore – Total	1125	1605	2545	3488	6,141	6,809
Lahore – Urban	849	1,296	2,170	2,953	5,143	5,656
Proportion of Urban	75.5	80.7	85.3	84.7	83.7	83.1
Province of Sindh						
Karachi – Total	1,138	2,049	3,607	5,438	9,802	10,883
Karachi – Urban	1,068	1,913	3,515	5,208	9,269	10,262
Proportion of Urban	93.8	93.4	97.4	95.8	94.6	94.3
Province of NWFP						
Peshawar – Total	386	516	784	1,084	2,039	2,265
Peshawar – Urban	152	218	273	566	988	1,090
Proportion of Urban	39.4	42.2	34.8	52.2	48.5	48.1
Province of Balochistan						
Quetta – Total	209	140	249	382	743	839
Quetta – Urban	84	107	158	286	560	631
Proportion of Urban	40.2	76.4	63.5	74.9	75.4	75.2

SOURCE: Government of Sindh, Development Statistics of Sindh (1998), Government of Punjab, Punjab Development Statistics (1998), Government of NWFP, NWFP Development Statistics (1998), Government of Balochistan, Development Statistics of Balochistan (1998), Government of Pakistan, Pakistan Statistical Yearbook, 2001, Federal Bureau of Statistics, Islamabad.

Table 4.12 gives the urban population and its proportion living in the capital cities of the provinces of Pakistan. It shows that, at present, of the total population of these cities, the urban proportion in Lahore is 83 per cent, in Karachi is 94 per cent, in Peshawar is 48 per cent and in Quetta is 75 per cent. Over the past half-century, these proportions have increased substantially in Balochistan, moderately in Punjab and NWFP. In Sindh, Karachi has consistently had more than 90 per cent of the urban population.

Finally, Table 4.13 reports the trend in population of the 10 largest cities of Pakistan, for the period 1951–98. Faislabad has shown the sharpest increase in the last 50 years, followed by Gujaranwala and Karachi. Hyderabad grew with the least pace of these 10 largest

TABLE 4.13   Trends in population of 10 largest urban agglomerations

Agglomerations	Population (in thousands)					Growth Rates			
	1951	1961	1972	1981	1998	1951–61	1961–72	1972–81	1981–98
Karachi	1,068	1,913	3,515	5,208	9,269	6.0	5.7	4.5	3.5
Lahore	849	1,296	2,170	2,953	5,063	4.3	4.8	3.5	3.2
Faisalabad	179	425	823	1,104	1,977	9.0	6.2	3.3	3.5
Rawalpindi	237	340	615	795	1,406	3.7	5.5	2.9	3.4
Multan	190	358	539	732	1,182	6.5	3.8	3.5	2.9
Hyderabad	242	435	629	752	1,151	6.0	3.4	2.0	2.5
Gujranwala	121	196	360	601	1,125	4.9	5.7	5.7	3.8
Peshawar	152	213	273	566	988	3.4	2.3	8.4	3.3
Quetta	84	107	158	286	560	2.5	3.6	6.8	4.0
Islamabad	-	-	77	204	525	-	-	11.4	5.7

SOURCE: Federal Bureau of Statistics, Pakistan Statistical Yearbook, April 2001.

TABLE 4.14   Population projections of urban agglomerations with 750,000 inhabitants or more in 2000

Agglomeration	Population (thousands)			Average Annual Rate of Change (%)		
	2005	2010	2015	2000–2005	2005–2010	2010–2015
Karachi	11,830	13,871	16,197	3.3	3.2	3.1
Lahore	6,379	7,458	8,721	3.1	3.1	3.1
Faisalabad	2,535	2,992	3,526	3.4	3.3	3.3
Rawalpindi	1,796	2,119	2,500	3.3	3.3	3.3
Gujranwala	1,581	1,877	2,223	3.5	3.4	3.4
Multan	1,460	1,702	2,000	2.9	3.1	3.2
Hyderabad	1,394	1,613	1,891	2.7	2.9	3.2
Peshawar	1,256	1,481	1,750	3.3	3.3	3.3

SOURCE: United Nations, 2002, World Urbanisation Prospects: The 2001 Revision, United Nations Secretariat, Population Division.

agglomerations though it ranks sixth in size. Islamabad was first counted in 1972 after this capital city was created.

Future Projections

As projected by the United Nations, the future population for the largest urban agglomerations of Pakistan, for the period 2005–15, are given in Table 4.14. The same source also points out that, presently, Karachi is the 16th largest city in the world and it will become the 10th largest city by the year 2015.

URBAN-RURAL DIFFERENCES

This section presents a rural-urban comparative analysis to look at the demographic and socio-economic differences between these two areas of Pakistan. In carrying out such an analysis, the point that must be kept in mind through out is the rural-urban share in the total population over the period. In 1998, in Pakistan, the total population was made up of two-thirds rural and one-third urban.

Demographic Differences

The selected indicators that portray the demographic picture of rural-urban areas are reported in Table 4.15.

The proportion of the population in the less than 15 years age group, which is not part of the labor force, is 45 per cent in rural areas, and 39 per cent in urban areas. In comparison to urban areas, children (under 15 years) and the elderly (over 60 years) account for a larger proportion of the rural population. This is true for both men and women. Consequently, in comparison to rural areas, the proportion of population of working age (in the age group 15–59) is higher in urban areas. Comparing the population distribution by marital status, the table shows that the proportion of population married is higher in rural areas (65.5 per cent) than in urban areas (59.4 per cent). This is mainly due to the difference in the proportion of married females.

The age dependency ratio, which is the ratio of the sum of population below 15 years and above 60 years to total population, is alarming in rural areas. More than 95 per cent of the population is dependent in rural areas where as in urban areas this ratio is just 75 per

TABLE 4.15   Rural-urban demographic differences, 1998

	Urban	Rural
Age Distribution (in %)		
a) less than 15 years		
Both	39.3	45.1
Male	37.8	45.8
Female	41.1	44.3
b) 15–59 years		
Both	56.0	49
Male	57.4	47.9
Female	54.4	50.1
c) 60 years & above		
Both	4.6	5.9
Male	4.7	6.2
Female	4.5	5.6
Married Population (in %)		
Both	59.4	65.5
Male	57.5	62.0
Female	61.6	69.2
Age Dependency Ratio (ratio of > 15 years +		
above 60 years to total population)	75.5	95.5
Sex Ratio (number of males per 100 females)	112.8	106.7
Crude Birth Rate (persons per 1000 population)	27.8	32.2
Crude Death Rate (persons per 1000 population)	7.1	9.2
Infant Mortality Rate (infants death over per	71.7	88.3
1000 live births)		
Total Fertility Rate (children per women of	3.7	5.4
reproductive age)		

SOURCE: Government of Pakistan, Pakistan Statistical Yearbook, April 2001, Federal Bureau of Statistics; Government of Pakistan, 1998 Census Report of Pakistan, Population Census Organization, Islamabad; Government of Pakistan, Statistical Supplement to Economic Survey, 200–2001.

cent. The number of males is higher than the number of females in both urban and rural areas, with urban areas in the leading position, as portrayed by the sex ratio. For every 100 females there are 113 males in urban areas, compared to 107 males in rural areas.

Both the crude birth rate and the crude death rate are higher in rural areas than in urban areas. The number of births in a year per 1,000 population is 32 and 28 in rural and urban areas, respectively. In the same order, the number of deaths in a year per 1,000 population is 9 and 7 in rural and urban areas. Even if the infant mortality rate is lesser in urban areas in comparison to rural areas, it is not pleasing. Out of 1,000 live births, infant mortality rates were 72 and 88 in urban and rural areas, respectively. Total fertility rate is also high in rural areas. Every woman of reproductive age, on average, gives birth to more than five children in rural areas compared to four children in urban areas.

Socio-Economic Differences

The selected socio-economic variables that examine the rural-urban disparity are presented in Table 4.16.

Labor force participation rates (LFPR) are almost equal in rural and urban areas. The male rate is, however, almost twice the female rate, again with no rural-urban difference.

Urban males have distinct advantages in both literacy and education. Urbanites have greater access to education and are more literate; on the whole, males have more access to education and literacy than do females. There is one anomaly, however. Both urban and rural females are higher than males in primary education. This is, however, in large part due to the greater male access to secondary and tertiary education.

As far as the quality of life is concerned, as expected, it is far better in urban areas. Percentages of population having facilities like electricity, piped water, and flush toilets in urban areas are 93 per cent, 65 per cent, and 88 per cent, respectively, whereas in rural areas these percentages are 60 per cent, 17 per cent, and 26 per cent, respectively.

Indicators of reproductive and health care coverage also reveal that rural populations are at a distinct disadvantage. For instance, the percentage of pregnant women with at least one Tetanus Toxoid injection is 66 per cent in urban areas, and only 31 per cent in rural areas; those with two or more injections, 53 per cent in urban areas, and 23 per cent in rural areas. The contraceptive prevalence rate is almost 40 per cent in

115

TABLE 4.16   Rural-urban socio-economic and health differences, 1998

	Urban	Rural
Socio-economic Conditions		
1. Labor Force Participation Rate (Refined) (in %)		
Both	32.1	31.9
Male	57.5	60.2
Female	2.9	1.9
2. Literacy Rate (in %)		
Both	64.7	34.4
Male	72.6	47.4
Female	55.6	20.8
3. Level of Education (in %)		
Below Primary (Male) (Female)	(13.3) (15.2)	(20.8) (27.0)
Primary (Male) (Female)	(23.7) (28.0)	(32.7) (40.2)
Secondary (Male) (Female)	(42.8) (39.3)	(38.1) (27.2)
Tertiary (Male) (Female)	(18.8) (16.9)	(7.8) (4.9)
Others (Male) (Female)	(1.3) (0.7)	(0.6) (0.7)
4. Households with electricity (in %)	93.1	60.1
5. Households with piped water (in %)	65.0	17.3
6. Households with flush toilet (in %)	88.0	26.0
Reproductive and Health Care Coverage		
1. Pregnant women with Tetanus Toxoid (in %)		
At least one Tetanus Toxoid	60	31
Two or more Tetanus Toxoid in last pregnancy	53	23
2. Contraceptive prevalence rate	39.6	21.7
3. Unmet need for family planning	30.1	34.4
4. Infants immunized (less than 10 years - in %)		
Punjab	79.9	73.8
Sindh	75.5	57.2
NWFP	80.3	69.6
Balochistan	65.7	48.4

SOURCE: Government of Pakistan, Pakistan Statistical Yearbook, April 2001, Federal Bureau of Statistics; Government of Pakistan, 1998 Census Report of Pakistan, Population Census Organization, Islamabad; Government of Pakistan, Statistical Supplement to Economic Survey, Finance Division, Islamabad, 2000-2001; Government of Pakistan, Interim population sector perspective plan 2012, Ministry of Population Welfare, Islamabad, 2002; Government of Pakistan, *Pakistan Integrated Household Survey (PIHS)*, 1998-99, Round 3, Federal Bureau of Statistics, Islamabad.

urban areas, and 22 per cent in rural areas. The unmet need for family planning is 30 per cent in urban areas, and above 34 per cent in rural areas. The percentage of infants immunized in the urban areas of Punjab, Sindh, NWFP, and Balochistan is 80 per cent, 76 per cent, 80 per cent, and 66 per cent, respectively, while in rural areas it is 74 per cent, 57 per cent, 70 per cent, and 48 per cent, respectively.

IMPLICATIONS

Highlights of the Urban Conditions

Although, in Pakistan, the total population growth rate increased from 1951 to 1972, it declined after that. This is also true for both urban and rural growth rates. The urban growth rates are higher than the overall population growth rates, indicating the fact that urbanization is growing in Pakistan. Despite this, the level of urbanization at the turn of the millennium (33 per cent) can be termed as moderate.

Sindh is the most urbanized province of Pakistan, where almost 50 per cent of the population live in urban areas. This is primarily because it contains Karachi which captures more than 21 per cent of the urban population of Pakistan. If the population of Karachi is excluded from Sindh, its level of urbanization declines to 28 per cent.

Another characteristic of urbanization in Pakistan is the high degree of concentration, and the presence of provinces and cities of unparalleled size. There are 14 cities where a large portion of Pakistan's urban population resides.[15] The combined share of the urban population of these major cities constitutes about 58 per cent of the total urban population of Pakistan. These characteristics yield problems of quality of life and health, management and institutional building, social cohesion, international industrial competitiveness, and stability.

Although migration contributed to urbanization in Pakistan, the natural increase in population has been the major source of increase in the urban population, followed by internal migration, and reclassification. This is true across all the provinces. However, the situation is greatly different when considering the major cities separately. During 1981–98, 58 per cent of the total increase in population in Islamabad was because of internal in-migration, and more than 38 per cent of the increase in the population of Karachi was because of in-migration. In Peshawar and

117

Lahore almost 26 per cent of the increase in population during the same period was also because of internal migration.

The proportion of migrants from other provinces is prominent in Sindh, while in Punjab and NWFP migration to urban areas takes place mostly from within the province. According to the 1998 population census, a large number of internal migrants originate from Punjab followed by NWFP. In Karachi, which is situated in Sindh, above 38 per cent of the immigrants are from Punjab, 29 per cent are from NWFP, while 24 per cent are from the other areas of the same province. In Lahore, Faisalabad, Gujranwala, and Multan, which are situated in Punjab, nearly 86 to 91 per cent of immigrants are from different parts of Punjab itself. However, in Hyderabad (Sindh), up to 84 per cent of the internal immigrants arise from Sindh.

During the period 1951–98, the number of cities has increased to more than twice the number. While the number of big cities (with populations of over 100,000) and medium–sized cities (with populations of 10,000–100,000) have increased, the number of small cities (with populations of under 10,000) has declined. The population living in big cities increased from 53 per cent to over 72 per cent while that in medium-sized and small cities declined from 35 per cent to 26 per cent and from 12 per cent to 1 per cent, respectively. Karachi is the only primate city of Pakistan, which accommodates more than 21 per cent of its total urban population.

According to theory, cities are important because they provide comparative advantage, internal scale economies, and agglomeration economies. They possess high development status, sizeable industrial bases, availability of infrastructure, large markets and trade, etc. Due to these characteristics, large development and industrial projects are aimed towards them. These projects provide a large number of employment and business opportunities, and fetch further investment, thus making cities the engines of economic growth.

Comparatively, the developed districts of Pakistan are Lahore, Rawalpindi, and Faisalabad in Punjab; Karachi and Hyderabad in Sindh; Peshawar in NWFP; and Quetta in Balochistan (Pasha et al. 1990). The highly urbanized areas of Pakistan are contained in these districts. However, even the relatively developed provinces, Punjab and Sindh, have large underdeveloped pockets (Pasha and Hassan 1982) and Pasha et al. 1990). This indicates that development in these provinces is primarily because of the development of their cities —Lahore,

Rawalpindi, Faisalabad, Karachi, and Hyderabad. It can be deduced from this that urbanization and regional development are related to each other. It has been found that "the most highly urbanized countries are generally the most 'developed' and the most economically 'advanced' countries must also be the most urbanized ones" (Asmatullah 1996, 130).

Pakistan's 10 major cities play a prominent role in the acceleration of its economic development. Of the total value added in large-scale manufacturing in Pakistan, about 48 per cent is generated from these cities. Of this 48 per cent, Karachi alone produces 29 per cent, while Lahore, Faisalabad, and Hyderabad produce 6.3 per cent, 5 per cent and 3 per cent, respectively.[16] Moreover, in these cities, the dominance of employment in commerce and services and a vast informal sector accommodating a large number of illiterate unemployed also imply that the share of urbanized cities in economic growth is fairly large.

Industrialization has made great progress in Karachi, Lahore, Faisalabad, Hyderabad, Gujranwala, and Multan. The main center of economic activities is Karachi, which accounts for 32 per cent of the total industrial establishments of Pakistan. Pakistan Steel Mill is the country's largest industrial unit, having a production capacity of 1.1 million tons of steel. Not only large manufacturing industries are established here but also the largest small-scale industry zone (having more than 3,000 industrial units) of Sindh is also located here. About 90 per cent of these units are export oriented. Textiles and garments manufactured in these urban centers are supplied not only to other parts of the country but are also exported abroad (more than 65 per cent of export earnings come from this sector). Moreover, Karachi and Lahore have numerous trade centers and markets with a variety of commodities ranging from food items to household items, computers, electrical goods, and motor-cars.

Karachi generates a large number of employment opportunities to local residents as well as to migrants from all over the country. More than 21,000 persons work on a regular basis, while 3,000 work as daily wage-workers and retainers in Pakistan Steel Mills. Places like Quaid-e-Azam International Airport Karachi, Kimari and Bin Qasim Ports, also provide many employment opportunities. The small-scale industry zone provides employment opportunities to more than 300,000 skilled, semi-skilled, and non-skilled workers. Moreover, the huge set-up of multi-national firms and large markets in the financial sector, particularly in Karachi and Lahore, absorb a large number of educated people.

119

Educational institutes imparting education from primary up to post-graduate level are located in most of these cities. In addition to government schools, these cities also have scores of private schools that provide quality education to the entire population of the city. The cities are also outfitted with a network of hospitals and dispensaries, established by both the government and the private sector. These cities provide education and health facilities, not only to their own habitants, but also for the people of adjoining districts. These cities are well served with a good network of roads compared to other cities of Pakistan and are also connected with other parts of the country by air and linked to the rest of the country through a railway network. They are also equipped with a modern communication network.

Major Problems

In fact, across the world, urban problems are primarily related to the increase in the demand for basic urban needs and infrastructure. One may deduce that these problems often offset the benefits of urbanization.

In Pakistan, the provision of housing is an increasing problem. The public sector housing schemes (particularly for the poor) are very minimal, while in the private sector the prices are very high. In major cities there are, on average, two rooms per housing unit which, on average, accommodate more than six persons. Thus, one room is shared by three or more persons (1998 district census reports). The inadequate supply and high cost of housing in the formal sector has lead to informal settlements, i.e., unplanned urban expansion (*katchi abadis*) and slums. About one-third of the urban population resides in 2,460 *katchi abadis* and 2,184 slums (Government of Pakistan Ten-Year Perspective Development Plan 2001–11). These houses are often overcrowded with unhygienic conditions—such as no proper sanitary facility, and limited access to water supply, electricity, and social services. This in turn results in the spread of diseases like tuberculosis and cholera.

The access to clean drinking water and to convenient sanitation facilities is also very limited, even to city dwellers in Pakistan. The quality of water supplied through the existing networks of water supply schemes does not meet the World Health Organization (WHO) standards (Government of Pakistan Ten-Year Perspective Development Plan 2001–11). Only half of the urban population of Pakistan enjoy indoor tap water facilities, whereas 5 per cent have tap water facilities outside the house, 38 per cent use hand pumps and motor pumps, and the rest use methods such as digging wells, public standpipes, water sellers, etc. to fulfill their water requirements (1998–99 Pakistan Integrated Household Survey). The accessibility of adequate sanitation and sewerage systems is low, as only 59 per cent of the urban population have these facilities (Government of Pakistan Ten-Year Perspective Development Plan 2001–11). The facility of flush toilets served by water-borne sewage systems is available to only 45 per cent of the houses while 33 per cent use flush toilets connected with septic tanks, and 7 per cent use covered dry toilets. Some 15 per cent of households use toilet facilities that leave human excreta exposed (1995 Multiple Indicators Clusters Survey of Pakistan).

The health services are also insufficient to fulfill the requirements of all the urban households. In Karachi, Lahore, Peshawar, and Quetta, the population per hospital is 7,037, 534, 601, and 261, respectively; and the population per doctor in Karachi, Peshawar, and Quetta is 2,885, 2,076, and 2,452, respectively.

These problems in turn create environmental problems. In addition, emission of chemicals and release of raw waste by factories, increasing traffic congestion, smoke-emitting vehicles, and tons of rubbish and filth burnt by the sanitary workers of metropolitan corporations in almost every part of the city further aggravate air and water pollution in the cities. Karachi is one of the most polluted (air and water) cities in the world where total suspended particulates (TSP) is three to four times higher than the level determined as safe by WHO. Also, sulphur dioxide and nitrogen dioxide, that are hazardous for human health, are notably above the safe levels. Similar conditions prevail in other major cities like Lahore, Faisalabad, Multan, Hyderabad, Rawalpindi, and Peshawar (Government of Pakistan Ten-Year Perspective Development Plan 2001–11).

Urban unemployment and poverty are the most potent problems with which people in the big cities are confronted. Poverty includes poor quality of life indicators as well as low income. Poverty is often accompanied by unemployment, malnutrition, illiteracy, low status of women, exposure to environmental risks, and limited access to social and health services. In Pakistan, unemployment and poverty have increased in recent years (particularly in the 1990s), as economic growth has lagged behind the rate of population growth. Unemployment is also harmful as it leads to social problems like crime, prostitution, and suicide.

Government's Overall Plan for Addressing Urban Issues

Urban development appears inevitable, even if efforts at rural development and decentralization were more successful, not least because many people have established themselves as more or less permanent urban residents. It is therefore essential to formulate and implement appropriate urban development policies.

Conversely, one cannot preclude the fact that large-scale urbanization also occurs as a result of weaknesses in the government's development policies, which fail to bring regional equity. The effect of such policies is to promote development only in the urban areas and neglect it in the rural areas. In Pakistan, one finds that, apart from the attraction of better employment, another pull factor is the provision of other facilities (for instance, education, health, transport and communication, and infrastructure facilities) which are far better in the urban areas. In rural areas, the status of such facilities is not only inferior but, in certain cases, these are not available at all.

Government Policies for the Uplift of Urban Areas

Below are mentioned the recent policies formulated by the government of Pakistan for the period 2001–11 (Government of Pakistan Ten-Year Perspective Development Plan 2001–11).

- Decrease the population growth rate from 2.16 per cent in 2001 to 1.82 per cent in 2004 and to 1.6 per cent in 2011.
- Increase the contraceptive prevalence rate (CPR) from the existing 30 per cent to 43 per cent in 2004 and to 53 per cent in 2011.
- Establishment of New Urban Centers, Industrial Estates, and Satellite Towns around major cities to disperse rural to urban migration.
- Construction of more than 0.5 million housing units annually to increase housing stock from 21 million to 26 million units, of which 40 per cent will be in urban areas. These will be largely comprised of new units of small plots in area development schemes.
- Completion of 1,000 walk-up flats annually for low income groups in new projects in Islamabad, Karachi, Lahore, and Peshawar etc.
- Construction of 1,000 houses each year in Islamabad, provincial capitals, and big cities for government employees.

- Regularization of all notified *Katchi Abadis* and slums upgrading, along with provision of essential utilities and environmental improvement therein.
- Additional 27 million people will be provided with drinking water supply. Also, new bulk water supply projects for Karachi and Quetta.
- Providing sanitation facilities, including water-borne sewerage systems to an additional 28 million people. Construction of sewage treatment plants in all major cities.
- Construction of urban roads and flyovers.
- Promoting reuse and recycling by privatization of collection, streamlining waste collection systems, establishing National Environmental Quality Standards (NEQS) for industrial solid waste, setting up regulations for transport and disposal of industrial solid waste.
- City governments in Karachi and Lahore for effective management of urban services.
- Create urban employment by promoting small-scale and informal sectors, increasing opportunities for self-employment, and expanding the existing employment sources in the private and public sectors.

Besides these, there are policies to improve and increase facilities like modern health care facilities, access to clean drinking water, and installed capacity of power generation. There are programs to strengthen the involvement of NGOs, through training, technical assistance, and selected operational inputs, to improve service delivery, particularly in urban slums, *Katchi Abadis* and labor colonies.

Presently, the ultimate aim of the population policy is to reduce poverty and to raise the quality of life of citizens. In the Social Action Program (SAP), January 1997 to June 2002, the government has taken initiatives to improve water and sanitation in the urban slums. Unfortunately, its progress remained slow due to difficulties in the implementation of service delivery, decentralization, availability of funds, and good governance. In January 2001, the National Rural Support Program (NRSP), in collaboration with the UNDP, has initiated an urban poverty reduction program. An amount of Rs.39.75 million was disbursed to 3,792 borrowers with a recovery rate of 99 per cent (Government of Pakistan Economic Survey 2000–1).

Shortcomings

The implementation of policies is the major hurdle in the way of economic and social development in Pakistan. The main economic factors behind this are shortage of financial resources, dependence on foreign capital (aid and investment), and disproportionately high current expenditures (with debt service taking the lion's share). Besides this, it can also be attributed to factors like mismanagement in the usage of available resources and lack of effective urban governance (surprisingly even in the primate city of Karachi).

Although Pakistan has achieved high economic growth in the past, its population has also grown at a high rate, so that per capita income has grown at around 3 per cent per annum (Government of Pakistan, Eighth Five-Year Plan, Part II). There is also a feeling that the benefits of growth have not been shared equally among the different regions and different sections of the society. The main economic factors behind this were high budget and balance of payments deficits, which resulted in accumulation of debt (both domestic and foreign). Also, this can be attributed to factors like neglect in improving social sectors (particularly education and health) and inadequate infrastructure development.

Suggestions

Successful urban development is, in fact, a combination of three essentials. These are improvement in urban governance, in management, and in finance.

Accountability of public sector staff, community participation, predictability of laws and regulations (especially in terms of contract law, dispute resolution procedures, and clear allocation of responsibilities), and transparency in private dealings are the major areas that need to be focused on for improvement in urban governance. It can be argued that in Pakistan governments are likely to neglect these preferences in consequence of taking up the new development approach that favors minimal government intervention and restricts reliance on the private sector.

Urban management can be improved by concentrating on four elements. These include: effective local authorities (i.e., appropriate institutions for delivery of services) and organizational structures for work (i.e., adequate availability of both human and financial resources); ensuring coordination and integration of development proposals, ranging from land use to service provision, with the urban plans, as cities get larger;

formulation and implementation of urban plans and policies/priorities; and involvement of local people in planning in order to get sustainable urban development (Connell 2000). The instrument that put into practice the urban development plans is the availability of adequate urban finance. In this regards, emphasis needs to be placed on policies that can generate sufficient urban resources, provided that they do not increase poverty.

At the same time, it is equally necessary to focus on the efficient allocation of resources, managing social safety nets, and building strong local institutions (Buckley and Mini 2002). Moreover, concentration on improvement of education, workshops, and the involvement of NGOs and the private sector will ensure participation and empowerment, which are crucial to all facets of development.

However, in order to proceed effectively, the first step is to create an appropriate strategy for economic growth leading towards development. This requires a favorable climate for investment (both public and private). Besides economic growth, it is also essential to adopt a population control program.

ENDNOTES

1   With the usual caveat emptor, the authors are indebted to Kaiser Bengali, G. M. Arif, and the Editors for comments and suggestions on an earlier draft.

2   In the Local Government Plan 2000, implemented on 14 August 2001, the local governments are formed at three levels in each province: district, tehsil, and union council (both in rural and urban areas). Tehsils consist of municipal committees and town committees, while union councils consist of a collection of villages, or mohallas. Moreover, large cities in a phased manner will be declared as city districts.

3   The relevant data for Northern Areas and Azad Jammu and Kashmir are not available in the public domain.

4   Annual observations of the same data may give fluctuations in the growth rates of the population. However, on average, these growth rates have declined in the 1990s. Moreover, since these growth rates are sensitive to the inclusion or exclusion of a particular year, the computation of average annual rate of growth for different sets of years may give different values.

5   "[T]his current level of urbanisation is much less than the level projected by different institutions and students of urbanisation during the last two and a half decades. For example, in the early 1970s, Burki estimated that by 2001 the nation's urban population will be 86 million and will make up nearly two-thirds of Pakistan's total population (Burki 1973). The United Nation's projection made in the 1980s and early 1990s showed the level of urbanisation around 40 per cent by 2001 (UN 1992). Even the Planning Commission's working group on urbanisation for the Ninth Five-Year Plan

estimated the share of urban dwellers at about 35 per cent in 1993 (Butt 1996)" (Arif and Ibrahim 1998).

6   The average annual rates of growth of total population for the intercensal periods 1951–61, 1961–72, 1972–81 and 1981–98 are 2.4 per cent, 3.7 per cent, 3.1 per cent and 2.6 per cent, respectively.

7   Internal migration means migration within Pakistan—from one district to another.

8   Bangladeshi patriot, Hamidul Haq Chowdhury, describes these events as follows: "If the Indian Army had not invaded and occupied East Pakistan in December 1971, Pakistan would have continued its legal existence. Taking advantage of the civil disturbances in East Pakistan during 1971, the Indian army marched into the Eastern Wing of Pakistan and occupied Dacca on 16 December 1971 ... The Indian forces remained in occupation from December 1971 to March 1972. A dozen or so leading members of the Awami League party who came back to Dacca with the Indian Army, on or about 16 December 1971, were installed in Dacca as the government and Bangladesh was declared an independent state by them, seceding East Pakistan from Pakistan." (Hamidul Haq Chowdhury 1989, 319).

9   According to the 1981 census, there were more than four million persons residing in Pakistan who moved from abroad, mostly from India and Bangladesh.

10   The 1998 population census does not report rural to urban migration separately. It rather shows the number of people who migrated from rural and urban areas (a combined figure) of one province/district to the urban areas of another province/district.

11   Parveen's research utilised data from the population census of Pakistan 1972 and 1981.

12   Barkley's analysis is based on data from the population census of Pakistan 1972 and 1981.

13   Irfan's findings came from the Population, Labor Force and Migration (PLM) Survey of 1979.

14   Primate economies are those in which the process of urbanization is at a stage where the size of the largest city (or the "primate" city) is very much larger than the size of the next largest city (or cities).

15   In addition to the cities cited in Table 13 (which accommodate 54.1 per cent of the urban population), four other cities (Sargodha, Sialkot, Bahawalpur, and Sukkur) account for 3.7 per cent of the urban population of Pakistan. This makes the total urban population of 14 cities nearly equal to 58 per cent of the total urban population of Pakistan.

16   Since data regarding the GDP generated by the cities is not available, data on value added in large-scale manufacturing has been taken as a measure of income in the urban areas of the district. This indicator has also been used by Pasha et al. (1990).

CHAPTER 5

Urbanization in Sri Lanka

A. T. P. L. ABEYKOON

The pace of urbanization in Sri Lanka over the past five decades has neither been spectacular nor comparable to the rate of growth of the urban populations of other developing countries in South Asia. The proportion of the population living in urban areas has increased only from 15.3 per cent in 1953 to an estimated level of about 24 per cent in 2000. It is, therefore, of interest to study the growth of the urban population, its pattern, and the various demographic and socio-economic factors that have contributed to the unusual rural-urban situation in Sri Lanka.

DEFINITION OF URBAN POPULATION

The census definition of "urban area" includes those localities categorized as town councils, urban councils, and municipalities; the other settlements, the village councils, are rural. Village councils get upgraded to town councils on the basis of population density, the existence of urban-type amenities such as water and electricity or the presence of urban functions such as shops, banks, government offices etc. However, these criteria have not been applied uniformly so that some settlements that have urban characteristics are considered rural and large village settlements with few amenities have sometimes been classified as town councils. To complicate matters further, the definition of "urban area" was changed in 1987 when urban areas were defined as comprising only municipalities and urban councils. The village councils and town councils were combined to form the *Pradeshiya Sabas* which are regarded as non-urban areas.

URBAN GROWTH IN SRI LANKA

Table 5.1 shows that the urban population has grown at a faster rate than the total or rural population during the period 1953–71. This was due in part to reclassification and upgrading of urban areas from 43 in 1953 to 135 in 1971. Natural increase played a slightly lesser role and migration was minimal, as is shown below. During the 1971–81 period, however, urban growth has been almost entirely due to natural increase and migration resulting in a growth rate slower than that of the total population. In the subsequent period 1981– 2001, the absolute size and the growth rate of the urban population has declined, both due to problems of coverage and changes in the definition of urban areas as indicated in the note to Table 5.1.

TABLE 5.1 Sri Lanka's population growth and urbanization, 1953–2001

Year	Population (000)%			No. Urban	Urb. Areas	Ave. Ann. Gr. %		
	Total	Urban	Rural	Urban	Areas	Total	Urban	Rural
1953	8,098	1,239	6,859	15.3	43			
1963	10,582	2,016	8,566	19.1	99	2.7	4.9	*1.95*
1971	12,690	2,848	9,842	22.4	135	2.2	4.2	*1.77*
1981	14,847	3,192	11,655	21.5	134	1.7	1.2	*1.83*
2001	16,865	2,467	14,398	14.6	44	1.2	–1.3	*0.60*
*2000**	*18,827*	*4,435*	*14,392*	*23.6*		*1.00*	*2.3*	*0.60*

SOURCE: Census of Population
* 2000 and Italics from UN World Urbanization Prospects, 1999 Revision
NOTE: the 2001 census was confined to only 18 of the country's 25 districts due to hostilities. It excluded an estimated 13 percent of the population. In addition, of the 18 districts enumerated, The Town Council, which was defined as an urban area in 1981, was now defined as rural. The decline in the urban population in 2001 is both due to the exclusion of 7 districts and designation of former Town Councils as rural areas. The Department of Census and Statistics has indirectly estimated the total population for the year 2001 as 18.7 million. If the UN estimate of urban proportion of about 24% is applied to this population, then the total urban population in 2001 is 4.488 million.

What is especially distinctive here is the low level of urbanization. More striking is that, in the period 1981–2001, the Sri Lankan census saw a negative urban growth, against a relatively low level of rural growth (0.60 per cent). This anomalous condition is due to two factors. One is the civil violence that has disrupted regular census processes; the second is a census reclassification of town councils as rural rather than urban areas. We shall have to live with the disruption and reclassification, which will continue to cause some uncertainty in the level of urbanization. What remains apparent, however, is that Sri Lanka has consistently shown a low level of urbanization in the sense of population density. On the other hand, it has also continued to show a high level of all social services in the rural areas, thus reducing the social distinction between urban and rural living standards.

Table 5.2 shows the level of urbanization by district from 1953–2001. Colombo is the only overwhelmingly urbanized district in the country. Jaffna and Trincomalee are the only other districts with a substantial (30 per cent or more) urban proportion. Jaffna has become

TABLE 5.2   Level of urbanization (%) by district 1953–2001

District	1953	1963	1971	1981	2001
Western Province					
Colombo	41.5	46.4	55.2	74.4	54.7
Gampaha	–	–	–	27.9	14.6
Kalutara	11.1	20.0	21.9	21.5	10.6
Central Province					
Kandy	10.8	11.4	12.4	13.8	12.3
Matale	8.6	11.5	11.9	10.7	8.2
Nuwara Eliya	5.5	6.2	6.1	6.2	6.1
Southern Province					
Galle	12.7	20.3	21.1	20.4	11.2
Matara	9.8	11.7	11.3	11.1	8.5

129

TABLE 5.2 (cont'd)

Hambantota	5.8	8.1	9.8	9.8	4.1
Northern Province					
Jaffna	15.7	24.6	33.3	32.6	--
Mannar	–	15.0	14.3	13.1	–
Vavuniya	–	16.3	21.7	19.4	–
Mullaitivu	–	–	–	9.3	–
Kilinochchi	–	–	–	–	–
Eastern Province					
Batticaloa	6.4	19.1	19.2	24	–
Ampara	0	0	0	13.7	19.1
Trincomalee	31.4	25.1	38.4	32.3	–
North Western Province					
Kurunegala	3.3	3.5	4.1	3.6	2.4
Puttalam	9.4	12.6	13.9	12.5	9.2
North Central Province					
Anuradhapura	8.0	9.9	10.0	7.0	7.6
Polonnaruwa				7.8	–
Uva Province					
Badulla	4.7	7.0	7.5	8.0	6.8
Moneragala				2.2	–
Sabaragamuwa Province					
Ratnapura	4.5	4.8	7.6	7.4	5.8
Kegalle	1.2	3.0	7.0	7.7	2.2

more urbanized over time; Trincomalee has remained at the same level throughout the past half-century. What is most striking about this distribution is both its stability over time and the low level of urbanization of most districts.

Table 5.3 shows urbanization levels by province. The Western Province, including Colombo, is the most urbanized region of the country, with nearly one-half of the population living in urban areas in 1981. The Northern and Eastern Provinces also show relatively higher levels of both urban growth (5+ per cent) and urbanization with 28 per cent and 22.1 per cent, respectively. All other provinces show levels of urbanization lower than the country as a whole. They also show relatively little change in the level over the past half-century. Like the districts, there is more stability than change and relatively little urbanization.

TABLE 5.3 Growth of urban population by province, 1953– 2001

Province	1953		1963		1971		1981		1953–8
	No. (000)	%	No (000)	%	No (000)	%	No (000)	%	Gr. (%)
Western	767	34.4	1150	45.5	1636	48.1	1831	46.7	3.1
Central	126	9.2	173	10.2	212	10.9	221	11.0	2.0
Southern	118	10.4	213	14.9	254	15.3	279	14.8	3.1
Northern	77	13.5	171	23.1	265	30.4	310	28.0	5.1
Eastern	44	12.4	113	20.6	174	24.2	215	22.1	5.8
North West	42	4.9	68	5.9	95	6.7	105	6.1	3.3
North Central	18	8.0	39	9.9	55	10.0	62	7.3	4.5
Uva	22	4.7	46	7.0	61	7.5	58	6.3	3.5
Sabaragamuwa	25	2.8	44	3.9	96	7.3	112	7.6	5.5
Sri Lanka	**1239**	**15.3**	**2016**	**19.1**	**2484**	**24.4**	**3192**	**21.5**	**3.4**

Components of Urban Population Growth

Table 5.4 shows the components of urban growth estimated for the intercensal period 1953–81. It is seen that creation of new urban places (town councils) and natural increase were the main components of urban population growth during the 1953–71 period. During the period 1971–81, natural increase was the only contributing factor. It is also of significance to note that internal migration has consistently been very low, and was even a negative contributor during 1971–81. It is to be noted that the number of urban places dropped from 135 to 134 during this period.

Characteristics of Migrant Populations

Table 5.5 provides some abbreviated data from ESCAP on Sri Lankan internal migration. This shows that migration in Sri Lanka has been mainly to short distance destinations. In the case of Greater Colombo and Colombo other urban, 43 and 36 per cent of migration movements come from the Colombo district. It is also evident that there are no important urban centers of attraction other than those around Colombo. In addition, it is reasonable to conclude that the vast majority of the migrants into the two major areas of the country, rural destinations and Colombo, are rural in origin. Unfortunately, the ESCAP study does not give us actual numbers of migrants, nor does it define large, small, and other urban areas.

Table 5,6 shows that the overwhelming majority of young migrants to urban areas are unmarried. Virtually all young male migrants are unmarried, regardless of the place of residence. Females show some differentiation by place of residence. The larger the city, the greater the proportion unmarried, with a range from 80 to 61 per cent.

Table 5.7 shows that migrants to urban areas have a higher level of fertility than non-migrants in urban areas. Fertility increases for both migrants and non-migrants as we move from the larger to the smaller urban areas, with no real difference between the two. Other urban areas show about 20 per cent higher fertility than Greater Colombo. The larger urban areas have more urban characteristics that contribute to low fertility such as more information on family planning and services. The lifestyles are also more "western" in outlook. In addition, in Sri Lanka the "Push" factors have not operated in full force as in other South Asian countries. Thus, the migrants to the smaller urban areas have been less enterprising

TABLE 5.4   Components of urban growth, 1953–1981

Period	New Urban Places		Natural Increase		Net Migration		Total Urban Growth
	No.	%	No.	%	No.	%	No.
1953–63	300,000	39	385,000	50	92,000	12	777,000
1963–71	420,000	51	306,000	37	106,000	13	832,000
1971–81			430,000	125	–86,000	–25	344,000

NOTES: Estimates for 2001 have not yet been made.

TABLE 5.5   Inter-regional and intra-regional migration (%)

Place of Birth	Place of Present Residence					
	Greater Colombo	Colombo Other Urban	Large Urban	Small Urban	Other Urban	Rural
Colombo District (Western)						
Migrants to same area	43.4	36.0	–	–	–	8.3
Migrants to other areas	–	8.6	16.2	15.7	13.8	7.8
Jaffna District (Northern)						
Migrants to same area	–	–	7.0	–	4.7	1.2
Migrants to other areas	6.1	2.4	2.9	11.1	7.1	1.2
High-density Region						
Migrants to same area	–	15.3	54.2	15.0	30.3	27.2
Migrants to other areas	38.5	22.8	2.9	29.3	18.7	17.5
Medium-density Region						
Migrants to same area	–	–	–	11.4	8.6	18.8
Migrants to other areas	9.2	12.5	10.8	6.7	8.6	9.1
Low-density Region						
Migrants to same area	–	–	–	8.9	5.2	6.8
Migrants to other areas	2.7	2.4	6.0	1.9	3.0	2.1

SOURCE: ESCAP, Migration, Urbanization and Development in Sri Lanka, 1980.

TABLE 5.6 Proportion of urban migrants aged 15–24 who where never married

Places of Residence	Male	Female
Greater Colombo	95.1	73.1
Colombo other Urban Areas	94.3	73.7
Large Urban Areas	95.1	80.6
Small Urban Areas	94.4	68.5
Other Urban Areas	93.8	61.3

SOURCE: Adopted from ESCAP Country Report 1980.

TABLE 5.7 Average number of children per 100 females aged 15–24, by migration status

Place of Residence	Migrants	Non-Migrants
Greater Colombo	186	155
Colombo other Urban Areas	177	153
Large Urban Areas	175	167
Small Urban Areas	224	166
Other Urban Areas	222	185

TABLE 5.8 Ethnic composition of urban migrants, 1971

Ethnic Group	Greater Colombo	Colombo Other Urban	Large Urban	Small Urban
Sinhala	70.9	78.2	65.4	64.8
Tamil	17.0	11.3	21.1	26.4
Moor	7.1	5.2	9.5	6.3
Other	5.0	5.3	4.0	2.5
Total	100.0	100.0	100.0	100.0

than those who have migrated to the large urban areas. Also, the small urban areas are more likely to have rural boundaries.

As regards the movements of the major ethnic groups, Table 5.8 shows that a higher proportion of Sinhalese migrate to Colombo and the surrounding suburbs, while Tamils, in addition to migrating to Colombo, prefer other large urban and small urban areas, especially in and around Jaffna.

Tables 5.9, 5.10, and 5.11 show the educational and employment conditions of migrants. For adults, just over half of the males and almost half of the females have a secondary education; about one-third have primary school education. It is striking that females are twice as likely as are males to have no schooling (about 10 to 20 per cent). It is assumed this includes older people, since there has been near universal education for boys and girls for some decades. For migrants 15–24 years of age, half the males are employed and another 20 per cent are students. Females show the same proportion of students, but only a fifth or less are employed while about a third are home-makers (Table 5.10). Half or nearly half of migrants 15–64 years of age are white collar employees, with little or nor difference between males and females. For males, the next most common occupational category is blue collar, while for women it is the service industries.

TABLE 5.9   Educational attainment of urban migrants 25 years and over, by sex

Education Level	Greater Colombo		Colombo other Urban		Large Urban	
	Male	Female	Male	Female	Male	Female
No Schooling	11.6	24.0	10.2	18.5	10.8	22.2
Primary	30.5	29.4	30.9	30.8	32.4	27.6
Secondary	51.5	42.8	53.1	45.8	47.3	43.5
Tertiary	6.4	3.9	5.8	4.9	9.5	6.7
Total	100.0	100.0	100.0	100.0	100.0	100.0

135

TABLE 5.10 Economic activity of urban migrants aged 15–24, by sex 1971 (%)

Education Level	Greater Colombo		Colombo other Urban		Large Urban	
	Male	Female	Male	Female	Male	Female
White Collar	48.4	45.1	41.3	50.3	51.8	48.4
Blue Collar	39.8	18.7	35.3	10.8	29.4	9.5
Service	12.7	29.9	14.5	25.9	12.6	37.0
Other	5.1	6.3	8.9	13.0	6.2	5.1
Total	100.0	100.0	100.0	100.0	100.0	100.0

TABLE 5.11 Occupation of urban migrants aged 15–24 by sex

Education Level	Greater Colombo		Colombo other Urban		Large Urban	
	Male	Female	Male	Female	Male	Female
White Collar Workers	48.4	45.1	41.3	50.3	51.8	48.4
Blue-collar Workers	39.8	18.7	35.3	10.8	29.4	9.5
Service Workers	12.7	29.9	14.5	25.9	12.6	37.0
Other	5.1	6.3	8.9	13.0	6.2	5.1
Total	100.0	100.0	100.0	100.0	100.0	100.0

A System of Cities

Tables 5.12 and 5.13 show the distribution of urban areas, their populations, and their proportion of total urban population by various size categories. Given Sri Lanka's persistently low level of urbanization, there are no really large cities, just a few with populations of over 100,000, and many in the 5,000 to 20,000 category. Still, time has brought the same kind of changes we see in other urbanizing countries, though on a much smaller scale. First, the number and populations of very small towns (less than 5,000) have steadily declined, and their proportion of the total urban population has also declined. Second, there has been some stability in the number of

TABLE 5.12 Distribution or urban population by size of towns, 1953–1981

Population	Number of Towns				Population in '000			
	1953	1963	1971	1981	1953	1963	1971	1981
<2000	30	17	6	3	42	29	10	5
2000–5000	35	32	34	28	113	103	110	90
5000–10000	29	29	27	28	216	209	191	199
10000–20000	25	29	34	35	351	391	486	511
20000–50000	9	21	26	31	219	576	800	977
50000–100000	6	5	2	3	383	379	411	195
>100000	1	2	3	6	426	622	824	1217
Total	**105**	**118**	**126**	**134**	**1750**	**2309**	**2832**	**3194**

SOURCES: Gadfrey Gunatilleke, Rural-Urban Balance and Development — The Experience of Sri Lanka" 1973; and Census of Population 1981.

NB: This table is not completely consistent with Table 5.1, because Dr. Godfrey Gunatilleke gives his own estimate of urban population and urban places after making adjustments for underestimation of urbanization in census data. He argues that some of the Village Councils that were upgraded to Town Council status during intercensal periods, in fact, had urban characteristics at the time of the previous census.

TABLE 5.13   Percentage share of urban population in cities of various size categories

Size	Percentage of Total Urban Population			
	1953	**1963**	**1971**	**1981**
< 2,000	2.5	1.3	0.4	0.2
2–5,000	6.6	4.5	3.9	2.8
5–10,000	12.6	9.2	6.8	6.2
10–20,000	20.6	17.1	17.2	16.0
20–50,000	12.6	25.3	28.3	30.6
50–100,000	22.4	16.6	14.6	6.1
> 100,000	24.9	27.3	29.2	38.1
(Urb Pop 000)	1708	2280	2822	3194

SOURCE: Gunatilleke 1981. See note for table 12 to note inconsistency with data in Table 1.

5,000–10,000 size towns, but they have lost population and the proportion of the total urban population. Third, the (relatively) larger towns, over 10,000, have grown in number, population, and proportion of the total urban population. The one exception to this rule is the decline in number, population after 1971, and proportion of urban population in the size class 50,000–100,000. This may be due to the fact that when the large urban areas with populations of 50,000– 100,000 reached saturation point, expansion occurred in the suburban areas or towns over 10,000.

Future Projections of Urban Population

Table 5.14 shows that the urban population of Sri Lanka is projected to increase from an estimated 4.4 million in the year 2000 to 10.2 million in 2030. The level of urbanization is expected to increase at a faster rate than experienced in the past. The proportion of the population living in

TABLE 5.14 Projections of urban population (000), 2000–2030

Sector	2000	2010	2020	2030
Total	18,924	20,699	22,057	22,887
Urban	4,314	5,552	7,312	9,098
Rural	14,610	15,147	14,745	13,788
Percentage Urban	22.2	26.8	33.2	39.8

SOURCE: UN 2001.

urban areas is expected to increase from 23.6 per cent in 2000 to about 42 per cent in 2030. The future pattern of urban expansion in Sri Lanka is more likely to occur due to upgrading of rural areas to urban status rather than due to rural-to-urban migration. This will become possible due to the emphasis given by government to decentralized development policies and programs.

Table 5.15 shows that the average annual growth rate of the urban population is expected to accelerate until 2015 and, thereafter, gradually

TABLE 5.15 Projected average annual growth rates (%) for urban and rural populations 2000–2030

Period	Urban Rate	Rural Rate
2000–2005	2.84	0.43
2005–2010	3.28	0.19
2010–2015	3.04	0.03
2015–2020	2.74	–0.19
2020–2025	2.46	–0.38
2025–2030	2.21	–0.54

SOURCE: UN 1999.

decline, but will remain at a much higher rate than that of the rural population. Thus, the future growth of the urban population in Sri Lanka will be mainly due to rural areas graduating to urban status and internal migration from rural to urban areas.

URBAN-RURAL DIFFERENCES

The urban and rural populations in Sri Lanka have distinct demographic and socio-economic characteristics. In this section, some of these differences are examined.

Demographic Characteristics

The sex ratio of urban and rural residents, in Table 5.16 shows that urban ratios are much higher, indicating a higher proportion of males among migrants into urban areas. However, there has been a decline in the sex ratios for both rural and urban areas since 1953, conforming to the overall national pattern. The decline in the urban areas has been faster than that of the rural areas, indicating that proportionately more females than in the past have moved into urban areas.

The age comparison of urban and rural populations by broad age categories is presented in Table 5.17. It can be seen that urban areas have a comparatively smaller percentage of those under 15 years of age, indicating both that fertility levels in urban areas have been lower than

TABLE 5.16   Urban and rural sex ration, 1953–2000

Year	Total	Urban	Rural
1953	111.5	131.0	108.3
1963	108.2	118.0	106.0
1971	106.1	113.3	104.0
1981	104.0	109.6	102.5
2001	97.9	102.2	97.2

TABLE 5.17   Urban and rural age composition, 1963–81

Category	0–14	15–64	65+
1963			
Urban	37.2	58.6	4.2
Rural	42.5	53.3	4.2
1971			
Urban	35.7	60.3	4.0
Rural	39.9	55.8	4.3
1981			
Urban	31.3	64.3	4.4
Rural	36.3	59.4	4.3

in rural areas, and that migrants have been of productive age. In both age categories, the rural-urban difference (about 5 percentage points) has remained stable over time. It is also interesting to note that the proportion of those under 15 years has declined in both rural and urban areas over time and, correspondingly, the proportion of those aged 15–64 years has increased. This reflects Sri Lanka's movement through the demographic transition, with falling fertility, due in part to the country's early and successful family planning program.

The marital composition, seen in Table 5.18, shows that there is no difference in marital patterns between urban and rural populations. We do see a higher proportion of males than females who are never married. However, the proportion of those who have never married among both sexes has declined between 1963 and 1981, and the gap between males and females has remained constant. As expected, a higher proportion of females are widowed. However, the widowed female proportion has declined slightly from 6.4 per cent in 1963 to 5.2 per cent in 1981. Divorce in Sri Lanka is very rare.

Mortality differentials by urban and rural residence are seen in Table 5.19. The difference in the crude death rate is very small, and reversed between the 1950s and 1960s. The infant mortality rate was slightly higher in urban areas, but all rates declined substantially; the urban rate has become slightly lower than the rural.

TABLE 5.18 Marital status by urban rural residence, 1963–81

	Never Married	Married	Widowed	Divorced
1963 Males				
Urban	65.6	32.4	1.7	0.2
Rural	64.4	33.4	2.0	0.1
Females				
Urban	58.3	34.9	6.4	0.2
Rural	57.2	36.6	6.0	0.2
1981 Males				
Urban	63.3	35.5	1.0	0.2
Rural	62.6	35.9	1.3	0.2
Females				
Urban	56.6	38.0	5.0	0.2
Rural	56.9	38.4	5.2	0.2

TABLE 5.19 Mortality by urban rural residence, 1952–2000

Period	Death Crude Rate		Infant Mortality Rate	
	Urban	Rural	Urban	Rural
1952–1954	11.6	10.8	79.5	72.8
1962–1964	7.8	8.8	64.6	53.4
1977–1987	36.5	29.9		
1983–1993	20.8	24.0		
1995–2000	14.9	17.4		

NOTE: The rates for the periods 1977-1987; 1983-1993; and 1995-2000 are based on indirect estimates of Demographic and Health Surveys of 1987, 1983-1993 and 1995–2000 are based on indirect estimates of Demographic and Health Surveys 1987, 1993, and 2000.

Table 5.20 shows that urban fertility levels, measured in terms of child woman ratios, have remained lower than rural fertility during the period 1953–81. Fertility measured by the total fertility rate (Table 5.21), however, shows that after 1981, while both rural and urban fertility levels declined, fertility in the rural sector has declined at a faster pace. In 2000, the fertility rate in the rural sector was slightly lower than in the urban areas.

As Table 5.22 shows, the fertility decline has been brought about by the substantial increase in contraceptive use. By 1987, there was little or no difference between rural and urban areas in contraceptive use. Between 1987 and 2000, modern temporary methods have increased substantially, while modern permanent methods have declined in both rural and urban areas. Traditional methods have declined slightly in urban areas, but have remained roughly stable in rural areas.

TABLE 5.20 Child woman ratios, 1953–1981

Sector	1953	1963	1971	1983
Urban	549	594	492	398
Rural	672	712	569	513
R as % of Urb	122%	120%	116%	129%

TABLE 5.21 Total fertility rate, 1987–2000

Period	Colombo Metro	Other Urban	Rural
1982–1987	2.2	2.3	2.9
1988–1993	2.0	2.4	2.3
1995–2000	2.2	2.2	1.9

SOURCE: Demographic and Health Surveys

TABLE 5.22   Contraceptive prevalence rates, 1987–2000 (% of married women of reproductive age)

Method	Colombo Metro		Other Urban		Rural	
	1987	2000	1987	2000	1987	2000
Modern Temporary	9.9	26.9	13.5	25.4	11.3	27.6
Modern Permanent	29.8	16.3	29.3	16.8	29.0	23.2
Traditional	23.0	20.9	25.5	23.3	21.6	21.2
Total	62.7	64.1	68.3	65.5	61.9	72.0

SOURCE: Demographic and Health Surveys 1987 and 2000.

Socio-economic Characteristics

Table 5.23 shows the levels of employment, unemployment, and participation for the labor force in rural and urban areas for three time periods. Except for 1972, all figures show little or no difference between

TABLE 5.23   Employment, unemployment and labor force participation rates, 1963–1981

	1963	1971	1981
Employment Rate			
Urban	91.0	76.6	80.8
Rural	92.7	82.7	82.5
Unemployment Rate			
Urban	9.0	23.4	19.2
Rural	7.3	17.3	17.5
Labor Force Participation Rate			
Urban	33.1	35.8	34.6
Rural	32.6	35.2	33.6

TABLE 5.24   Industrial distribution of the labor force 1981

Industry	Urban	Rural
Primary	7.4	57.2
Secondary	20.2	11.7
Tertiary	72.4	31.1

urban and rural areas. In 1971 alone, urban unemployment was greater than rural, and urban employment was less than rural. Aside from this relatively minor difference, rural and urban areas have shown the same patterns of employment and unemployment.

In the industrial distribution of the labor force, we see major rural-urban differences. As expected, the large majority (72.4 per cent) living in the urban sector are engaged in the tertiary sector or in service-related industries. On the other hand, 57 per cent of residents in the rural sector are engaged in the primary industries such as agriculture, fisheries, and mining (Table 5.24). Despite the low levels of urbanization and the relative penetration of urban lifestyles into the rural areas, Sri Lanka still shows the major rural-urban industrial difference. Rural areas are predominantly agricultural, though much of that agriculture is the highly modernized tea plantation industry. Still, overall, urban living implies service activities, rural living implies agricultural industries.

Table 5.25 shows literacy rates by gender in the country as a whole, and in urban and rural areas. Urban and male advantages are clear, but those advantages have been cut in half in the two decades 1962–81. In total, urban areas showed 15 percentage points higher literacy than rural areas in 1963. That discrepancy was reduced to 8 percentage points by 1981. For males, the discrepancy was reduced from 10 to 5 percentage points; for females it was reduced from almost 20 to just over 10. Urban areas retain a slight advantage in literacy, but it is safe to say that today Sri Lanka is a totally literate society, for both males and females, in both rural and urban areas.

TABLE 5.25 Urban and rural literacy rates

	1963	1971	1981
Total			
Urban	84.1	86.2	93.4
Rural	68.7	76.2	85.4
U–R	15.4	10.0	8.0
Male			
Urban	87.9	90.3	95.3
Rural	77.1	84.1	89.9
U–R	10.8	6.2	5.4
Female			
Urban	79.4	81.5	91.4
Rural	59.6	67.9	80.9
U–R	19.8	13.6	10.5

IMPLICATIONS OF URBANIZATION

Over the past five decades, the pace of urbanization in Sri Lanka has been rather slow. Between 1963 and 1981, while the total population of the country increased by 4.3 million, the urban population increased by only 1.2 million. While there is some uncertainty today, due to the hostilities, it appears that the total population may have increased by another 4.3 million, and the urban population by some 3 million. Sri Lanka is indeed becoming more urbanized, but only slowly. On the other hand, the differences between urban and rural life are declining dramatically, except in the industrial distribution of the labor force. Rural people remain in agricultural pursuits, urban people concentrate on the service industries. But all other measures—education, literacy, mortality, fertility—have shown dramatic declines in rural-urban differences. If Sri Lanka remains largely rural, the lifestyles of its population have become highly urban.

The slow urbanization in Sri Lanka is due to a number of reasons. One important factor is the absence of a sharp urban-rural dichotomy. During the past five decades, the rural sector has been the focus of interest and most government programs have been directed towards the uplifting of rural communities. The social development policies and programs have included free education and health services, and producer subsidies and guaranteed prices for the produce. A nationwide network of institutions enabled the equitable distribution of these services. These policies and programs have contributed towards narrowing the disparities between urban and rural living conditions. In addition, subsidized transport and a good network of roads and railways have made travel within the country convenient and relatively inexpensive. This has further prevented people from permanently migrating to urban areas. The government programs of land settlement in the dry zone also relieved population pressures in the densely populated districts through rural-to-rural migration.

The pattern of urbanization that took place in the more developed countries, where an increasing share of the labor force shifted from agriculture to industry and subsequently to the service sector, is unlikely to occur in the same manner in Sri Lanka. It is possible that there will be a faster growth of the service sector resulting in the development and growth of small and medium-sized towns.

As evident from the projections of urban population, the pace of urbanization in the future is likely to be rapid. What is expected to take place is a pattern of "decentralized urbanization," where there will be a rapid growth of medium-sized towns, both in number and size, as a result of the decentralized development policies and programs that are being pursued.

The following policies and programs that are being formulated and planned by the government will contribute to the process of what we can call sub-urbanization in Sri Lanka.

One of the goals of the National Population and Reproductive Health Policy formulated by the government in 1998 is to promote the economic benefits of migration and urbanization while controlling their adverse social and health effects.

The policy document noted that, although the pace of urbanization in Sri Lanka in the past has been slow, it is expected to accelerate in the future due to the growth of small towns around the major cities. The following are some of the strategies and actions outlined in the Policy and Action Plan documents.

Strategy: Strengthen the legal framework and provide facilities to improve environmental sanitation and reduce pollution.

Action: Promote the development effective environmental management strategy though legal reforms and provision of facilities.

Strategy: Establish mechanisms to impart health education to population living in urban areas.

Action: Strengthen health education activities in under-served urban areas.

Action: Involve the private sector in improving health and environmental education for the working population.

Strategy: Create an enabling environment for economic investment to take place in small towns and in rural areas so as to encourage the redistribution of population.

Action: Promote economic investment in small towns that support rural areas.

The National Physical Planning Policy of the government presented in May 2002 outlines the following policies to bring about a more balanced urban settlement structure in the country.

(1)   Develop a second major metropolitan region in the north central and eastern parts of the country.
(2)   Develop three small-scale metropolitan areas centered on districts in the north, south and east of the country.
(3)   Within the metropolitan regions/areas thrust areas will be developed as metro urban centers.
(4)   Each of the metro urban centers will be developed to meet the needs of the hinterland area. The identified centers will not only provide higher order urban services, amenities, and facilities to meet the needs of their wider catchments areas/hinterlands, but also act as locational points for industrial development.
(5)   Within each metro urban center:
    (a)   Conservation areas and cultural and recreational activities will be treated as important land uses.

(b) Spatial aspects of defense establishment will be given due consideration.

(c) Provision of social infrastructure facilities will be given high priority.

(d) High and medium density concentrated residential development will be promoted.

(6) All other urban centers will be developed in a hierarchically structured manner. At each level, the necessary services will be provided in relation to the hinterland population and the required thresholds for the services.

(7) Provision of social infrastructure will be accorded high priority within urban areas.

(8) High and medium density, concentrated, residential development will be promoted (both vertical and horizontal) in the core areas of urban clusters to optimize land use.

(9) Conservation areas and cultural and recreational activities will be treated as important land uses and integrated into urban physical planning.

(10) All urban development activities in the future will be considered as part and parcel of the integrated regional structure plans prepared on the basis of the National Physical Planning Policy guidelines.

(11) All development activities of a specific urban area will be covered in a single integrated plan. Specific urban agglomeration plans will be prepared for a wider demarcated area on the hierarchy of metropolitan regional/areas/metro urban centers and other urban centers.

(12) Legislation will be introduced to promote the functional coordination and the management of national regional and urban land uses.

(13) Private sector, large and medium scale settlement development projects will be encouraged with the necessary legal protection provided by the government to promote investment. Development of green fields as new model cities will be encouraged within identified areas.

CHAPTER 6

Urbanization and Urban Growth in Indonesia

PRIJONO TJIPTOHERIJANTO AND
EDDY HASMI

In the past half-century, Indonesia embarked on the great modern urban demographic revolution. It is not yet complete and will continue well into the current century. In 1950, Indonesia's population stood at only 80 million; today (2002) it is about 218 million; by 2050, the population is expected to reach 311 million (UN 2000). In 1950, Indonesia's urban population numbered less than 10 million, accounting for only 12 per cent of the population (UN 1999). Today, the urban population stands at 87 million and constitutes 41 per cent of the population. By 2030, Indonesia's projected 180 million urbanites will constitute over two-thirds of the population.

The urbanization process in Indonesia should be considered seriously since many studies show that the level of population concentration in large cities has been increasing over time. For example, in 1990, the 55.4 million people in urban areas constituted 31 per cent of the nation's total population. About 40 per cent of these urban dwellers lived in metropolitan areas with populations greater than one million and large cities (with populations of 500,000 to one million), 20 per cent lived in medium-sized cities (with populations of 100,000–500,000), and another 40 per cent lived in small cities (with populations of less than 100,000). As might be expected, given regional economic patterns, most of Indonesia's cities, particularly the large cities, are located on Java.

There are tendencies among several of the large cities to keep growing larger, and then to become metropolitan cities. The capital, Jakarta, for example, has long been the largest city in Southeast Asia, with an estimated 9 million people in 1995. If it continues to grow at its present rate, it will become one of the largest cities in the world within the next 15 years. The present living and working conditions in Jakarta and in the other large and small cities of the country leave a great deal to be desired, and further growth of these cities will pose formidable problems of urban management, finance, and provision of services. The wide range of complex issues faced by the national planners requires that a broad range of studies must be undertaken and applied to specific planning issues.

The most common picture in large and medium-sized cities is the fact that many of the city dwellers are living below subsistence level. Therefore, the poverty incidence appears greater in the urban than rural areas; even though, as a general figure, the urban people are always better off than the rural. If urban poverty is not greater than rural poverty, it is at least more visible, and, possibly, also more politically volatile.

URBAN GROWTH IN INDONESIA

Urban Definitions

Since independence was proclaimed in 1945, Indonesia has conducted five population censuses: in 1961, 1971, 1980, 1990, and 2000. In 1961, the Central Bureau of Statistics (CBS) defined urban area as (1) all villages in the capital district, (2) all villages in administrative districts, and (3) villages with 80 per cent or more of the population working outside the agricultural sector. In the 1971 census, the CBS defined urban areas as (1) all villages that were classified as urban areas in the 1961 census,

151

(2) villages with 50 per cent or more of the population working outside of the agricultural sector, and (3) villages with two urban facilities: a school and electricity.

Since 1980, the CBS has used the following definition of urban areas:

(1) The population density is 5,000 people or more per square kilometer.
(2) The number of households that work in the agricultural sector is 25 per cent or less.
(3) The area has eight or more urban facilities:
    * elementary school or equivalent
    * junior high school or equivalent
    * senior high school or equivalent
    * cinema
    * hospital
    * maternity hospital/mother and child health center
    * public health center/clinic
    * roads that can be used for three and four wheeled vehicles
    * telephone/post office/supporting post office
    * market building
    * shopping center
    * bank
    * factory
    * restaurant
    * electricity
    * party utilities rental.

Urbanization

Table 6.1 shows the growth of Indonesia's total, urban, and rural population. The decline of fertility since the 1970s has reduced overall population growth. At the same time, urbanization has continued rapidly. The rate of urban growth has typically been a few percentage points greater than rural growth. Today, Indonesia is above average in the percent urban for all Southeast Asia. Only Malaysia, Philippines, and Singapore (and tiny Brunei) are more urbanized than Indonesia.

TABLE 6.1   Urbanization and population growth in indonesia, 1961–2000

Census	Population (000)			Percent Urban	Rate of Growth		
	Total	Urban	Rural		Total	Urban	Rural
1961	96,945	14,385	82,660	14.8	2.28	1.8	1.9
1971	119,139	20,465	98,674	17.2	2.33	3.6	1.8
1980	146,755	32,845	113,930	22.4	2.14	5.4	1.5
1990	179,321	55,460	123,861	30.9	1.77	5.4	0.8
2000*	208,126	82,851	125,275	42.2	1.43	4.22	0.30

SOURCES: CBS, 1966, 1975, 1983, 1992, 2002
* UN, 2000; CBS just released the final report of 2000 census only for total population.

REGIONAL DIFFERENCES

Indonesia has long known extremes of regional difference throughout the islands. In particular, Java's rich volcanic soils have always supported high population densities (945 persons per square kilometer in 2000). The Outer Islands, on the other hand, have always shown much lower levels of density (from 8 to 124 persons per square kilometer in 1990).

TABLE 6.2   Population density by region, 1971–2000

Region	Year				
	1971	1980	1990	1995	2000
SUMATRA	44	59	76	85	88
JAVA	530	690	843	900	945
KALIMANTAN	9	12	17	19	20
SULAWESI	45	55	66	72	75
MALUKU+IRIAN JAYA	3	6	7	8	8
OTHER ISLAND	56	70	116	125	124*

SOURCES: State Ministry for Population & Environment, 1992 CBS, 2002
* excluding East Timor

153

Thus, it should be no surprise that the patterns of urban growth differ markedly between Java and the Outer Islands. The growth rate of the population in urban areas in Java showed a decrease from 5.74 per cent per year during the period 1971–80 to 5.14 per cent per year during the period 1980–90. In Sumatra, the rate increased from 4.80 per cent to 5.29 per cent; in Kalimantan, it increased from 3.53 per cent to 5.54 per cent; and in Sulawesi, from 2.07 per cent to 5.22 per cent during the same period. The reason for the decrease in the rate of urban growth in Java is that those areas are already saturated, especially because of the limited land and the high population density as shown in Table 6.2. This saturation is not yet seen in urban areas in the Outer Islands. In the area of DKI Jakarta, the saturation is more obvious, producing a decrease in the rate of growth from 3.94 per cent per year during the period 1971–80 to 0.84 per cent during the period 1985–90. According to the data on migration, during the period 1985–90, DKI Jakarta experienced a negative net migration. So, the population growth of 0.84 per cent is the excess of the natural population growth in DKI Jakarta minus the outgoing net migration.

Regional population densities are shown in Table 6.2. Densities in Indonesia will continue to increase. Java is still the most densely populated area. In 2020, the density level in Java island is projected to rise to 1,903 persons per square kilometer. The most sparsely settled areas are Maluku and Irian Jaya (24 persons per square kilometer). Table 6.3 shows the changing level of urbanization in each province from 1971 to 2000. Every region experienced an increase, with the sole exception of Lampung during the period 1980–90. For each of the major island groupings, we have constructed an index based on the level of urbanization in 1971. This shows the comparative rates of growth. For all Indonesia, the level of urbanization rose almost two and a half times over these 30 years (index 245). Nusa Tenggara, starting from the lowest level, not surprisingly showed the largest increase, trebling its level of urbanization. Next comes Java (319), followed by Sulawesi (208), Sumatra (200), and Kalimantan (184). Individual provinces show greater variance. Bali shows the greatest increase with a index of 478, followed by West Nusa Tenngara (424), West Java (405), and Yogyakarta (350). DI Yogyakarta has become the second most urbanized area after DKI Jakarta. Yogyakarta is known as a student city for its centers of higher education. This is one of its attractions. Its fine educational institutions and opportunities are supported by a low cost of living, attracting many in-migrants.

TABLE 6.3 Percentage of urban population by province and region

No	Province/Region	% of Urban Population					
		71*	80*	85*	90*	95*	2000**
1	D.I. Aceh	8.44	8.94	9.9	15.81	20.54	22.75
2	North Sumatra	17.15	25.48	29.62	35.49	41.09	42.64
3	West Sumatra	17.17	12.72	14.08	20.22	25.06	27.62
4	Riau	13.28	27.18	28.95	31.92	34.36	42.30
5	Jambi	29.09	12.66	16.88	21.43	27.16	28.12
6	South Sumatra	27	27.38	28.39	29.34	30.31	35.22
7	Bengkulu	11.73	9.43	10.96	20.37	25.71	28.16
8	Lampung	9.83	12.47	14.39	12.44	15.71	20.74
	SUMATRA	17.10	19.58	21.83	25.52	27.49	34.26
	Index	**100**	**115**	**128**	**149**	**161**	**200**
9	DKI Jakarta	100	93.69	90.66	100.00	100.00	100.00
10	West Java	12.41	21.02	26.85	34.51	42.69	50.22
11	Central Java	10.73	18.75	25.5	26.98	31.90	39.26
12	D.I. Yogyakarta	16.33	22.08	26.1	44.43	58.05	57.25
13	East Java	14.48	19.61	23.21	27.45	32.06	40.62
	JAVA	17.99	25.13	30.36	35.66	52.94	57.47
	Index	**100**	**140**	**169**	**198**	**294**	**319**
14	Bali	9.81	14.71	18.42	26.44	34.31	46.87
15	West Nusa Tenggara	8.11	14.08	18.06	17.13	18.85	34.39
16	East Nusa Tenggara	5.64	7.51	8.82	11.39	13.88	15.45
17	East Timor				7.79	9.51	
	NUSA TENGGARA	7.80	12.01	20.67	17.14	19.14	31.15
	Index	**100**	**154**	**265**	**220**	**245**	**399**
18	West Kalimantan	11.02	16.78	19.61	19.97	21.66	26.49
19	Central Kalimantan	12.36	10.30	14.06	17.57	22.47	27.66
20	South Kalimantan	26.65	21.37	22.23	27.07	29.96	35.06
21	East Kalimantan	39.15	39.95	41.80	48.82	50.22	56.88

TABLE 6.3 (cont'd)

KALIMANTAN	22.11	24.45	28.37	31.08	36.52	19.79
Index	**100**	**111**	**123**	**143**	**156**	**184**
22	North Sulawesi	19.5	16.77	18.49	22.79	26.28	33.11
23	Central Sulawesi	5.66	8.99	9.31	16.50	21.87	20.17
24	South Sulawesi	18.16	18.09	19.04	24.53	28.27	29.17
25	South East Sulawesi	6.33	9.35	9.75	17.02	22.38	20.97
	SULAWESI	12.41	13.30	14.14	20.21	24.70	25.85
	Index	**100**	**107**	**113**	**162**	**199**	**208**
26	Maluku	13.28	10.86	12.64	19.02	24.57	
27	Irian Jaya		21.43	22.74	24.24	25.76	26.47
	MALUKU+ IRIAN JAYA	15.51	17.28	21.47	25.16		
	INDONESIA	17.18*	22.38	26.23	30.93	35.91	42.15
	Index	**100**	**130**	**152**	**177**	**209**	**245**

SOURCES: * Calculated from CBS, 1997.
    ** Calculated from CBS, 2002.

The urbanization level in East Kalimantan has also gone beyond the 50 per cent level. Urbanization has been taking place for quite a long time in regions with industry as the base of the economy. East Kalimantan has been developing timber, oil, and natural liquid gas industries and gold mining, all of which provide job opportunities and attract urban in-migrants.

Table 6.4 shows the changing rates of urban growth for all provinces and major island groups. First, note that the all-Indonesia rate peaked in 1980–85 (the all-Indonesia rate of population growth peaked 20 years earlier, in 1961–70). There is considerable variation among the provinces and island groups, however, in their trajectories of growth. Nusa Tenggara and Java peaked in 1971–80, and have shown declining rates of growth since then. Most provinces (13 of the 27), however, peaked in 1985–90 and have declined since then. Thus, it appears that the rate of urban growth is declining, following the decline in overall population growth in about 20–25 years.

TABLE 6.4   Growth rate of urban population by province and region, 1971–1995

No	Province/Region	Rate of Growth (Yearly)				
		1971–1980	1980–1985	1980–1990	1985–1990	1990–1995*
1	D.I. Aceh	3.56	4.62	8.38	12.13	7.92
2	North Sumatra	6.97	5.43	5.37	5.31	4.65
3	West Sumatra	–1.13	3.69	6.24	8.78	6.02
4	Riau	11.03	4.53	5.77	7.01	5.07
5	Jambi	–5.22	9.53	8.61	7.70	8.27
6	South Sumatra	3.46	3.70	3.72	3.73	3.36
7	Bengkulu	1.92	7.12	11.99	16.86	8.57
8	Lampung	8.32	7.75	2.59	–2.57	6.93
	SUMATRA	4.80	5.22	5.29	5.37	6.34
9	DKI Jakarta	3.21	3.27	3.03	2.80	2.06
10	West Java	8.51	7.22	7.49	7.77	6.51
11	Central Java	7.86	7.35	4.81	2.27	4.22
12	D.I. Yogyakarta	4.46	4.61	7.57	10.52	5.52
13	East Java	4.86	4.75	4.44	4.12	4.00
	JAVA	5.74	5.59	5.14	4.70	4.46
14	Bali	6.20	5.91	7.04	8.16	6.24
15	West Nusa Tenggara	8.49	6.88	4.18	1.47	3.56
16	East Nusa Tenggara	5.13	5.45	5.94	6.43	5.94
17	East Timor	6.52				
	NUSA TENGGARA	6.80	6.21	5.7 a)	5.18 a)	5.56
18	West Kalimantan	6.97	5.64	4.33	3.02	4.09
19	Central Kalimantan	1.38	9.40	9.15	8.90	8.32
20	South Kalimantan	–0.30	2.72	4.66	6.61	4.28
21	East Kalimantan	5.86	5.28	6.35	7.41	4.89
	KALIMANTAN	3.53	4.96	5.54	6.21	5.39
22	North Sulawesi	0.63	3.75	4.65	5.56	4.28
23	Central Sulawesi	8.93	3.94	8.90	13.85	8.56

TABLE 6.4 (cont'd)

24	South Sulawesi	1.70	2.76	4.30	5.85	4.53
25	South East Sulawesi	7.40	4.30	9.59	14.87	9.11
	SULAWESI	2.07	3.14	5.22	7.29	6.62
26	Maluku	0.62	5.69	8.35	11.01	7.79
27	Irian Jaya	5.04	5.45	5.10	4.74	4.83
	MALUKU+ IRIAN JAYA	3.09	5.55	6.50	7.45	6.31
	INDONESIA	5.26	5.40	5.22	5.05	4.76

SOURCES: Alatas, 1993
*CBS: 1997
a) Not including East Timor

Sources of Urban Growth

Urban growth is due to natural increase of the urban population, migration of people to urban areas, and reclassification of areas from rural to urban, or the expansion of urban administrative boundaries. Three different calculations have estimated the relative role of each of these in Indonesia's urbanization. These are shown in Tables 6.5, 6.6, and 6.7.

The recalculation of the data collected by Speare (1976a) for 1961–71 is shown in Table 6.5. This shows that natural increase was the major source of growth, followed in most areas by net migration. Only in the urban areas of Sumatra did reclassification contribute more (15 per cent) than net migration (4 per cent). Note also, however, that the prominence of net in-migration is largely caused by the large urban agglomerations, in which 43 per cent of the growth is due to net in-migration. For all other urban areas, natural increase produced 89 per cent of the growth, net in-migration only 5 per cent, and reclassification 6 per cent. Thus, in this early period, natural increase contributed most to urban growth; and migration was a feature primarily of the large urban agglomerations.

Table 6.6 shows Hugo's (1980) estimates excluding reclassification. Without including the element of reclassification, which has been relatively minor, urban growth throughout the cities in Indonesia in 1971–

TABLE 6.5 Components of urban growth in Indonesia, 1961–1971

		Reclassification		Migration (Netto)		Natural Growth	
Urban Categories	Growth (%)	Population (Thousand)	(%)	Population (Thousand)	(%)	Population (Thousand)	(%)
Indonesia							
Agglomeration	49,5	223,8	9	1.028,5	43	1.162,8	48
Other Urban Areas	27,0	105,4	6	67,8	5	1.428,0	89
Total Urban Areas	37,2	329,2	8	1.096,3	27	2,590,8	65
Java							
Other Urban Areas	17,9	–	–	69,7	–	571,3	–
Sumatra							
Total Urban Areas	37,2	105,4	15	30,6	4	564,3	81
Other Islands							
Total Urban Areas	32,1	–	–	106,8	27	292,0	73

SOURCES: Speare 1976 in Hugo, 1981.

76 was still dominated by natural increase, which contributed almost three times as much as net migration. This table also shows that there is little difference between males and females in sources of growth. In Indonesia, women move as easily as men in the process of urban migration.

Hugo also shows, however, that the urban growth in Jakarta in the period 1961–71 was due to 2.3 per cent natural increase and 2.6 per cent net migration. During 1971–76, the net migration component declined to 1.18 per cent per year while the natural rate remained 2.3 per cent per year. The decrease in net migration during this period was possibly due to the government's policy that made Jakarta a restricted city. This was supported by the increased transportation facility between Jakarta and West Java, which allowed people to make circular migration across the border of West Java and Jakarta.

Comparing Tables 6.5 and 6.6 shows a major change in Sumatra's urbanization process after 1971. Natural increase declined to 2.28 per cent per year, and the net migration increased dramatically to 3.28 per cent per year. This is closely related to the acceleration of the exploitation

159

TABLE 6.6 Components of urbanization in Indonesia by region, 1971–1976

Region		Growth per Year 1971-1976		Ratio of Netto
		Natural Growth (%)	Migration Netto (%)	Migration to Natural Growth
Jakarta	Male	2,30	1,18	0,49
	Female	2,30	1,16	0,49
	Total	2,30	1,18	0,49
Outside Java-Bali	Male	2,11	1,37	–
	Female	1,91	1,05	–
	Total	1,93	1,18	–
Sumatra	Male	2,28	3,01	1,34
	Female	2,30	3,33	1,48
	Total	2,28	3,28	1,41
Kalimantan	Male	2,50	5,56	2,36
	Female	2,52	5,22	2,18
	Total	2,52	5,42	2,28
Sulawesi	Male	2,25	2,11	0,94
	Female	2,30	2,69	1,16
	Total	2,28	2,40	1,05
Total Urban	Male	2,21	0,71	0,31
	Female	2,11	0,88	0,40
	Total	2,16	0,78	0,35

SOURCE: Hugo, 1981.

of the natural resources in Sumatra during the mid-1970s. The growth of oil mining and other minerals produced a rapid urbanization in cities such as Pekanbaru.

During the period 1971–76, Kalimantan and Sulawesi had rates of natural increase that exceeded the national rate, and net migration rates that exceeded those of Jakarta. Kalimantan also showed an exceptionally high rate of net migration at that time.

The World Bank made an estimate of the sources of urban growth in Indonesia berween 1961 and 1980, which is shown in Table 6.7. The study shows that between the 1960s and the 1970s, the absolute growth from natural increase did not show any evident change, but the number

TABLE 6.7   Components of urbanization in Indonesia, 1961–1980

	Natural Growth		Migration Netto		Total	
	1961-1971	1971-1980	1961-1971	1971-1980	1961-1971	1971-1980
Number (Million)	4,59	4,63	2,17	5,0	6,76	9,63
Percentage	68	48	32	52	100	100

SOURCE: World Bank, 1984.

of net migrants more than doubled. According to the percentage contributions, however, there was a substantial change. Urbanization in Indonesia in the 1960s was dominated by natural increase, and in the 1970s, especially towards the end of the decade, net migration played a more important role.

For the 1980s, a United Nations estimate (ESCAP 1993, 11–16) showed that Indonesia's urbanization was primarily due to net in-migration (64.8 per cent); natural increase only contriuted one-third (35.2 per cent) to the process.

Overall, these studies show that urbanization before 1970 was doninated by natural increase. This was also the period when the country showed an overall high rate of natural increase. After the mid-1970s, the national rate of natural increase declined, due in part to the success of the national family planning program. As the overall rate of natural increase declined, net migration came to dominate the urbanization process.

Characteristics of Migrants

Table 6.8 provides a picture of the total migration pattern in Indonesia in 1995. There is movement in all directions: urban to urban, rural to rural, rural to urban and urban to rural. There were 14 million people classed as migrants in 1995. More than half (8.5 million or 61 per cent) were residing in urban areas. Of the urban migrants, more than half (55 per cent) came from other urban areas, and 45 per cent from rural areas. Most of the rural migrants (65 per cent) came from other rural areas, but as many as 2 million (or 35 per cent of migrants in rural areas) came from urban areas. Unfortunately, there is no data to show who these

161

TABLE 6.8   Distribution of migrants by place of residence five years ago and currently, 1995

Residence 5 Years Ago	Current Place of Residence		
	Urban Areas	Rural Areas	Total
Urban Area	4.756.078 (55%)	1.902.470 (35%)	6.659.048 (48%)
Rural Area	3.580.865 (45%)	3.429.684 (65%)	7.010.549 (52%)
Total	8.516.721 (100%)	5.457.174 (100%)	13.973.895 (100)

SOURCE: CBS, 1997.

urban-to-rural migrants are, but it is believed they are older people retiring to rural areas. The 1995 study did show that almost half of the rural-to-urban migrants are younger and moved for education and employment. One other main reason for migration to urban areas is family (41 per cent), as most of the workers who move to urban areas bring their families with them.

Another study done by the State Ministry for Population and the Asian Urban Information Centre of Kobe (AUICK) in Surabaya (1995) found that most respondents (95.8 per cent) stated that job opportunities in Surabaya were the main reason for their move to the city. Socio-economic development in Surabaya was becoming a very attractive factor for rural people. This finding is very similar to research done by the State Ministry for Population and Environment in 1991. As in the previous study, it found that 92 per cent of respondents reported moving to Surabaya in response to job opportunities in the city. Only 8 per cent moved to Surabaya for other reasons such as education, family considerations, transfer of job, and following the family. Both studies had samples of 324 persons.

In 1995, the CBS conducted a comprehensive survey on rural-urban migration, the Survey of Urbanization. In this survey, the CBS reported characteristics of incoming migrants to the six largest cities in Indonesia: Medan, Jakarta, Bandung, Semarang, Surabaya, and Ujung Pandang. Table 6.9 shows the prior place of residence of incoming migrants currently living in those six cities. The majority of migrants (62 per cent) came from other urban areas (including abroad). The rest were from rural areas. Medan is the highest city for migrants from other urban

162

TABLE 6.9   Incoming migrants according to place of residence five years ago in Indonesia's six largest cities

Current Place of	Place of Residence 5 years ago			Total
Residence	Urban*	Rural	Don't know	
Total				
(%)				
Medan	240.008	80.711	17.727	338.446
(%)	(70.9)	(23.8)	(5.2)	(100.0)
Jakarta	616.509	359.445	23.895	999.89
(%)	(61.7)	(35.9)	(2.4)	(100.0)
Bandung	246.50	145.360	3220	395.140
(%)	(62.4)	(36.8)	(0.8)	(100.0)
Semarang	139.464	58.365	0	197.829
(%)	(70.5)	(29.5)	(0.0)	(100.0)
Surabaya	263.464	202.444	29.700	495.608
(%)	(53.2)	(40.8)	(6.0)	(100.0)
Ujung Pandang	101.024	79.069	1869	181.962
(%)	(55.5)	(43.5)	(1.0)	(100.0)

SOURCE: CBS, 1997a.

areas (70.9 per cent), followed by Semarang (70.5 per cent), Bandung (62.4 per cent), Jakarta (61.7 per cent), Ujung Pandang (55.5 per cent), and finally Surabaya (53.2 per cent). Thus, for these large cities, more than half of the migrants come from other urban areas. This supports the theory of chain migration. People from rural areas migrate first to small cities then to medium-sized cities and finally to very large cities.

A 1995 intercensal survey asked about changes in the level of welfare in relation to migration. The great majority of migrants, 70 per cent, reported that their level of welfare had improved; 20 per cent felt there had been no change, and only 10 per cent reported a decline in their level of welfare.

Table 6.10 shows the educational characteristics of rural-to-urban migrants in those six big cities. There is a striking difference between migrants in Java's cities and the Outer Island Cities. Java's cities (Jakarta, Bandung, Semarang, and Surabaya) have rural migrants with lower levels of education compared to the two cities outside Java (Medan and Ujung

163

TABLE 6.10 Percentage of in-migration from rural areas according to level of education

Level of Education	City					
	Jakarta	Bandung	Semarang	Surabaya	Medan	Ujung Pandang
No education/not yet completed primary school	46.2	48.6	55.6	50.2	29.4	20.6
Completed primary school	19.0	15.1	12.1	19.3	27.7	24.6
Completed Junior High	29.0	30.7	30.3	23.3	36.7	50.9
Completed Senior High Academy + University	5.8	5.6	2.0	7.2	6.2	4.0
Total	100.0	100.0	100.0	100.0	100.0	100.0

SOURCE: CBS, 1997a.

Pandang). Semarang had the laregst proportion with little or no education. Ujung Pandang showed the highest quality of migrants followed by Medan. It is interesting to note that in all cases, Junior High School migrants were greater than primary school migrants. Further analysis shows that migrants who are moving to those cities are mostly literate young people. Surabaya seems to receive more illiterate migrants from rural areas compared to the other cities (Table 6.11).

A System of Cities

The urbanization process leads us to the further question of how the urban population is distributed across the cities. This question is very important since the high concentration of population in one city may lead to economic problems for the nation. Unfortunately, there are not many studies that analyze the development of the cities in Indonesia.

A comprehensive study of city distribution in Indonesia was performed in 1985 through the National Urban Development Strategy Project (NUDSP). Using data from NUDSP, Werner Rutz in 1987 (Karyoedi 1993) analyzed 400 cities in Indonesia based on the total population in each city. Rutz found that the number of small cities (with

TABLE 6.11 Percentage of in-migration from rural areas according to age and literacy

Characteristics	City					
	Jakarta	Bandung	Semarang	Surabaya	Medan	Ujung Pandang
Age						
10–19	30.6	34.1	42.4	27.8	37.3	38.3
20–29	47.2	46.4	40.4	53.4	37.9	49.1
30–39	13.0	15.1	13.1	14.3	16.9	9.1
40–49	5.0	1.7	2.0	2.2	2.8	2.9
50+	4.1	2.8	2.0	2.2	5.1	0.6
Total	100.0	100.0	100.0	100.0	100.0	100.0
Literacy	97.7	98.3	99.0	93.7	98.9	98.9
Latin	0.4	0.0	0.0	0.0	0.0	0.0
Others	1.1	1.7	1.0	6.3	1.1	1.1
Illiterate	100.0	100.0	100.0	100.0	100.0	100.0
Total						

SOURCE: CBS, 1997a.

less than 100,000 inhabitants) is enormous (291 cities) compared to medium-sized (with 100,000–500,000 inhabitants) and large cities (with 500,000 to one million inhabitants), which number only 109.

Table 6.12 shows the growth and distribution of cities with populations of over 100,000. Two things are especially noteworthy in these data. First, there has been a rapid growth of very large cities (with over one million inhabitants). There were just two in 1961 (Jakarta and Surabaya) and by 1990 there were eight. Second, there has been substantial growth in the Outer Islands as well as in Java. Sumatra and Sulawesi now have cities with populations greater than one million. Moreover, there has also been a rapid development of medium-sized cities (with populations of 100,000 to one million) in both Java and the Outer Islands. Despite the lower concentration of the total population in the Outer Islands (35 per cent), by 1990, they had as many medium-sized cities as Java (26 vs. 27).

165

TABLE 6.12   Urban centers with more than 100,000 inhabitants, 1961–1990

City Size	Location	Year			
		1961	1971	1980	1990*
1 Million +	Java	Jakarta, Surabaya	Jakarta, Surabaya Bandung	Jakarta, Surabaya Bandung	Jakarta, Surabaya, Bandung, Semarang Yogayakarta
		2	2	3	5
	Outer Islands			Medan	Medan, Ujung Pandang, Palembang
		0	0	1	4
100,000-999,000	Java	11	23	24	27
	Outer Islands	3	17	16	26

SOURCE: Hugo, et al. 1986; *Firman 1996.

Table 6.13 shows the percentage of urban population across the different city sizes compared to the total population living in urban areas in 1971–80. Clearly from the table, we can see that the share of the population living in metropolitan and large cities (with populations above one million) as well as medium-sized cities (with populations between 100,000 to one million) tends to increase while the share of the population living in small cities tends to decline. This implies that the role of metropolitan and large cities, as well as medium-sized cities, is becoming more important in urbanization and urban growth in Indonesia. Furthermore, the study performed by Firman (1996) also discovered that the segment of the country's urban population in Jabotabek (Jakarta-Bogor-Tangerang-Bekasi) reached 22.45 per cent in 1980 and 23.62 per cent in 1990, or approximately almost a quarter. Also, the proportion of the urban population in the four largest metropolitan areas (Jabotabek, Gerbangkertasusila, Bandung Raya, and Mebidang) reached 40.2 per cent in 1980 and 40.63 per cent in 1990. In general, all studies indicate that

TABLE 6.13 Percentage of urban population by city size-class, 1971–1980

City Size	Year	
	1971	1980
1,000,000 and above	32.6	34
500,000 – 1,000,000	9.8	11
250,000 – 500,000	11.5	13
100,000 – 200,000	9.0	10
100,000 and below	37.1	32
Total	100.0	100

SOURCE: Hugo,et al., 1986.

the urban population in Indonesia is very much concentrated in the large cities, especially in Jabotabek.

One of the indicators often used to determine the distribution of the urban population is the primacy index. There are various versions of this index. First, the ratio between the population of the main (largest) city against the population of the second largest city; second, the ratio between the population of the main city and the total population of the next three largest cities. Firman (1996) made a calculation of the primacy index using the second method of calculation.

There will be an underestimate in this calculation, however, when the administrative area of Jakarta (or any other city) is used to count the population. The urban population, especially in Java, spills out beyond the administrative boundaries of the city itself. Some correction can be made by using the greater metropolitan area. A rough estimate of the amount of underestimation can be made by comparing the data in Tables 6.13 and 6.14. With 34 per cent of the 1980 urban population living in cities with populations greater than one million (Table 6.13), the population in these cities would be roughly 11.2 million (based on the 32.8 million total urban population). But Table 6.14 shows a total of 13 million living in these four greater metropolitan areas surrounding the large cities, giving an underestimate of about 14 per cent. Thus, for example, for the main city of Jakarta, the population to be used in the calculation is the number within the larger metropolitan area.

167

TABLE 6.14   Urban population, Java and outside Java

Metropolitan Areas	Administrative Unit	Urban Population, 1980 (Thousand)	Urban Population, 1990, (Thousand)	Growth Rate (%)
Jabotabek	DKI Jakarta	7.373,6	13.096,2	5,9
	Kab.Bogor			
	Kodya Bogor			
	Kab. Bekasi			
	Kab. Tanggerang			
Bandung Raya	Kodya. Bandung	2.099,3	3.317,0	4,7
	Kab. Bandung			
Gerbangkertosusilo	Kab. Gresik	2.301,5	3.697,8	4,7
	Kab. Bangkalan			
	Kab. Mojokerto			
	Kodya Surabaya			
	Kab. Sidoarjo			
	Kab. Lamongan			
Mebidang	Kodya Medan	1.416,9	2.409,4	5,4
	Kodya Binjai			
	Kab. Deli Serdang			
Indonesia		32.845,8	55.433.8	
Primacy Index		1.27	1.39	

SOURCE: Fiman, 1996.

The result of the calculation (from data in Table 6.14) shows that the primacy index of the urban areas in Indonesia in 1980 was 1.27, which then increased slightly to 1.39 in 1990. This coefficient basically shows that the urban population in Indonesia is still very much concentrated in Jabotabek, although it is not as large as the concentration of the urban population in Thailand or the Philippines, for example, which are models of high primary rates.

When we examine specific regions, however, it is clear that the *primacy rate* varies greatly. The development of Ujung Pandang in South Sulawesi, for example, is not supported by any medium-sized city. Mamuju is the closest city to Ujung Pandang, but it is only a very small city. The other truly medium-sized cities, Kendari and Palu, are too far from Ujung

Pandang to be a part of it. This shows how dominant the development of Ujung Pandang has been to its surrounding cities.

The government's urban development policy also stimulates the development of large cities and metropolitan areas. The concept of interlinked cities such as Jabotabek (Jakarta-Bogor-Tangerang-Bekasi) promotes the development of very large cities and neglects the development of the medium-sized cities nearby. The period 1971–90 showed that the distribution of cities in Indonesia was heading towards an integrated and dispersed urban system. The development of cities tended to create mega-urban areas. In addition to Jabotabek, these include Mebidang (Medan-Lubuk-Pakam-Binjai-Stabat-Tebing-Tinggi), Bandung Raya (Bandung-Cimahi-Lembang-Banjaran-Majalaya), and Gerbangkertosusilo (Gresik, Bangkalan, and Mojokerto).

In general, economic growth is concentrated in several urban areas which have better environments for industrial activities such as the availability of reliable power, telecommunications, water supply and other public utilities, banking and credit institutions, intra and inter urban transportation, and human resources. As a result, although economic growth is increasing, its spread is inequitable.

Urban Projections

Urbanization is expected to continue in the future. Ananta et al. (1994) used the 1995 Intercensal Population data to project future urban growth, which is shown in Table 6.15. This predicts that by 2025 the level of urbanization in Indonesia will reach 57 per cent. The projection for the year 2000 is very similar to the actual level of urbanization found in the 2000 population census, providing some validation for the projection to 2025.

The rural population, on the other hand is expected to decline. According to Table 6.14, above, starting 2015 the proportion of the population living in urban areas will be larger than the proportion of the population living in rural areas. The UN estimates (UN 2001) project an absolute decline in the rural population beginning in 1995–2000 and continuing beyond that time. Furthermore, it is assumed that in 2020 there will be 23 urban areas with populations of more than one million people, 11 of them will be in Java. Five out of the 23 cities are expected to have populations of more than five million people, including Jabotabek, which is expected to have 35 million people at that time (Kartasasmita 1995, 5).

169

TABLE 6.15 Indonesia's urban population projection 2000–2025

Year	Number	Percentage
2000	87,577,1	41,80
2005	102,534,1	46,01
2010	116,481,0	49,55
2015	129,245,3	52,60
2020	140,309,9	55,19
2025	150,052,0	57,39

SOURCE: Ananta dan Anwar, LDFE UI (1994).

TABLE 6.16 Basic demographic and social development indicators

Year	Characteristics											
	IMR			TFR			CBR			CPR		
	Urban	Rural	U–R	Urban	Rural	U–R	Urban	Rural	U–R	Urban	Rural	U–R
1971	106	141	35									
1970–6				4.72	5.34	-0.62						
1980	79	102	23									
1981–4				3.53	4.27	-0.74						
1987										54.3	45.3	9.0
1991	57.2	81.0	23.8	2.60	3.24	-0.64	24	25.6	-1.6	55.7	47.2	8.5
1994	43.1	75.2	32.1	2.31	3.15	-0.84	21	24.2	-3.2	60.2	52.5	7.7
1997	35.0	58.0	23.0	2.40	2.98	-0.58	22	23.6	-1.6	59.8	56.5	3.3

SOURCES: *State Ministry for Population/NFPCB, 1995.
** Indonesia Demographic and Health Survey, 1987, 1991, 1994, 1997.

RURAL-URBAN DIFFERENCES

Basic Demographic Differences

Table 6.16 shows some basic demographic data on Indonesia's rural-urban differences. As in most developing countries, urban reproductive and health conditions are better than those in the rural areas. Urban infant mortality rate (IMR), total fertility rate (TFR) and crude birth rate (CBR) are lower; and contraceptive use rates are higher. Some of these gaps between urban and rural areas are narrowing, others seem more stable. The IMR gap was reduced considerably in the 1970s, but has remained stable since then at about 23 points (with the notable and unexplainable exception of the 1994 survey). The TFR gap was about two-thirds of a child until 1997, when it dropped to 0.58 of a child. The gap in the CBR has vacillated from 1.6 points in 1991 to 3.2 points in 1994 and then down again to 1.6 points in 1997. We have no explanation for this aberrant position in the 1994 survey. Finally, the gap in the contraceptive prevalence rate has shown a steady decline from 9 to 3.3 percentage points, reflecting the success of the Indonesian family planning program.

Economic differences between urban and rural areas are shown in Table 6.17. These data show both a familiar pattern and some conditions that are distinctive to Indonesia. First, living standards are higher in urban than rural areas. The proportion under the poverty line is consistently slightly lower in urban than in rural areas. The differences have remained relatively stable over the years at about 2 percentage points. Second, and perhaps more important, both the numbers and the proportions under the poverty line have declined dramatically in both urban and rural areas. Urban poverty declined from 38 to 10 per cent, and rural poverty declined from 40 to 12 per cent. This is somewhat distinctive to Indonesia, where economic progress in the last three decades has been quite remarkable both for its speed and for the decline of poverty.

The data also show, however, the impact of the economic collapse of 1997. From 1996–99, the urban poor grew by almost 10 million (10 to 19 per cent) and the rural poor doubled from 16 to 32 million; the proportion also doubled from 13 to 26 per cent.

Finally, the Gini index coefficients show that economic inequality has consistently been higher in urban than in rural areas. The differences have not changed much over the period of observation, except for the slight rise in inequality after 1997.

171

TABLE 6.17   Poverty and economic equality in urban and rural areas, 1976–1999

| Year | Poor People | | | | | | Gini Coefficient | | |
| | Urban | | Rural | | Total | | Urban | Rural | Total |
	Million	%	Million	%	Million	%			
1976	10.00	38.80	44.20	40.40	54.20	40.10	0.32	0.28	0.33
1981	9.30	28.10	31.13	26.50	40.60	26.90			
1984	9.30	23.10	25.70	21.20	35.00	21.60			
1985	9.70	20.10	20.30	16.40	30.00	17.40			
1987			0.32	0.27	0.32				
1990	9.40	16.70	17.80	14.30	27.20	15.08	0.34	0.25	0.32
1993	8.80	13.40	17.20	13.80	25.90	13.67			
1996	6.90	10.10	15.70	12.60	22.60	11.39	0.36	0.26	0.35
1999*	15.6**	19.41**	32.3**	26.03**	48.0**	23.42**			

SOURCES: Tjiptoherijanto, 1997.
*CBS 2000: Statistical Year Book of Indonesia.
** without East Timor.

Table 6.18 shows an abbreviated analysis of educational services in urban and rural areas for 1990 and 1998. Children in urban areas are clearly advantaged. Smaller percentages had no schooling and larger percentages were currently attending school, in both 1990 and 1998. At the same time, there has been considerable improvement over the past decade (which would be even more dramatic if we could extend the data back further in time). A decade ago, one quarter of the rural children were not attending school; in 1998 that fell to 16 per cent.

If we examine only the most recent figures, it is clear that considerable progress has been made in providing education for all Indonesia's young people. As might be expected, more progress has been made in urban than in rural areas. By 1998, the great majority of both urban and rural children aged 5–9 were attending school. Even more impressive are the figures for the 10–14 age group, those at the end of primary and the beginning of secondary schooling. Almost all urban children and two-thirds of the rural children were attending school. At

172

TABLE 6.18 Percent of urban and rural children in different educational conditions

Educational Activity	1990		1998	
	Urban %	Rural %	Urban %	Rural %
All ages 5 +				
No School	13.3	24.3	7.4	16.0
Attending	31.4	24.5	29.4	24.6
Finished	55.0	51.2	63.3	59.4
Ages 5–9 Yrs				
No School			28.3	33.5
Attending			71.4	64.0
Finished			0.3	0.5
Ages 10–14 Yrs				
No School			0.3	1.3
Attending			95.0	64.0
Finished			4.7	11.1
Ages 15–19 Yrs				
No school			0.4	1.9
Attending			66.4	38.5
Finished			33.2	59.6

SOURCE: Statistical Yearbooks, 1998 and 1990.

the secondary level, ages 15–19, two-thirds of the urban and one–third of the rural children were attending school.

Two points are prominent here. First, there has been substantial progress in providing primary and secondary education for all children. Second, the progress has been greater for urban than for rural children.

A study by the World Bank (1994) provides more evidence of both overall progress and urban advantages in the availability and use of health services (Table 6.19). This shows the percentage among the poorest 40 per cent of the population who reported being ill in the past week and who used various health services (either the government health center or another modern provider, such as a private doctor or a pharmacist).

TABLE 6.19 Utilization of health services among the poor, 1978–87*

	Java				Outer Islands			
	Urban		Rural		Urban		Rural	
	1978	1987	1978	1987	1978	1987	1978	1987
Hlth Cntr	19	27	17	31	27	31	11	26
Other Modern	13	40	24	21	24	30	24	25
Total	32	67	41	52	51	61	35	51

* % among the poorest 40% who reported being ill in the last week and who used various services World Bank 1994.

There is an interesting difference here between Java and the Outer Islands. In Java, the urban poor moved from government health centers to "other modern" providers, while the rural poor tended to rely more and more on government health services. This was a period in which government health services were being expanded rapidly in the rural areas, and it is evident that the rural poor took advantage of those servcices. The urban poor, on the other hand, appeared to be using their increased income on other private health providers. The same was true in the Outer Islands, though the change was less dramatic. Still, the urban poor tended to shift slightly to other modern providers, while the rural poor tended to rely more and more on the expanding government services.

Despite many problems, there has been a rapid growth of modern infrastructure in both urban and rural areas; always, of course, with urban areas leading the way. For example, according to the report from the World Bank, the provision of electricity between 1981–89 increased from 47 to 84 per cent in urban areas and 6 to 28 per cent in rural areas. The availability of clean water increased from 39 to 52 per cent in urban areas and from 4 to 10 per cent in rural areas. The indicator of the housing in Indonesia in 1993 also shows that the houses are generally in good condition. Ownership and occupation rates of houses have inceased dramatically. The floor area per person reached 14 square meters in 1992 and every house is occupied by 1.08 households. The provision of healthy houses, including for the poor, also shows a significant improvement. This is supported by the Slums Upgrading Program. However, the lowest income groups still face a shortage of housing in both rural and urban areas.

IMPLICATIONS

Highlights

From 1950 (especially after 1966) to 1997, Indonesia has made significant progress in all forms of development and welfare. Income has risen, the country has become self-sufficient in rice, a whole range of new urban industries have arisen, and human welfare has increased dramatically. And with this has come rapid urbanization. In a sense, the urban-industrial revolution is now in full swing, and with it has come a substantial rise in human welfare. All death rates have declined, life expectancy has risen, and educational opportunities have rapidly expanded to reach the great majority of the population. Since the economic collapse of 1997, of course, the economic and welfare situation has deteriorated, but it is still far ahead of where the country was half a century ago.

We have seen that the urban growth was first driven primarily by population growth, until about the 1970s. Since then,, it is in-migration that has become the major driver of urban growth. We have seen that this migration appears to be a two-step (or more) process, with people first moving from rural areas to small towns, and then on to larger urban areas. The majority of migrants in the larger cities come from other urban areas.

We have also seen that urban growth first occurred in Java, but it has rapidly spread to the Outer Islands, especially to Sumatra, Sulawesi, and Kalimantan. Urbanization has been associated with economic growth and industrialization, with causal forces no doubt running in both directions.

Problems

If there has been progress, there remain many problems in the urbanization process. One of the most serious is urban industrial pollution. Industrial wastes pollute water supplies and the air. Although

175

there are laws protecting the environment, implementation and enforcement are lacking. Urban areas feel the brunt of this pollution problem. Added to this is the pollution from the human population. Due to great shortages in waste collection and sewage treatment, human waste pollutes water and the land.

The general category of weak infrastructure development covers many of the problems of urban areas. Lack of sewage treatment and clean water supplies means both pollution and reduced welfare. Here it is especially the poor who suffer, often spending substantial portions of their income on simple clean water. Housing is another area where shortages reduce the quality of life. Rapid urbanization has often meant the rapid growth of slums with low-grade housing and no urban amenities. Finally, the transportation infrastructure is not well developed. Mass transit systems are not well developed, giving rise to massive traffic jams and long hours spent moving from home to work. All of these problems fall more heavily on the urban poor, whose numbers have risen as fast as or faster than the urban centers themselves.

Government Plans and Policies

The government of Indonesia is not unaware of the urban problems it faces. Along with various policies and programs to promote economic development and human welfare, it has devised a series of plans and projects to improve the urban sector.

One of the fundamental policies concerns attempts to *improve urban administration*. The government has created a series of administrative structures for towns and cities at different stages of development. These focus on helping urban administrators address their most urgent problems: providing the basic urban infrastructure and services that are needed. In addition, the government has established bodies to deal with *regional planning*. These bodies attempt to link different cities together for joint planning to ensure a more balanced development of a larger region. The government also seeks to *expand urban boundaries* to give urban governments the larger extent of land that they need for more effective planning. The government has also instituted a series of *local (sometimes Kampung) improvement projects*. These attempt to mobilize local communities (villages, neighborhoods, and towns) to enagge in their own infrastructure development and improvement. In these projects, the

176

government is attempting to decentralize the planning and improvement process and to increase the participation of the local population.

Perhaps one of the most interesting set of projects and policies is aimed at *supporitng the informal sector*. It is well recognized that the informal sector (street merchants etc.) absorbs a great deal of the new urban labor force and provides ways for people to earn a living, and to find food and shelter. There are programs for micro-credit, for training and skill development, and innovative programs to link formal and informal structures. For example, lagre urban department stores are encouraged to provide stalls for individual vendors, and to build eating areas staffed by individual sellers. The government also constructs market areas for informal producers and sellers through a program called *Pujasera (Pusat Jajan Serba Ada)*.

Finally, the government is attempting to create *new urban centers* to draw off growth from the large and overcrowded cities. This attempts to distribute the urban growth more evenly throughout the country. Along with the new urban centers, the government promotes many programs of *rural development*. These are aimed both at increasing the development and welfare of rural people and at reducing the heavy migration to the cities.

CONCLUDING REMARKS

Urbanization must be recognized as a natural modern process by which humans attempt to improve their welfare. The level of urbanization in Indonesia is still increasing. It is projected that the number of metropolitan areas in 2020 will increase to 23 compared to the current eight metropolitan areas. The major factor contributing to the level of urbanization is migration from rural to urban areas. To help ensure that this growth *responds* to the people's desire for a better life, it is the government's responsibility to provide the policy so that the level and direction of urbanization across the nation is effectively managed. Policy is very important in order to avoid an extreme primacy rate and the imbalance of urban distribution. In Indonesia, the urgent urban and regional policy is to stimulate the development of medium-sized cities.

7

Trends and Patterns of Urbanization in Malaysia, 1970–2000

TEY NAI PENG

Malaysia consists of 11 states in Peninsular Malaysia, and Sabah and Sarawak on the north-western coast of Borneo Island. The two regions are separated by about 530 kilometers of the South China Sea. There are three federal territories (Kuala Lumpur, Labuan, and Putra Jaya, the last became a federal territory in 2001). The states are sub-divided into administrative districts, and are further sub-divided into mukim. Urban and rural areas are defined to distinguish areas with certain socio-economic characteristics.

The population of Malaysia consists of three major ethnic groups in Penninsular Malaysia: the Malays, Chinese, and Indians (and others). In Sabah and Sarawak, there are other indigenous groups such as the Kadazan/Dusun and Murut in Sabah, Iban, Bidayuh and Melanau. In 2000, there were about 1.3 million foreigners out of a total population of about 23 million.

Urbanization and population redistribution in multi-ethnic Malaysia have been an important policy instrument in achieving the goals of the New Economic Policy (1970–90), the National Development Policy (1990–2000), and National Vision Policy (2001–2010). In formulating and implementing development policies and programs, the government has placed great importance in restructuring the society for a more balanced ethnic distribution in the urban areas, and a more balanced distribution in occupation.

At the time of Independence in 1957, the Malays made up about half of the population and were mainly engaged in agricultural activities in the rural areas. The Chinese, who had migrated from southern China in the early part of the 20th century, made up about 37 per cent of the total population in 1957. They were mainly engaged in urban commercial activities. The Indians, who also migrated to Malaysia at about the same time as the Chinese, made up about 12 per cent of the total population in 1957, and were divided between the plantation sector and urban services. Ethnic segregation and income disparity led to the racial riots on 13 May 1969, right after the general election. This induced the government to construct a new policy to address the unbalanced ethnic distribution in location and vocation.

The New Economic Policy was implemented in the aftermath of the racial riots to eradicate poverty, irrespective of race, and to restructure the society by eliminating the identification of ethnicity with location and vocation. In each of the successive five-year development plans within the framework of the New Economic Policy (and later the National Development Policy in 1990 and National Vision Policy in 2000), great emphasis has been given to the implementation of distributional strategies, aimed at increasing effective Bumiputera (i.e., indigenous peoples) ownership and participation in the corporate sector, improving Bumiputera participation in high-income occupations, strengthening the development of the Bumiputera Commercial and Industrial Community (BCCI), narrowing income inequality, and eradicating poverty. Programs to restructure employment have focused on increasing the number of Bumiputera professionals, managers, and skilled workers in various occupations and sectors.

Past development plans placed great emphasis on rural development, partly because poverty had been identified as more of a rural problem. Rural development programs in Malaysia have been widely acclaimed (Ness 1967). The Federal Land Development Schemes (FELDA) resulted in the mass intra-rural migration in the 1960s and 1970s, and improvement of the standard of living of the landless people. However, with rapid urbanization, urban poverty and various social, economic, and environmental issues have gained increasing attention. Urban poverty, high cost of urban living, congestion, lack of inter-personal interaction, social tension, feeling of relative deprivation, change of lifestyle and aspirations, violence, and public safety are issues that need to be addressed urgently.

This paper examines the trends and patterns of urbanization in Malaysia since 1970 when pan-Malaysia population census data are available.[1] Given the importance of the ethnic factor in urbanization and socio-economic development, this chapter will shed some light on the ethnic trends and differentials in urbanization. This will be followed by a discussion on the implications of the urbanization process, with an examination of the socio-economic differences between the urban and rural areas. Salient findings from a 2001 survey on the squatter areas in five major cities in Peninsular Malaysia and a 1997 survey on the Consequences of Rural Depopulation will be presented. The paper concludes with a discussion of some of the problems and challenges of Malaysian urbanization.

Malaysia is one of the more urbanized countries among the developing countries. Between 1957 and 2000, its urbanization level has increased from about 27 per cent to 62 per cent. However, wide variations in the level of urbanization can still be observed across regions and ethnic groups.

URBAN GROWTH IN MALAYSIA

Definition of Urban Areas

Urban areas were defined as gazetted local authority areas with a specified population threshold. In both the 1970 and 1980 population and housing censuses, the criterion for a gazetted area to be classified as urban was that it should have a population of 10,000 persons or more.

To provide a more realistic level of urbanization in keeping with rapid socio-economic development, the definition of urban areas in the 1991 and 2000 population and housing censuses was extended to include areas having urban characteristics around the periphery of the boundaries of the gazetted towns (Department of Statistics 2001). In general, urban areas are defined as follows:

- Gazetted areas with their adjoining built-up areas which had a combined population of 10,000 or more at the time of the population census.
- Built-up areas were contiguous to a gazetted area and had at least 60 per cent of their population (aged 10 years and over) engaged in non-agricultural activities as well as having modern toilet facilities in their housing units.

In comparing the urbanization level before and after 1980, it has to be borne in mind that a large part of the change is due to the redefinition of urban areas. For instance, by adopting the urban definition of the 1980 population census to the data in the 1991 population census, the level of urbanization would have been just 36 per cent instead of 51 per cent as reported, since the new definition included the built-up areas.

Levels and Trends of Urbanization

The level of urbanization in Malaysia increased from 28.4 per cent in 1970 to 34.2 per cent in 1980, 50.7 per cent in 1991, and 61.8 per cent in 2000. During the three decades between 1970 and 2000, the number of urban dwellers increased more than four times from 2,962,795 persons to 13,725,605 persons (see Table 7.1). A sizeable proportion of this increase can be attributed to changes in definition and reclassification of rural areas as urban centers, as well as the agglomeration of surrounding areas.

While the rate of growth of the total population hovered around 2.3 per cent to 2.6 per cent during the last three decades, the urban population grew much more rapidly, at about 4.2 per cent per annum during the 1970s, and accelerated to 6.2 per cent per annum in the 1980s before slowing to 4.8 per cent per annum in the 1990s. In contrast, the rural population was growing slowly at 1.5 per cent per annum in the 1970s, remained almost stationary in the 1980s, and registered a decline of 0.24 per cent per annum in the 1990s.

TABLE 7.1 Population by urban rural location, level of urbanization and rate of population growth

Year	Population			%	Ave. Ann. % Growth		
	Total	Urban	Rural	Urban	Total	Urban	Rural
1970	10439430	2962795	7476635	28.4			
1980	13136109	4492408	8643701	34.2	2.30	4,16	1.45
1991	17563420	8898581	8664839	50.7	2,64	6.21	0.02
2000	22202614	13725609	8477005	61.8	2.60	4.82	-0.24

Regional/State Differentials in the Level of Urbanization

The level of urbanization varies widely across region and state, as shown in Table 7.2. In terms of region, Peninsular Malaysia is more urbanized than Sabah and Sarawak. The level of urbanization in Peninsular Malaysia has increased from 27 per cent in 1957 to 29 per cent in 1970, 37 per cent in 1980, 54 per cent in 1991, and 65 per cent in 2000. Sabah and Sarawak have also been urbanising rapidly, from around 16 per cent in 1970 to close to 50 per cent by 2000. Within Peninsular Malaysia, the level of urbanization ranges from less than 40 per cent in Kedah, Kelantan, and Perlis, to 80 per cent and 88 per cent in Pulau Pinang and Selangor, respectively. Kuala Lumpur has been classified as 100 per cent urbanized since 1957.

Up until 1970, Pulau Pinang was the only state with an urbanization level of about 50 per cent, except for Kuala Lumpur, which was 100 per cent urbanized. By 1980, however, Selangor had become the most urbanized state, with 60 per cent of its population living in urban areas. By 2000, the urbanization level was 60 per cent or higher in five states: Perak (60 per cent), Johor (64 per cent), Melaka (67 per cent), Pulau Pinang (80 per cent), and Selangor (88 per cent).

There are 83 districts in Peninsular Malaysia. In 2000, 1.3 million people were living in 19 districts which did not have any urban population. There were only about 400,000 urban inhabitants in the

TABLE 7.2 Population size and level of urbanization by state, 1957–2000

	Total Population					Percent living in urban areas				
	1957	1970	1980	1991	2000	1957	1970	1980	1991	2000
Johor	927000	1,277,180	1580423	2069740	2,565,701	21.8	26.3	35.2	47.8	63.9
Kedah	702000	954,947	1077815	1302241	1,572,107	13.3	12.7	14.4	32.5	38.7
Kelantan	506000	684,738	859270	1181315	1,289,199	9.8	15.1	28.0	33.5	33.5
Melaka	291000	404,125	446769	506321	602,867	24.0	25.1	23.4	38.7	67.3
N. Sembilan	275000	481,563	551442	692897	830,080	17.8	21.5	32.6	42.0	55.0
Pahang	313000	504,945	768801	1045003	1,231,176	22.2	19.0	26.1	30.4	42.1
Perak	1221000	1,569,139	1743655	1877471	2,030,382	25.0	27.5	32.2	53.6	59.5
Perlis	91000	121,062	144782	183824	198,335	–	–	8.9	26.6	33.8
P. Pinang	572000	776,124	900772	1064166	1,225,501	56.7	50.9	47.5	75.0	79.5
Selangor	1013000	776,124	1426250	2297159	3946527	43.0	45.0	60.0	75.2	88.3

TABLE 7.2 (cont'd)

Terengganu	278000	405369	525255	766244	879691	19.0	27.0	42.9	44.5	49.4
WPKL	–	648276	919610	1145342	1297526	100.	100.0	100.0	100.0	100.0
P. Malaysia	6179000	8819000	10944800	14185964	17670092	26.6	28.7	37.2	54.3	65.2
Sabah		636431	929299	1734685	2449389	–	16.5	20.6	33.2	48.3
Sarawak		976,269	1,235,553	1,642,771	2,012,616	–	15.4	17.6	37.5	47.9
WP Labuan		17173	26413	54241	70517	––	0	46.3	48.4	76.8
Malaysia		10439430	13136109	17563420	22202614	–	26.7	34.2	50.7	61.8

NOTE: States in italics are classified as less developed states, all others are classified as more developed states in the Eighth Malaysia Plan.

18 districts with an urbanization level of less than 30 per cent, one million in 15 districts with an urbanization level of between 30 and 50 per cent, and 1.5 million in 14 districts with an urbanization level of between 30 and 70 per cent. More than half of the total population of Peninsular Malaysia (8.6 million) were in the 17 districts with an urbanization level of 70 per cent or higher. Out of the 20 districts in Sabah, 11 did not have any urban population, and none had urbanization levels of 70 per cent or higher. Out of the 29 districts in Sarawak, 20 did not have any urban population, and four had an urbanization level of 70 per cent or higher (table not shown).

During the past three decades (1970–2000), the rate of growth of the urban population has been significantly higher than that of the general population, and this is true for all the states (Table 7.3). The rate of growth of the urban population for the country as a whole increased from 4.2 per cent in the 1970s to 6.2 per cent in the 1980s and then declined to 4.8 per cent in the 1990s. In comparison, the average annual rate of population growth was about 2.3 per cent in the 1970s and 2.6 per cent during the 1980–2000 period.

The urban population of Kelantan, the least urbanized state on the east coast of Peninsular Malaysia, registered the most rapid growth at 8.5 per cent per annum in the 1970s, slowed down to 4.5 per cent in the 1980s and grew at a mere 1 per cent between 1991 and 2000 (the same as in the rural areas). The rate of growth of the urban population in Terengganu, another east coast state, also registered a sharp decline from 7.2 per cent in the 1970s to 2.7 per cent in the 1990s, despite having oil fields. On the other hand, the urban population of Melaka, which remained practically stationary between 1970 and 1980, increased very rapidly at 5.7 per cent per annum in the 1980s and 8.1 per cent in the 1990s. Prior to 1980, there was no urban center in Perlis, the smallest state located on the north-western coast of Peninsular Malaysia. Consequent upon the reclassification of urban areas, the urban population of Perlis grew rapidly at 12.5 per cent in the 1980s, but this declined to 3.5 per cent in the following decade.

The numerical increase in the urban population has great relevance for development planning in terms of provision of employment opportunities, housing, transportation, and basic amenities such as water, electricity, education, health services, and environmental and sewerage management. Knowledge of urban population growth and distribution will also be needed for business planning.

TABLE 7.3 Average annual rate of growth of the total and urban population by state

	Average annual rate of population growth			Average annual rate of urban population growth		
	1970-80	1980-91	1991-2000	1970-80	1980-91	1991-2000
Johor	2.13	2.45	2.39	5.1	5.2	5.6
Kedah	1.21	1.72	2.09	2.6	9.1	4.0
Kelantan	2.27	2.89	0.97	8.5	4.5	1.0
Melaka	1.00	1.14	1.94	0.3	5.7	8.1
Negri Sembilan	1.35	2.08	2.01	5.5	4.4	5.0
Pahang	4.20	2.79	1.82	7.4	4.2	5.5
Perak	1.05	0.67	0.87	2.6	5.3	2.0
Perlis	1.79	2.17	0.84	–	12.1	3.5
Pulau Pinang	1.49	1.52	1.57	0.8	5.7	2.2
Selangor	6.08	4.33	6.01	6.4	11.5	7.8
Terengganu	2.59	3.43	1.53	7.2	3.8	2.7
F.T. KL	3.50	2.00	1.39	3.5	2.0	1.4
P. Malaysia	2.16	2.36	2.44	4.1	5.8	4.5
Sabah	3.79	5.67	3.83	5.4	10.4	8.0
Sarawak	2.36	2.59	2.26	3.9	9.3	5.0
F.T. Labuan	4.31	6.54	2.92	–	7.0	8.0
Malaysia	2.30	2.64	2.60	4.2	6.2	4.8

SOURCE: Reports from various population censuses.

During the three decades beginning in 1970, the total urban population increased from 2.9 million to 13.7 million, an increase of about 10.8 million (Table 7.4). The largest increase was in Selangor— from about a quarter million to 3.5 million. The urban population also increased dramatically in three other states—from 336,000, 100,000, and 151,000 to 1.6 million, 1.2 million, and 963 thousand, respectively, in Johor, Sabah, and Sarawak. It is worth noting that the urban population had also increased substantially even in the least urbanized states— about 330,000 in Kelantan and 488,000 in Kedah over the 30-year period.

The urban population for the whole country increased by about 1.5 million in the 1970s, but increased much more rapidly, by about 4.4 million, between 1980 and 1991, and 4.8 million between 1991 and 2000. The rapid increase in the urban population in Selangor, Sabah, Melaka, and Johor that began in the 1980s continued into the 1990s.

Components of Urban Population Growth

The three components of urban growth are natural increase, rural-urban migration, and reclassification of rural areas and agglomeration of built-up areas. The rate of growth of the urban population has been much higher than that of natural increase, and the rate of growth of the rural population. This implies that there was a substantial influx of migrants from the rural areas. The rapid rate of population growth in the urban areas also results from reclassification, changes in the administrative boundaries, and annexation of the suburbs into urban agglomerations.

The relative importance of each of these components of urban population growth should be taken into account in development planning. Rapid population growth in the urban areas arising from natural increase would require different policy responses compared to urban growth resulting from rural-urban migration.

A study by Fernandez et al. (1975) found that between 1957 and 1970, natural increase accounted for about 61 per cent of the urban population growth, with migration and reclassification each contributing about one-fifth. During the following decade, natural increase accounted for only about 40 per cent of urban population growth, while the other two components accounted for about 30 per cent each (Kok and Chan 1988). The relative importance of each of these components varied significantly across the states. During both periods, migration accounted for about 40 per cent of urban growth in Selangor (including the Federal

187

TABLE 7.4 Increase in urban population by state, 1970–2000

	1970 total	1970 urban	Increase in urban population			
	population	population	1970-80	1980-91	1991-2000	1970-2000
Johor	1,277,180	336,051	220,785	433,074	648,862	1,302,721
Kedah	954,947	120,337	35,166	267,747	185,446	488,359
Kelantan	684,738	103,250	137,778	154,457	36,376	328,611
Melaka	404,125	101,442	2,939	91,617	209,919	304,475
N.Sembilan	481,563	103,914	75,600	111,322	165,699	352,621
Pahang	504,945	95,880	104,983	116,324	200,989	422,296
Perak	1,569,139	432,294	129,908	444,611	201,135	775,654
Perlis	121,062	0	12,949	35,889	18,242	67,080
P.Pinang	776,124	395,615	32,190	370,471	176,503	579,164
Sabah	636,431	107,621	76,934	391,771	606,564	1,075,269
Sarawak	976,269	151,137	71,392	394,308	346,395	812,095
Selangor	982,090	257,540	229,693	1,239,327	1,757,205	3,226,225
Terengganu	405,368	109,438	115,743	115,471	93,618	324,832
Kuala Lumpur	648,276	648,276	271,334	225,732	152,184	649,250
Labuan	17,173	0	12,219	14,052	27891	54,162
Malaysia	10,439,430	2,962,796	1,529,612	4,406,173	4,827,028	10,762,813

Territory of Kuala Lumpur), the most dynamic growth center. Kedah, Melaka, and Pulau Pinang, on the other hand, lost urban population through migration during both periods.

A substantial proportion of urban population growth between 1980 and 1991 is due to the changes in the definition of urban as well as administrative boundaries, as alluded to above. Due to the unavailability of data, a decomposition of the components of urban growth between 1980 and 1991 will not be attempted here. However, it is possible to estimate the component of urban population growth between 1991 and 2000 based on published reports, as the two population censuses adopted the same definition of urban areas.

Table 7.5 shows that, for the country as a whole, natural increase is still the most important factor in urban population growth, accounting for 46 per cent between 1991 and 2000, while reclassification and migration accounted for 21 per cent and 33 per cent, respectively. Natural increase accounted for 25 per cent to 33 per cent of urban population growth in Melaka, Selangor, Sabah, and Labuan; about 40 to 50 per cent in Negri Sembilan, Johor, Pahang, and Sarawak, and more than 50 per cent in all the remaining states. The rate of population growth lagged behind the rate of natural increase in Kelantan and the Federal Territory of Kuala Lumpur.

No new urban centers emerged between 1991 and 2000 in four states/territories (Kedah, Kelantan, the Federal Territory of Kuala Lumpur, and Labuan). Reclassification of rural to urban localities accounted for about three-quarters of the increase in urban population in the two smaller states (Melaka and Perlis), and around one-third in Pahang, Terengganu, and Sabah. During this period, net migration accounted for about 71 per cent of the urban growth in the Federal Territory of Labuan, 49 per cent in Selangor, and between 30 to 45 per cent in Johor, Kedah, Negri Sembilan, Pahang, Sabah, and Sarawak. The urban population in six of the states/territories (Kelantan, the Federal Territory of Kuala Lumpur, Terengganu, Perlis, Perak, and Melaka) had a net loss through out-migration (see Table 7.5).

The rapid urban population growth in Selangor, the most dynamic commercial and industrial center, was largely due to the inflow of migrants. On the other hand, the growth of the urban population in Melaka was due mainly to the reclassification of rural urban areas.

Comparing the rate of population growth and the crude rate of natural increase, it can be seen that there were substantial out-flows of rural population to urban areas, although part of the differentials in the two rates may be attributed to reclassification. It is worth noting that

TABLE 7.5 Rate of population growth and crude rate of natural increase of urban and rural population, and component of urban population growth by state, Malaysia, 1991-2000

State/territory	Urban population							Rural population	
	Rate of growth	% of population increase due to			% contribution to rate of growth			Rate of growth	Natural increase
		Natural increase	Reclassi-fication	Migration	Natural increase	Reclassi-fication	Migration		
Johor	5.6	2.5	0.9	2.2	44.6	16.1	39.3	-1.7	1.9
Kedah	4.02.7	0	1.3	67.5	0	32.5	1.0	1.9	
Kelantan	1.0	2.7	0	-1.7	270.0	0	-170.0	1.0	2.8
Melaka	8.1	2.1	6.3	-0.3	25.9	77.8	3.7	-5.1	2.0
N.Sembilan	5.0	1.9	1.2	1.9	38.0	24.0	38.0	-0.8	1.9
Pahang	5.5	2.3	1.6	1.6	41.8	29.1	29.1	-0.23	2.1
Perak	2.0	1.8	0.3	-0.1	90.0	15	-5.0	-0.63	1.7
Perlis	3.5	2.4	2.6	-1.5	68.6	74.3	-42.9	-0.31	1.7
P. Pinang	2.2	1.5	0.4	0.3	68.2	18.2	13.6	-0.65	2.0
Selangor	7.8	2.6	1.4	3.8	33.3	19.7	48.7	-2.3	2.3
Terengganu	2.7	2.4	1.0	-0.7	88.9	37.0	-25.9	0.5	2.6
Kuala Lumpur	1.4	2.0	0	-0.6	142.9	0	-42.9	0	–
P. Malaysia	**4.5**	**2.2**	**0.9**	**1.4**	**48.9**	**20.0**	**31.1**	**-0.5**	**2.1**
Sabah	8.0	2.3*	2.8	2.9	28.8	35.0	36.3	1.0	n.a.
Sarawak	5.0	2.2*	0.6	2.1	44.0	12.0	40.0	0.3	n.a.
FT Labuan	8.0	2.3	0	5.7	28.8	0	71.3	-6.0	n.a.
Malaysia	**4.8**	**2.2**	**1.0**	**1.6**	**45.8**	**20.8**	**33.3**	**-0.2**	**n.a.**

NOTE: The crude rate of natural increase was obtained by taking the average figure for the period 1991 and 1998 for which data are available. The estimated rate of growth due to reclassification is computed as follows: ln[(urban population in 1991+ population of new urban centres in 2000)/ urban population in 1991/9. The residual is taken as the estimated rate of urban growth due to migration.

nine states/territories had registered a reduction in rural population in the 1990s.

Between 1991 and 2000, the population living in central areas of towns increased from about 6.6 million to about 8.1 million, but those living in built-up areas increased much more rapidly from 2.3 to 5.6 million (Table 7.6). Consequently, the proportion of urban population living in built-up areas increased from 25.7 per cent to 40.8 per cent. In 2000, at least half of the urban population in the following states were in built-up areas: 51.5 per cent in Johor (up from 28.5 per cent in 1991), 74 per cent in Melaka (up from 47.4 per cent in 1991), 80 per cent in Perlis (up from 70.8 per cent in 1970), 62.6 per cent in Pulau Pinang (up from 46.2 per cent in 1991), 50 per cent in Selangor (up from 33 per cent in 1991), and 85 per cent in the Federal Territory of Labuan.

Trends and Patterns of Migration

Migration has a varied impact on the populations of the receiving and sending areas. In Malaysia, migration is seen as a means of social restructuring to urbanise the Bumiputera (including the Malays and other indigenous population), and to bring about more balanced participation among the different ethnic groups in the various economic sectors. As migration data from the 2000 population census have not been released, the following discussion will be based on the 1991 population and housing census and the migration surveys.

In the 1970s, the pattern of internal migration was bi-polar. Selangor attracted a large number of migrants to the commercial/industrial centers; Pahang drew migrants to the Federal Land Development Schemes (FELDA). In the 1990s, about 2 per cent of the total population of Malaysia were international migrants, 7 per cent were inter-state migrants, and 5 per cent were inter-district intra-state migrants. Inter-state migration during the 1986–91 period was dominated by the state of Selangor, with a net gain of 155.3 thousand persons, followed by Johor, a distant second, with a gain of 19.3 thousand persons. The states that registered the largest net loss were Perak (70.2 thousand), the Federal Territory of Kuala Lumpur (41.86 thousand, mainly to neighboring Selangor), Kelantan (28.7 thousand) and Melaka (13.9 thousand). In terms of percent of state population, the Federal Territories of Labuan and Kuala Lumpur had the highest in-migration

TABLE 7.6 Urban population in central areas and built-up areas by state, 1991 and 2000

	1991				2000		
	Total	Central areas	Built-up areas		Total	Central areas	Built-up areas	
			Number	%			Number	%
Johor	989910	708044	281866	28.5	1638772	794404	844368	51.5
Kedah	422150	317667	104483	24.8	608696	357090	251606	41.3
Kelantan	395485	351137	44348	11.2	431861	374649	57212	13.2
Melaka	195998	103166	92832	47.4	405917	105347	300570	74.0
N.Sembilan	290836	240377	50459	17.3	456535	301835	154700	33.9
Pahang	317187	288589	28598	9.0	518176	380255	137921	26.6
Perak	1006813	747336	259477	25.8	1207948	790409	417539	34.6
Perlis	48838	14247	34591	70.8	67080	13413	53667	80.0
P.Pinang	798276	429755	368521	46.2	974776	364196	610580	62.6
Sabah	576326	393162	183164	31.8	1182890	653137	529753	44.8
Sarawak	616837	407352	209485	34.0	963232	615313	347919	36.1
Selangor	1726530	1158394	568136	32.9	3473154	1744395	1728759	49.8
Terengganu	340652	290465	50187	14.7	434270	328171	106099	24.4
FT Kuala Lumpur	1145342	1145342	0	0.0	1297526	1297526	0	0.0
FT Labuan	26271	26271	0	0.0	54162	8197	45965	84.9
	8897451	6621304	2276147	25.6	13714995	8128337	5586658	40.7

rates of 19.1 per cent and 13.2 per cent, respectively, but the latter also had the highest out-migration rate of 16.9 per cent, resulting in a net loss of 3.7 per cent. Most inter-state migrants were from neighboring states. For instance, more than one-third of the migrants to Selangor were from the Federal Territory of Kuala Lumpur, and another 17 per cent from Perak (Table 7.7).

Studies by Kok and Chan (1988) and the Department of Statistics (1996) show that rural-urban migration accounted for about 30 per cent of the urban population growth in the 1970s and 1980s, and this is also true in the 1990s, as shown in Table 7.5, above. These studies show that Malaysia has not been experiencing the emergence of one all-dominant mega city, as in other Southeast Asian countries.

TABLE 7.7 Net migrants by state of destination and selected period of migration, Malaysia, 1975–1993

State of destination	Census data		Survey data	
	1975-80	**1986–1991**	**1991–92**	**1992–93**
Johor	−7.4	19.3	12.6	22.5
Kedah	−41.0	−5.3	9.4	5.7
Kelantan	−19.2	−28.7	−4.7	2.8
Melaka	−19.4	−13.9	8.3	6.3
N.Sembilan	−12.8	−2.3	2.5	−2.4
Pahang	3.6	−10.0	−13.9	−7.2
Perak	−71.1	−70.2	3.0	−11.2
Perlis	−0.3	2.5	−2.1	3.5
Pulau Pinang	0.5	1.8	2.1	5.4
Sabah	2.0	−1.1	−5.7	−5.5
Sarawak	−1.4	−3.5	−0.4	1.9
Selangor	91.6	155.3	18.2	13.3
Terengganu	−0.1	−5.5	0.3	−12.6
FT Kuala Lumpur	44.2	−41.6	−28.8	−23.3
FT Labuan	–	3.3	−1.0	1.0

SOURCE: Department of Statistics, Internal Migration in Malaysia. Population Census Monograph Series, No. 2, August, 1996.

Table 7.8 shows that urban-ward migration during the 1986–91 period was more prevalent among inter-state migrants (55 per cent urban-urban and 16.1 per cent rural-urban) as compared to inter-district migrants (24.1 per cent urban-urban and 23 per cent rural-urban). Of the urban-ward migrants, 71 per cent of the inter-state migrants and 64 per cent of intra-state migrants headed for metropolitan cities (with 75,000 persons and above).

The 2001 migration survey shows that urban-ward migration has become even more dominant in inter-state migration, accounting for 77.6 per cent of the migrants (65.7 per cent urban-urban and 11.9 per

TABLE 7.8   Percentage distribution of inter-state and inter-district intra-state migration by migration direction and population size classes of urban areas, Malaysia, 1986–1991

Migration direction/ size class of	Size class of urban destination				Rural	Total
	75,000 and above	25,000–74999	10000–24999	Urban		
Inter-state migration						
Urban	39.3	11.0	4.7	55.0	18.5	73.5
75000 and above	27.7	8.3	3.2	39.2	12.2	51.4
25,000-74,999	5.8	1.4	0.7	8.0	3.0	10.9
10,000-24,999	5.7	1.4	0.8	7.8	3.3	11.2
Rural	10.8	3.5	1.8	16.1	10.4	26.5
Total	50.1	14.5	6.5	71.1	28.9	100.0
Inter-district intra-state migration						
Inter-state migration						
Urban	15.4	5.4	3.3	24.1	21.2	45.3
75000 and above	7.9	3.7	1.9	13.6	13.6	27.2
25,000-74,999	3.8	1.0	0.5	3.3	3.3	8.6
10,000-24,999	3.7	0.8	0.8	4.3	4.3	9.6
Rural	16.5	3.4	3.1	31.7	31.7	54.7
Total	31.9	8.8	6.4	52.9	529	100.0

SOURCE: Department of Statistics, 1996.

cent rural-urban). Rural-rural and urban-rural migration each accounted for 4 per cent and 18.5 per cent, respectively. As many as 85 per cent of the urban migrants in Selangor had come from other urban centers, and this is true for both inter-state and intra-state migration streams.

Migration in Malaysia is generally dominated by males, particularly those heading for rural areas. With rapid industrialization, however, the sex ratio in urban-ward migration is declining, as more women are taking up jobs in the factories. Between 1986 and 1991, female migrants from the rural areas within the same state outnumbered the males, as indicated by a sex ratio of 95 (Department of Statistics 1996).

Migration in Malaysia tends to be selective of the young adults between the ages of 15 and 34 years, especially those in the 20–24 age group. The 1991 population census shows that nearly 60 per cent and 54 per cent of inter-state and intra-state migrants were aged between 15 and 34 years, as compared to 32 per cent for the non-migrant population.

Responding to the government's policy to urbanize the Bumiputera, Malays had the highest inter-state migration rate of 8.9 per cent as compared to 7.2 per cent among the Indians and 4.9 per cent among the Chinese. The other Bumiputera had the highest inter-district migration rate (9.8 per cent), followed by the "Others" (5.9 per cent), the Malays (5.5 per cent), the Indians (4.1 per cent), and the Chinese (3.1 per cent).

A higher proportion of the migrants had secondary or tertiary education as compared to the non-migrants. Among inter-state and intra-state migrants, about 11.8 per cent and 6 per cent had tertiary education, as compared to 4.2 per cent of the non-migrants. The inter-state migration among those with tertiary education was 22.7 per cent between 1986 and 1991, as compared to 9.2 per cent among those with secondary education, 4.2 per cent among those with primary education, and 3.2 per cent among those with no schooling.

Between 1986 and 1991, the male labor force participation rate among inter-state migrants of 80.3 per cent was slightly lower than that of non-migrants (83.7 per cent) and inter-district migrants (85.4 per cent). However, among the females, the labor force participation rate among inter-state migrants (45 per cent) was slightly higher than the non-migrants (41.3 per cent) and inter-district migrants (41.7 per cent). The male labor force participation rate for migrants was generally lower than that of the non-migrants at all ages. Female migrants aged 15–19 years had a higher labor force participation rate than non-migrants, but the reverse is generally true for all other ages. Census data also show that

195

migrants were also more concentrated in service and production-related work. Of those who were employed, about 40 per cent and 21 per cent of the migrants were in production-related work and services, respectively, as compared to 34 per cent and 10.1 per cent of the non-migrants.

The migration and employment survey conducted in 1986 shows that about half of the migrants to the urban centers of the Klang Valley (Kuala Lumpur and the urban parts of Selangor), Johor Bahru, and Melaka had come from rural areas. The sex ratio of the migrants was about 91, indicating that relatively more females than males had migrated to these three urban centers. The migrants are more likely to be aged 24 to 39 as compared to the non-migrants. The survey found that the propensity to migrate was very much higher among those with upper secondary or tertiary education as compared to those with lower education. In this survey, overall, about 52 per cent of the moves to the Klang Valley were job related, 3 per cent followed family, and about 11 per cent to pursue education. The survey shows that 74 per cent of the males were responsible for their own decision to migrate to the Klang Valley, 17 per cent were on job transfer, and 9 per cent followed families. Of the females, 43 per cent had made their own decision to move, 54 per cent followed spouses, 7 per cent followed parents, and 3 per cent were on job transfer. Younger women were twice as likely as older women to make their own decision to migrate. Migration has beneficial effects on the individuals. It has allowed the better educated migrants to take up more lucrative jobs in the modern sector which are concentrated in the large urban centers (Tey 1988 and 1994).

A 1997 survey on out-migration from four rural districts in Peninsular Malaysia, that registered negative population growth, shows that about half of the household heads had stayed in their present place since birth, and only 10 per cent had migrated from other states. The survey data show that 72 per cent of the households in these four districts had at least one adult child who had migrated, and 61 per cent had at least two children who had migrated, with a mean of about 2.8 (Tey et al. 2000).

The 1997 survey shows that most of the migrant children from the four rural districts had moved to the urban areas in other states, especially to Kuala Lumpur and Selangor. Reasons for migration differed markedly between male and female migrants. Among male migrants, employment was by far the most important reason, with education and marriage as distant second and third reasons. As for female migrants, more than half had cited marriage as the main reason for moving, and about 30 per cent had migrated to take up jobs. Males were the main decision-makers in the migration process. However, such scenario may be changing with the increased propensity of younger females to migrate.

The sex ratio of children who stayed back was about 103, while that of migrant children was about 100. This indicates that rural out-migration is only slightly selective of the males. A majority of the co-resident children were below 20 years of age. In contrast, more than 90 per cent of the migrant children were aged 20 years and older. The survey data also show that almost 15 per cent of the adult children (aged 18 and above) who stayed behind had no schooling, in sharp contrast to only 1.1 per cent among those who had migrated. On the other hand, while more than 10 per cent of the adult migrant children had tertiary education, merely 1.1 per cent of those who stayed behind had achieved this level. The activity status of migrant children differed markedly from those who stayed behind. Few migrant children were currently engaged in the agricultural sector (6.3 per cent), as compared to about one-quarter of the non-migrant children. Migrant children were relatively more likely than non-migrant children to work as employees, while the reverse is true with respect to self-employment. Among daughters, the non-migrants were more likely than migrants to be housewives.

Urban Population Distribution

Consequent upon the different rates of urban population growth across the states/territories, there has been a substantial shift in the distribution of the urban population, as shown in Table 7.9. In 1970, about 93 per cent of the urban population were in Peninsular Malaysia and 7 per cent were in Sabah and Sarawak. However, with a more rapid increase in the urban population in Sabah and Sarawak, the corresponding figures have changed substantially to 84 per cent and 16 per cent in 2000. Within Peninsular Malaysia, the distribution of the urban population has also changed significantly between 1970 and 2000, with sharp declines in Kuala Lumpur (from 21.9 per cent to 9.5 per cent), Perak (from 14.6 per cent to 8.8 per cent), and Pulau Pinang (from 13.4 per cent to 7.1 per cent), while Selangor registered the sharpest increase from 8.7 per cent to 25.4 per cent. Since the 1980s, a large number of residents from Kuala Lumpur

TABLE 7.9 Percentage distribution of urban population in Malaysia

	1970	1980	1991	2000
Johor	11.3	12.4	11.1	11.9
Kedah	4.1	3.5	4.8	4.4
Kelantan	3.5	5.4	4.4	3.1
Melaka	3.4	2.3	2.2	3.0
N. Sembilan	3.5	4.0	3.3	3.3
Pahang	3.2	4.5	3.6	3.8
Perak	14.6	12.5	11.3	8.8
Perlis	0	0.3	0.5	0.5
Pulau Pinang	13.4	9.5	9.0	7.1
Selangor	8.7	10.8	19.4	25.4
Terengganu	3.7	5.0	3.8	3.2
FT Kuala Lumpur	21.9	20.5	12.9	9.5
Peninsular Malaysia	91.3	90.6	86.3	84.0
Sabah	3.6	4.1	6.5	8.6
Sarawak	5.1	5.0	6.9	7.0
FT Labuan	0	0.3	0.3	0.4
Malaysia	100.0	100.0	100.0	100.0

TABLE 7.10   Population of Federal Territory of Kuala Lumpur and surrounding areas*, 1970–2000

	1970	1980	1991	2000
Central Kuala Lumpur	451,810	961,019	1,145,342	1,297,526
Surrounding areas	253,998	477,195	1,567,810	2,945,225
Total for Klang Valley	705,808	1,438,214	2,713,152	4,242,751

*Surrounding areas include Petaling Jaya, Subang Jaya, Ampang Jaya, Shah Alam, Kajang, Selayang Baru, Ceras, Semenyih and Gombak Setia.

central city have migrated to the suburbs, as reflected in the rapid increase in the population of the surrounding areas (Table 7.10). Between 1970 and 2000, the total population of the Klang Valley, comprising Kuala Lumpur and the urban centers of the four surrounding districts, increased rapidly from a little more than 700,000 in 1970 to 4.24 million in 2000. During this period, the population of Kuala Lumpur central city increased from about 450,000 to 1.3 million, but that of the surrounding areas increased much more rapidly from about a quarter million to close to three million. Rapid population growth in the suburbs began in the 1970s, accelerated in the 1980s, and continued into the 1990s.

The capitals are the main urban centers in all the states, and a large proportion of the population reside in the national and state capitals. Table 7.11 shows that for the country as a whole, 23.7 per cent of the total population and 38.4 per cent of the urban population live in the capital towns. More than half of the urban population of Kelantan, Negri Sembilan, Pahang, Perlis, and Terengganu live in the capital towns. In Negri Sembilan, up to 35 per cent of the state population live in Seremban, the capital town. About 23 per cent to 28 per cent of the state population live in the capitals of the states of Johore (Johor Bahru), Melaka (Melaka town), Pahang (Kuantan), Perak (Ipoh), and Perlis (Kangar).

The Local Authority Areas (LAAs) are usually consolidations of towns and other gazetted areas. They are administered by a City Hall, City Councils, Municipal Councils or District Councils. In total, there are 148 local authority areas, of which three are City Halls, three City Councils, 25 Municipal Councils, 112 District Councils, two Town

199

TABLE 7.11   Total population, urban population, and the number and proportion of population living in in national and state capitals according to state, 2000

State	Total population	Urban population	Population in state/ national capitals	% of total population in state capital	% of urban population in state capital
Johor	2,565,701	1,638,772	630,603	24.58	38.48
Kedah	1,572,107	608,696	186,524	11.86	30.64
Kelantan	1,289,199	431,861	252,714	19.60	58.52
Melaka	602,867	405,917	149,518	24.80	36.83
Negri Sembilan	830,080	456,535	290,999	35.06	63.74
Pahang	1,231,176	518,176	289,395	23.51	55.85
Perak	2,030,382	1,207,948	574,041	28.27	47.52
Perlis	198,335	67,080	54,390	27.42	81.08
Pulau Pinang	1,225,501	974,779	180,573	14.73	18.52
Selangor	3,947,527	3,483,765	319,612	8.10	9.17
Terengganu	879,691	434,270	255,109	29.00	58.74
Kuala Lumpur	1,297,526	1,297526	1,297,526	100.0	100.0
Sabah	2,449,389	1,182,890	305,382	12.47	25.82
Sarawak	2,012,616	963,232	423,873	21.06	44.01
Labuan	70517	54162	54162	76.8	100.0
	22,202,614	13,725,609	5,264,421	23.7	38.4

Boards, one Rural District Council, one Development Board, and one Local Authority. Municipal Council areas are usually comprised of state capitals or other large towns.. There are 25 Municipal Councils for the whole of Malaysia.

The number of urban centers with populations of at least 10,000 increased from 49 in 1970 to 58 in 1980, 123 in 1991, and 170 in 2000 (Table 7.12). Over the 30-year period, the number of mega cities with populations of 150,000 and above increased from three to 26, and the population living in cities of this size class increased from about 970,000 (or 38 per cent of the urban population) to 8.8 million (or 64 per cent of the urban population). The number of metropolitan areas with populations of 75,000 to 149,999 also increased rapidly from five in 1970 to 14 in 1991 and 2000, and these accounted for about 11 per cent of the

TABLE 7.12 Number of urban centers and population by size class, Malaysia, 1970, 1980, 1991 and 2000

Size of towns	Number of urban centers				Population			
	1970	1980	1991	2000	1970	1980	1991	2000
10,000-24999	26	33	64	82	371679 (14.7)	513629 (12.6)	1027757 (1.6)	1346341 (9.8)
25000-49999	8	8	20	35	273309 (10.8)	287765 (7.0)	734827 (8.3)	1287030 (9.4)
50000-74999	7	4	9	13	405045 (16.0)	249628 (6.1)	473376 (5.3)	773134 (5.6)
75000-149999	5	5	14	14	511425 (20.2)	575,936 (14.1)	1,479,104 (16.7)	1,525,178 (11.1)
150,000+	3	8	17	26	969026 (38.3)	2,456,148 (60.2)	5,166,376 (58.2)	8,783,315 (64.0)
Total	49	58	124	170	2,530,484 (100.0)	4,083,106 (100.0)	8,881,440 (100.0)	13714998 (100.0)

NOTE: Figures in parentheses refer to percentages of population living in towns of various size class.

urban population in 2000, down from 20 per cent in 1970. The number of smaller and medium-sized urban centers increased less rapidly. Not surprisngly, the proportion of the population living in these centers declined from about 41 per cent in 1970 to about 25 per cent in 2000.

As with the urban population, the number of urban centers is not evenly distributed across the states. In 1991, out of the 17 mega cities (with at least 150,000 persons), four were in Selangor. The rest were mainly state capitals. By the year 2000, eight out of 26 mega cities of this size class were in Selangor, and all these were in the surrounding areas of Kuala Lumpur. It is interesting to note that the number of mega cities in East Malaysia (Sabah and Sarawak) doubled from three to six between 1991 and 2000 (Table 7.13).

The number of metropolitan towns with populations of between 75,000–149,999 persons remained at 14 between 1991 and 2000. The number of urban centers of this size class increased from two to five in Johor, and from three to four in Pulau Pinang. However, the number of these metropolitan centers decreased from four to two during the same period, as two of these, along with two smaller urban centers in the state, were upgraded to the class size of 150,000 and above. In Kelantan, eight out of 10 urban centers were of the smallest size class (10,000–24,999 persons) in 2000, the same as in 1991.

Table 7.14 shows the 30 largest urban centers in Malaysia as of 2000. The Federal Territory of Kuala Lumpur, the nation's capital, remains the largest urban center, with a population of about 1.3 million. Between 1991 and 2000, the population of Kuala Lumpur increased by only 152,000, and it is only twice as large as neigboring Klang, the second largest center, whose population size more than doubled during the same period. Johor Bahru, on the southern tip of Peninsular Malaysia, has become the third largest urban center. Its population size increased from about 385,000 in 1991 to 630,000 in 2000, about the same size as Klang. Ipoh, the second largest urban center in 1991, was ranked fourth in 2000. Four of the urban centers surrounding Kuala Lumpur registered very rapid increases in population—Petaling Jaya is ranked fifth, Subang Jaya seventh, Ampang Jaya eighth and Shah Alam ninth largest urban centers in the country. Kuching in Sarawak and Kota Kinabalu in Sabah are ranked sixth and tenth respectively. It is interesting to note that, with the exception of Kuala Lumpur, the population living in built-up areas constitutes a sizable proportion of the urban population of most of the major towns in Malaysia—up to 85 per cent and 61 per cent of the

202

TABLE 7.13 Number of urban centers in all the states in Malaysia by size class, 1991 and 2000

State	1991					2000				
City Size (000)	10–25	25–50	50–75	75–150	150+	10–25	25–50	50–75	75–150	150+
Johor	10	4	1	2	1	10	6	1	5	1
Kedah	4	1	1	1	1	3	2	0	1	2
Kelantan	8	1	0	0	1	8	1	0	0	1
Melaka	2	1	0	1	0	8	4	0	1	0
N.Sembilan	3	1	0	0	1	3	1	1	0	1
Pahang	5	1	0	0	1	4	5	0	0	1
Perak	11	3	1	0	2	9	6	1	0	2
Perlis	0	1	0	0	0	1	0	1	0	0
P. Pinang	4	1	3	3	1	5	2	1	4	2
Sabah	4	1	1	1	2	6	3	3	0	3
Sarawak	3	0	1	2	1	5	1	0	1	3
Selangor	8	2	1	4	4	16	4	2	2	8
Terengganu	2	2	0	0	1	4	0	2	0	1
FT Kuala Lumpur	0	0	0	0	1	0	0	0	0	1
FT Labuan	0	1	0	0	0	0	0	1	0	0
Total	64	20	9	14	17	82	35	13	14	26

TABLE 7.14   Thirty largest urban centers in 2000 (and the population size in 1991) according to population size in the central areas and built-up areas, Malaysia

Urban centers	State	1991 urban population			2000 urban population		
		Central areas	Built-up areas	Total	Central areas	Built-up areas	Total
Kuala Lumpur	FT Kuala Lumpur	1145342	0	1145342	1297526	0	1297526
Klang	Selangor	243355	125024	368379	317538	314138	631676
Johor Bahru	Johor	328436	113267	411703	384613	245990	630603
Ipoh	Perak	382853	85988	468841	451558	122483	574041
Petaling Jaya	Selangor	254350	96645	350995	220676	217408	438084
Kuching	Sarawak	148059	129846	277905	163846	260027	423873
Subang Jaya	Selangor	53800	25202	79002	255523	167815	423338
Ampang Jaya (1)	Selangor	41935	153225	195160	51608	297186	348794
Shah Alam	Selangor	119564	38875	158439	166623	152989	319612
Kota Kinabalu	Sabah	76120	84064	160184	230761	74621	305382
Seremban	N.Sembilan	182869	10368	193237	246441	44558	290999
Kuantan	Pahang	199484	2961	202445	276339	13056	289395
Sandakan	Sabah	125841	30834	156675	162489	112886	275375
K. Terengganu	Terengganu	228119	0	228119	250528	4581	255109
Kota Bharu	Kelantan	219582	14999	234581	233673	19041	252714
Tawau	Sabah	86289	38654	124943	102226	111677	213903
Kajang	Selangor	46269	54228	100497	86072	121250	207322
Taiping	Perak	183261	17063	200324	183495	15835	199330

TABLE 7.14 (cont'd)

Selayang Baru	Selangor	124228	9969	134197	164812	22921	187733
Alor Setar	Kedah	124412	40032	164444	114949	71575	186524
Georgetown	P.Pinang	219603	0	219603	180573	0	180573
Cheras	Selangor	21278	29674	50952	32664	144857	177521
Sungai Petani	Kedah	114763	2214	116977	156575	18034	174609
Miri	Sarawak	87167	15711	102878	138119	29416	167535
Sibu	Sarawak	126381	7098	133479	151582	14740	166322
Bukit Mertajam	P.Pinang	25798	96194	121992	18164	147258	165422
Melaka	Melaka	75909	37843	113752	64626	84892	149518
Kluang	Johor	49005	49664	98669	48848	86032	134880
Ampang Jaya (2)	Selangor	90488	4804	95292	108195	18264	126459
Batu Pahat	Johor	70749	13351	84100	75723	47514	123237

population of Ampang Jaya and Kuching live in built-up areas, and close to half of the population of Klang, Petaling Jaya, Shah Alam, and Tawau also live in the built-up areas.

Projection of Urban Population

Population projections at the national level have been made by the United Nations and other researchers. Leete (1996) projected the total population to reach 21.9 million by 2001, 26.8 million by 2011, and 31.6 million by 2021. Compared to figures from the 2000 population ccensus, his projected population appears to be slightly under-estimated. An earlier projection of the urban population by the United Nations (2001) placed the urbanization level of Malaysia at about 57.4 per cent in 2000. This has proven to be slightly under-estimated as compared to the findings from the population census. According to the UN projection, the urbanization level of Malaysia is projected at 63.8 per cent in 2010 (or 16.5 million), 68.6 per cent (or 20.1 million) in 2020, and 72.7 per cent in 2030 (or 23.7 million).

On the basis of projections for the total population, the urban and rural populations are projected using the exponential rate of growth. Some rough estimates of the future urban and rural populations were obtained by making several assumptions (Table 7.15). Rural population is assumed to decrease at a rate of about 1 per cent per year for the period 2001–20, as more rural areas will be reclassified as urban centers, and rural-urban migration is also expected to continue as more job opportunities are available in the large urban centers. The rate of growth of the urban population is assumed to decline to 3.8 per cent for the 2001–10 period and further to 2.3 per cent for the 2011–20 period, such that the overall rate of growth would be close to that assumed for the national population projection. The urban population is projected to increase to 20 million by 2010 and 25 million by 2020. The urbanization level is projected to increase to 72 per cent and 78 per cent during the same period.

The Federal Territory of Kuala Lumpur has been classified as fully urbanized since the 1970 population census. In 2000, more than three-quarters of the population in Selangor, Pulau Pinang, and the Federal

TABLE 7.15 Actual and projected urban and rural population and level of urbanization, Malaysia, 2000–2020

	Population (million)			Percentage urban
	Urban	Rural	Total	
2000	13.7	8.5	22.2	62
2005	16.5	8.1	24.6	67
2010	20.0	7.6	27.6	72
2015	22.3	7.3	29.6	75
2020	25.0	7.0	32.0	78

Territory of Labuan were living in urban areas. On the basis of the current level of urbanization and rate of growth, Johor and Melaka are expected to have an urbanization level of at least 75 per cent. By 2020, all states/territories, except Kedah, Kelantan, Terengganu, Perlis, and Pahang, are expected to be at least 75 per cent urbanized.

RURAL-URBAN DIFFERENCES

Differentials in the Rates of Growth of Urban and Rural Populations

Between 1970 and 2000, the urban population increased by about 10.72 million or 4.6 times, while the rural population increased by just one million or 1.13 times. The average annual rate of growth of the urban population ranges from 4.2 per cent per annum in the 1970s to 6.2 per cent in the 1980s. Data show that 82 per cent of the increase in the urban population during the 1970–2000 period was in Peninsular Malaysia, increasing by 8.9 million or about 4.3 times (Table 7.16).

The average annual rate of growth of the urban population in Peninsular Malaysia ranges from 3.6 per cent between 1957 and 1970 to 5.8 per cent in the 1980s. In contrast, the rate of growth of the rural population in Peninsular Malaysia has been declining steadily from 2.3 per cent per annum between 1957 and 1970 to a negative 0.6 per cent in the 1990s. Consequently, the rural population in Peninsular Malaysia remained practically unchanged during the 1970–2000 period.

In the 1980s, the rate of growth of the urban population averaged 10.4 per cent and 9.3 per cent in Sabah and Sarawak, respectively, the highest rate ever recorded in any region. However, while the high rate of growth of the urban population in Sabah continued into the 1990s (at 8 per cent per annum), that of Sarawak decelerated somewhat to 5 per cent per annum. Reflecting the higher tempo of urbanization, Sabah's urban population increased from about 108,000 in 1970 to 1.18 million by 2000, an increase of 11 times, as compared to a 2.4 fold increase in the rural population. The urban population of Sarawak increased by about 812,000 during the 30 years between 1970 and 2000, or 6.4 times, as compared to a much smaller increase of less than a quarter million in the rural population, or 1.3 times.

TABLE 7.16   Population growth in urban and rural areas by stratum and region, Malaysia 1957, 1970, 1980, 1991 and 2000

Malaysia

Year	Population			%	Ave. Ann. % Growth		
	Total	Urban	Rural	Urban	Total	Urban	Rural
1957*	6,268,000	1,667,000	4,601,000	26.6	2.50	5.80	1.50
1970	10,439,430	2,962,795	7,476,635	28.4	2.3%	4.2%	1.5%
1980	13,136,109	4,492,408	8,643,701	34.2	2.6%	6.2%	0.0%
1991	17,563,420	8,898,581	8,664,839	50.7	2.6%	4.8%	–0.2%
2000	22,202,614	13,725,609	8,477,005	61.8			

* Peninsular Malaysia only

Peninsular Malaysia

Year	Population			%	Ave. Ann. % Growth		
	Total	Urban	Rural	Urban	Total	Urban	Rural
1957	6,268,000	1,667,000	4,601,000	26.6	2.6%	3.6%	2.3%
1970	8,819,000	2,650,400	6,168,600	30.1	2.2%	4.3%	1.1%
1980	10,944,800	4,073,100	6,871,700	37.2	2.4%	5.8%	–0.5%
1991	14,185,964	7,705,418	6,480,546	54.3	2.4%	4.5%	–0.6%
2000	17,670,092	11,525,325	6,144,767	65.2			

TABLE 7.16 (cont'd)

Sabah

Year	Population			%	Ave. Ann. % Growth		
	Total	Urban	Rural	Urban	Total	Urban	Rural
1970	636,431	107,621	528,810	16.9	3.8%	5.4%	3.4%
1980	929,299	184,555	744,744	19.9	5.7%	10.4%	4.0%
1991	1,734,685	576,326	1,158,359	33.2	3.8%	8.0%	1.0%
2000	2,449,389	1,182,890	1,266,499	48.3			

Sarawak

Year	Population			%	Ave. Ann. % Growth		
	Total	Urban	Rural	Urban	Total	Urban	Rural
1970	976,269	151,137	825,132	15.5	2.4%	3.9%	2.1%
1980	1,235,553	222,529	1,013,024	18.0	2.6%	9.3%	0.1%
1991	1,642,771	616,837	1,025,934	37.5	2.3%	5.0%	0.3%
2000	2,012,616	963,232	1,049,384	47.9			

Differences in the Socio-economic Conditions Between Urban and Rural Areas

Migration tends to draw the working-age population from the rural areas to the urban areas. Consequently, the age structure differs markedly between urban and rural areas. The 2000 population census shows that 63 per cent of the urban population were in the "working-age group" of 15—59 years, as compared to 44.8 per cent in the rural areas. Owing to the differences in the age structure, the dependency ratios and ageing index are significantly higher in the rural areas as compared to the urban areas (Table 7.17).

The sex ratio in the urban areas (103) is slightly lower than that of the rural areas (105). Among those aged 15—59 years, the sex ratio is 102.6 in the urban areas and 106.5 in the rural areas. This indicates that females in the working-age group are slightly more likely than the males to have migrated from rural to urban areas. Many younger women are now working in factories in the urban areas.

In 1970, the average household size in the urban areas (6.1) was higher than that of rural hosuseholds (5.3), but there was no difference in the household size between urban and rural areas in 1980 and 1991 (about five each). However, by 2000, the urban household size was slightly smaller than that of the rural areas (4.4 and 4.7 respectively).

The ethnic distribution differs markedly between urban and rural areas. In 2000, the Malays made up 43.9 per cent of the urban population and 64.6 per cent of the rural population. Relative to the total population, the Malays are still under-represented in the urban areas. The Chinese and Indians made up 33.9 per cent and 9.3 per cent of the urban population but only 9.7 per cent and 4.1 per cent of the rural population. The other Bumiputera are still predominantly rural; they made up only 6.1 per cent of the urban population but 20.5 per cent of the rural population. Non-Malaysians made up 5.7 and 6.9 per cent of the urban and rural populations, respectively.

The crude birth rate in the urban areas is slightly higher than that of the rural areas. Part of this diffferential may be attributed to the younger age structure of the urbanites. The crude death rate has declined to a relatively low level in both urban and rural areas (5.0 and 4.5 per thousand population respectively).

In terms of family formation variables, data from the 1994 Malaysian population and family survey show that urban women marry later and have fewer children as compared to rural women. Urban women are also more likely than rural women to use contraceptive methods (Table 7.17).

The educational level is higher among the urban than the rural population, as reflected by the higher literacy rate (94.3 per cent as compared to 85.4 per cent). Data also show that about one in four workers in Kuala Lumpur and Selangor had tertiary education, as compared to about 10–15 per cent among workers in other states. However, it must

TABLE 7.17   Demographic and socio-economic indicators for urban and rural areas, Malaysia, (circa 2000)

Indicators	Urban areas	Rural areas
Age distribution (%)		
Less than 15	31.1	47.7
15–59	63.4	44.8
60+	5.4	7.5
Sex ratio		
All ages	103	105
<Less than 15	106.2	105.7
15–59	102.6	106.5
60+	89.8	93.2
Dependency ratio		
Youths	47.5	63.1
Old	5.1	8.2
Ageing index	10.7	12.9
Average household size		
1970	6.1	5.3
1980	5.2	5.2
1991	4.9	5.0
2000	4.4	4.7
Ethnic distribution		
Malays	43.9	64.6
Other Bumiputera	6.1	20.5
Chinese	33.9	9.7
Indians	9.3	4.1
Others	1.2	1.2
Non-Malaysians	5.7	6.9
Crude birth rate	25.9	23.1
Crude death rate	5.0	4.5
Mean age at marriage among women aged 30 and over (1994)	21.6	19.8

TABLE 7.17 (cont'd)

Mean number of children ever born (1994)	3.0	3.9
Contraceptive prevalence rate		
All methods	55	48
Modern methods	30	27
Literacy rate	94.3	85.4
% with tertiary education among working population	25	
Most urbanized region (Kuala Lumpur and Selangor)		10 to 15
All other states		
% with tertiary education among working population	25	
Most urbanized region (Kuala Lumpur and Selangor)		10 to 15
All other states		
Occupation		
Legislators, senior officials and managers	8.7	3.3
Professionals	7.3	2.6
Technicians and associate professionals	13.9	8.3
Clerical workers	12.3	4.5
Service workers and shop and market sales	15.4	8.4
workers Skilled agriculture and fishery workers	2.5	37.8
Craft and related trade workers	10.0	7.6
Plant and machine-operators and assemblers	16.2	15.8
Elementary occupations	13.7	11.7
Mean monthly gross household income (1990)	1,374	951
Mean monthly gross household income (1999)	3,103	1,718
Mean monthly gross household income (2002)	3,652	1,729
Incidence of poverty (2002)		
Number of poor households (2002)	2.0	11.4
Incidence of hardcore poor households (2002)	69,600	198,300
Number of hardcore poor households (2002)	12,600	40,300

SOURCES: 2000 Population and Housing Census; 1994 Malaysian Population and Family Survey; Malaysia Plans.

be mentioned that some of those higher-educated workers in Kuala Lumpur and Selangor have moved from the rural areas, upon completing their studies.

Urban workers are more likely than their rural counterparts to work in the formal sector. A much higher proportion of urban workers (78.1 per cent) are working as employees as compared to rural workers (59.3 per cent). On the other hand, rural workers are much more likely than their urban counterparts to work as "own account" workers (35.6 per cent and 17.0 per cent, respectively). Relatively few are employers or unpaid family workers. Nevertheless, as expected, urbanites are relatively more likely than their rural counterparts to be the employers, and the reverse is true for unpaid family workers.

The occupational structure differs markedly between urban and rural workers. As expected, the most striking difference between urban and rural occupational structures is the proportion working in agriculture: 2.5 per cent among the urban workers and 37.8 per cent among the rural workers. Urban workers are more likely than rural workers to be engaged in all other occupations, particularly as officials and managers, professionals, technicians, clerks, and services and sales workers.

The income level in the urban areas has always been higher than that of the rural areas, and there has been a tendency for the disparity to widen in recent years. Between 1990 and 2002, the mean monthly household income always tripled in the urban areas (from RM1,374 to RM3,652) but it barely doubled in the rural areas, from RM951 to RM1,729. During the three years between 1999 and 2002, when the economy staged a recovery from the Asian financial crisis that hit the region in 1997, urban household income increased by more than RM500 a month, as compared to an increase of RM11 among rural households. In 1997, the number of poor households was 55,400 in the urban areas and 239,000 in the rural areas, and these represented about 2.1 per cent and 10.9 per cent of the total households in the urban and rural areas, respectively. The incidence of hardcore poor of 0.4 per cent in the urban areas was much lower than that of the rural areas (2.5 per cent).

IMPLICATIONS OF RAPID URBANIZATION AND STATE INTERVENTION

Implications on Restructuring of Society—Changing the Ethnic Composition of the Urban Population

As stated earlier, one of the main objectives of Malaysian development policies has been to eliminate the identification of race with vocation as well as location. Hence, urbanization by ethnic group assumes great importance in Malaysia.

The wide ethnic differences in urbanization has been changing dramatically. In 1970, 14.9 per cent of the Malays were living in urban areas, as compared to 47 per cent of the Chinese and 35 per cent of the Indians. With rapid industrialization and socio-economic development, the urbanization level of all ethnic groups has been increasing rapidly. However, the tempo of Malay urbanization has been significantly higher than that of the other ethnic groups, increasing from 2.2 per cent in 1957 to about 5 per cent in the 1970s and 1980s, before decelerating to 2.5 per cent in the 1990s. In contrast, the tempo of urbanization among the non-Malays, especially the Chinese, has been much more gradual (Table 7.18). Consequently, ethnic differences in the level of

TABLE 7.18 Percentage of urban to total population and tempo of urbanization by ethnic group

Census Year	Percent Urban to Total Population			Tempo of Urbanization (in the decade ending)		
	Malays	Chinese	Indians	Malays	Chinese	Indians
1970	14.93	47.38	34.68	2.20	0.40	0.90
1980	25.20	56.12	41.02	5.20	1.70	1.70
1991	43.29	75.78	63.78	4.91	2.73	4.01
2000	54.2	85.9	79.7	2.50	1.37	2.48

NOTE: Tempo of urbanization is calculated as: [ln (percent urban in later period divided by percentent urban in earlier period)/number of years between the two period*100)].

214

urbanization has been reduced substantially. The more rapid pace of urbanization among the Malays can be partly attributed to the various programs of the government to facilitate rural-urban migration, such as provision of scholarships and loans for starting businesses. Responding to the various incentives provided by the government, the tempo of urbanization of the Malays reached a peak in the 1970s. Be that as it may, the level of urbanization is still much higher among the Chinese (86 per cent) and the Indians (80 per cent) as compared to the Malays (54 per cent) as of 2000.

Consequent upon the differential rate of urbanization, the ethnic distribution of the urban population has changed siginficantly. While the Malays (and a small number of other Bumiputera) made up only 28 per cent of the urban population in 1970, their proportionate share of the urban population has increased to about 50 per cent (43.9 per cent Malays and 6.1 per cent other Bumiputera) in 2000. On the other hand, the Chinese proportion of the urban population has been declining rather sharply from about 59 per cent to 34 per cent between 1970 and 2000. The Indian proportion of the urban population has also been decreasing, although at a slower rate as compared to that of the Chinese, from 12.8 per cent to 9.3 per cent during the same period (Table 7.19). The decline

TABLE 7.19   Ethnic composition of urban population, Malaysia, 1970, 1980, 1991 and 2000

Census Year		Proportion of Urban Population (%)			
	Urban Population	Malays	Chinese	Indian	Others
1970	2,962,795	27.6	58.5	12.8	1.1
1980	4,492,408	37.9	50.3	11.0	0.7
1991	8,898,581	41.5	39.4	9.4	9.7*
2000	13,725,609	43.9	33.9	9.3	12.9**

* Include other Bumiputera, other ethnic groups and non-Malaysians.
**Include 6.1 per cent Other Bumiputera, 1.2 per cent others and 5.7 per cent non-Malaysians)

215

TABLE 7.20   Employment by sector for total population and Bumiputera, 1980 and 2000

	1980		2000	
	Total population	Bumiputera	Total population	Bumiputera
Agriculture, forestry, livestock and fishing	35.7	51.3	15.2	18.2
Mining and quarrying	1.1	1.0	0.4	0.5
Manufacturing	15.1	11.3	27.6	26.3
Construction	6.9	3.9	8.1	6.0
Electricity, gas and water	0.7	0.8	0.8	1.1
Transport, storage and communication	4.8	4.0	5.0	5.4
Wholesale and retail trade, hotels and restaurants	15.5	9.2	17.1	12.7
Finance, insurance, real estate and business services	1.9	1.1	5.5	4.8
Other services (including government services)	18.2	17.5	20.3	25.0
Total	100.0	100.0	100	100

in the Chinese and Indian proportions of the urban population results from lower rates of natural increase and rural-urban migration as compared to the Malays. At the national level, the proportionate share of the Chinese population to the total population has decreased from about 36 per cent in 1970 to 25 per cent in 2000; while that of the Indians has decreased from 11 per cent to 7 per cent during the same period. Furthermore, the Chinese and Indian migrants are more likely to move from one urban center to another urban center, while the Malays have been relatively more likely to move from rural areas to the urban centers.

With the rapid urbanization of the Malays, most major towns now have a rather balanced ethnic composition, with the exception of Kota Bharu (in Kelantan) and Kuching Utara (in Sarawak) where the population are predominantly Bumiputera/Malays. In Georgetown, Subang Jaya, Kucing Selatan, and Ipoh, the Chinese population is significantly more than the Bumiputera. Compared to the national figure, the Indians tend to be over-represented in some major cities in Peninsular Malaysia, such as Klang, Seremban, Petaling Jaya, Selayang, Shah Alam, Ipoh, and Sungei Petani. This partly reflects their occupational structure as many Indians work as professionals.

Implications on Restructuring of Society—Changing the Employment Stucture by Ethnic Group

In 1970, about two-thirds of the Malay workers were engaged in the agricultural sector. However, with industrialization and rapid urbanization, the employment structure of Malaysians has been changing from the primary sector to the secondary and tertiary sectors, such that the agricultural sector accounted for only a little more than one-third of employment in 1980 and 15.2 per cent in 2000. The Malays and other Bumiputera have also moved out from their traditional sector. In 1980, a little more than half of the Bumiputera were still engaged in agriculutral activities, but this decreased sharply to only 18.2 per cent in 2000.

The manufacturing sector, which accounted for only 9.4 per cent of employment in 1970, increased its share to 15.1 per cent in 1980 and 26.3 per cent in 2000. The proportion of Bumiputera engaged in the manufacturing sector also increased rapidly from 5.3 per cent in 1970 to 11.3 per cent in 1980 and 26.3 per cent in 2000. Along with other Malaysians, relatively more Bumiputera are now engaged in the business and services sectors. However, the Bumiputera are still under-represented in businesses and over-represented in the services sector.

Effects of Urbanization on the Socio-economic Conditions of Urban and Rural Areas

Malaysia has achieved remarkable economic growth since Independence. The transformation from a rural agrarian economy to an urban-based economy has lifted the income level and standard of living of both urban and rural populations, largely by transferring excess labor from the lower to the higher productivity sectors. In 1960, rubber constituted 55 per cent of the country's export earning, but this had declined to a mere 2.2 per cent by 1997, while the contribution from manufactured goods jumped from 16 per cent to 80 per cent during the same period. The

TABLE 7.21 Household income and incidence of poverty in the urban and rural areas, Malaysia, various years

	Urban areas	Rural areas
Mean monthly gross household income		
1970	428	200
1979	975	550
1984	1,541	824
1990	1,374	951
1995	2,589	1,326
1999	3,103	1,718
2002	3,652	1,729
Incidence of poverty		
1970*	21.3	58.7
1980*	15.8	43.1
1985	8.2	24.7
1990	7.3	19.3
1997		2.1
10.9		
1999	3.4	12.1
2002	2.0	11.4
Number of poor households		
1985	81,300	402,000
1990	77,500	371,400
1997	55,400	239,000
1999	86,800	264,300
2002	68,600	198,300

strong economic foundation enabled the country to stage a strong recovery from the 1997 Asian financial crisis.

The income level rose substantially in both urban and rural areas. Between 1970 and 2002, the mean monthly household income (at current prices) increased from RM428 to RM3,652 in the urban areas and from RM200 to RM1,729 in the rural areas (Table 7.22).

The government is determined to eradicate poverty, and the various poverty eradication programs have succeeded in reducing the incidence of poverty in both urban and rural areas. Under the Eighth Malaysia Plan (2001–5), households with monthly income of RM1,200 and below are targetted for assistance. Between 1970 and 2002, the incidence of poverty declined from 21.3 per cent to 2.0 per cent in the urban areas, and from 58.7 per cent to 11.4 per cent in the rural areas. The number of poor households is estimated at about 267,000 (about 69,000 in urban areas and 198,000 in rural areas) in 2002. Given the sharp differences in the incidence of poverty between urban and rural areas, urbanization has contributed significantly to the overall decline in the number of poor households. Assuming that the urbanization level remained at about 30 per cent, the number of poor households would be around 420,000 in 2002 rather than 267,000, *ceteris paribus*.

The standard of living among urbanites is further enhanced with the provision of basic amenities and services by the government. Along with urbanization, there has been significant improvement in the provision of basic amenities. Almost all houses have access to electricity, piped water, and toilet facilities. This is a marked improvement from 1970 when less than half of the total population and about a quarter of the rural population had access to piped water and electricity.

On the other hand, rapid urbanization has also brought about some untoward consequences. Existing infrastructures may be inadequate to cope with the influx of migrants and rapid population growth in the large urban centers. For instance, many urban schools are over-crowded, while there are only a few students in some of the rural schools. Traffic is also a major problem. The Eighth Malaysia Plan (2001–5) recognizes that traffic congestion has reached a critical level in Kuala Lumpur and the Klang Valley (urban Selangor). Quoting a 1997 survey, the Plan stated that travel speed on most of the major radial roads in Kuala Lumpur had been reduced to 10 kilometers per hour or less during the morning peak hours due to the high traffic volume.

The Squatter Population of Major Urban Centers

The squatter population was estimated at about 582,000 in 1999, and was concentrated in a few states: Selangor (171,000), Sabah (148,000), and the Federal Territory of Kuala Lumpur (134,000). The average household size of about five in the squatter areas of Selangor and Kuala Lumpur is slightly higher than that of the non-squatter population of the respective state/territory.

There has been a significant shift in the ethnic composition of the squatter population. For instance, in 1980, the Chinese made up about half while the Malays made up a little more than a third of Kuala Lumpur's squatter population (Kok and Chan 1988). A 2002 survey in Kuala Lumpur, Petaling Jaya, Johor Bahru, Ipoh, and Sungei Petani (NPFDB 2004) found that the Malays made up about 58 per cent while the Chinese just about one-quarter of the squatter population in Kuala Lumpur. The changes in the ethnic composition can be explained by the fact that many of the Malays are new migrants to the cities, while some Chinese squatters have moved out to the housing estates, low-cost apartments or condominiums. The 2002 survey showed that the Malays, Chinese, and Indians made up 54 per cent, 16 per cent, and 27 per cent of the squatter population in these five towns. Clearly, the Indians, many may have migrated from the estates, are over-represented in the squatter settlements.

The squatter settlements in urban Malaysia are much more favorable than those in some neighboring countries. Close to 90 per cent of the squatters are provided with piped water and electricity. Nearly half of the squatter families in the five urban centers own motor cars and 70 per cent own motorcycles. Modern objects and amenities such as television, washing machines, refrigerators, telephones, and handphones are rather common among the squatter population.

Effects of Urbanization on Social Structures

Concomitant with urbanization and socio-economic development, there have been increasing opportunities for higher education and job opportunities in the urban labor markets for both males and females. The female labor force participation rate has been increasing steadily from 31 per cent in 1970 to about 50 per cent in the mid-1990s. As alluded to above, there has been a shift from the traditonal to the modern sector. The proportion of women who worked as unpaid family workers has been falling, from about 40 per cent in 1970 to about 10 per cent in 2000. More than three-quarters of the women workers are now working as employees. Increased female labor force participation has impacted their roles within the family. Traditionally, the women were the main care providers for ageing parents, but this source of family support is fast eroding. While the young migrate from the rural areas, most older people prefer to stay back in the countryside. Consequently, the extended families are giving way to nuclear families. Working women now lack the traditional support for child care.

Urbanization has also impacted on family formation. With higher education, women are marrying ever later and some have opted to remain single. The traditional norm for large families has also given way to small families, and this will have a significant impact on future population growth and population ageing.

Role of the Government in Urban Planning and Management

The government has always played a very important role in shaping urban development in Malaysia. With increasing urbanization, the government has recognized the need to ensure that urban centers have the necessary social facilities, such as adequate housing, and educational and recreational facilities, in order to improve the quality of life. More efforts will be undertaken to ensure that new urban centers are properly planned to provide for these facilities to ensure a more comfortable, friendly, and healthy environment. Various strategies were implemented in all major urban areas to alleviate local traffic congestion. Kuala Lumpur and the Klang Valley continued to be given priority in efforts to ensure an efficient and effective road network and public transportation service.

The Eighth Malaysia Plan also took cognizance of the fact that migration from the rural sector to areas within, and the outskirts of, urban centers has created pockets of urban poverty, and the government has instituted measures to alleviate the situation. Under the urban policy that is being formulated, the urban areas will be evaluated in terms of size, roles, functions, population targets, as well as human settlement planning and development. Efforts will be carried out to encourage greater community participation, in line with the Habitat Agenda and Local Agenda 21.

ENDNOTES

1   Malaysia was formed in September 1963 when Sabah, Sarawak, and Singapore joined the Federation. Singapore left Malaysia and became an independent country in 1965.

CHAPTER 8

Urbanization in
the Philippines

NIMFA B. OGENA
EDITED BY GAYL D. NESS[1]

The Philippines is among the world's fastest urbanizing countries, with heavily over-crowded cities. With some 59 per cent of the population living in urban areas compared to the 37.5 per cent average in the Southeast Asian Region in 2000, only two of 11 countries in the region, Singapore and Brunei Darrusalam, exhibited a higher level of urbanization (UN 2001).

URBAN GROWTH

Urbanization in the Philippines has been rapid and this process is expected to continue in the future. The number of people living in urban areas increased from a fourth in 1950 to 59 per cent 50 years later. About 36.8 million of the 76.5 million population counted during the recent 2000 census were living in urban barangays, which comprise less than a fourth of the 9,998 barangays in the country. (See Table 1 for a note on discrepancies.) Eleven of its 16 highly urbanized barangays are entirely urban and 11 of its 79 provinces have 50 per cent urban population (NSO 2003).

Definition of "urban" areas

The 1939, 1948, 1956, and 1963 urban definitions used varying levels of the following criteria: population density rule, minimum population size, and administrative center. The 1970 definition, which was used until the 2000 census, utilized the density rule with a combination of urban characteristics like street pattern and presence of establishments and facilities for basic services, among others.

"Urban" areas in this definition include those with the following characteristics (NSO 2003):

(1) In their entirety, all cities and municipalities which have a population density of at least 1,000 persons per square kilometer.

(2) *Poblaciones* or central districts of municipalities and cities which have a population density of at least 500 persons.

(3) *Poblaciones* or central districts, not included in (1) and (2) above, regardless of population size which have the following characteristics:

    (a) street pattern, that is, network of streets in either parallel or right angle orientation;

    (b) at least six establishments, either commercial, manufacturing, recreational and/or personal services; and

    (c) at least three of the following:

        (i) a town hall, church or chapel with religious service at least once a month;

        (ii) a public place, park, or cemetery;

        (iii) a market place or building where trading activities are carried on at least once a week;

        (iv) a public building like a school, hospital, child or health center or library.

(4) Barangays [barrios], having at least 1,000 inhabitants which meet the conditions set forth in (3) above and in which the occupation of the inhabitants is predominantly non-farming/fishing.

All areas not falling under any of the above classifications are considered rural.

Studies that reviewed these criteria indicated that some were no longer applicable, hence the need to formulate a more up-to-date, practical, and realistic definition of urban areas in the Philippines. In

October 2003, the National Statistical Coordination Board (NSCB) approved a new definition of urban areas, which will be adopted starting with the 2005 census of population:

(1) if a barangay has a population size of 5,000 or more, then a barangay is considered urban; or

(2) if a barangay has at least one establishment with a minimum of 100 employees, a barangay is considered urban; or

(3) if a barangay has five or more establishments with a minimum of 10 employees, and five or more facilities within the two-kilometer radius from the barangay hall, then a barangay is considered urban

All barangays in the National Capital Region are automatically classified as urban, and all highly urbanized cities would be subjected to the urban-rural criteria in order to determine its urban-rural classification. All other barangays that do not satisfy the three criteria above are classified as rural. The change in definition is intended to improve the statistical measurement of urban areas but will not change the general concept of an urban area.

The new definition was subjected to an open and rigorous process of evaluation and revalidation through a series of inter-agency discussions and consultations with experts, stakeholders and other concerned agencies, including the Technical Committee on Population and Housing Statistics (TCPHS) of the NSCB.

The Urban Population of the Philippines

In the span of half a century, the Philippines was transformed from a predominantly rural to a predominantly urban society. From five million in 1950, the urban population increased more than seven or eight fold (37 or 44 million), while the total population grew by less than four fold, from 20 to 77 million. The proportion urban increased from just over one-quarter to substantially over 50 per cent, as Table 8.1 shows.

Rapid mortality declines following the end of the war in 1945 pushed the Philippines' total population annual growth rate to over 3 per cent. This represents the familiar beginning of the demographic transition. Then fertility began to decline slowly, bringing a secular decline in the total growth rate to its current level below 2 per cent per year. During this period, urbanization moved very rapidly. Urban growth rates were

TABLE 8.1 Population growth and urbanization

Year	Population (in million)			Percentage	Annual Growth Rates		
	Total	Urban	Rural	Urban	Total	Urban	Rural
1950	20	5	15	27	2.99	4.11	2.56
1960	27	8	19	30	3.09	3.39	2.71
1970	37	12	25	31	2.79	4.30	2.00
1980	48	18	30	37	2.43	5.20	0.56
1990	61	29	32	47	2.26	4.30	1.49
2000	77	37	40	48	2.30	2.70	2.56
2000 UN	76	44	31	59	1.86	3.19	−0.19

NOTE: Growth rates are for Y to Y+5. The Philippines NSO and UN figures agree until 2000, when the NSO estimate shows a dramatic slowing of urban growth and 7 million fewer urbanites than estimated by the UN. Some redefinition of urban areas is largely responsible for this, but it does not seem plausible that any real decline in urbanization actually took place. Thus we tend believe that the UN estimates more accurately reflect the real situation. GDN

steadily higher than rural growth rates, usually by 1 to 2 percentage points. The rural growth rate has declined steadily and has now become negative. This is a not unfamiliar pattern for societies undergoing rapid change in the past half-century.

The urban population of the Philippines continues to be concentrated in the National Capital Region (NCR) or Metro Manila (MM) and its surrounding regions of Central Luzon (Region III) and Southern Luzon (Region IV). Nearly 60 per cent of the country's urban population resides in these areas. Metro Manila, the only region in the country that is 100 per cent urban, is the financial, educational, commercial, and political hub of the country.

Since 1990, more than half of the population in Regions III and IV lived in urban areas. These two regions consistently exhibited high urban growth rates between 1970 and 2000. The urban growth rate of the majority of the regions in the country slackened after reaching a peak during the period 1970–80. Metro Manila still retains the highest proportionate share of the urban population. One of every three urban dwellers in 2000 was residing in the metropolitan area. Almost two out of every three lived in regions abutting on Metro Manila.

Between 1970 and 2000, Southern and Central Luzon exhibited the highest urban growth rates. These two regions also registered the highest number of urban barangays together with Metro Manila, resulting partly from the establishment of the CALABARZON economic zone during the past decade. In 2002, Region IV was divided into two: CALABARZON (Region IV-A) and MIMAROPA (Region IV-B). This can be seen in Table 8.2.

Many regions in the country reveal large increments and decrements in the number of urban barangays after 1990 (see Table 8.3). Southern and Central Luzon regions gained many urban barangays during this decade as many rural barangays were reclassified as urban, partly as a spillover effect of industrial developments in Metro Manila and CALABARZON. Mindanao exhibited large reductions in the number of urban barangays in 2000 after the creation of the CAGARA and ARMM regions. Urban to rural transitions, resulting from the economic slump during the decade, were also noted in some barangays in the Visayas. Hence, the Visayas and Mindanao regions experienced the largest change in proportion urban.

Sources of Growth: Natural Increase, Migration, Changes in Administrative Boundaries

Only one definition of "urban" areas was used during the 1970–2000 period. Hence, urban growth and trends can be analyzed as the data are comparable. Urban growth may be accounted for by three possible sources: natural increase or the difference between births and deaths, rural-urban migration, and change in administrative boundaries.

The 1997 study conducted by Cabegin and Arguillas documented the importance of the reclassification process in explaining urban growth in all regions, regardless of their speed or urbanization. Even out-migration regions registered positive urban growth as a result of the reclassification. Ilocos, Cagayan Valley, Western Mindanao, and ARMM posted about three-fourths of their urban growth due to reclassification

TABLE 8.2   Percent urban and annual growth rate of the urban population by region, 1970–2000

Region and Province	Percentage Urban Population				Urban Population Growth Rate			
	1970	1980	1990	2000	1970–1980	1980–1990	1990–2000	2970–2000
National Capital Region (Metro Manila)	100.0	100.0	100.0	100.0	0.20	0.20	0.20	0.20
Cordillera Administrative Region (CAR)	17.9	20.1	30.1	36.3	0.01	0.02	0.02	0.01
Region I - Ilocos Region	18.7	23.6	32.3	38.2	0.02	0.05	0.05	0.04
Region II - Cagayan Valley	15.2	17.7	21.5	22.2	0.01	0.02	0.01	0.01
Region III - Central Luzon	30.2	41.8	54.3	60.5	0.09	0.14	0.15	0.13
Region IV - Southern Tagalog	30.6	37.1	52.9	58.4	0.09	0.21	0.25	0.18
Region V - Bicol Region	19.2	21.9	26.8	27.7	0.02	0.03	0.02	0.02
Region VI - Western Visayas	26.7	28.4	37.1	30.3	0.03	0.07	-0.01	0.03
Region VII - Central Visayas	27.9	32.1	42.5	46.4	0.04	0.07	0.07	0.06
Region VIII - Eastern Visayas	19.4	21.8	28.1	19.4	0.01	0.02	-0.02	0.01
Region IX - Western Mindanao	15.7	17.4	30.2	25.0	0.01	0.05	-0.02	0.02
Region X - Northern Mindanao	20.9	27.1	39.4	40.5	0.03	0.06	-0.03	0.02
Region XI - Southern Mindanao	26.6	33.9	39.7	38.3	0.05	0.06	0.02	0.05
Region XII - Central Mindanao	15.6	18.9	28.1	32.7	0.01	0.05	0.00	0.02
Region XIII - Caraga				27.2				
Autonomous Region in Muslim Mindanao (ARMM)				21.2				

SOURCE: National Statistics Office, Manila, Philippines.

TABLE 8.3 Distribution of urban barangays by region, 1990 and 2000

Region	Urban Barangays			Percent Urban Barangays		
	1990	2000	Change	1990	2000	Change
Philippines	10030	10,031	1	26.22	23.93	–2.28
NCR	1670	1694	24	100.00	100.00	0.00
CAR	211	222	11	19.43	18.94	–0.49
Region I	815	809	–6	26.34	24.81	–1.53
Region II	281	285	4	13.23	12.35	–0.88
Region III	1218	1286	68	43.36	43.65	0.29
Region IV	1560	1937	377	31.36	34.52	3.15
Region V	679	579	–100	20.99	16.69	–4.30
Region VI	784	671	–113	21.57	16.58	–4.99
Region VII	561	649	88	19.48	21.68	2.20
Region VIII	828	522	–306	22.54	11.90	–10.64
Region IX	278	210	–68	11.18	9.94	–1.23
Region X	542	292	–250	23.70	19.29	–4.41
Region XI	327	205	–122	18.75	13.48	–5.27
Region XII	276	258	–18	10.79	18.04	7.26
Caraga		156	156		11.94	11.94
ARMM		256	256		11.97	11.97

FIGURE 8.1 Contribution of reclassified areas to urban growth (%),
1980–1990

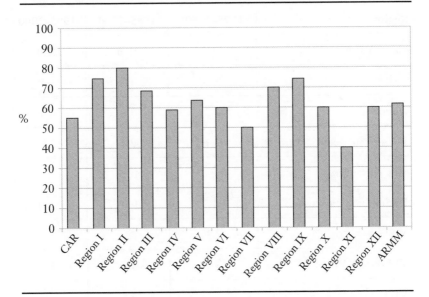

of rural areas to urban, while most regions indicated percentages greater
than 50 per cent (see Figure 8.1).

For areas that did not need rural-urban reclassification, the main
engine of urban growth was natural increase, which accounted for nearly
47.2 per cent of the urban growth, on average. Net migration did not
account for urban decentralization as was initially expected.

Characteristics of Incoming and Outgoing Populations

The proportionate share of inter-regional migrants in Metro Manila has
been declining (see Table 8.4), which somehow corroborates earlier
findings on metropolitan deconcentration and migration being relegated
in recent years as a marginal ground for urban growth. The increasing
share of inter-regional migrants in Southern and Central Luzon, Central
Visayas, as well as Western, Southern, and Northern Mindanao likewise
documents the emergence of new agglomeration areas challenging the
traditional dominance of Metro Manila.

TABLE 8.4 Percentage distribution of inter-regional migrants, 1970–1975, 1985–1995 and 1995–2000

Region	1975–1980*	1985–1990	1995–2000
Metro Manila	51.2	30.6	22.0
CAR		1.7	1.1
I Ilocos	2.2	3.3	4.0
II Cagayan Valley	1.1	2.1	1.5
III Central Luzon	7	10.5	9.5
IV Southern Tagalog	11.7	19.9	20.0
V Bicol	2.3	2.9	4.0
VI Western Visayas	3.9	3.4	4.3
VII Central Visayas	5.1	4.8	5.9
VIII Eastern Visayas	1.6	2.7	2.9
IX Western Mindanao	1.5	2.1	4.8
X Northern Mindanao	4.6	6.6	4.5
XI Southern Mindanao	6	6.0	4.8
XII Central Mindanao	1.8	3.4	2.5
ARMM			6.1
CARAGA			2.2
*REGION IV/NCR (Disputed)			0.1

* Inter-regional migrants to urban Areas 15 years old and over.

Migrants were relatively younger than non-migrants in urban areas, and female migrants were also relatively younger than their male counterparts in 1980 (see Table 8.5). A higher proportion of single females than males have chosen to reside in urban areas, and more so in Metro

TABLE 8.5 Percentage distribution of population 15 years old and over, by migration status, sex, and selected characteristics in Metro Manila and Other urban areas in the Philippines, 1980

Characteristics	METRO MANILA				OTHER URBAN			
	MALE		FEMALE		MALE		FEMALE	
	Migrant	Non-Migrant	Migrant	Non-Migrant	Migrant	Non-Migrant	Migrant	Non-Migrant
N	294,388	1,480,476	387,208	1,664,584	297,180	3,116,888	353,528	3,379,140
Age group								
15–19	15.5	17.4	24.3	19.3	14.8	20.7	23.2	20.6
20–29	43.5	35.6	45.5	36.4	39.1	30.5	42.5	31
30–39	23.8	22.6	16.4	21.1	23.6	21.1	18.6	20.2
40–54	13.8	18.7	10.3	17.4	16.1	20.1	12	20
53–64	3.4	5.7	3.5	5.8	4.4	7.6	3.7	8.2
Total	100	100	100	100	100	100	100	100
Marital Status								
Single	46.4	55.1	54.3	53.6	47	57.3	49.3	53.8
Married	50.4	43.5	41.2	41	51.4	40.8	46	40
Widowed	1.2	1.4	4.5	5.4	1.6	1.9	4.7	6.2
Total	100	100	100	100	100	100	100	100

TABLE 8.5 (cont'd)

Education								
Elementary	27.6	33.2	37.5	38.5	41.9	48.8	45.7	51.2
High School	35.5	36.1	32.9	32.5	30.8	29.4	30.1	26.1
College	36.5	30.7	29.6	29.1	27.3	21.8	24.2	22.7
Total	100	100	100	100	100	100	100	100
With Gainful Occupation								
Yes	74.2	68.1	45.5	35	79	70.2	35.9	28.3
No	25.8	31.8	54.5	65	21	29.8	64.1	71.7
Students	14.6	18.4	11.8	16.3	11.6	18.3	11.8	16.6
Housekeepers (own home)	0.5	0.5	38.6	43.8	0.5	0.7	49.3	50.7
All others	10.7	13	4.1	4.9	8.9	10.8	3	4.4
Total	100	100	100	100	100	100	100	100

SOURCE: NSO unpublished special tabulations.

Manila than in other urban areas of the country. The majority of migrants, on average, have attained at least high school education compared to non-migrants. This pattern is more pronounced among male migrants than female migrants.

The majority of males in urban areas in 1980 found gainful occupation compared to less than half of their female counterparts. Males were more likely to be in production process and crafts or in professional, technical, and administrative occupations, while females were likely to be in service and clerical/sales occupations. Migrant females are more likely to get a job in Metro Manila than in other urban areas, while migrant males have better chance of getting a job in other urban areas than in

Metro Manila. Among those who were not gainfully employed in 1980, non-migrants were more likely to be studying in school than migrants. Housekeeping was more prevalent among non-migrant than migrant females.

The Urban Structure

The scale of urbanization may be further understood by examining the urban structure in terms of type of urban area and city-size categories. Urban areas in the Philippines consist of cities and towns. Cities may be further categorized into *large* cities, which include cities with an urban population of at least 500,000; *intermediate* cities, which include cities with an urban population of between 100,000 and 499,999; and *small* cities, which include those having an urban population of less than 100,000. Towns are urban areas with populations greater than 1,000 and having certain urban characteristics. Table 8.6 shows the urban population by size group of city, the proportion of the urban population in each size category, and the annual growth rate of each size category for the years 1970–2000.

First, we note that the cities and towns each had about 50 per cent of the total urban population in 1970. In the next three decades, the cities slowly lost their share, accounting for only 45 per cent of the urban population in 2000. The smaller towns steadily gained those 5 percentage points. With the different city-size categories, there has been considerable fluctuation. The large cities first increased their share of the urban population by 5 percentage points, then steadily lost nearly twice that much. The intermediate cities mirrored that pattern. They first lost 4 percentage points then gained 10 points by 2000. The smaller cities have steadily lost their share of the urban population, dropping from 12 per cent in 1970 to only 5 per cent in 2000.

It is difficult to make much sense of this pattern. One of the problems, of course, lies in the changing units of analysis and administrative boundaries. In effect, it appears that suburban sprawl, especially around the greater Manila Metropolitan area (including Regions III and IV) may be leading to more rapid growth of the "towns." It may be more accurate, however, to see an increasing concentration of the urban population in that region. Somewhat the same thing may be happening on a smaller scale in other urban centers in the Visayas and the South. The growth of the towns may reflect only suburban sprawl, in

233

TABLE 8.6 Urban population in the Philippines by type, 1970–2000

Decade & Measure	Philippines	Cities				Towns
		Total	Large	Interm.	Small	
1970						
Pop (000)	11,678	5,919	2,085	2,330	1,504	5,759
% of Urban	100	50	18	20	12	50
Ann. Gr. Rate %	—	—	—	—	—	—
1980						
Pop (000)	17,826	8,721	4,163	2,946	1,612	9,105
% of Urban	100	49	23	16	10	51
Ann. Gr. Rate %	5.3	4.7	10.0	2.6	0.7	5.8
1990						
Pop (000)	28,550	12,361	5,242	5,621	1,498	16,189
% of Urban	100	43	18	20	5	57
Ann. Gr. Rate %	6.0	4.2	2.6	9.1	-0.7	7.8
2000						
Pop (000)	36,757	16,77	5,240	9,558	1,579	20,380
% of Urban	100	45	14	26	5	55
Ann. Gr. Rate %	2.9	3.2	0.0	7.0	0.5	2.6

NOTE: The Philippines NSO population figure for 2000 is used here, since that figure is disaggregated by city size.

which the new areas become incorporated as separate towns, though they are really parts of spreading metropolitan areas.

Future Projections

The United Nations data are used for the future projections. The form of Table 8.1 is used in Table 8.7, giving five-year intervals for the projections of total, urban, and rural population sizes and growth rates. The Philippines' total population is expected to top 112 million by 2030, at which time some 75 per cent of the population will live in urban areas. All growth rates are expected to decline, however. The total growth rate

TABLE 8.7 UN projections, world urbanization prospects, 2001 revision

Year	Population (in million)			Percentage	Annual Growth Rates		
	Total	Urban	Rural	Urban	Total	Urban	Rural
2000NSO	77	37	40	48			
2000 UN	75.7	44.3	31.4	59	1.86	3.19	−0.19
2005	83.0	51.9	31.1	63	1.59	2.68	−0.37
2010	89.9	59.4	30.5	66	1.29	2.16	−0.53
2015	95.9	66.2	29.7	69	1.12	1.81	−0.49
2020	101.4	72.5	29.0	71	1.08	1.61	−0.29
2025	107.1	78.5	28.6	73	1.00	1.48	−−0.37
2030	112.6	84.6	28.0	75			

is expected to fall to 1 per cent per year by 2030. The rural growth rate is already negative and is projected to remain so throughout the period. Urban growth rates are projected to remain substantially higher than the rural rates, but they, too, are projected to decline from over 3 per cent today to about 1.48 per cent.

URBAN-RURAL DIFFERENCES

Demographic Characteristics

The Philippine population growth continues to remain high at 2.26 per cent per year from 1990 to 2000 (see Table 8.1). This is higher than all of the more developed Southeast Asian countries except Malaysia (2.3) and Singapore (2.84), which is experiencing the echo effect of past fertility decline. This implies that the Philippine population is relatively young, with 37 per cent of the 76.5 million counted in the 2000 census being less than 15 years of age (see Table 8.8). The rural population is slightly younger than the urban population, with 39 vs. 34 per cent under 15 years. This 5 percentage-point rural-urban difference is the same for male and female populations. There is no rural-urban difference in the proportion over 65 years.

On marital status, half of the Philippine population, 10 years old and over, were married in 2000. Both legally married and common law/live-in arrangements are included in the married category. Single people

TABLE 8.8 Selected demographic indicators, Census 2000

Demographic Indicators	Population (in thousands)			Percentage		
	Total	Urban	Rural	Total	Urban	Rural
Sex / Age Group						
Philippines	76503	36756	39746	100	100	100
<15	28314	12633	15680	37	34	39
15–64	45257	22824	22432	59	62	56
65+	2932	1299	1634	4	4	4
Male	38524	18232	20291	100	100	100
<15	14455	6442	8013	38	35	39
15–64	22760	11241	11518	59	62	57
65+	1309	549	760	3	3	4
Female	37979	18523	19455	100	100	100
<15	13859	6191	7667	36	33	39
15–64	22497	11583	10914	58	63	56
65+	1623	749	874	4	4	4
Marital Status*	57140	28031	29109	100	100	100
Single	25079	12158	12921	44	43	44
Married	28527	14046	14481	50	50	50
Others	3533	1826	1707	6	7	6

*Total population 10 years old and over.

accounted for the next largest group (44 per cent) while widowed, divorced/separated, and those with unknown marital status accounted for about 6 per cent. There is no rural-urban differential by marital status that is discernible from the 2000 census data.

The female population aged 10–49 amounted to 63 per cent of the total female population in 2000 (not shown). The proportion of urban women in this age-group was slightly higher than that for rural women (65 per cent vs. 61 per cent). The total fertility rate (TFR) in the country declined slightly from 4.1 in 1991 to 3.7 in 1996, and to 3.5 children in 2001 (NSO and Macro International 1994, NSO et al. 1999, NSO 2004).

Given its still high fertility rate, and with about one-child difference in the desired fertility and actual fertility of women in 1996 (POPCOM 2000), achieving replacement level fertility of about 2.1 children by 2020 will be quite a tall challenge considering the elevation of the population issue to political discourse and the dwindling donor funds for the procurement of contraceptive supplies in the country.

Rural women have a higher unmet need for Family Planning (FP) services than do urban women (see Table 8.9), which reflects a relatively weak primary health care and fertility limitation program. The unmet demand for FP services is greater for limiting the number of children than for spacing children. This implies a considerable need for fertility limiting services among older women who have already born the number of children they desire. This pattern is reflected in both urban and rural areas.

There are marked improvements in the past decade specifically in child and maternal health. However, the rates of decline for MMR and IMR have slowed down in recent years and have remained unacceptably high relative to the ideal. The infant mortality rate (IMR) declined from 45.6 to 35.3 deaths per 1,000 live births between 1985 and 1998; the under-five mortality rate decreased from 72.3 to 48.4 deaths between 1985 and 2000; and the maternal mortality ratio (MMR) declined from 209 deaths per 100,000 live births during the 1987–93 period to 172 for the 1991–97 period. Since the IMR decline is much faster than the decline in maternal mortality, some sectors are inclined to believe that the Maternal and Child Health Program is biased in favor of the children. At present we have no data on rural-urban differences in this critical area of reproductive health care.

TABLE 8.9   Unmet need for family planning services, Philippines, 1998

| Residence | Unmet Need for Family Planning (%) | | |
	For Spacing	For Limiting	Total
Urban	7.3	9.0	16.3
Rural	9.8	13.4	23.3
Total	8.6	11.2	19.8

SOURCES: 1998 National Demographic and Health Survey (NSO, DOH and MI, 1999).

Social and Economic Characteristics

The relatively high fertility, and, therefore, the number of school-age children, has partly affected the ability of the country to achieve high survival rates in elementary and secondary education in the face of the boom-bust economy of the country. Nevertheless, the government continues to give basic education the highest budgetary priority, which partly explains the high levels of schooling participation that have been achieved.

Statistics provided by the Department of Education (DepEd) show that the elementary school participation rate (i.e., the proportion of the school-age population who are enrolled) is generally high, averaging 91 per cent during the SY1990–91 to SY2000–1 period. Data from the National Demographic Surveys show that female participation rates are slightly higher than male participation rates in both urban and rural areas. Children of both sexes in urban areas have higher participation rates than children in rural areas. Data from these surveys also show variations in enrollment rates by income groups. As expected, the poorest income groups show much lower levels of enrollment of children aged 6–14 years.

While participation rates are high, cohort survival rates have remained low. At the elementary level, the cohort survival rate averaged 68 per cent during the period 1990–2001, with very little variation. At the secondary level, the cohort survival rate averaged 73 per cent during the same period, also with little variation around this average. In fact, the cohort survival rates barely rose over the last 20 years at both levels of education. Cohort survival rates vary by region and are generally higher in private schools than public schools at both the elementary and secondary levels.

Data from the 1998 NDHS reveal that children aged 15–19 years belonging to the poorest families have much lower educational attainment compared to children in the richest group. Only 74 per cent in the poorest group completed grade 6, compared to 97 per cent in the richest group, while only 29 per cent in the poorest group completed grade 9 (or third year high school), compared to 68 per cent in the richest group.

The high value placed on education by both the Philippine government and its citizens is reflected in its near universal literacy rate (see Table 8.10). The 7-percentage point difference in the rural and urban literacy rates in 2000 (96 per cent vs. 89 per cent, respectively), however,

TABLE 8.10   Selected education indicators, Census 2000

Demographic Indicators	Population (in thousands)			Percentage		
	Total	Urban	Rural	Total	Urban	Rural
Literacy Status*	56975	27892	29083	100	100	100
Literate	52579	26825	25755	92	96	89
Illiterate	4396	1068	3328	8	4	11
Highest Grade Completed**	66834	32278	34556	100	100	100
Elementary and No Education	33475	12544	20931	50	39	61
Secondary	21533	11944	9589	32	37	28
Tertiary	9874	6742	3131	15	21	9
Not Stated	1952	1047	905	3	3	3

* Household population 10 years old and over based on 10% sample.
** Total population 5 years old and over.
SOURCE: NSO special tabulations.

indicates underlying inequities in social and economic conditions in the country.

The urban advantage in terms of education is further validated by the highest grade completed of the population five years and older. Thirty-seven per cent of the urban population has at least secondary education compared to only 28 per cent of the rural population. Unlike many other countries in the world, females do better in terms of education than their male counterparts. Available data show that women and men have the same simple literacy rate. Moreover, female children tend to have higher elementary completion rates than male children (72 per cent vs. 62 per cent), as well as higher secondary completion rates (76 per cent vs. 66 per cent). The advantage is carried forward to post-basic education. The proportion of women with college or higher education was 58 per cent compared to only 42 per cent of the men.

Unfortunately, existing policies appear to have created incentives for more rapid and unbalanced migration, both to urban areas, especially to the metropolis, thus increasing slum dwellers and aggravating environmental problems, and to upland areas and other fragile ecosystems, thus contributing to resource depletion and environmental degradation.

The Philippines' uneven economic performance (boom-bust cycle) partly explains the lack of sustained reduction in poverty incidence, which consistently shows a higher proportion of families below the poverty threshold in rural than urban areas. Figure 8.2 shows that the rural poverty level in 2000 was more than twice the urban level.

Economic growth has occurred without much impact on the reduction of the high unemployment rate. Much of the employment problem can be traced to the rapid growth of labor supply (the working-age population grew annually by 2.6 per cent in the 1990s) and the slow increase in labor demand owing to the effects of inward-looking economic policies such as low agricultural productivity and capital intensive manufacturing. There was also a steady increase in the participation of women in the workforce from 49 per cent in 1970 to 60 per cent in 1980, and then to 65 per cent in 2000, which was partly due to increased education of women and a response by married women to the inadequacy of household income resulting from unemployment and/or under-employment of family breadwinners. Unemployment has typically been higher in urban than in rural areas, among the young, and among women.

The high level of unemployment in the Philippines has naturally made overseas employment an attractive option. The number of overseas Filipino workers (OFWs) increased from 214,590 in 1980 to 1.06 million in 2002. The 2002 Survey of Overseas Filipinos (SOF) reported that most OFWs worked in Asia (78 per cent), of which the largest percentage were in Saudi Arabia (33 per cent), followed by Hong Kong (15 per cent), Japan (12 per cent), and Taiwan (11 pre cent). About one-third of the total OFWs worked as laborers and unskilled workers. The OFWs remitted a total of 67.7 billion pesos from April to September 2002 (NSO 2002). While overseas employment may augment household income, the temporary absence of the overseas worker creates numerous stresses and strains that frequently result in social costs like marriage breakdown, contracting STI and/or HIV/AIDS, among others, that affect the welfare of individuals and families.

IMPLICATIONS

Urbanization in the Philippines is not having the positive influences expected or experienced elsewhere in the region. Urbanization is moving ahead steadily, and the expected rural-urban differences are apparent. The country is now more than half urbanized, and within a generation threequarters of the population will live in urban areas. Yet the accompanying conditions one has come to expect are not materializing.

First, alone among the more developed nations in Southeast Asia, the Philippines has experienced more than two decades of economic stagnation. Total GDP growth has done no more than match population growth for the past quarter-century (WB 2004). Along with economic stagnation has come relative weakness in a variety of population and welfare measures. Given its level of education and urbanization, the Philippines has an unusually high total fertility rate (TFR), recorded at 3.7 in the 1998 Demographic and Health Survey (DHS 2004). Moreover, this is one full child greater than the reported desired fertility level. By contrast, Vietnam, which is much poorer and only half as urbanized, has a much lower TFR (1.9) and a lower desired fertility level (1.6). This indicates less of an "unmet need" for contraceptive services than in the more wealthy Philippines.

Not only is rapid population growth slowing economic development, it also has a negative effect on welfare conditions. The infant mortality rate stands at 35 and the under-five mortality rate stands at 48 (DHS 2004). Again, the contrast with poorer Vietnam (18 and 24) is striking. Moreover, although abortion is illegal, there are an estimated 320,000 to 480,000 abortions per year, or about one in six pregnancies. Abortion is estimated to be the fourth leading cause of maternal deaths in the country (CPDF 2002, as reported in ICOMP 2003).

The rapid growth of smaller cities and towns presents something of a problem for Philippines urban planning. On the one hand, there is a tendency for Philippine cities to be "overbounded" or to include large areas of rural populations. This occurs because mayors and city councils are induced to include as large an area as possible, since the size of the tax base determines the salary of city officials (Fleiger 2000). This leads to large numbers of towns and cities with distinctive urban administrations. On the other hand, many of these cities and towns are drawn together into larger regional planning Commissions. Unfortunately, these Commissions often lack the capacity to act effectively for urban planning.

Finally, the high levels of urban unemployment, especially among males, leads to extensive overseas migration for employment. Some one million Filipinos are now overseas workers. This represents about 2 per cent of the population aged 15–64. The Philippines education system, which provides extensive education in English, gives Filipinos an advantage in overseas employment. While this provides a substantial amount of foreign exchange through remittances, it deprives the country of what could be a highly productive work force. Of course, that this work force is not employed at home is one of the implications of the slow economic growth.

ENDNOTE

1   For personal reasons, Professor Ogena was unable to complete this chapter. Thus it was revised and edited by the senior editor. This also implies that the sources of data and statements are not available, except where the editor has included references.

The Urban Scenario in Singapore

PAUL CHEUNG

The transformation of Singapore from a small trading settlement on a tropical island to a modern city-state with global economic links is a multi-faceted process. One key dimension is the growth of its population over time and the changes in the urban landscape to accommodate the expansion of the population and the economy. As a city, Singapore is well known for its careful urban planning, characterized by intensive utilization of land in accordance with market principles and the desire to preserve a high quality of life. Such planning efforts have resulted in a living environment that is comparable to the developed countries. As the population has expanded over time to the present size of 4.2 million, the city has also evolved with the development of new towns and major urban amenities.

Among the Asian countries, Singapore's urban scenario is unique as it is 100 per cent urbanized. The distinction between urban and rural areas was largely diminished by 1980. In 1990, Singapore's physical landscape resembled a conglomeration of urban clusters in close proximity rather than a juxtaposition of urban and rural areas. Today, new towns and regional centers, industrial estates, and business parks have been developed all over Singapore. These are well connected by extensive road and rail transport networks, and linked through green corridors of parks and open spaces.

This chapter provides a brief analysis of the growth and characteristics of the population of Singapore as it grows into an international city. The visioning of the urban landscape in Singapore is described to give a sense of the direction of future development. In addition, differences among existing urban clusters are examined.

THE URBANIZATION OF SINGAPORE'S POPULATION

Singapore comprises the main island and several small, off-shore islands. Prior to the 1950s, Singapore was administered as two broad units. One unit covered the central city area which was administered by the City Council and the other unit covered the remaining part which was administered by the Rural Board. After 1963, the administration of the city and rural areas was integrated into the central government administration. Since then, there has been no administrative division of Singapore into urban and rural areas.

Increase in Density and Urban Population

Singapore's total population numbered 4,163,700 in 2002 (Table 9.1). The total population has almost tripled since 1957. In comparison, the total land area has increased by only 18 per cent. Population density has

TABLE 9.1   Total population

Year	Total (Thousand)	Per Cent Urban & Suburban	Land Area (Sq Km)	Population Density (per sq km)	Average Annual Population Growth (%)
1957	1,445.9	78	582	2,486	4.4[1]
1970	2,074.5	75	586	3,538	2.8
1980	2,413.9	Above 90	618	3,907	1.5
1990	3,047.1	Near 100	633	4,814	2.4
2000	4,017.7	100	683	5,885	2.8
2002	4,163.7	100	685	6,075	1.8

1   Refers to population growth between 1947 and 1957.

increased markedly, with 6,000 persons for each square kilometer of land in 2002. The increased population density reflects the intensification of the urbanization process in Singapore, as low-density squatter areas were cleared in the 1960s and 1970s for the development of high-density, low-cost public housing estates and new towns. With the establishment of the Housing and Development Board in 1960, several large public housing estates have been developed around the periphery of the city area. Slum clearance and rehabilitation of the central city area under the Urban Renewal Program also contributed to the mushrooming of high-density public housing within the city. Old shophouses made way for high-density public housing in various parts of the central area.

Population Growth Through Migratory Inflows

Since Singapore's founding in 1819, migration has been an important source of population growth. Historical records show that the inflows of immigrants from China and India resulted in substantial population growth in the 19th century and the first half of the 20th century. These immigrants arrived in Singapore to take advantage of the employment opportunities available in the development of the rubber and tin industries. With the outbreak of the Second World War, inflows of immigrants dwindled in the ensuing years.

Migratory inflows became increasingly important in the last two decades of the 20th century. This was because of the manpower shortages in various sectors as the Singapore economy developed. The latest population census data showed that almost half of the total population increase (46 per cent) during the last decade 1990–2000 was contributed by non-residents (Table 9.2). Non-residents comprised foreign workers, students, and other foreigners who were not granted permanent residence in Singapore, excluding tourists and transients. The remainder of the population increase came from the Singapore resident population comprising Singapore citizens and permanent residents. With large inflows of foreigners into Singapore, the share of the non-resident population increased from 10 per cent in 1990 to 19 per cent in 2000.

245

TABLE 9.2   Total population by residential status

Residential Status	Number ('000)		Percentage	
	1990	2000	1990	2000
Total Population	3,047.1	4,017.7	100.0	100.0
Resident Population	2,735.9	3,263.2	89.8	81.2
Citizens	2,623.7	2,973.1	86.1	74.0
Permanent Residents	112.1	290.1	3.7	7.2
Non-Resident Population	311.3	754.5	10.2	18.8

TABLE 9.3   Resident population by country of birth

	1970	1980	1990	2000
Resident Population ('000)	2,013.6	2,282.1	2,705.1	3,263.2
Born in Singapore	1,542.9	1,883.8	2,292.6	2,667.1
Born Outside Singapore	470.7	398.3	412.5	596.1
As % of Resident Population	23	18	15	18
Among Residents Born Overseas (Percentage)	100.0	100.0	100.0	100.0
Malaysia	35.3	38.0	47.3	51.5
China, Hong Kong & Taiwan	45.9	46.0	36.4	27.4
India, Pakistan, Bangladesh & Sri Lanka	9.6	9.0	8.5	10.3
Indonesia	5.1	5.3	5.2	5.5
Others	4.2	1.8	2.7	5.3

Larger Proportion of Residents Born Overseas

With the sustained inflow of immigrants, the proportion of the resident population born outside Singapore increased between 1990 and 2000 (Table 9.3). This was a reversal from two decades of decline. In absolute terms, the number of overseas-born residents in 2000 was the highest in the last 30 years. Among the residents who were born overseas, an increasing proportion were born in Malaysia and the Indian sub-continent. With the passing away of the old generation of migrants, the proportion born in China declined.

Young, Educated New Immigrants

Of the overseas-born residents in 2000, slightly more than half arrived in the last three decades. Some 28 per cent arrived during the last decade in the 1990s. This was the same proportion as those who arrived during the earlier two decades in the 1980s and 1970s. Young adults formed the bulk of recent immigrants and had a better education profile than the older generations of immigrants (Table 9.4). Among those who came in the 1990s, six in 10 arrived in Singapore when they were in their 20s and 30s. Seven in 10 of the recent immigrants had upper secondary or higher qualifications. The proportion declined for the older generation of immigrants. Being better-educated, proportionately more of the recent immigrants were literate in English, which is the working language for administration and business in Singapore. About seven in 10 immigrants who arrived in the 1990s and 1980s were literate in English.

TABLE 9.4 Selected characteristics of resident population born outside Singapore, 2000

Year of First Arrival	Total	Before 1971	1971–1980	1981–1990	1991–2000
Age at First Arrival (%)	100.0	100.0	100.0	100.0	100.0
Below 20 years	51.3	70.7	47.6	37.5	30.6
20–29 years	34.3	22.9	41.4	47.2	41.6
30–39 years	11.2	5.2	8.4	11.9	21.4
40 years & over	3.2	1.2	2.6	3.4	6.4
Percentage with Upper Secondary or Higher Qual.	35.0	13.2	35.3	50.2	69.7
Post Secondary	16.7	8.8	18.5	25.2	26.2
University	18.3	4.4	16.8	25.0	43.5
General Literacy Rate (%)	88.6	77.7	96.7	98.9	98.9
Percentage Literate in English*	54.8	36.8	56.3	67.4	73.4

* Literate in English only or multi-language.

DEMOGRAPHIC IMPACT OF IMMIGRANTS

Increased Quantity and Quality of Labor Supply

The inflows of young migrants into Singapore in the last two decades have helped increase the number of persons at prime working age. The residents who arrived in the 1980s and 1990s accounted for more than 14 per cent of resident persons aged 25 to 39 years in 2000 (Figure 9.1). The arrival of better-educated immigrants in the last two decades has expanded the pool of university graduates in Singapore. Overseas-born residents who arrived in Singapore between 1981 and 2000 accounted for 27 per cent of the resident graduate population in 2000 (Figure 9.2). The increase in the quantity and quality of the labor supply has facilitated the rapid and high rates of economic growth.

THE URBAN ECONOMY

Changing Occupational and Industrial Structure

The Singapore economy has grown more sophisticated. With rising demand for skilled manpower, there has been significant upgrading of the resident workforce, with larger concentrations in more highly skilled and better-paid occupations. The proportion employed in managerial, professional, and technical jobs jumped from 27 per cent in 1990 to 44 per cent in 2000 (Table 9.5). The upgrading of the occupation profile was faster for younger working adults than their older counterparts. Between 1990 and 2000, the increase was 23 percentage points for those aged 25–39 years compared with 9 percentage points for the older ones aged 40–54 years. The change in occupational structure reflects the emerging trend towards a services-oriented economy, with more persons working in the business and financial services sectors in 2000 (19 per cent) than in 1990 (13 per cent). In comparison, the proportion of working persons in the manufacturing sector declined from 26 per cent to 20 per cent. Singapore residents have also become more enterprising, with more working persons venturing out to operate their own businesses. In 2000, 14 per cent of working persons were self-employed, up from 12 per cent in 1990.

FIGURE 9.1   Components of resident population by age, 2000

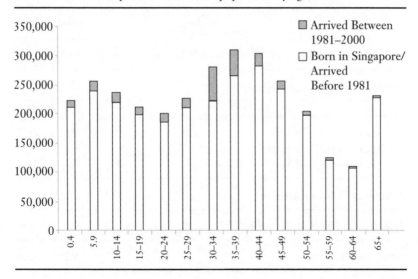

FIGURE 9.2   Components of resident population by highest qualification attained, 2000

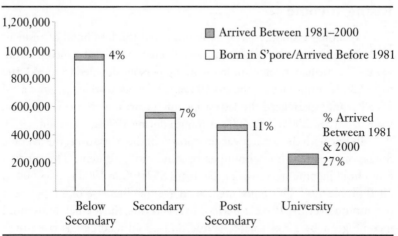

TABLE 9.5 The Singapore resident workforce

	1990	2000
Percentage in Managerial & Professional Positions	14.7	24.4
Percentage in Technical & Related Positions	12.2	19.1
Percentage in Managerial, Professional & Technical Positions	27.0	43.5
Age Group 15–24 Years	15.5	29.1
Age Group 25–39 Years	30.8	53.8
Age Group 40–54 Years	29.3	38.5
Percentage in Manufacturing	26.2	19.5
Perentage in Financial Services	4.5	5.9
Percentage in Business Services	8.2	12.9
Percentage Self-Employed	11.5	14.0

Rising Income

The expanding economy has greatly improved the livelihood of resident working persons in the last decade, as reflected in the rising income from work. The median income among working persons doubled from S$1,100 to S$2,200 per month over the last 10 years. Younger working persons aged 25–39 years experienced the fastest income growth, with median income rising from S$1,200 to S$2,600 per month during 1990–2000 (Figure 9.3).

In line with the greater earning power of the workforce, the average Singapore resident household has become more affluent. The median household income from work grew from S$2,300 in 1990 to S$3,600 in 2000 (Table 9.6). This amounted to an average increase of 4.6 per cent per annum over the 10-year period. In real terms, the median household income grew by 2.8 per cent. While household income has risen over the past 10 years, the average number of working persons in households has not increased in tandem. The average number of working persons in households was smaller at 1.6 persons in 2000, compared with two persons in 1990. Thus, the rise in living standard of households had been achieved with fewer income earners in the household.

FIGURE 9.3   Median monthly income from work among resident workforce

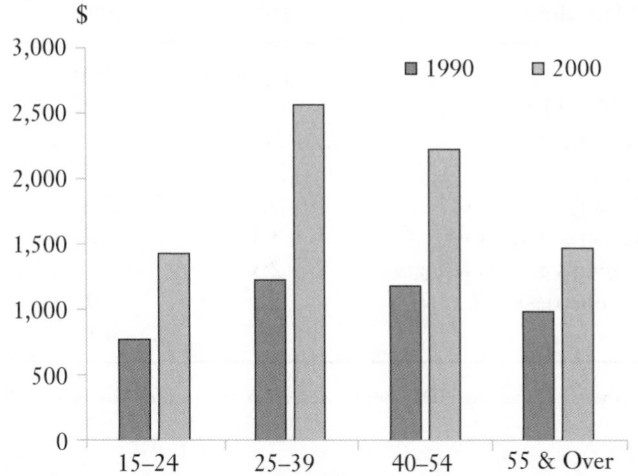

TABLE 9.6   Household income from work

	1990	2000
Median Monthly Household Income ($)	2,296	3,607
Average Number of Working Persons in Household	2.0	1.6

IMPROVEMENTS IN URBAN LIVING CONDITIONS

Increased Home Ownership and Better Housing

Home ownership was almost universal among resident households in 2000. A high proportion of 92 per cent of households owned the dwelling units they occupied in 2000, up from 88 per cent in 1990 and 59 per cent in 1980. Concomitantly, housing conditions had improved with urban redevelopment and the building of bigger and better public flats to meet the people's aspirations. In 2000, 68 per cent of Singapore resident households were living in public four-room or larger flats, condominiums and private flats, and landed properties (Table 9.7). The proportion living in better housing was a lower 52 per cent in 1990 and 24 per cent in

TABLE 9.7   Resident households by dwelling type (Percentage)

Type of Dwelling	1980	1990	2000
Total	100.0	100.0	100.0
HDB (Public) Flats	68.5	84.6	88.0
1- & 2- Room	21.9	8.2	5.0
3- Room	32.2	35.4	25.7
4- Room	9.8	27.4	33.2
5- Room & Executive	3.5	13.0	23.7
Condominiums & Private Flats	2.3	4.1	6.0
Landed Properties	8.5	7.0	5.1
Others	20.7	4.3	0.9

NOTE: Others include non-HDB shophouses, attap/zinc-roofed houses and other public flats.

1980. With households upgrading to bigger dwellings and the decline in household size, there is now more living space per person. Among households in public flats, the average number of rooms per person increased from 0.68 in 1980 to 0.99 in 1990 and 1.29 in 2000.

Increased Car Usage and Ownership

The car has become a more popular mode of transport in 2000. The proportion of working persons commuting to work by car rose from 18 per cent in 1990 to 24 per cent in 2000 (Table 9.9). More students also travelled to school by car in 2000. The proportion of those who did so increased from 4.5 per cent in 1990 to 7.8 per cent in 2000. The increased car usage reflects the growing affluence and ownership of cars. Over the past 10 years, households have had greater means to own cars. The proportion of households with cars rose from 28 per cent in 1990 to 32 per cent in 2000.

Despite increased car usage, public transport was still the main mode of transport to work among working persons and students. There was only a slight decline in the proportion of working persons and students who took public transport to work or school between 1990 and 2000. This was largely due to the extensive development of the MRT system and improvement of public bus services over the decade.

TABLE 9.8 Mode of transport and car wwnership

	1990	2000
Among Working Persons		
Percentage Using Public Transport to Work	55.0	52.4
Percentage Commuting by Car to Work	18.1	23.7
Percentage Requiring No Transport to Work	8.0	6.1
Among Students		
Percentage Using Public Transport to School	46.3	45.1
Percentage Commuting by Car to School	4.5	7.8
Percentage Requiring No Transport to School	29.6	30.1
Household Ownership of Cars (%)	28.0	31.7

POPULATION DISTRIBUTION
IN URBAN CLUSTERS

Enduring Predominance of Central Region

Historically, the majority of Singapore's population was concentrated in the central region. With the redevelopment of old pre-war residential buildings and shophouses into commercial and office complexes over the decades, the central region still had 28 per cent of the resident population in 2000 (Table 9.8). Developments of new townships in the north, north-east, west, and east regions have led to more residents living in these regions. In 2000, 23 per cent and 20 per cent of the resident population lived in the western and eastern regions, respectively. The northern region was the least populated region in 2000.

Central Region with Better Socio-Economic Profile

The residents in the central region appear to be better off than those in the other regions. In 2000, the central region had the highest average monthly household income from work (Table 9.9). Residents in the region also had higher proportions of the better-educated and more highly skilled workers.

TABLE 9.9   Resident population by geographical region, 2000

	Thousand	Per Cent	Rank
Total	3,263.2	100.0	
Central	896.8	27.5	1
West	742.1	22.7	2
East	654.2	20.0	3
North East	567.3	17.4	4
North	397.1	12.2	5
Others	5.7	0.2	

NOTE: Others include water catchment areas, and not stated.

FUTURE DIRECTIONS IN URBAN PLANNING

Urban planning can be traced back to the early years of Singapore's founding in the early 19th century. A formal plan for the Singapore settlement was drawn up in October 1822, soon after Sir Stamford Raffles' first arrival in 1819. This plan provided for the development of Singapore along the seafront around the harbor and extended inland for 1 to 2 kilometers. The original core center of settlement has, since then, developed and expanded into Singapore's Central Business District.

Physical planning for Singapore is constrained by several factors. The most important constraint is the scarcity of land. Singapore has a total land area of only 685 square kilometers. While future land reclamation can increase existing land size, there is a limit to how much can be reclaimed. Future reclamation can increase Singapore's land size by only another 15 per cent. Other considerations in planning include the need to ensure sufficient land for infrastructure needs, water catchment, and military uses. There are also some technical constraints, such as the height constraints imposed by our airports.

Given the physical constraints in Singapore, urban planning goes beyond safeguarding land for housing, industry, and recreation for the future. It involves development blueprints to promote Singapore's economic growth and improve the quality of life for the population. Some new initiatives are listed below:

TABLE 9.10 Selected socio-economic indicators, 2000

Region	Average Monthly Household Income from Work ($)	Rank	% Residents with Upper Secondary or Higher Qualifications	Rank	% Residents with Managerial, Prof/Technical Jobs	Rank
Central	5,300	1	35	1	48	1
East	5,200	2	33	2	45	2
North East	5,100	3	32	4	43	3
West	4,700	4	33	2	41	4
North	4,000	5	29	5	37	5

(1) *New homes in familiar places.* Provisions will be available for people to set up new homes in established housing estates, close to their parent's home and ready amenities such as markets, mass transit, and schools. One to two new towns will be developed to cater to those who want to live in a new area.

(2) *High-rise city living.* In areas with less stringent height constraints, housing can rise to 30 storeys and higher. More homes will be built in the city, with an estimated 90,000 more units envisaged in the New Downtown. By increasing the average plot ratio for housing in the New Downtown, the proportion of population living in the city will be increased from the current 3 per cent to 7 per cent.

(3) *More choices for recreation.* Open spaces will double from the existing 2,500 ha to 4,500 ha. The park connector network will be extended to link parks with town centers, sports complexes, and homes. More areas will be opened up within the Central Catchment for low-impact recreational uses such as hiking and cycling. Reservoirs will also be opened up for organized non-motorized water activities such as canoeing, rowing, and sailing. There will be new arts spaces both in the city and within housing estates.

(4) *Greater flexibility for businesses.* A new zoning system will be put in place. Industrial and business activities will be grouped according

to their impact on the surrounding environment. New business zones will be introduced for non-pollutive uses and for pollutive uses. A new "White" zone will be introduced, allowing all uses except pollutive ones. The White zone will create the potential for mixed-used buildings and work-live-learn-play environments.

(5) *A global business center.* A majority of the financial and services sectors will be concentrated within the Central Area for greater synergy and critical mass. This concentration will help to position Singapore as a global financial hub. The current three regional centers will continue to be built up. These three regional centers will be sufficient to provide for the needs of commercial space outside the Central Area.

(6) *An extensive mass transit rail network.* To support the increase in activities in the Central Area, there will be a denser and more comprehensive rail network. The existing 93 kilometers of rail lines will increase to about 500 kilometers in the future.

(7) *Focus on identity.* New towns of the future will be smaller, more compact, and personal, so that residents will have a greater sense of ownership and identity. Natural elements and landmarks will be retained and integrated as part of the new towns. To build regional identity, an identity map will be incorporated into each development guide plan. The identity map will show icons, activity nodes, focal points, essential routes, and gathering places, which could provide the landmarks for change and renewal.

CONCLUDING REMARKS

Singapore has grown to become a cosmopolitan city with global links. With its compact size and a relatively smaller population compared to other Asian mega cities, the realization of a high standard of living has been achieved much earlier. Being 100 per cent urbanized and having no rural-urban migration problems to grapple with, urban redevelopment has been able to proceed in a structured, planned manner. Yet, significant challenges remain. The limited land resources continue to pose a challenge in Singapore's commitment to provide a variety of housing choices. There is a need to provide more land to satisfy demands for low-rise or landed properties in land-scarce Singapore.

Another major challenge is the need for Singapore to develop and distinguish itself as a city with character and more recreation choices. As other cities in the Asian region grow and compete for internationally mobile talent, Singapore has to step up efforts to further improve its living environment to remain attractive. To this end, the new initiatives

10

Globalization and Urbanization: Focus for the Future of Thailand

KRASAE CHANAWONGSE

We are now in the new millennium and the countries of the world, whether industrially developed or still in the stages of development planning, face a variety of challenges. In Asia, the demographic challenge and the issues regarding urbanization need special attention. This chapter concentrates on the experience and perspective of Thailand.

The population projections for Thailand for the period 2003–16 as well as the appropriate data from the UN Population Division for Urbanization covering the years 1950–2030 are also referred to in this chapter. It is hoped that this will provide a basis for comparison of perspectives from selected countries of Asia, and give some clues to interested sectors and policy makers who need to take into account the challenges we all face in the contemporary world.

Table 10.1 provides some basic current information about Thailand. The country's population of 62 million people shows a slightly larger number of women. Just under half of the population lives in urban areas. Thailand is still primarily rural, but it has come through the demographic transition and

TABLE 10.1 Basic data on Thailand 2002

1	Total Population (000l)	62,376
2	Population by Sex (000)	
	Male	30,971
	Female	31,405
3	Population by Residence (000)	
	Urban	19,399
	Rural	42,977
4	Population by Region (000)	
	Bangkok Metropolis	7,610
	Central (Excluding Bangkok)	13,404
	Northern	11,698
	Northeastern	21,362
	Southern	8,302
5	Population by age group	
	Under 15	15,045
	Labor Force (15–59)	41,449
	Elderly (60–79)	5.314
	Oldest Old (80 and over)	568
	School Age	17,022
	Women of Reproductive Age (15–44)	16,221
	Ever married women of reproductive age	
	Number (000)	10,614
	Percent	65.6
	Eligible Voters (18 and over)	44032
6	Vital Rates (per 1000)	
	Crude Birth Rate	14.0
	Crude Death Rate	6.0
	Natural growth Rate	0.8
	Total Fertility Rate	1.8
	Contraceptive Prevalence Rate (percentage)	72.2

TABLE 10.1 (cont'd)

7	Basic Welfare Measures	
	Infant Mortality Rate (per 1000 live births)	20.6
	Life Expectancy at birth (years)	
	Male	69.9
	Female	74.9
	Life Expectancy at 60 (additional years)	
	Male	20.3
	Female	23.9

is moving rapidly towards becoming an urban industrial society. The young have declined form nearly half to about a quarter of the population. The aged are increasing in number and proportion. Crude birth and death rates are now quite low, the rate of natural increase is less than 1 per cent per year, and the total fertility rate (TFR) is 1.8, less than the replacement level. Mortality and fertility have been brought down dramatically by government health and population policies, and by the rapid expansion of health and family planning services throughout the country. All of this has been accompanied by a rise in the basic indicators of welfare. Infant mortality has dropped dramatically and is now approaching that of the more wealthy countries. Along with this, life expectancy has increased to levels near those of the more wealthy industrial nations. This is a remarkable transition that has occurred in just the past half-century.

Definitions

Thailand's urban system is dominated by a primate capital city. Bangkok, with a population in 2002 of 7.6 million people, is about 20 times larger than the next biggest city, Korat. Just over one-third (29 per cent) of the urban population in Thailand is located in Bangkok. There are also intermediate and smaller cities throughout the country. Though different countries may define the key terms such as urban, city, rural, village, and migrant, with a variety of emphases according to the context in which the statements are made, we believe we could have a common denominator with comparable connotations to make sense of the findings referred to in this compilation.

In line with the statement of Dr. Prem Talwar, the Thai concept of an *urban area* involves the size and/or density of habitation. To be considered urban in the Thai census, an area must have 400 persons per square kilometer, the predominant activity (75 per cent of the male working force) being in non-agricultural pursuits, and a population numbering more than 4,000 persons. In Thailand, the term *rural population* implies those dwelling in villages in the countryside.

In 2000, the Thai government changed the administrative boundaries of what it called urban areas. This substantially increased the proportion urban, from 19 per cent in 1995 to 31 per cent in 2000 (see Table 2). This was a purely administrative definitional change, not a real increase in urbanization. The new figures may, however, be a more accurate reflection of the real level of urbanization in Thailand. We shall see this shortly when we discuss rural-urban differences. In effect, despite the relatively low level of percent urban, much Thai rural behavior is very much like urban behavior.

The definition of *migrant* is also specified. In Thailand, a migrant is identified as someone who has stayed continuously for at least six months in a village or town (rural or urban) before moving to the current place of residence (rural or urban). We will refer to this later.

Number and Percentage of Urban Population 1951–2001

Like many countries in the "Less Developed Regions," Thailand is now undergoing a major transformation from rural-agrarian to urban-industrial society. As Table 10.2 shows, Thailand has become more urbanized over the past half-century.

In 1950, only 10 per cent of the population lived in urban areas. Thailand has experienced the demographic transition discussed in the first chapter. Its mortality rate fell rapidly after 1945, while fertility remained high. This gave us a period of rapid rate of population growth. This reached its peak at 3.18 per cent per year during the period 1960–65. After 1965, fertility began to decline, both from local economic pressures, and from policy and programmatic changes, namely the introduction of a national fertility limiting policy and the creation of a very effective national family planning program. As fertility fell, the rate of national increase fell, and continues to fall today.

261

TABLE 10.2 Population growth and urbanization in Thailand, 1950–2030

	Population (000)			%	Ave. Ann Growth (%)		
Year	Total	Urban	Rural	Urban	Total	Urban	Rural
1950	19,626	2,056	17,570	10.5			
1955	22,759	2,610	20,149	11.5	2.96	4.77	2.74
1960	26,603	3,329	23,274	12.5	3.12	4.86	2.88
1965	31,190	4.011	27,178	12.9	3.18	3.73	3.10
1970	36,145	4,802	31,343	13.3	2.95	3.60	2.85
1975	41,067	6.200	34,867	15.1	2.55	5.11	2.13
1980	46,015	7,841	38,174	17.0	2.28	4.70	1.81
1985	50,541	9.030	41,511	17.9	1.88	2.82	1.68
1990	54,736	10,244	44,492	18.7	1.60	2.52	1.39
1995	58,729	11,315	47,415	19.3	1.41	1.99	1.27
2000	62,806	19,560	43,246	31.1	1.34	11.6	-1.8
2005	66,500	21,716	44,784	32.7	1.14	2.11	0.70
2010	68,681	23,970	44,711	34.9	0.94	1.99	-0.03
2015	72,490	27,401	45,089	37.8	0.79	2.71	0.16
2020	75,097	31,315	43,782	41.7	0.71	2.70	-0.59
2025	77,480	36,028	41,452	46.5	0.63	2.84	-1.09
2030	79,525	41,035	38,490	51.6	0.52	2.63	-1.47

SOURCE: Dr. Peerasit Kamnuansilpa, Kohn Kaen University, personal communication.
NOTES: 1950–1995 population growth and urbanization rates in Thailand were from
UN 2002. In 1995 the Thai government redefined urban areas by including a substantial
number of small towns. Thus the increase 1995–2000 from 19 to 31 per cent is largely
due to a redefinition of "urban."[1]

1   2000-2030 population growth and urbanization rates in Thailand were estimated by
adjusting the new definition of urban population promulgated by the law in 2000.
The estimation was done by keeping the same total population from 2000-2030 as
estimated earlier by UN 2002. The distributions of urban-rural population from
2000 to 2030 were done by observing the same pattern of acceleration of urbanization
of Thailand indicated in UN 2002.

The average annual growth rates were estimated using the formula:

P = C(1+r)ᵗ when

P = Projected population

C = Current population (Initial population)

R = Growth rate

T = Number of years in the interval (in this case = 5)

Throughout this past half-century, urbanization has increased. Urban growth rates have been 1 to 3 percentage points higher than rural growth rates until the last decade of the century. The gap has narrowed in the past decade, but as we shall see with projections later, it is expected to grow.

Between 2000 and 2005, it is expected that the rural growth rate will turn negative, though the "echo" effect of past high fertility will bring two more periods of rural growth. Then, in 2020, it is expected that the rural growth will enter a period of constant decline.

Sources of Growth

There are at least three factors which can contribute to the growth of urban population. Firstly, the overall demographic growth may be attributed to natural increase viz. the excess of births over deaths. Secondly, net migration from rural to urban areas may also contribute to the growth.

Thirdly, the growth in urban population may also be due to changes in demarcation of city boundaries, or definition of former rural areas. As noted above, the redefinition of boundaries in 2000 brought many previously rural areas into urban administrative units.

The spread of urbanization, as in the Bangkok area, is also happening in the intermediate-sized urban areas, especially around the rapidly growing cities like Khon Kaen, Ubon Ratchathani, Nakorn Rachasima, Hatyai-Songkhla, and Phitsanulok.

One of the important factors for urban growth is foreign direct investment (FDI). Since 1984, Thailand has kept the country open to international capital inflows and foreign investment. The Thai currency also remains internationally convertible. Liberal economic policies and mobility of capital contributed much to the drive for urbanization.

Another factor that contributed toward urban growth is the ready acceptance and spread of new technology, such as the use of the internet, mobile phones, and fiber optic networks. Container ports and aviation facilities in Thailand are recognized as being world class. During the early 1950s, many klongs (canals) were filled in to make way for arterial motorways. Motorization expedited regional urbanization.

During the rapid urbanization over the past two decades, Thailand's centralized administrative policies enabled the urban economy to develop closer links with the global economy. Area-based administration, however, separated rural from urban development, with no systematic links between rural and urban policies and implementation. The gaps in terms of the distribution of income, economic activities, and social services widened. Rural growth and prosperity has not been adequately enhanced by growth and prosperity in the urban areas, leading to uneven growth, poverty, and backward conditions in the rural areas. The key production areas of the agricultural sector and natural resources have deteriorated and need systematic conservation. Along with this, weak city planning and uncontrolled urban growth have resulted in deterioration of the environment and quality of life for both urban and rural people.

Recognizing the problems caused through overly centralized administrative policies, decentralization has been a priority policy objective of the Royal Thai Government since the Eighth Plan for National Economic and Social Development. The initiation of a Regional Urban Development Fund has helped to implement the plan for decentralization and the spread of urbanization.

In the current Ninth Plan for National Economic and Social Development, the Royal Thai Government continues with decentralization as a priority policy objective by promoting initiatives in support of employment creation opportunities in all regions of the country, with the focus on the faster growing non-agricultural sector. With the new development orientation, in accordance with "the sufficiency economy philosophy", emphasis is placed on the fostering of supportive links between urban and rural economies, to more equitably distribute economic and social opportunities. The aim is to strengthen local administrative organizations to effectively carry out decentralized development functions, so that the benefits of development are better distributed among the people, particularly the poor and the underprivileged, and to contribute to Thailand's long-term goal of sustainable economic and social development.

Migrant Composition

We referred earlier to the migration from rural to urban areas. It must be noted that there is also migration from urban to rural areas, although it is proportionally small. The urban to rural migration can be attributed to two main factors: firstly, there are those from the villages who are attracted to employment opportunities in the cities and who logically return to their rural families and roots as the period of urban employment concludes. Secondly, there are the rural young people who go to the urban centers for education and then return to their home villages after securing the education they went to get. There are also the urbanites with a social conscience (e.g., health and educational personnel), who choose to devote their lives to promote rural development, who can also be added to this migration.

Rural-to-rural migration is influenced by a series of factors. One is that migrants may consider one rural area more accessible for employment than the villages where they lived in the past. The living conditions in urban slums, where rural migrants may stay while holding down available employment, may discourage rural people from migrating to urban areas. The construction of arterial motorways, mentioned earlier, has enabled rural people to commute, as necessary, between rural areas and from rural to urban areas. Hence, settling down in urban slums is avoidable. Another factor influencing rural-to-rural migration has a cultural element. The extended family system still prevails, especially in the rural areas. Women who migrate from rural areas to other villages are usually motivated by circumstances of marriage or family situations which make it convenient for them to be near relatives for support or child rearing. All political parties consider rural areas as their support power base and, accordingly, maintain a "rural bias." This encourages the rural people to stay in rural areas, even if this means the need to move from one rural location to another. Funds for assistance to Thailand, e.g., from the World Bank, during the economic crisis, were directed towards economically marginal areas, which meant that priority was given to the rural areas. Rural-to-rural migration has also been prompted by trouble in areas bordering neighboring countries experiencing ethnic or political conflicts, such as Cambodia, Laos, and Myanmar. Borders are also opportunity regions for overland trade and often become areas of refuge asylum. All these factors contribute much to rural-to-rural migration.

As shown in our previous data on the population of Thailand, the female population exceeds that of the male population by 434,000. The male migrant component, however, can be assumed to exceed the female component as, culturally, males are expected to be more mobile and ready to migrate to places where employment is available. Wives usually accompany husbands as they migrate. Single women migrants may make a small portion of the overall migration figure; however, due to the sex industry migrants, women may form the majority in rural-to-urban migration. This study encompasses both males and females for the rural-to-urban and urban-to-urban categories.

Projections

Table 10.2, above, provides one set of data on estimated projections for the next three decades. Table 10.3 presents another set of projections to 2010. One point needs to be made regarding these two tables and their differences. Table 10.2 is based on the UN 2002 estimates, with new projections calculated on the new urban area definitions. Table 10.3 shows the official Thai estimates to 2010. Together, these show an interesting condition. Note first that the Thai estimates are lower than those of the United Nations. In fact, the UN 2002 estimates are lower than their own 2000 estimates. At almost every biannual UN revision of World Population Prospects (or World Urbanization Prospects), the estimates for Thailand (as well as for most of Asia) have been revised downward. We fully expect that the next round of UN estimates, due in 2004, will be more in line with the lower Thai estimates.

From Table 10.2 we see that the overall Thai population is expected to grow from 62.8 million in 2000 to 79.5 million in 2030. Almost all of that growth will take place in the urban areas. The urban population is expected to grow from 20 to 41 million in the next three decades;[1] that is, it will more than double. The rural population peaked at 47 million in 1995, declined for five years, then rose again. It is expected to grow to a second peak of 45 million in 2020 and then begin an absolute decline to 38 million in 2030. In effect, the rural population will reach a peak and decline while the urban population continues to grow. Thailand is making the common transition from rural agrarian to urban industrial society.

From Table 10.3, we see that the total population is expected to grow from 62.4 million in 2000 to 67.2 million in 2010 (1.4 million less than the UN estimate for 2010). All of that growth will be in the urban population, which will grow from 25.8 million to 35.3 million. The proportion urban is expected to grow from 41 per cent in 2000 to 52 per cent in 2010. That is, by the end of this next decade, more than half the Thai population will be found in the urban areas. The rural areas are expected to show an absolute decline from 36.6 million in 2000 to 31.9 million in 2010. This is an earlier and faster decline than projected by the United Nations.

We also see from Table 10.3 that urbanization will continue throughout the country, though at rather different rates. The Northeast has typically been the least urbanized up until 1995, when 18 per cent of its population lived in urban areas. By 2010, however, it is expected to be the second most urbanized region, after the Eastern Seaboard area. The urban population will grow continuously throughout this decade. The rural population, however, will be in absolute decline in all areas except the South, where it is expected to remain roughly stable at around 6.5 million.

IMPACT OF URBANIZATION OF THE THAI POPULATION

While the rural population was larger than the urban population at the beginning of 2002, the 1999 study by Kaothien and Webster predicted that within the next 10 years the majority of Thailand's population would be urban. This has many implications for national policy. We can only make estimates at present and it will require select and well-planned research for the formulation of future urban and rural policies, and plans covering the whole nation. The following sub-sections are intended to provide relevant hints.

Rural/Urban Interaction

National development plans involving location of dams, industrial zones, and export-oriented or aviation complexes influence migration between rural and urban areas. Obviously these provide employment opportunities for relevant members of the labor force.

Undoubtedly, contact with urban conditions affect the values and lifestyles of the migrants from rural areas. Traditionally, the rural people in Thailand are oriented towards agriculture which determines their style of life and relaxed use of time. Migrants to the urban areas, however, have to conform to the routines of factories or construction firms, within set time-frames and schedules of daily work. Unlike the traditional communities in their villages, their neighbors or work-mates with whom they associate in their urban work-settings may come from a variety of backgrounds with different interests. The urban setting exposes them to a wider circle of friends and media access, and gives them ready

TABLE 3 Population and urbanization forecast for Thailand, 1995–2010
(Population figures given in millions)

	1995	2000	2005	2010
Whole Kingdom	59.4	62.4	65.0	67.2
Urban	21.9	25.8	30.6	35.3
Rural	37.5	36.6	34.4	31.9
Percentage Urban	36.9%	41.0	46.9%	52.8%
BMA	8.0	9.1	10.3	11.5
BMR Perimeter	19.4	19.9	20.0	20.1
NORTHEAST	19.4	19.9	20.0	20.1
Urban	3.4	4.5	5.9	7.5
Rural	16.0	15.4	14.1	12.6
Percentage Urban	17.5%	22.6%	29.5%	37.4%
SOUTH	7.8	8.2	8.6	8.7
Urban	1.5	1.7	2.0	2.2
Rural	6.3	6.5	6.6	6.5
Percentage Urban	19.1%	20.8%	23.2%	25.2%
NORTH	10.9	11.1	10.8	10.6
Urban	2.6	3.0	3.4	3.7
Rural	8.3	8.1	7.4	6.9
Percentage Urban	23.8%	27.1%	31.6%	35.0%
ESB II [What does ESB II mean?]	5.8	6.3	6.9	7.2
Urban	2.0	2.7	3.5	4.0
Rural	3.8	3.6	3.4	3.2
Percentage Urban	34.5%	42.9%	50.7%	55.6%
WEST & UPPER CENTRAL	4.2	4.3	4.3	4.2
Urban	1.1	1.2	1.3	1.4
Rural	3.1	3.1	3.0	2.8
Percentage Urban	26.1%	28.1%	30.2%	33.0%

opportunities for gaining general knowledge. There is also improvement in terms of the level of literacy among the rural migrants.

Whether they have better sanitation and clean water, and more acceptable living conditions in the urban setting can be debated, depending on work situations and the location of the migrants. Considering the living conditions of slum-dwelling migrants, claims can be made that their original rural environment provides them with a better sanitary setting and cleaner air, as well as cleaner water. On the other hand, it can also be said that the urban setting provides them with chlorinated piped water, electric power, and modern facilities mot readily available in many of their rural habitats.

It is often assumed that these rural migrants in urban slum settings (e.g., Bangkok) are wretched and poor. But studies have shown that a third of the slum dwellers have higher than (mean) average family income of those regular citizens in the area of the Bangkok Metropolitan Administration. There is also the sacrificial commitment of the rural migrant wage-earners to ensure that they can set aside funds to take care of their children's education or to invest in some small businesses. Their urban experiences also influence their attitude toward family size. The family planning information and program of Thailand has been acknowledged as successful and effective. The rural migrants have practical experience of the value of such programs, and with a new sense of value with regard to children (e.g., quality not quantity), the family size of these people has been reduced. In this sense, the social impact of urbanization and the effects of rural/urban interaction can be viewed as both significant and beneficial, even for the whole country.

Population and Differentials

It is recognized in the Ninth National Economic and Social Development Plan (2002–6), that "Thailand's population is aging and becoming increasingly urbanized. It is expected that the proportion of young people will decrease from 23.0 per cent in 2002 to 21.9 per cent in 2006 while the proportion of older persons will increase from 9.8 per cent to 10.7 per cent over the same period. Based on these demographic trends, Thailand will become an ageing society within the next 15 years. At the same time, there is a transformation of households from extended families to nuclear families of various types.

These trends present an opportunity to modify population development policies toward improving the quality of children's education and health, and augmenting health, welfare, and social security provision for the elderly. Increasing urbanization constitutes an opportunity to strengthen rural development potential through the creation of rural-urban linkages and more effective management of development resources." It is thought that these improvements "will enhance the sustainable and livable development of urban and rural areas."

The quality of life targets of the Ninth National Economic and Social Development Plan (2002–6) are: "Focus on maintaining a balanced demographic structure and appropriate family size. Fertility will stay at a replacement level. Every Thai person should have access to resources to achieve good health, develop abilities to adapt to change, and practise high moral standards and social responsibility. Young people should have an opportunity to receive at least nine years of education by the year 2006. By the same year, at least 50 per cent of Thai workers will have completed lower secondary education. Health insurance schemes will be extended to cover all of the population on an equitable basis. The social protection system will be improved to provide social insurance for all age groups, thereby strengthening communities and civil society. Community empowerment will create an enabling environment that fosters people participation in the development of livable cities and communities, as well as sustainable management of natural resource and environment."

Economic and Social Issues

Urban/rural interaction covers both the differentials as well as the economic and social issues arising from urbanization.

We referred earlier to the domination of Thailand's urban areas by Bangkok, the primate capital city. The slums of Bangkok, occupied by rural migrants, have an impact on both the urban and the rural communities concerned. The presence of ugly slums in the setting of a rapidly progressive metropolis like Bangkok affects the urban communities. Slum dwellers are not all poverty-stricken and some may have more economic advantages (income) than the average inhabitant in the capital, as mentioned earlier. The rural migrants (in terms of women in the sex industry) can be factors for increased problems in health, crime, and morality for the urban community. The effect of the urban experience on the lifestyles, sense of value, general knowledge, and financial situations of the rural migrants, and even of the rural sector at large, has also been mentioned earlier.

As in other developing countries, Thailand can see the disparity in many areas of life between urban and rural communities. Educational facilities and level of education in the rural areas are very low in comparison with those in the urban centers. Civic amenities in the villages, though much fewer and less available than those in the urban areas, can be viewed with some sense of satisfaction, as decentralization of the urban system helps the spread of amenities and facilities; even providing access to these by rural communities. It is also useful to note that not all amenities and facilities which urban people cherish are necessarily priority items for rural communities.

There is more *male* migration from rural areas to the urban centers, and, as indicated earlier, those of working age and students constitute the majority. This means that the composition, age-wise and gender-wise, of the urban and rural populations is also affected by such factors. Older workers, after retirement or on completion of their employment in urban centers, tend to return to their rural roots, and consequently contribute to the age profile differential between the rural and urban populations.

In spite of the availability of transport for urban people, their social life or connectedness is not necessarily better (or warmer) than for their counterparts in rural settings, where cultural ties and traditions provide them with a closer and warmer sense of connectedness.

Though more will be said about health later, it is useful to note here that health conditions and facilities are better in urban areas then those in the rural areas. Accordingly, the infant mortality rate in village communities exceeds that in the urban areas.

Having noted these differentials, it is necessary to state here, and also later, that, in Thailand, the differences between the urban and rural communities are dwindling with the passage of time.

From the foregoing statements, the impact of urbanization on the Thai population is already apparent. There are both positive and negative aspects in the process of urbanization in any country; but there are differences. Urbanization comes with modernization. The new is not necessarily always better than the old. One thinks of the negative consequences in the development of some primate capitals or

271

metropolitan cities in the world, e.g., New York, resulting in the death of neighborhoods, destruction of some historical land marks, increase in chaos and despair, and a rise in crime rates. The saddest part of the negative aspects of urbanization is that those affected are usually the most vulnerable: the poor.

Some models for industrialization and urbanization pay scant attention to community, social, and environmental factors. A case in point is a school in Map To Phut, in the Eastern Seaboard area, which had to be moved because of severe air pollution from a petro-chemical complex in the vicinity.

On the positive side, we may make reference to increased civic amenities, employment and education opportunities, and the continuing acquisition of new technology.

Research findings show evidence of the net benefits to Thailand in the process of peri-urbanization supported by foreign direct investment (FDI). By net benefits we mean the growth in Gross Domestic Product (GDP), poverty reduction, and job creation.

The differentials in the socio-economic structures between and within urban areas, between urban and rural communities, and the implications of these variations for the populations concerned, need to be studied further. In Thailand, however, the gap between styles and quality of life is narrowing.

Hopes and Challenges

Although the levels of expectation may not be the same between urban and rural communities, members of both certainly aspire to enjoy better and more productive lives, thus yearning for improved quality of life for themselves and their families. Even for people in urban environments, the issue for urban planners is the way to manage urbanization so that such people may have a higher standard of living and better quality of life, and contribute to the overall Thai competitiveness in regional and world markets.

For policy makers and development planners, the improvement of inadequate infrastructure and the increase of civic amenities require constant attention, especially for rural communities. The improvement of inadequate infrastructure, however, does not imply pre-occupation with indiscriminate motorization. Development of reliable, comfortable, and efficient *public* transport systems is what is important for a positive impact of urbanization on the Thai population at large. Attention also needs to be given to the prevention, or reduction, of the *brain drain* from key areas in the urbanization process.

HEALTH AND ENVIRONMENT

Urbanization and Health

Messrs Wongboonsin and Indaratna in their paper presented at the Kobe meeting on "Cities and Health" said the following:

"It has now been commonly accepted that health can refer to both physical and mental health. What constitutes physical and mental health? First, living conditions: housing, food, and a healthy lifestyle concerning consumption patterns including food, drinks, and leisure. Second, the broader physical environment: sanitation, waste management and treatment; health and safety legislation and enforcement: helmets for motor cyclists, seat belts, levels of emission, petrol content, working or business hours; and recreation and park areas. Third, a happy family and social environment, which can affect the work and living relationships. Fortunately, most negative attributes of health can be prevented, but they need to be recognized. In addition, preventive and promotive actions need to be advocated."

"All of the attributes of health require recognition of the importance of health as a major element of living and productive life. It is necessary to realize that bad health is costly both to individuals and countries and that is preventable. It is a win-win situation because no one loses in a good health game. However, health, if left to individuals, especially at a young age or in lower socio-economic groups, may be assigned a low priority. Therefore, actions at a broader level than the individual are sometimes necessary."

"Still, individuals should take steps to promote their health and to prevent unhealthy conditions whenever possible. Some health problems can only start with the lack of self-awareness and discipline, and others can start in families. Where broader environments, such as schools, workplaces, and hospitals, are the appropriate sources of a healthy life, they can play an important role in prevention of health problems and promotion of healthy living conditions."

"A City as a vehicle for healthy living. All cities have major, basic systems in common: transport, environmental management, education, public health services, and community participation. Each of those systems requires planning both in the long run and the short run, in order to respond to the increasing population and demand for resources, at least to maintain healthy basic living conditions such as clean water and environment, fresh air, pleasant scenery, food hygiene, and safety in life and property. If those systems are not developed and maintained, there would be major immediate and long-term impacts on health. Making a city health-concerned will provide multiple and wide effects upon the population. This will improve the value of land and good living habits as it can raise an awareness of good living standards and the desire to protect them."

Rural Health

Alongside the urban context, we should also take note of the health care situation in rural areas.

Over the past few years, many research studies have addressed social, cultural, and economic issues in an attempt to understand people's health behavior. In the field of primary health care alone, uncountable research investigations have been conducted in the area of selecting, training, and utilizing village health volunteers, as well as providing a variety of health education programs at the community level. Although some studies have addressed community participation and the psychological aspects of rural health services, they were somewhat inadequate in trying to understand the hearts, minds, and immediate environment of the people. Many of these used quantitative techniques and the "over-used" method of "Knowledge, Attitude, and Practice (KAP)" surveys. The latter are wonderful in telling the investigator what is going on, but are very limited in understanding the underlying processes of *why* they are occurring. For this aspect, qualitative investigations using case studies are exceedingly valuable.

Concerns for an Ageing Population

The population of Thailand is ageing at a very rapid rate, allowing only a relatively short period of time to deal with the issue of old age and older persons. While the populations of developed countries usually become affluent before they grow old, Thailand will become an ageing society at a time when it is neither affluent nor prepared.

Table 10.4 provides the basic data on ageing in Thailand. In the broad age categories we see that the population under 15 will decline from its current 26 per cent to 17 per cent by 2050. Note that the decline of the past quarter-century, from 42 to 26 per cent is associated with the rapid decline of fertility and the completion of the demographic transition. The population over 60 is expected to rise from 5 to 22 million, or from 8 per cent to 27 per cent of the population in the next half-century. This will surely tax the country's government and social institutions.

TABLE 10.4   Aging in Thailand

Indicator	Age	1950	1975	2000	2025	2050
Population (thousands)						
Total		19,626.0	41,067.0	62,805.6	77,480.4	82,490.7
Broad age groups (%)	0-14	42.1	42.6	26.7	19.6	17.1
	15-59	52.8	52.4	65.2	63.3	55.8
	60+	5.0	5.0	8.1	17.1	27.1
Detail of the Aged						
Total	60+	5.0	5.0	8.1	17.1	27.1
	65+	3.2	3.2	5.2	11.4	21.1
	80+	0.4	0.3	0.6	1.7	5.5
Female	60+	5.6	5.4	8.8	18.6	29.6
	65+	3.6	3.5	5.8	12.7	23.6
	80+	0.5	0.4	0.7	2.2	7.1
Male	60+	4.5	4.6	7.4	15.5	24.5
	65+	2.8	2.8	4.7	10.0	18.5
	80+	0.3	0.2	0.5	1.2	3.9

On the brighter side, usually most of the older persons in Thailand remain independent well into very old age. They continue to work and earn, or help with housework until they are quite old. They are an important source of family support. In other words, their work is not always recognized as being productive input into the GDP. However, when they eventually reach a disabled and dependent state towards the end of their lives, they may not be able to get the support they need. Industrialization, urbanization, migration, socio-economic development, HIV/AIDs, drug abuse, and the phenomenon of high morbidity expansion are major factors affecting the capacity of families and communities.

We reiterate Thailand's support for the Macao Recommendation; the outcome from the Asia and Pacific Regional Preparatory Consultation for the Second World Assembly on Ageing in Macao, in September 2001. It called upon the United Nations to:

(1) effectively expand the existing institutional capacity of the United Nations to address the challenges of ageing and to meet the concerns of older persons, including the creation of a separate agency and fund it within the UN system;

(2) place mainstream ageing related issues into the work of the relevant UN agencies. In this connection, focal points on ageing and inter-generational issues should be set up and/or maintained in these UN agencies, and in relevant international financial institutions; and

(3) develop, sponsor, support, and promote regional and international exchange of ageing programs, and approaches to ageing related issues.

Preparation for old age security is a life long process. We need to promote knowledge about the contribution to society old people continue to make. At the same time, there is a need for family life education. It is especially important to strengthen inter-generational ties through such education. It is especially important to emphasize the need for an ageing-friendly environment. The provision of comprehensive community services and public health care are key approaches for the old people to have access to preventive and curative services. In Thailand, it took five years to collect and build up the data used in the Second National Long-term Plan for the Old People. It emphasized crucial issues, including preparation for old age, promotion and maintenance of contributions to society by old people, and the development of appropriate long-term care services for old people and their care-takers.

Environment

Reference has been made in this section to the health of both the city and the rural populations. These are related, of course, to the health of the environment. Urbanization affects not only the population in the cities and villages, but also the environment itself. The problems with regard to waste treatment, clean water supply, and controlling the pollution of waterways and the air, all point to an urgent need to give attention to environmental quality control and management.

Even if we look only at Bangkok, the primate city of Thailand, and its air pollution problem, we can see the fundamental importance of the environmental concern. The paper on "Environmental health and air quality in the City of Bangkok" presented at the WHO meeting at Mississauga, Canada, last year, speaks volumes about the environmental implications of urbanization. In this paper, Praphan Kitisin , the Deputy Governor for Public Health, Bangkok Metropolitan Administration, provided detailed data on the adverse effects of motor vehicles on the environment and, consequently, on the health of the population concerned. Bangkok has a third of the total number of cars in the whole country, not to mention one and a half million motorcycles, aggravating the city's air pollution. It is not only the environment and health, but also the national economy that is adversely affected because of the negative image the city gets abroad which affects tourism. Again those who suffer the most are the poor, especially in terms of their health. He stated that "concentration in the (city) atmosphere of particulate matter of less than 10 microns (PM_{10}) and carbon monoxide (CO) have been found to exceed the acceptable standards, while concentrations of nitrogen oxide (NOx), hydrocarbon (HC) and ozone have also been increasing. It has been found that over one million citizens of the Bangkok Metropolitan Area suffer from air-pollution-related illnesses. These particles, and the highly reactive chemicals they absorb, are known causes of respiratory, neurological and carcinogenic health disorders."

277

In 1999, the government undertook a campaign to reduce air pollution, the effects of which can be seen in Table 10.5.

Out of 10 million citizens, as many as 4,000–5,500 pre-mature deaths each year in the metropolitan area may be attributed to short-term exposure to outdoor airborne particulate matter! A study on decreasing lung capacity of traffic police in Bangkok found that of 174 policemen, 30 had constricted lungs and 14 had airway obstruction; 25.29 per cent had abnormal pulmonary function.

The condition of the environment does not only affect the health of the community, but also implies a very high cost in the form of pre-mature deaths, hospitalization, other health care, and loss of productivity.

National economic and social development plans encourage the implementation of capacity building for environmental improvement. The Environmental Quality Control and Management Division has initiated measures to be undertaken by agencies of the Bangkok Metropolitan Authority and other relevant bodies. There is encouragement for motorists to avoid heavily congested routes during peak hours; for motorcyclists to use batteries, solar cells, and electrical

TABLE 10.5 Comparison of 24-hour average concentration of PM_{10} on 8 pollution-free roads before the campaign (1998) and after the campaign (May 2000)

Roads	24-hr average concentration of PM_{10}		% Difference
	Before campaign (1999)	May 2000	
1 Rachapralop *	242	182	–24.8
2 Phetburi	283	213	–24.7
3 Silom *	195	112	–42.6
4 Si Paya	225	112	–50.2
5 Ramkumhang	332	182	–45.2
6 Rama 9	304	120	–60.2
7 Ajanarong	205	146	–28.8
8 Paholyothin *	395	207	–47.6

*NOTE: Campaign initiated on 1 March 1999; in the rest, on 2 August 1999. The legal standard for the 24- hour average concentration of PM_{10} is that it should not exceed 120 ug/m³.

or water energy; and for government departments to substitute their two-stoke motorcycles with four-stroke ones. There are also attempts to improve fuel quality; for example, the Office of National Energy Policy to inspect fuel quality regularly.

SUMMARY SCENARIO

As the factors and interpretations regarding urbanization have been discussed in the foregoing sections, the following summary underlines only some important points under each heading which may require further attention and reflection.

Globalization and Urbanization

The fact that the world is becoming a global village reinforces the trend for urbanization in Thailand. There are, however, both centrifugal and centripetal influences which affect urban/rural interaction in the country. Interestingly enough, it is globalization which stimulates both of these influences for Thailand.

Thailand's rural population is, at present, much larger than its urban population, and it has been pointed out that Thailand, as a whole, has a rural bias, or is relatively underurbanized. But the study on globalization and urbanization in Thailand also pointed out that within a decade, Thailand's population will be predominately urban. Advice given in the study was that importance should be given to the rural-urban transition (which in most countries only happens once in their history) and to take advantage of it to set the urbanization pattern and direction for the new century.

Growth of the Urban Population

Urbanization will grow and gain momentum, but it is also important to note that the differentials between urban and rural in Thailand will likely diminish in terms of quality and styles of life, in education, and in health.

The role urban centers in the Eastern Seaboard play as a manufacturing base for the Southeast Asian region, is an opportunity which national policy makers have to reckon with. The challenges rural migrants face, especially in the slum areas, are challenges for policy makers and national planners to contend with.

279

Urbanization is a matter of enjoying mixed blessings. Is progress in its positive connotation only to be considered in economic terms? The human cost, the price paid in the form of new forms of illnesses, and the deterioration of the environment, are just a few areas for informed reflection.

Toward Preventive and Remedial Measures

Living in a globalized world, steps toward prevention and remedy of problems and challenges will have to be coordinated, both within the country and with relevant agencies abroad. As we have seen with the air pollution problem in Metropolitan Bangkok, remedies had to be taken in coordination with many relevant agencies, such as the Traffic Police Division of the Royal Thai Police, the Pollution Control Department, the Department of Land Transport, Bangkok Mass Transit Authority, and the Petroleum Authority of Thailand.

In the matter of upgrading motor cycles to reduce air pollution in Bangkok, the participating groups included not only representatives of national agencies, such as the Thailand Automotive Institute, the Traffic Police Division, etc., but also the World Bank, Kenan Institute Asia, and NGOs. If the matter involves motor cars, we can be sure that the representatives of the dominant foreign car companies will have to be involved too.

The National Plans of the State always give attention to development, and the Current Ninth National Economic and Social Development Plan began with what H.M. the King had referred to as "Sufficiency Economy." The Plan envisaged Thai Society in terms of Quality Society, Knowledge-based and Learning Society, and "United and Caring Society." One emphasis in the strategies is restructuring of management for sustainable *rural* and *urban* development. Major targets in this connection are: livable cities and communities, poverty alleviation, linkages between rural and urban development with equitable distribution of economic and social opportunities, and management of area-function-participation development.

Participatory development was repeatedly emphasized in the Ninth Plan, and it is, for the purpose of the theme of this volume, a key principle for reflecting on creative consideration of the impact of globalization on the Thai population.

RECOMMENDATIONS

Using some of the insights arising out of the Kaothien/Webster case study of Thailand regarding globalization and urbanization, some of the following points, lifted from their study, merit early adoption and action.

(1) With the impending and growing urbanization of the Thai population, proactive strategically-oriented partnership initiatives by the public and private sectors, to prepare urban areas for *competitive, high quality of life, and environmentally sensitive* urbanization, are needed.

(2) There is a need to encourage the development of dynamic regional centers in the three regions (North, Northeast, and South) distant from Bangkok, to provide highly developed local services in support of development, and to provide alternative migration destination opportunities to the local people.

   N.B. The careful homework and study already done in Khon Kaen province is a good example for implementing such recommendations.

(3) Very high rates of urbanization (e.g., in excess of 4.5 per cent annually) are in most cases undesirable. This is because local authorities cannot cope with such growth dynamics in terms of delivery of infrastructure and services.

(4) Industries relevant to the select regions with potential (tourism, agro-based industries, etc.) need to be provided for. As the Ninth Plan indicated, integrated area-function-participation development, with rural-urban linkages in mind, will be very much in order.

(5) Much Thai urban development (especially in peri-urban areas) has been exogenously driven. The goal needs to be to endogenize it, particularly linked and induced activity associated with leading firms. The key to achieving this objective is to rapidly develop human resources.

(6) Coordinated purpose-oriented programming and management, increasingly at local and regional levels, based on an understanding of new urban realities, need top priority attention and action.

(7) It is also crucial that tried and exemplary implementers of the proposals in this paper are trained and entrusted to take the needed initiatives.

(8) Some of the thoughts and suggestions mentioned in this paper still need to be updated with supplementary research. With such support, they can be put into effect, as an outcome of the present cooperative effort.

ENDNOTE
1 Under the new 2000 definition of urban areas.

CHAPTER **11**

Urbanization and Urban Growth in Vietnam

TRINH DUY LUAN, NGUYEN HUU MINH,
AND DANG NGUYEN ANH

Vietnam is now urbanizing fairly rapidly. The past half-century, however, has seen both increases and decreases in the level of urbanization. The level rose from 1960 to 1975, then fell until 1985 when it began to rise again. In the past five years (1994–99), the level of urbanization rose from 20.5 to 23.5 per cent. Though urbanization is proceeding rapidly, the level of urbanization remains low for Southeast Asia. Only Cambodia and Laos have lower levels of urbanization than does Vietnam. The current "new wave of urbanization" is expected to continue and even to accelerate in the near future. It brings both advantages and problems for the country. This chapter will examine various aspects of the urbanization process and comment on the advantages and problems.

Most of the data used in this chapter are based on both national censuses and a census sample of approximately 3 per cent of the total population.[1]

Urban Classification

In the Vietnam 1999 census, the urban population is defined as including those persons who are living in urban districts of cities, urban quarters, and towns. All others living in local administrative units (communes) are classified as rural. The definition of what is an urban or rural place is an administrative procedure and the designated status has been attached to the sample records available from the census.

Among urban places, there is an official hierarchy of urban status, with five levels of urban places being defined. There are five principal criteria that are theoretically used for determining urban status: The size of the population, the percentage of the labor force in non-agricultural occupations, population density, the level of infrastructure, the administrative role, and the position of urban centers within regions (MOC 1992; 1999). In general, urban status classification is done on the basis of population size, with other criteria sometimes being employed.

For example, regarding the size of population there are five levels:

- The first level: Cities with more than one million persons.
- The second level: From 350,000 to one million persons.
- The third level: From 100,000 to less than 300,000 persons.
- The fourth level: From 30,000 to less than 100,000 persons.
- The fifth level: From 4,000 to less than 30,000 persons.

However, available sample data from the 1999 census do not allow us to use the official classification of urban as the codes for urban places within provinces were not made available for the analysis. Therefore, we were not able to match urban places with the official classification. In order to examine differentials among various categories of urban places, we have created a provincial level index of the degree of urbanization. This index aggregates the individual-level census data to characterize the level of urbanization of a province. Four levels of urbanization are created as follows:

- Level 1: Percent of urban population of province greater than 50 per cent (includes Hanoi, Ho Chi Minh City, and Hai Phong).

- Level 2: Percent of urban population of province greater than 30 per cent but less than or equal to 50 per cent.

284

- Level 3: Percent of urban population of province greater than 20 per cent but less than or equal to 30 per cent.

- Level 4: Percent of urban population of province less than or equal to 20 per cent.

Urban Population

The process of urbanization involves a redistribution of the population between rural and urban areas. After a relatively long period with a low and stable proportion of the population living in urban areas, the level of urbanization began to climb in the early 1980s after an initial decline that occurred after reunification (see Figure 11.1). The initial pace of change was slow, with the urban population only constituting 20.1 per cent of the total population in 1990. During the 1990s, the increases in urbanization became more rapid and, by 1999, 23.5 per cent of the population were living in places classified as urban (CCSC 2000).

FIGURE 11.1 Total, urban and rural population growth in Vietnam, 1951–2030

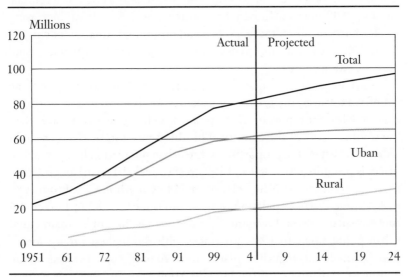

SOURCE: Tables 11.1, 11.7 and UN 2001.

285

TABLE 11.1 Total, urban and rural population in Vietnam, 1951–2000

Year	Population (000)			Pct Urban	Ave. Ann Growth Rates		
	Total	Urban	Rural	Urban	Total	Urban	Rural
1951	23,061*				0.5		
1960	30,172**	4,527	25,645	15,0	3.93		
1970	41,063**	8,787	32,276	21,4	3.24		
1980	53,722***	10,094	42,368	19,1	2.18	2.50	2.10
1990	66,017****	12,880	53,137	19.5	1.92	2.41	1.80
2000	77,635****	18,805	58,830	24.2	1.36	4.00	0.54

SOURCE: * Vietnam Population Census 1989: Detailed Analysis of sample results. General Statistical Office, Hanoi 1991.
** Annual Statistical Data Book 1993. General Statistical Office, Hanoi 1994.
*** Annual Statistical Data Book 1981. General Statistical Office, Hanoi 1982.
**** Annual Statistical Data Book 2001. General Statistical Office, Hanoi 2002.

Although the proportion urban remains low, there are now over 600 urban centers in Vietnam, with four cities under the direct management of the central government,[2] 83 cities and provincial centers, and over 500 towns (Ministry of Construction 1999). With increasing levels of urbanization, there has been an on-going formation of clusters of urban centers along rivers, the seacoast, and important road transportation routes.[3]

Urban places are distributed relatively evenly throughout the country. However, the process of urbanization is uneven. The northern part has a lower proportion of the population living in urban places than the southern part of the country. This difference can be clearly seen in Table 11.2, where the proportion of the urban population living in urban places is presented for 1989 and 1999 respectively.[4] The urban growth is most apparent for Da Nang, Hanoi, and Ho Chi Minh City. From 1989 to 1999, the urban population of these cities increased 2.6, 1.6 and 1.4 times, respectively, and accounted for nearly one-third of Vietnam's total urban population.[5] In 1989, provinces with the highest proportion of population living in urban places were mainly concentrated in the Southeast, radiating out from Ho Chi Minh City. In 1999, this pattern can still be seen, with an increase of levels of urbanization in some Central Highland provinces. In the North, high levels of urbanization are

TABLE 11.2 Percent of urban population by province and district, 1989 and 1999

Province	Percentage Urban 1989	Percentage Urban 1999
Red River Delta	**8.6**	**9.7**
Ha Tay	10.2	8.0
Hai Duong	5.0	13.8
Hung Yen	5.0	8.7
Ha Nam	10.7	6.1
Nam Dinh	10.7	12.4
Thai Binh	5.3	5.8
Ninh Binh	10.7	12.8
Northeast	**11.3**	**16.0**
Ha Giang	8.9	8.4
Cao Bang	9.7	10.9
Lao Cai	16.0	17.1
Bac Kan	18.8	14.5
Lang Son	7.6	18.7
Tuyen Quang	8.9	11.1
Yen Bai	16.0	19.6
Thai Nguyen	18.8	20.9
Phu Tho	7.0	14.2
Vinh Phuc	7.0	10.2
Bac Giang	5.0	7.4
Bac Ninh	5.0	9.4
Quang Ninh	43.1	44.1
Northwest	**11.3**	**13.0**
Lai Chau	13.2	12.2
Son La	13.1	12.8
Hoa Binh	10.2	13.8
North Central Coast	**9.5**	**12.3**
Thanh Hoa	7.2	9.2
Nghe An	8.3	10.2
Ha Tinh	8.3	8.9
Quang Binh	7.7	10.8
Quang Tri	13.6	23.5
Thua Thien Hue	26.7	27.6

TABLE 11.2 (cont'd)

South Central Coast	20.0	21.7
Quang Nam	30.1	14.3
Quang Ngai	8.2	11.0
Binh Dinh	18.0	24.0
Phu Yen	18.2	18.9
Khanh Hoa	37.4	36.4
Central Highlands	17.0	22.8
Kon Tum	15.8	32.1
Gia Lai	19.3	24.9
Dac Lac	16.2	20.0
Southeast	19.7	29.0
Lam Dong	34.2	38.7
Ninh Thuan	22.2	23.6
Binh Phuoc	4.7	15.2
Tay Ninh	10.6	17.9
Binh Duong	4.7	32.6
Dong Nai	24.9	30.5
Binh Thuan	22.2	23.4
Ba Ria Vung Tau	91.5	41.6
Mekong River Delta	15.1	17.1
Long An	12.7	16.5
Dong Thap	11.4	14.5
An Giang	18.8	19.7
Tien Giang	12.4	13.3
Vinh Long	9.6	14.4
Ben Tre	7.4	8.5
Kien Giang	21.1	22.1
Can Tho	18.0	21.3
Tra Vinh	9.6	12.9
Soc Trang	18.0	17.9
Bac Lieu	18.9	24.5
Ca Mau	18.9	18.7
4 cities	48.7	68.0
Ha Noi	35.7	57.6
Hai Phong	31.1	34.0
Da Nang	30.1	78.6
Ho Chi Minh	73.6	83.5

FIGURE 11.2 Total, urban and rural population growth in Vietnam, 1951–2030

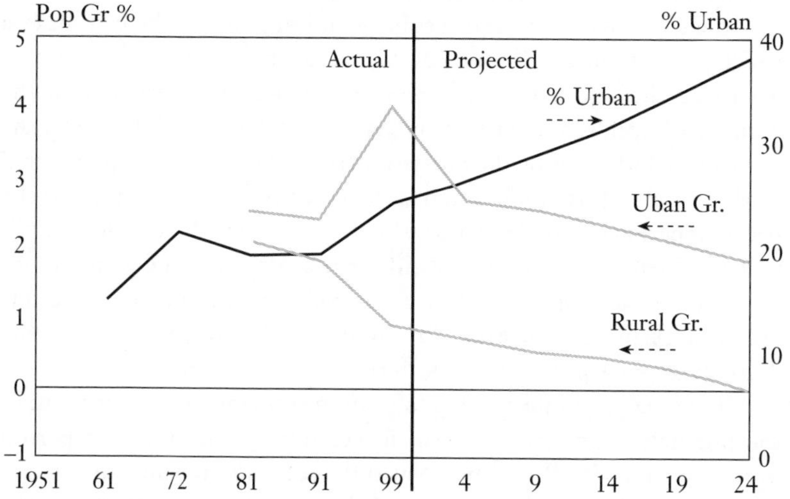

SOURCE: Tables 11.1, 11.7 and UN 2001.

associated with the main cities of Hanoi and Hai Phong. The lowest levels of urbanization are found in the North Central Coast and several provinces in the Northeast.

Sources of Growth: Decomposition of Urban Growth

Because of changes in urban boundaries and classification criteria over the decade 1989–99, and also because of our inability to identify specific urban areas from the 3 per cent sample data, it is not possible to fully analyze levels of urban growth. It is also not possible for us to adequately answer the fundamental policy question of the amount of urban growth that can be attributed to migration, the amount attributed to natural increase, and that amount of change which results from urban reclassification or urban boundary expansion. To adequately examine this issue we would need to match urban areas classified in 1989 and 1999, something that we are unable to do.

However, because of the importance of this question, we present a simplified decomposition that is based only on the 1999 census data. Population change for a fixed area can only result from natural increase—the balance of mortality and fertility—and migration. We can make a rough estimate of the amount of change in the population of an area occurring through natural increase over a five-year period from the number of children aged 0–4 in that particular area. These are the survivors of births during the five-year period.[6] The amount of population change resulting from migration is the number of net-migrants for the five-year period before the census. What we cannot include in the analysis is the influence of mortality at older ages. Although the assumptions required for the analysis result in a relatively crude estimate, the results are interesting and useful. In Figure 11.2, the outcome of the decomposition is provided for both rural and urban areas.

Our analysis indicates that migration contributed 34.7 per cent of the population growth in urban places during the five-year period preceding the 1999 census. Natural increase, at the same time, accounted for over 65.3 per cent of the growth. For rural areas, the situation is reversed. Natural increase contributed 111.4 per cent of rural population growth. However, migration helped to reduce the growth of rural population by over 11.4 per cent. The results indicate that if there has been no net loss of population through migration, the rural population of Vietnam could have increased by more than 11 per cent during the 1994–99 period. Indeed, rural-to-urban migration has contributed significantly to the lessening of population pressure in rural areas. Similar analyses undertaken for Ho Chi Minh City and Hanoi show that migration contributed 50.78 per cent of the growth in Ho Chi Minh City during the period 1994–99 and 35.64 per cent of the growth in Hanoi.

An alternative, and again somewhat crude, decomposition can be made based on information found in the population projections undertaken by the General Statistical Office (GSO 2000). It was estimated that during the period 1994–98 the urban population of Vietnam increased by 1.4 million as a result of reclassification of administrative units, i.e., 280,000 persons per year. If we assume that this level of reclassification existed over the period 1989–99, the proportion of the increase of 5,454,992 persons in the urban population over the same period that can be attributed to reclassification is 27 per cent. If we assume that the increase in urban growth due to migration for the period 1994–99 can be extrapolated for the period 1989–99, the contribution of migration to urban growth over the period would have been 32 per cent, a very similar estimate to the one obtained above. The remaining 41 per cent of urban growth is accounted for by natural increase of the population.

Migration

Definition
Recent migrants are defined here as persons who changed their place of residence (regions, provinces, and districts) within the five years preceding the census date. Only persons aged five years or over are considered in the analysis. Inter-regional migrants are migrants whose last place of previous residence was in a different region from their current region of residence. Inter-provincial migrants are those whose last place of previous residence was in a different province from their province of residence. Likewise, intra-provincial migrants are movers whose last place of previous residence was in a different district (commune/ward) from their district (commune/ward) of residence at the census date.

Levels and patterns of migration
Overall, during the five years preceding the 1999 census, 4.5 million people over five years of age changed their place of residence (rural commune or urban ward) in Vietnam. These people constituted 6.5 per cent of the total population aged five and over. Among these migrants, 55 per cent (i.e, 3.6 per cent of the population) moved within a province, and 45 per cent (2.9 per cent of the population) moved across provincial boundaries within Vietnam.

It is noteworthy that the majority of those who had migrated between provinces also moved between regions, which predominantly involves long distances and is associated with changes in work place and other labor market attributes such as income and work status. More than two-thirds (67 per cent) of the migrants who crossed provincial boundaries also crossed regional boundaries.

These patterns, however, did not characterize all regions to the same degree. The proportion of inter-provincial migrants to each region varied substantially. Because of their attractiveness as destinations, the Southeast and the Central Highlands had proportionately more inter-provincial migrants in their populations in 1999 than did any other region of Vietnam. Over 921,000 persons (8 per cent of the population of the Southeast) had moved there since 1994. The figure for the Central Highlands during the same period was 248,000 persons and that accounted for 9.5 per cent of its 1999 population. With abundant natural resources and cash crops, the Central Highlands attracted many in-migrants from other regions. The levels of migration for all other areas were similar and very small, ranging from 0.7 to 2.9 per cent (see Figure 11.3).

Characteristics of Migration Streams

Population movements can be broadly classified into four migration streams: rural-to-rural migration, rural-to-urban migration, urban-to-rural migration, and urban-to-urban migration. Analysis of migration streams helps in understanding the origin and destination of internal migrants and the underlying patterns of migration. The 1999 census data allow measurement of migration streams between rural and urban places. In the following analysis, migration streams include both intra-provincial and inter-provincial migration, excluding those who migrated from outside the country. Although all migrants were concentrated in the age group 20–4, the patterns show a very high concentration of young migrants in the rural-to-urban stream (see Figure 1.4).

As noted above, the 1999 census found that 4.3 million persons had moved during the census interval (and for whom data on the rural/urban status of origin is available). Of these, about 1.6 million moved from rural to rural areas, nearly 1.2 millions persons migrated from rural to urban places, 1.1 million from urban to urban, and about 422,000 individuals migrated from urban to rural places. About 27 per cent of the whole five-year migration took place between urban places. Indeed, the number of urban-to-urban migrants is almost as large as that of rural-to-urban migrants (1.13 and 1.18 millions persons respectively). Another striking feature is the major streams of rural-to-urban and urban-to-urban migration to major cities, especially to Ho Chi Minh City (over 867,000 persons). This movement is likely motivated by better employment and income opportunities, and better higher educational facilities in the urban centers.

Table 11.3 presents data on migration types and streams for Vietnam as a whole, for males and females, and for different lengths of migration. As in other developing countries with large rural populations, rural-to-

292

FIGURE 11.3   Decomposition of urban and rural population growth, 1994–99

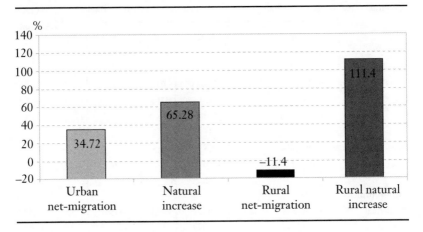

FIGURE 11.4   Percentage of migrants by areas, 1994–99

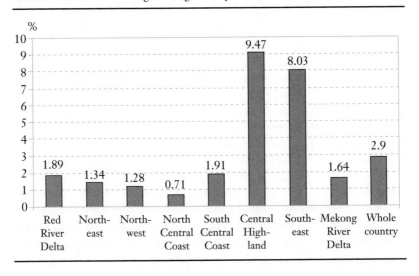

TABLE 11.3   Sex ratio of migration streams: Vietnam, 1994–99

Migration Streams	Male		Female		Total		Sex ratio (M/100F)
	N	%	N	%	N	%	
Population Age 5+							
Non-Migrant	31,614,357	94.0	32,878,954	93.4	64,493,309	93.7	96.2
Urban	6,897,037	(21.8)	7,174,570	(21.8)	14,071,607	(21.8)	96.1
Rural	24,717,319	(78.2)	25,704,383	(78.2)	50,421,702	(78.2)	96.2
Intra-Prov. Migrant	1,042,816	3.1	1,354,008	3.8	2,396,824	3.5	76.1
Inter-Prov. Migrant	975,604	2.9	978,575	2.8	1.954,179	2.8	99.7
Total Population	33,632,776		35,211,536		68,844,312	100.0	95.5
Intra-provincial							
Rural-rural	329884	31.6	515917	38.1	845801	35.3	63.94
Rural-urban	215746	20.7	259795	19.2	475541	19.8	83.04
Urban-rural	116168	11.1	125521	9.3	241689	10.1	92.55
Urban-urban	381018	36.5	452775	33.4	833793	34.8	84.15
All	1,042,816	100.0	1,354,008	100.0	2,396,824	100.0	77.02
Inter-provincial							
Rural-rural	381860	39.1	381362	39.0	763222	39.1	100.13
Rural-urban	336797	34.5	369949	37.8	706746	36.2	91.04
Urban-rural	102692	10.5	77571	7.9	180263	9.2	132.38
Urban-urban	154255	15.8	149693	15.3	303948	15.6	103.05
All	975,604	100.0	978,575	100.0	1,954,179	100.0	99.70

NOTE: Population ages 5 and over only.

rural movements were most frequent in terms of number of moves, accounting for over one-third of all moves reported by the census. Rural-to-urban and urban-to-urban streams each represented 26–7 per cent of all migration. In addition, more females than males are represented in these streams. When combined, these two streams of urban ward migration accounted for about 54 per cent (2.3 million persons) of all recent migrants.[7] The results indicate the importance of migration to urban areas in Vietnam. Major urban places are not only economically efficient locations for producing and distributing a wide range of services, they also provide the highest returns for those with higher education and skills. Because of the different sizes of the rural and urban populations, with the vast majority of the population being rural, the demographic impact of migration on urban areas is much greater than for rural areas.

Another important stream, often overlooked in migration studies, is the urban-to-rural-stream. This stream accounted for approximately 9 per cent of all movement. As a substantial percentage of the stream was likely to have been return migration (IOS 1999), careful attention is warranted to such movement as a factor that affects the social and economic conditions in rural origins.

Table 11.3, above, also shows the sex composition of the recent migration flows. The figures indicate the dominance of female migrants in all intra-provincial (or short distance) migration streams. Here females outnumber males by about 300,000, or about 13 per cent of all short distance migrants. Beyond this, however, what is striking about numbers and percentages is the similarity of males and females in all other categories. There are slight male advantages in longer distance urban-to-rural and urban-to-urban moves, and slight female advantages in longer distance rural-to-urban, but these are less striking than the similarities. In Vietnam, women apparently move as easily as men.

The changes (or lack of them) in the sex composition of migration streams are clearly seen in Figure 11.5. Data from 1989 displayed in this figure are from published data (see CCSC 1991). In order to ensure comparability with the 1989 data, intra-district movement is not treated as migration in the 1999 data. The results demonstrate the major changes in inter-provincial migration that took place between 1984–89 and 1994–99: males declined slightly and females rose to near equality with males. There was little change in intra-provincial movement. The increases in levels of longer distance female migration are a result of related changes in the social and economic renovation in Vietnam over the last 15 years. It can be expected that these changes will continue and that, consequently, levels of female migration will increase further in the future.

Migration by Sex and Age
In most regions of the world, internal migrants are preponderantly young adults. Vietnam is no exception. Over half of all migrants (52 per cent) were less than 25 years old, and only 10.5 per cent were aged 45 years and older, compared to 48 and 20 per cent, respectively, of the non-migrant population. Figures 6 and 7 present the age-sex specific migration rates for both intra-provincial and inter-provincial movements. The

295

FIGURE 11.5   Age specific migration rate of migration stream, 1994–99

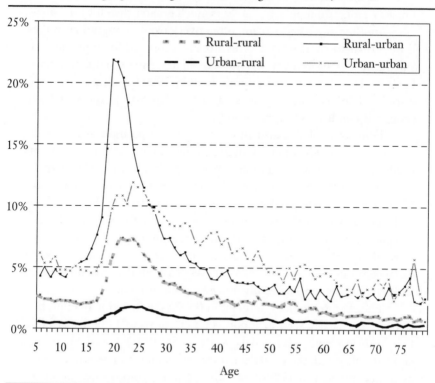

typical skewed bell-shaped distribution of migration by age is also observed for Vietnam.

These figures further display the sex differences seen in Table 3, above. The dominance of females in intra-provincial migration clearly comes from the age 20–30 group. Moreover, the lack of sex differences in inter-provincial migration is seen here in the dominance of both young males and females in the longer distance stream.

Migration by Marriage Patterns

Migrants and non-migrants differ with respect to marital status. Although relatively more married persons than single persons were recent migrants, the single males exceeded females in longer distance migration. The proportion of inter-provincial migrants is considerably higher among

FIGURE 11.6   Percentage of population migrating by type of migration and sex, 1984–89 and 1994–99

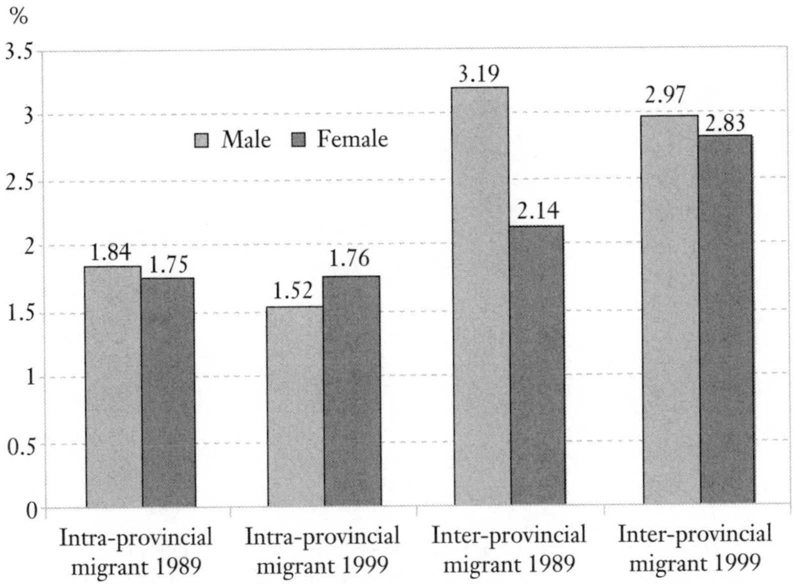

%

NOTE: Intra district migrants are treated as non-migrants.

single males than among the married. The proportion is almost equal between single males and females who moved between provinces (4.9 and 4.7 per cent, respectively). There is a relatively higher proportion of the currently married women (5.1 per cent) than single women (3.7 per cent) undertaking intra-provincial migration. These differences strongly indicate that being married is associated with shorter distance migration, probably because a considerable part of the movement is related to the relocation to new places following marriage.

Although the widowed, divorced, and separated comprise a very small share of the Vietnamese population, the pattern of their movement is distinctive. Widowed persons, both male and female, had among the lowest migration rates, while the divorced/separated had some of the highest rates. This is true both for inter-provincial and intra-provincial migration. Divorced males experienced the highest rate of intra-provincial migration (5.3 per cent), with the dissolution of the marriage likely to be responsible

297

FIGURE 11.7 Age specific intra-provincial migration rate by sex, 1994–99

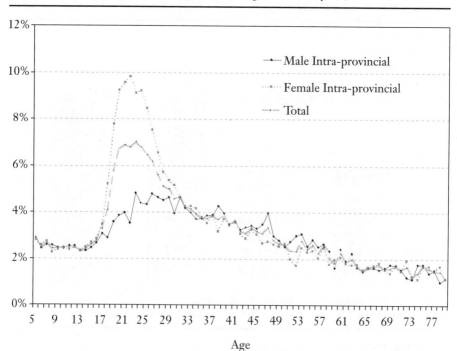

for many of these moves. This may reflect two different migrant patterns. Since we do not have data on the time of movement or divorce, we cannot speculate on the causal direction. It is equally possible that migration and separation lead to divorce, and that divorce leads to migration.

Migration by Education

In general, women showed the same patterns as men in the relationship between migration and education. Migration rates were very low among people with no or little education. As the level of education increases, the proportion of migrants, both inter-provincial and intra-provincial, rises. Completed secondary school marks a threshold in migration patterns. More than one in every five persons with a secondary school education (21 per cent) migrated in the five years before the census. For persons with university/college or higher level of education, migration was even more prevalent. The mean number of years of schooling was highest for inter-provincial migrants (8.2 years) compared with that of intra-provincial migrants (7.8 years) and non-migrants (5.9 years) (data not shown). Differentials in migration by education appear to be somewhat greater for intra-provincial than for inter-provincial migration, suggesting that much of the migration in search of educational opportunities occurs within provinces.

Migration by Occupation

Table 11.4 shows that considerable variation in migration status by occupation is noticeable. The highest proportion of non-migrants is found working in agriculture/forestry/fishery. This reflects the nature of work and the lack of opportunities for employment in agriculture. At the other extreme, migrants comprise a larger proportion of workers in the industrial and construction sector. Of these workers, 15.9 per cent were classified as five-year migrants, with over one-half of these migrants having moved between provinces. This was greater than for commerce and service workers, of whom 12.3 per cent were migrants, mainly moving within provincial boundaries. As the economy develops a shift from agricultural to other occupations, industrial and service occupations especially will fuel migration in Vietnam.

A System of Cities: Distribution of Urban Population by City-size Categories

Tables 11.5 and 11.6 show the growth of cities of different sizes, and the growth of the country's eight largest cities. We see first an increase in the number and share of the urban population in the largest cities, over one million: Ho Chi Minh City and Hanoi. But we also see a substantial growth in the number of cities and the proportion of urban population in the smaller towns (under 20,000) as well. Table 11.6 shows the growth of Vietnam's eight largest cities. Here, we have included index numbers, with 100 as the 1979 population. The index number is also shown for all Vietnamese urban population. Here, we see that from 1979 to 1986 the larger cities grew at roughly the same rate as the overall urban population. While the overall urban population grew by 128 per cent, most cities fell in the range of 120 to 133 per cent. The two exceptions were Hue (150) and Bienhoa (152). By 1997, however, the situation had changed

TABLE 11.4 Percentage distribution of main occupation in the last 12 months by sex and migrant status: Vietnam, Census 1999

Main occupation	Migrant status							
	Non-migrant		Intra-provincial migrant		Inter-provincial migrant		Total	
	N	%	N	%	N	%	N	%
Total	50541804	92.9	2111236	3.9	1759050	3.2	54412090	100.0
Student, unemployed housework	16667736	92.5	719186	4.0	633489	3.5	18020411	100.0
Agriculture/forestry/ fishery	24389380	96.1	531368	2.1	446831	1.8	25367579	100.0
Industry/construction	3710809	84.1	308758	7.0	391623	8.9	4411190	100.0
Commerce/services	4180926	87.7	362989	7.6	222149	4.7	4766064	100.0
Health/education science/art	1212434	86.3	143437	10.2	48506	3.5	1404377	100.0
National defense/ security	380519	86.0	45498	10.3	16452	3.7	442469	100.0

NOTE: Population ages 13 and over only.

remarkably. The total urban population grew by 186 per cent over 1979, while all of the eight largest cities grew at lower rates (124–62 per cent). Thus, it seems that there may be a more balanced growth, with cities of all sizes growing rapidly, with no major concentration in only the largest cities

There may be a substantial error, however, in this analysis, if suburban growth around the largest cities is not counted as part of those conurbations. In the future, we must examine these larger conurbations, as standard metropolitan statistical areas, to understand more fully the degree of urban concentration that is occurring.

TABLE 11.5   Number of cities and towns by population category, 1979, 1989, and 1997*, showing % of the urban population in each category

No. of Population (1000)	1979		1989		1997*	
	No.	% of urban pop	No.	% of urban pop	No.	% of urban pop
1000+	1	26.7	1	22.8	2	30
500–<1000	1	8.9	1	7.7	1	3.7
200–<500	2	6.9	6	13.6	5	9.6
100–<200	11	16.0	12	12.2	16	13.8
50–<100	18	12.6	18	10.0	28	11.9
20–<50	21	7.1	24	6.4	23	4.8
<20		21.8		27.3		26.2

SOURCES: GSO 1991: Detailed Analysis of Sample Results, p. 39. Ministry of Construction 1999: Guidelines on Master Planning of Urban Development in Vietnam Toward 2020, pp. 81–89.

Projection

A projection for the urban population should take into account the population changing as a result of reclassification of administrative units in addition to the three components of fertility, mortality, and migration. As mentioned above, each year there are 280,000 people who change their status from rural to urban residents. In recent years, many towns that are the center of state-agricultural enterprises have been disintegrated. Residents who are living in these towns become registered as rural residents. Taking into account this factor, there are only 150,000 people who change their status from rural to urban residents each year.

Based on two sources of data, provided above, a projection of the urban population in Vietnam is done with two variants: (1) assuming that urban population increase due to reclassification will be about 150,000 per year; (2) assuming that urban population increase due to reclassification will be about 280,000 per year.

In addition, projection will be different depending on the variants of assuming future fertility trends. In this paper, we provide results estimated by the VIE/97/P14 Project using a medium variant of fertility

TABLE 11.6   Urban population of cities and towns of more than 200,000 inhabitants, 1979, 1989, and 1997 (population unit: thousand)

City	1979*	1989*	1997**
Ho Chi Minh City	2,633	3,1169	3,252
Index	100	120	124
Hanoi	821	1,089	1,151
Index	100	133	140
Haiphong	343	456	540
Index	100	133	157
Danang	294	371	476
Index	100	126	162
Bienhoa	180	274	291
Index	100	152	162
Nhatrang	167	214	216
Index	100	128	129
Hue	141	211	215
Index	100	150	152
Cantho	178	208	220
Index	100	117	124
All Vietnam Urban	10,094	12.880	18,805
Index	100	128	186

* GSO 1991: Detailed Analysis of Sample Results, p. 39.
** Ministry of Construction 1999; Guidelines on Master Planning of Urban Development in Vietnam Toward 2020, pp. 81-89.

(TFR) for urban areas: 2.15 in 1999–2004; 2.00 in 2004–9; 1.95 in 2009–14; 1.90 in 2014–19 and 2019–24. The result is presented in Table 11.7 (see GSO, VIE/97/P14, 16 and 41).

Although the percentage of urban population increased following this projection, the growth rate of the urban population will decline as a result of projected declines in all three components: TFR, net migration rate, and growth rate resulting from reclassification (see GSO, VIE/97/P14, 43).

TABLE 11.7 Urban population projections, medium fertility variant, and two assumptions of reclassification

Year	1st assumption of reclassification			2nd assumption of reclassification		
	Number (1000)	Percent (%)	Growth rate (%)	Number (1000)	Percentage (%)	Growth rate (%)
1999	17918.2	23.5		17918.2	23.5	
2004	20494.9	25.4	2.69	21158.0	26.2	3.32
2009	23265.6	27.2	2.54	24627.9	28.8	3.04
2014	26136.2	28.9	2.33	28231.4	31.2	2.73
2019	28994.9	30.5	2.08	31851.0	33.5	2.41
2024	31757.1	32.1	1.82	35386.4	35.8	2.11

SOURCE: GSO, VIE/97/P14 Project 2000, p. 41.

URBAN-RURAL DIFFERENCES

Demographic Characteristics

Table 11.8 presents the percentage distribution of some demographic characteristics for urban and rural areas. Overall urbanization is associated with slightly smaller households. The modal household size in both urban and rural areas is four persons. The second most frequent household size is five for rural areas and three for urban areas. Mean household size is 4.36 for urban areas and 4.56 for rural areas. The percent of households with five or fewer persons in urban areas is slightly higher than in rural areas (77.6 vs. 72.4). However, an exception to this pattern is found for the most highly urbanized provinces, where the percent of households with six or more persons is higher in urban than in rural areas (23.9 per cent compared to 20.6 per cent—results not shown here). A possible reason is that in highly urbanized areas, such as Ho Chi Minh City and Hanoi, the housing market is very tight and some families have to share houses.

According to the censuses of 1979 and 1989, Vietnam had among the lowest sex ratios of any country in the world. One of the reasons for the low sex ratio in Vietnam is that significant numbers of men died during the wars for independence from the 1940s to 1975. In recent

TABLE 11.8 Percentage distribution of demographic characteristics (%)

Characteristics	Rural	Urban
Household size		
1	4.2	4.7
2	8.8	10.1
3	15.9	20.5
4	23.9	26.4
5	19.6	16.2
6	13.1	9.5
7	7.3	5.2
8	4.2	3.5
9	1.5	1.5
10	1.5	2.4
Mean	4.56	4.36
Sex ratio (M/100F)		
Total		
96.9		
96.1		
0–4	108.4	109.7
5–9	106.7	110.6
10–14	106.5	110.2
15–19	101.1	99.4
20–24	94.8	92.8
25–29	100.4	96.4
30–34	100.8	93.9
35–39	94.6	95.1
40–44	89.4	93.8
45–49	90.5	87.5
50–54	82.9	81.1
55–59	75.9	86.5
60–64	77.7	80.3
65–69	79.8	83.6
70+	61.5	62.2

TABLE 11.8 (cont'd)

Percent never married	Male	Female	Male	Female
Total	35.2	29.0	40.0	33.3
10–14	99.8	99.7	99.9	99.8
15–19	97.4	89.6	98.8	94.7
20–24	62.3	39.0	83.5	63.2
25–29	22.3	13.9	45.3	26.3
30–34	6.4	8.0	17.8	14.4
35–39	2.4	6.5	7.5	9.4
40–44	1.2	5.7	3.8	8.5
45–49	.8	5.1	2.1	7.6
50–54+	2.2	8.7	5.4	17.7
SMAM	**24.5**	**22.3**	**27.6**	**24.7**

years, the sex ratio has gradually become more balanced. In 1989, the overall sex ratio was 94.7; in 1999, it was 96.7. Due to the impact of war, the sex ratios for the age groups of those who were adults during the wars are lower than the sex ratios for the other age groups (Table 11.9)

In general, the sex ratio for urban areas is similar to the sex ratio for rural areas (96.11 compared to 96.85). However, for some age groups, there is a clear difference. The rural male surplus is greater than the urban through ages 10–14, but the urban male surplus continues through ages 30–34, while the rural surplus becomes a deficit at ages 15–19. This reflects migration for work. At the older ages, the sex ratio for the age group 55–9 in urban areas is 86.5, whereas in rural areas it is 75.86. The possible reason is that a larger number of men in this age group from rural areas may have died in the war than from urban areas.

In Vietnam, as in most other societies, men marry at later ages than do women, and urban residents tend to marry at later ages than do rural residents. The singulate mean age at first marriage (SMAM) for urban residents is 27.6 for men and 24.7 for women, while SMAM for their rural counterparts is 24.5 and 22.3, respectively.

There are also differences between urban and rural areas in the marital status composition of the population. For example, the proportion of the population never married in rural areas is much lower than in urban areas. Differences between urban and rural areas in age-specific proportions never married are also clear (see Table 11.8). While 83.5 per

TABLE 11.9 Crude birth rates and total fertility fates for Vietnam, 1959-1999

Period	CBR	TFR
1959–64	43.9	6.39
1964–69	42.3	6.81
1969–74	38.8	6.45
1974–79	33.2	5.25
1979–84	33.5	4.70
1984–89	31.0	3.98
1989–94	27.4	3.27
1994–94	20.5	2.45
4/98–3/99	19.9	2.30

SOURCE: *Marriage, Fertility, and Mortality in Vietnam: Level, Trend and Differentials*, (Monograph). Statistical Publisher, Hanoi, 2001, p. 46.

cent of urban men in the age group 20–4 are never married, the figure for rural areas is only 62.3 per cent. The proportion never married for urban men in the age group 25–9 is twice that of rural areas (45.3 per cent compared to 22.3 per cent). Similar differences can be observed for women. This suggests the importance of features of urban living that act to delay marriage.

In most societies, there are clear differentials in fertility among urban and rural places. Data from the 1999 census (CSCC 2000) indicate that the crude birth rate (CBR) in 1999 (19.9 per 1,000) has declined considerably compared to 1989 (30.1 per 1,000) and that CBR for urban areas was 15.9 compared to 21.2 in rural areas. The difference is greater in less developed regions, such as in the Northwest (CBR for rural areas is twice that of urban areas) and the Central Highlands (CBR for rural areas is 1.5 times the figure for urban areas). In other regions, the differences in CBR between urban and rural areas were not great.

Comparisons of age-specific fertility rates (ASFR) and Total Fertility Rates (TFR) between urban and rural areas show clear differences. For young women, fertility is much lower in urban than in rural areas. Women in the age groups 20–4 and 25–9 play an important role in reducing the fertility level in urban areas to lower than the replacement level. Overall, the TFR for urban areas is 1.7 whereas for rural areas it is 2.6 (CCSC

TABLE 11.10 Changing age specific fertility* in urban and rural areas, 1989–1999

Age Group	Urban ASFR		Rural ASFR	
	1989	1999	1989	1999
15–19	19	14	38	33
20–24	126	93	217	181
25–29	147	106	229	146
30–34	99	73	117	44
35–39	50	34	117	44
40–44	19	13	59	20
45–49	4	2	17	7
TFR	2.2	1.7	4.3	2.6

*births per 1000 women in tha age category.
SOURCE: *Marriage, Fertility, and Mortality in Vietnam: Level, Trend and Differentials,* (Monograph). Statistical Publisher, Hanoi, 2001, p. 51.

2000). At the same time, both urban and rural fertility have declined remarkably since 1989. The urban TFR fell by 23 per cent (2.2 to 1.7) while rural TFR fell by 40 per cent (4.3 to 2.6). The rural urban gap was two children in 1989 and fell to one-half a child in 1999.

Completed family sizes for urban and rural areas are also different. In 1999, the mean number of children ever born (CEB) for women aged 45–9 in rural areas was 1.3 times that of women in urban areas (3.92 and 2.92, respectively). The CEB for younger age groups shows even more variation. For example, the rural-urban ratio of differences in CEB for age groups 40–4, 35–9, and 30–4 are 1.43, 1.43, and 1.48, respectively.

Socio-economic Characteristics

Dwelling conditions and facilities typically vary between urban and rural places. In Vietnam, where housing is generally available for all, the main issue is the quality of housing. Table 11.11 provides data on housing conditions in rural and urban areas for 1999. In general, the level of co-residence in households in urban areas is higher than that in rural ones; however, this difference is not great, with 7.7 per cent of urban households

TABLE 11.11 Percentage with specified housing characteristics by place of residence (%)

Characteristics	Rural	Urban
1. *Sharing house*	5.8	7.7
2. *Type of house*		
Permanent	8.8	26.6
Semi-permanent	48.7	53.7
Wood frame	15.9	8.4
Simple cottage	26.6	11.3
Total	100.0	100.0
3. *Housing area per head**		
a. **Not shared house**		
<4 m2	2.5	4.3
4–6	11.6	10.4
6–10	33.6	25.3
10+	44.5	51.3
b. Shared house	7.8	8.7
Mean (m²)	11.75	15.14
4. *Year of construction**		
Before 1976	19.2	26.4
1976-1986	19.6	16.7
1987-1992	23.1	21.8
1993-1997	29.0	27.1
1998-1999	9.1	8.0
5. *No electricity*	27.5	4.1
6. *Source of drinking water*		
Running water	2.0	47.0
Rain water	12.0	3.2
Other hygienic water	59.6	42.1
Other	26.5	7.7
7. *Type of toilet*		
Flush toilet	4.3	55.8
Suilabh toilet	.8	1.9
Simple toilet	76.4	33.8
No toilet	18.5	8.4
8. *Have a television set*	46.1	76.5

NOTE: *Applied to three types of housing: Permanent, semi-permanent, and wood frame with specified housing characteristics, by level of urbanization and place of residence.

308

sharing residences compared to only 5.8 per cent of rural households. The results indicate a tighter housing market in urban than in rural areas. The percentage of households living in permanent or semi-permanent housing is much higher in urban areas than in rural areas. The percentage of urban residents living in permanent houses is three times that of rural dwellers, while the percentage living in a simple cottage is only 11.3 per cent in urban areas compared to 26.6 per cent in rural areas.

Urban dwellers are not only more likely to live in more permanent housing than are rural dwellers, they also generally have more housing area per household.[8] On average, the dwelling area per person in urban areas is about one and a half times that of the countryside. This reflects both higher demand for space and better living conditions of the urban population compared with the rural population. Houses in rural areas are mainly one-story while urban residents often build houses with several stories. The percentage of urban residents living in households built before 1976 is relatively high (26.4 per cent), although not much higher than that in rural areas (19.2 per cent).

It is notable, however, that there is more polarization of indicators of housing quality in urban areas compared to rural areas. While urban households generally have more living space per person than do rural households, there is also a greater proportion of persons with access to very small areas of living space. This is especially pronounced in the most highly urbanized provinces, and reflects the competition for living space in these urban areas.

Perhaps the clearest difference between urban and rural living conditions is found when we examine access to basic facilities. Overall, 22 per cent of the population live in households that do not have electricity. However, this percentage is seven times higher in rural areas compared to urban areas (27.5 per cent vs. 4.1 per cent). The percentage of residents of urban areas living in households with running water is 23 times higher than that of rural residents (47 per cent vs. 2 per cent). It is notable that there remain 7.7 per cent of urban residents using unhygienic water sources, although this figure is dwarfed by the 26.5 per cent of rural residents using unhygienic sources of water (see Table 11.9, above).

Over one-half of urban households live in houses that have hygienic latrines such as septic tank and semi-septic tank (suilabh). This percentage is much higher than that of rural families (5.1 per cent). However, the percentage of urban households using rudimentary latrines (including

309

double septic tank or just simply dug holes) remains high (33.8 per cent). In particular, 8.4 per cent of urban households live in houses that have no latrine. This reflects the very low living standards of a segment of the urban population

The percentage of households having at least one television is an indicator of the material quality of life, but it also reflects a different style and mode of living and thinking between rural and urban residents. Access to a television provides information about lifestyles that can influence behavior. At the present, the percentage of urban residents living in households with a television is as almost twice as high as those in rural areas (76.5 per cent vs. 46.1 per cent).

Educational attainment is a basic indicator of development. Census data indicate considerable progress in education levels in Vietnam over the past decade. The percentage of the population who never attended school decreased from 18 per cent in 1989 to below 10 per cent in 1999 (CCSC 2000). The rate of illiteracy also decreased, and, although rural/urban differentials in literacy remain pronounced (see Figure 11.8), the gap between them has decreased with time. For the age group 10–14, the percent illiterate in rural areas is twice that as for urban centers. For the older age groups, the difference is even greater. The rural/urban differential is most obvious for females. The higher level of variation for female children between rural and urban areas is also seen for children in the age group 6–14 who never attended school or who have already dropped out of school. The percentage of urban children aged 6–14 who have dropped out is 5 per cent and that for those who never attended school is also 5 per cent. The respective percentages for rural areas are 7 and 7 per cent (CCSC 2000)

Education differentials can also be viewed from the aspect of the percentage of the population who attended specified levels in the school system or the percentage that have completed a certain school level. In general, urban residents have more opportunity than rural residents to attend school, especially at higher levels. For attendance at primary school, the difference between rural and urban areas is not substantial, but the difference is much larger at the secondary school level. The percentage attending secondary schools in urban areas is more than double that of rural areas. For the age group 18–19, the percentage attending the final level of secondary school in urban centers is 70 per cent and in rural areas is 50 per cent (CCSC 2000).

FIGURE 11.8   Age specific inter-provincial migration rate by sex: 1994–99

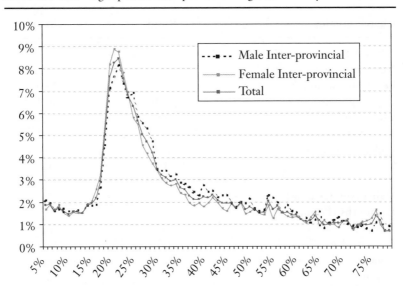

The percentage of the urban population who completed secondary school level is three times that of the rural population (20.2 per cent vs. 5.9 per cent). This indicates the advantage of cities as educational centers and is instrumental in attracting a "brain flow" from rural areas. The most substantial difference between urban and rural areas is the percentage that completed college, university or higher, with 6.3 per cent of the urban population age 10 or over graduating from college or higher compared to 0.9 per cent in rural areas. A significant factor in explaining the difference is the concentration of universities and colleges in urban areas (see Table 11.12). Many of these differences, of course, reflect migration patterns, as we have seen more educated rural people migrating to the urban areas, where they continue their education and thus increase the rural urban gap.

A comparison of economic activity status between rural and urban areas is presented in Table 11.12. The unemployed are defined here as persons who, during the year before the census, wanted to work but were not able to find work. The unemployment rate for those aged 13 years of age and above is 5.4 per cent in urban areas and 2.1 per cent in rural

TABLE 11.12 Urban rural educaitonal and occupational characteristics (%)

Characteristics	Rural			Urban		
Education (population 5+)						
Never attended	12.7			7.1		
Less than low primary	36.8			24.0		
< upper primary	37.9			30.4		
< secondary	5.8			11.9		
Secondary	5.9			20.2		
College/university	0.9			6.3		
Higher	0.0			0.2		
Main activities in last 12 months (Population 13+)						
Working	70.3			56.7		
Housework	6.3			11.3		
Student	12.1			16.2		
Invalid	3.2			2.7		
Unemployment demand for work	2.1			5.4		
Unemployment no demand for work	6.0			7.6		
Sector of work (Population 13+)	**M**	**F**	**Tot.**	**M**	**F**	**Tot.**
Government	5.1	4.8	5.1	26.4	27.3	27.0
Collective	29.1	36.1	32.8	5.2	6.6	5.8
Capital	0.5	0.3	0.4	2.0	1.7	1.9
Private	64.9	57.7	61.1	62.4	58.9	60.7
Mixed	0.3	0.4	0.3	3.0	3.5	3.3
Foreign	0.1	0.5	0.3	0.8	1.9	1.3

areas. These rates are 8.7 per cent and 2.9 per cent in terms of economically active population (according to the definition of the 1999 census). The difference in the unemployment rates in urban and rural areas is consistent for all age groups and both sexes. The higher level in urban areas may be attributed to a more strict definition of employment in cities, where employment focuses on earning a wage. For the whole country, the unemployment rate accounts for 3 per cent of the population or 4.2 per cent of the economically active population.

The working-age population can be divided into the economically active (employed and unemployed) and economically inactive. In

FIGURE 11.9   Percent illiterate by age and place of residence: total population and female population

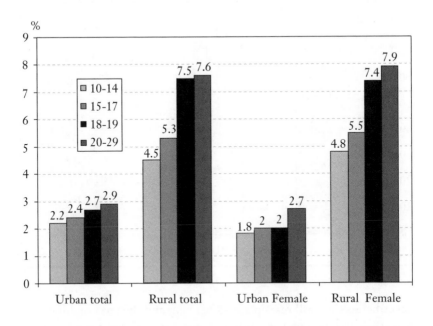

Figure 11.9, economic activity status is classified according to sex and urban-rural residence. There are large differences between urban and rural areas in the level of economic activities. Participation rates for both sexes in rural areas are higher than those in urban areas. Furthermore, the participation rate of males is higher than that of females in both urban and rural areas. Especially noteworthy is the differential of 18 percentage points between male and female participation rates in urban areas. A possible cause is the large number of urban women who are involved in home duties in urban areas, or the larger number of students in the urban areas.

Age is related to urban-rural differences in the unemployment rate (see Figure 11.10). High unemployment rates are found mainly for the young, particularly in urban areas. The unemployment rate of those aged 15–19 in urban areas is 25.8 per cent and of the 20–4 age group is 15.1 per cent. For the remaining age groups, unemployment rates are lower,

313

FIGURE 11.10   Economically active, by sex and place of residence

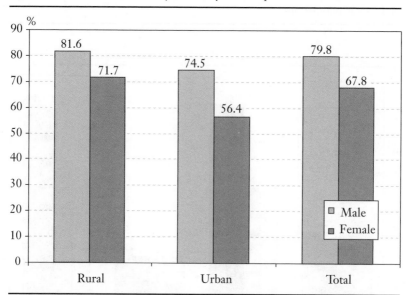

nevertheless they still remain at 4–5 per cent and the level of difference from the corresponding age groups in rural areas is about three times.

There is a significant difference in the structure of economic sectors between urban and rural areas (see Table 11.12). In urban areas, the state and private sector play the most important roles in employment. The proportion of the employed population in urban areas who work in the government sector is 27 per cent compared with 5.1 per cent in rural areas. The proportion employed in the private sector is 60.7 per cent, almost equal to the 61.1 per cent employed in this sector in rural areas. In rural areas, a significant proportion of the labor force works in the collective sector (32.8 per cent). In urban areas, the emergence of private and mixed economic sectors and 100 per cent foreign-invested establishments is also evident. Although the proportion of population engaging in these sectors and establishments is not high, the sectors employ a significant proportion of the urban labor force in the most highly urbanized provinces (9.5 per cent). Finally, with the exception of a substantial female dominance in rural collectives and male dominance in the rural private sector, there is little difference between men and women in their occupational distribution.

CONCLUSION AND IMPLICATIONS

Highlights

Unlike most of its Southeast Asian neighbors, Vietnam has experienced very low levels of urbanization. For decades, the government has discouraged rural-urban migration and actively organized rural resettlement. However, the rate of urbanization increased markedly during the 1990s, with 23.5 per cent of the population living in urban areas in April 1999, an increase from 19.4 per cent in 1989. The urban population is expected to grow more rapidly than the rural population over the next quarter of a century, when the level of urbanization is expected to be above 30 per cent.

The increasing level of urbanization observed in Vietnam during the 1990s is undoubtedly associated with the transformation in the economic and social fabric of Vietnamese society during that period. These changes included increases in levels of educational attainment, diversification of the occupational structure, and increasing spatial integration. The changes, which began with the economic reforms in 1986, have touched all areas of life.

The development efforts of Vietnam have focused on industrialization and urbanization, which makes it difficult to restrict migration to urban areas. Much of the foreign investment entering the country has been concentrated in the urban core and this has strengthened the *pull* factors attracting rural labor to the major cities. The growth of the service and informal sector continue to provide jobs for migrant workers. This process has had a profound impact on the urban cores of Hanoi and Ho Chi Minh City.

Although we cannot be precise about the various sources of urban growth, we assume that through the 1980s urban areas grew primarily by natural increase with net migration and reclassification playing minor roles. After 1990, however, overall national fertility declined rapidly, in part due to a successful national family planning program. From the 1990s therefore, it appears that net migration has played a more important role in increasing urbanization, though natural increase is still the major source of urban growth.

This increasing urban migration includes especially the young, better educated, and people not in the primary industrial sector. Short distance (intra-province) migration is dominated by young women; longer

315

distance migration (inter-province) is dominated by the young, both men and women.

Urban Benefits and Problems

Residents of urban areas have benefited from the uneven development. Urban residents have smaller family size, later marriages, better housing, greater access to amenities such as electricity and clean water, and better access to education and more skilled occupations. These urban advantages have become even more pronounced in the areas that are most highly urbanized. This makes the major cities more attractive. Without a change in current development trends, rapid urban growth of cities, such as Ho Chi Minh City and Hanoi, can be expected to continue.

However, it should also be noted that within the urban areas there are segments of the population who still do not have access to basic infrastructure such as toilet facilities and access to hygienic water supplies. Furthermore, in the most highly developed urban areas, especially Ho Chi Minh City, crowding and a tight housing market result in relatively high proportions of households sharing dwellings. There is a need to continue targeting poor and marginal populations in cities.

These results suggest that, although rapid urban growth in the largest cities and urban centers is a response to high levels of development and does generally lead to improved living standards, a small segment of the urban dwellers do not have opportunities to share in these benefits. The results of our analysis also indicate that the situation of large cities needs to be carefully monitored and addressed.

Government Policies

Despite the increasing scale of migration and the importance of its socio-economic and demographic impacts, migration is the least well-understood demographic process in Vietnam. The lack of reliable data on migration has forced program managers to make numerous assumptions when making policies on migration. For example, in policies and regulations regarding population and labor relocation, migrants have generally been seen as a homogeneous population with uniform needs, goals, and abilities, whereas the reality is that they are composed of people with heterogeneous characteristics. Government policy measures have therefore been designed without taking account of whether they are consistent with the individual goals of migrants. Consequently, macro policies aimed at creating socially optimal distribution between population and resources may not be consistent with, or may even conflict with, the desires of migrants and hence limit the success of the policies.

Although population size remains one of the central concerns of Vietnamese planners and policy-makers, the more recent policies of the government have been more oriented to the nature of migration process (see Nguyen 1998). Recognizing the spatial problems of regional disparities, the government policy of agriculture-based organized migration and new economic zone development has been the main government migration policy over the last three decades. Efforts in this area have met with some success but have also involved large financial costs (Population Council 1998). Unfortunately, urban ward migration has not been adequately placed in migration policies in Vietnam.

Rising under-employment, low incomes, and the lack of resources in rural areas continue to function as a push factor to stimulate out-migration. A lack of incentives for the growth of the private sector in the countryside makes it difficult for entrepreneurs to set up the labor-absorbing businesses and non-farming jobs that rural areas desperately need to absorb labor. In this situation, the government's efforts to invest in selected peripheral and rural poor areas certainly may not be effective enough to halt the pressure for out-migration.

However, providing the conditions that facilitate the growth of rural off-farm employment is important in reducing the pressure for migration of certain groups of the population, such as the young, more highly educated people. We can expect that rural development will further facilitate the movement of this group of the population as they do not have strong social ties to bind them to the rural areas, and opportunities for them are much greater in the urban areas. For unskilled or married persons, many of them have strong ties to their rural places of residences, and are seasonal migrants to earn a living in the major cities. Effective policies to promote rural off-farm employment will impact most on reducing the pressure for this population group to migrate to cities.

Levels of urbanization are increasing in Vietnam. Following *Doi Moi*, regional differences in income and opportunities have grown and the government's relaxation in granting residential permits has contributed to an increase in rural-urban migration. As documented in the present study, migration to major cities is increasing in Vietnam. However, urban growth per se is not a critical problem, as the population size is not necessarily correlated with the severity of its negative impacts. The key challenge is to manage city growth efficiently and in a sustainable way.

Realizing this situation, the government approved a guideline for urban management and development in 1998.[9] This guideline is based on the estimation that the urban population rate will increase from 24 per cent (present level) to 45 per cent in 2020, which implies that the rate of growth in urbanization would be approximately 3 per cent per year, a relatively rapid, but manageable, level of change. The guideline is the very first step in planning to manage and develop urban areas. However, within this plan, little attention has been paid to the consideration and provision of the social welfare of migrants. Policy should facilitate and accommodate migration rather than trying to regulate or plan population movements. In the years to come, it would be necessary to ensure migrants' access to the basic social, legal, and economic facilities available to non-migrant residents and their equal participation in credit, employment, and education and health services.

The migration and urbanization data collected in the 1999 census provides us with basic information on migration and urbanization in Vietnam. This information will be very useful in developing spatial plans and policies over the next decade. Future research needs to take into account the full range and types of mobility that is occurring in Vietnam, look at the impact of migration on the lives of migrants, their families and communities, and explore more fully the unknown social linkages that migration both depends on and further develops.

ENDNOTES

1   Sample size was determined on the basis of representation of each of the 61 provinces and major cities in Vietnam. Urban and rural areas were cross-classified as separate strata with a fixed number of enumeration sites from each strata. The census used a stratified cluster sampling design. Within each province, two clusters were selected with equal probability to represent rural and urban sites, which resulted in the selection of 122 area clusters. The sample has been weighted to ensure national representation. Because of the large differentials in sizes of populations and in sex ratios of enumeration areas, the weights are based on rural/urban as well as male/ female divisions. When applied to the data, the weights adjust the sample distribution to the distributions of Vietnamese population as obtained from the 1999 census. Complete details of sample design, selection, and the data coverage are provided in the census report (see CCSC 2000). Our analysis focuses primarily on the information aggregated from individual-level data.

2   These cities are Hanoi, Ho Chi Minh City, Da Nang, and Hai Phong.

3   The apparent discrepancy with the figures in Table 5 is due to the fact that some of the 83 provincial centers mentioned here have populations below 20,000.

4   The number of provinces changed from 1989 to 1999. Where a province in 1989 contained two 1999 provinces, the recorded 1989 level was assigned to both provinces.

5   Data collected by the two censuses show a population increase from 3,989,513 to 5,743,565 for urban Hanoi and Ho Chi Minh City combined (CCSC 1991; 2000).

6   We make the further assumption of no migration for the age group 0–4. Although migration does occur in the youngest age group, the low levels of mobility of the very young means that the amount of error that we introduce with this assumption is small.

7   The percentage may be underestimated as many persons who migrated to areas with urban characteristics but which were still classified as rural, were counted as rural ward migrants.

8   Information on housing area was collected for permanent, semi-permanent, and wood-frame houses only. Simple houses are not considered.

9   Decision 10/1998/QD-TTg, dated 23 January 1998.

CHAPTER 12

Four Countries: Cambodia, Laos, Myanmar and Nepal

GAYL D. NESS AND PREM P. TALWAR

Treating these four countries together in one brief chapter requires an explanation. It does not lie in country characteristics. Nepal is a landlocked mountainous *South* Asian Himalayan country abutting India on the south and Tibet and China on the north. Myanmar, Laos, and Cambodia are wet rice riverine ecosystems that lie in the heart of mainland *Southeast* Asia. In geography, landscape, and ecosystems they differ considerably. Yet we squeeze them together in one brief chapter.

There are two reasons which we hope will be acceptable. One is to keep the size of the overall manuscript more reasonable. Another 50 pages for each country would make this volume too large. More important, however, is that these are not only the poorest and least urbanized countries in Asia, they have also been wracked by internal and external turmoil, and they lack much of the basic physical and administrative infrastructure of a modern state. The major outcome of this for our study is the scarcity and weakness of data. Compared to the other countries in this volume, these have relatively little data and what they do produce is often of questionable validity.

Thus, for each country, we begin with United Nations (2001) estimates of the past 50 years and projected next 30 years of urbanization. This gives us the first table for each country. Where we have data from the countries themselves, we add these to the tables in bold type. Next, we attempt to say something about migration, and the system of cities, following the format of the other chapters. Finally, we describe urban-rural differences with whatever data the countries provide.

Let us first provide a broad statistical overview of the four countries. The basic data are shown in Table 12.1.

These are all small, poor countries. The three Southeast Asian countries total 63 million people, just over a tenth of the region's total. Nepal's 24 million are completely dwarfed by India, Pakistan, and Bangladesh. All four show very low measures of monetary wealth and their high infant mortality rates indicate a low level of human welfare as well. They all show very low levels of urbanization, even by regional standards. In 2000, South Asia was 30 per cent urban; Nepal was less than half that. Southeast Asia was 37 per cent urbanized; these three countries were all below that level. As we shall see, however, they are all moving ahead in urbanization.

TABLE 12.1   Size, population, wealth and welfare measures in cambodia, Laos, Myanmar and Nepal

Item	Cambodia	Laos	Myanmar	Nepal
Area (000 Sq Km)*	56	231	658	143
Pop 2000 (mill)+	11.2	6.2	45.6	23.9
Density (P/ sq.km)+	72	22	71	164
GNP/cap (2000) US$*	300	400	?	125
IMR (2000)+	83	97	92	83
% Urban**	16	24	28	12

* World Bank 2002.
** UN 1999.
+ UN 2000.

CAMBODIA

Cambodia is an ancient kingdom lying at the southern edge of the Southeast Asian mainland land mass. It was a great kingdom from the 9th to the 13th centuries, controlling much of mainland Southeast Asia and leaving behind the great monuments of Angkor. The mighty Mekong River flows through the eastern part of the country, but has a major impact through one of its tributaries, the Tonle Sap River. This meets the Mekong at Phon Penh, linking the mighty river to the shallow bowl of Central Cambodia. During the (summer) rainy season, this river flows from the Mekong to the central lake, the Tonle Sap, expanding that lake to four times its dry season size. In the dry season, the Tonle Sap river flows back into the Mekong, increasing its volume by draining the Tonle Sap. This Monsoonal variance regulated rice production in Central Cambodia, making it a rich land that could support a rich kingdom.

Cambodia succumbed to French imperial conquest in the 19th century, the vicissitudes of national independence movements, and the turmoil of the French and American Vietnamese wars from 1945 to 1975. After 1975, it experienced one of the bloodiest internal revolutions under the Khmer Rouge, which left more than a million dead. This was followed by a Vietnamese invasion and more turmoil. Today, as an independent kingdom with a constitutional monarchy, it attempts to build a new nation,

TABLE 12.2 Population growth and urbanization in Cambodia, 1950–2030

	Population			%	Ave. Ann Growth (%)		
Year	Total	Urban	Rural	Urban	Total	Urban	Rural
1950	4.3	0.44	3.86	10.2			
1955	4.8	0.50	4.30	10.2	2.33	2.73	2.14
1960	5.4	0.56	4.84	10.3	2.50	2.40	2.30
1965	6.1	0.66	5.44	10.8	2.59	3.57	2.33
1970	6.9	0.81	6.09	11.7	2.62	4.55	2.24
1975	7.1	0.73	6.37	10.3	0.58	-1.98	0.77
1980	6.5	0.80	5.70	12.4	-1.69	1.92	-2.23
1985	7.4	0.93	6.47	12.6	2.77	3.25	2.51
1990	8.7	1.09	7.61	12.6	3.51	3.44	3.17
1995	10	1.41	8.59	14.2	2.99	5.87	2.50
2000	11.2	1.78	9.42	15.9	2.49	5.25	1.83
2005	12.2	2.19	10.01	17.9	1.79	4.61	1.28
2010	13.3	2.68	10.62	20.2	1.80	4.47	1.09
2015	14.4	3.28	11.12	22.8	1.65	4.48	1.01
2020	15.5	3.99	11.51	25.6	1.53	4.33	0.78
2025	16.5	4.74	11.76	28.7	1.29	3.76	0.39
2030	17.4	5.54	11.86	31.9	1.09	3.38	0,09

SOURCE: UN 2001.

hoping for some measure of economic development and social welfare. While it remains largely rural and very poor, it is urbanizing rapidly, with all the social change, progress, and dislocation that implies.

Table 12.2 provides the basic data on population growth and urbanization in Cambodia from 1950 through projections to 2030.

For the first two decades, the country followed the path of all poor, less developed countries. Mortality fell, but fertility remained high, giving a period of rapid population growth, with rates of total population growth reaching 2.6 per cent. At first, through 1960, rural and urban growth rates were roughly equal. In the 1960s, rapid urbanization began and urban growth rates outpaced rural rates by 1 or 2 percentage points, implying urbanization growth rates up to twice that of rural areas. Then came the deluge of the Khmer Rouge; first emptying the cities to produce near 2 per cent *negative* urban growth rate, followed by an even larger absolute decline in the rural areas. The Cambodian "Holocaust" cost one or two million lives, though the UN estimates show only a 0.6 million decline between 1975 to 1980. Note, however, how quickly the society bounced back, at least in reproductive terms. Total growth rates rose quickly to nearly 3 per cent by 1980, and to 3.5 per cent in the next five years. Since 1990, the total growth rate has apparently slowed, and is projected to slow over the next three decades. But urbanization after the holocaust shows a higher and more sustained growth. From 1980–85, the urban growth rate was about 1 percentage point above the rural growth rate. Since then, though the urban growth rate declined slightly, it remains about 3 percentage points above, or more than twice the rural growth rate. Urbanization moves inexorably. The following charts make these changes dramatically clear.

Unfortunately, we have no further data to present on Cambodia. There will undoubtedly be studies and surveys that will illuminate some of the details of the coming changes. But the extent of the social destruction wreaked by the Khmer Rouge will certainly be felt for some years or decades to come. We cannot expect to find effective government, nor effective public data collection, for some time into the future. Thus, the current projections must be for the present the best guesses of what will happen in the future.

LAOS

Like Cambodia, Laos is also an ancient kingdom, Buddhist from at least the 8th century. It is Southeast Asia's only landlocked city. It is, however, traversed by the mighty Mekong River, which forms much of its border with Thailand. The river gives it a useful physical condition for trade and communication. Indeed, for all of its history, up to the past few years, the river was the only really effective means of communication. The ancient capital of Luang Prabang lies on the river, as does the modern capital, Vientiane.

Along the river and its broad valley, the Lao have lived for centuries as wet rice farmers. The highlands rising up to the east from the river, have been the ancient home of the Maung peoples, only recently relocated to the river valley for security reasons. Like Cambodia, Laos was embroiled in French Imperial thrusts, wars of independence, and the

FIGURE 12.1   Cambodian population growth and urbanization

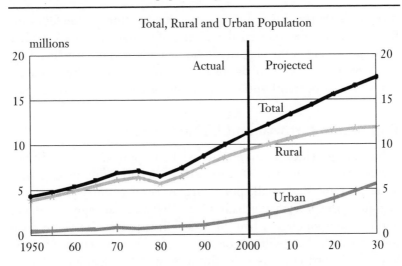

Total, Rural and Urban Population

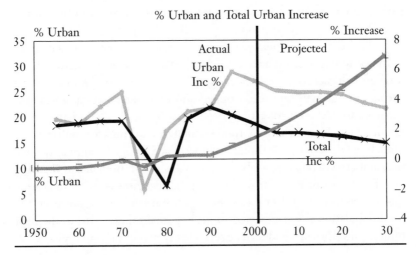

% Urban and Total Urban Increase

American Vietnam war. It remains a nominally Communist nation; the king having been deposed in 1962.

It is one of the poorest countries in Southeast Asia, as well as one of the most rural. At the same time, it is now experiencing the early transition to an urban society.

(N.B. In what follows we cite sources by table number in Laos 1997.)

Urban definition

A village is classified as an urban village if it has three of the following five conditions: a market, road, majority of households are electrified, tap water supply in the majority of households, and it must "lie in the municipality vicinity where the district or provincial authority is located" (Laos 1997). Apparently, other "obviously" urban areas are considered.

Population Growth and Urbanization

Table 12.3 provides the basic data on Laos' population growth and urbanization for the past 50 years, with projections for the next three decades. Laos is a small, poor, largely rural country that is just beginning the process of urbanization. Half a century ago, less than a tenth of the population lived in urban areas, and even those areas were more like large villages or small towns than the cities we could find in other parts of Asia. By the turn of the millennium, about a fifth of the population lived in urban areas. It is projected that in the next three decades that proportion will rise to just over 40 per cent.

The pattern of population growth rates is characteristic of a country in the early stages of urbanization. As mortality has been controlled, the total growth rate rose, peaking at over 3 per cent in 1985–90. In the past decade, the growth rate has dropped almost 1 percentage point and is expected to decline further to 1.65 per cent by 2030. The urban growth rate has been higher than the rural or total rate for the past half-century, often by a factor of two or three. It is now over 5.8 per cent annually, while the rural growth rate is probably less than 2 per cent. Both urban and rural growth rates are projected to decline over the next three decades. Indicating that the country is still in the early stages of urbanization, however, the rural population is not expected to decline in absolute terms in the near future. These broad trends can be seen clearly in the charts in Figure 12.2.

Migration

There are few data provided on migration. The Basic Statistics Report shows the proportion of the population considered migrants by province. Questions were asked in the census about the place of birth and place of current residence. These data showed that 81 per cent of the population currently lived in the district in which they were born. Only 19 per cent

TABLE 12.3   Population growth and urbanization in Laos

Year	Population (mill.)			% Urban	Ann Growth Rate (%)		
	Total	Urban	Rural		Total	Urban	Rural
1950	1.8	0.13	1.67	7.2			
1955	1.9	0.15	1.75	7.6	1.11	3.08	1.97
1960	2.2	0.17	2.03	7.9	3.16	2.67	2.18
1965	2.4	0.2	2.2	8.3	1.82	3.53	2.13
1970	2.7	0.26	2.44	9.6	2.50	6.0	1.9
1975	3	0.34	2.66	11.4	2.22	6.15	1.78
1975*	**2.9**						
1980	3.2	0.43	2.77	13.4	1.33	5.29	0.71
1980*	**3.2**						
1985	3.6	0.56	3.04	15.6	2.5	6.05	1.77
1985*	**3.6**						
1990	4.2	0.75	3.45	18.1	3.33	6.79	2.29
1990*	**4.1**						
1995	4.8	0.99	3.81	20.7	2.86	6.40	2.14
1995*	**4.6**	**0.78**	**3.79**	**17.1**			
2000	5.4	1.28	4.12	23.5	2.50	5.86	1.88
2000*	**5.2**						
2005	6.2	1.63	4.57	26.4	2.96	5.47	1.72
2010	6.7	2.06	4.94	29.5	2.58	5.28	1.6
2015	7.8	2.57	5.23	32.7	2.29	4.95	1.45
2020	8.8	3.15	5.65	36	2.56	4.51	1.2
2025	9.7	3.79	5.91	39.3	2.05	4.06	0.88
2030	10.5	4.47	6.03	42.6	1.65	3.59	0.53

SOURCE: UN 2001; * Laos 1997.

of the people currently lived in a district in which they were not born. This percentage varies considerably, however. The highest proportion of migrants are found in the Vientiane Municipality and Xaysomboon Special Region adjacent to Vientiane (both 44 per cent) and Vientiane Province (28 per cent). This implies that of the 385,000 people in larger Vientiane some 162,000, or 42 per cent, were not born in the city. Other provinces showed much lower levels of in-migration, ranging from 7.8 per cent to 42.7 per cent. These differences did not follow the pattern of

FIGURE 12.2   Population growth and urbanization in Laos

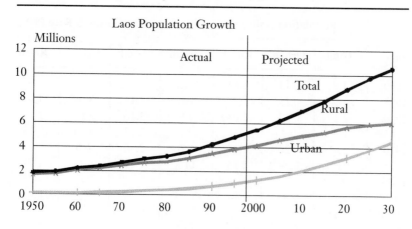

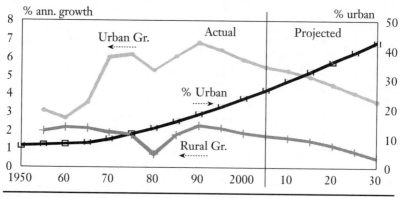

urbanization. For example, the five most urbanized provinces had an average of 18.8 per cent in-migrants; and the five least urbanized provinces had an average of 18.9 per cent in-migrants (Laos 1997, Table 2.4).

A System of Cities

This would better be titled a system of towns, since, as we shall see shortly, even the largest city, Vientiane, retains many rural characteristics which make it more like a large town than a city.

TABLE 12.4 Population and proportion of urban population in Laos five largest towns

City	Population	% of Urban	Cu % Urban	% Total	Cu % Total
Vientiane	385,470	49	49	8.4	8.4
Savanakhet	100,278	13	62	2.2	10.6
Luang Prabang	71,353	9	71	1.6	12.2
Champasek	64,463	8	79	1.4	13.6
Thakhek	36,605	5	83	0.8	14.4
Salakhan	21,110	3	86	0.5	14.9

Vientiane is the largest city in Laos. Its municipal boundaries have an estimated 331,000 *urban* residents, with perhaps another 55,000 living in suburban areas outside the municipal boundaries. But the municipal boundaries also contain another 193,309 people, about a third of the population, who are considered rural (see Table 12.4 for more details). The next largest town is Savanakhet, with an estimated population of 100,000. Below that there are only four more towns with populations greater than 20,000. Table 12.4 shows these six towns and their proportion of the total urban population

It must be noted that these numbers are estimates. The 1995 census report (Laos 1997) publishes a list of the country's 18 provinces with their total population and percent urban for each. These raw data are shown in Table 12.5. We have assigned the total urban population in each case to the largest town in that province. This may somewhat overestimate the size of these five cities, and overlook some smaller towns. We do not believe that the errors will be very large, however. The main point to be derived from these data is that Laos is a small, poor nation, in the very early stages of urbanization. Even its capital is more a larger town than a city. More than four-fifths of its (small) urban population lives in just five towns. And this urban population represents only about 15 per cent of the country's total population. Table 12.5 shows the details of the urban and rural population by provinces.

TABLE 12.5 Urban and rural population by province

Province	Population	Urban	% Urb	Rural	% Rural	Town > 20,000
Vient. Munic.*	524,107	330,798	63	193,309	37	Vientiane
Vient. Prov.*	286,564	50,065	18	246,499	82	Vientiane
Xaysomboon SR*	54,068	4,607	9	49,461	91	Vientiane
Phongsaly	152,848	8,658	6	144,190	94	-
Luangnamtha	114,741	19,621	17	95120	83	-
Oudomxay	210.207	31,678	15	178,529	85	Luang Prabang
Bokeo	113,612	5,870	5	107,742	95	-
Luang Prabang	364,840	39,675	11	325,165	89	Luang Prabang
Huaphanh	244,651	14,404	6	230,247	94	-
Xayaboury	291,764	21,110	7	270,654	93	Salakhan
Xiengkhuang	200,619	14,103	7	186,516	93	-
Borikhamxay	163,589	10,218	6	153,371	94	-
Khammuane	272,463	36,605	13	235,858	87	Thakhek
Savanakhet	671,758	100,278	15	571,480	85	Savanakhet
Saravane	256,231	16,073	7	240,158	93	-
Sekong	64,170	9,968	16	54,202	84	-
Champasek	501.387	64,463	13	436,924	87	Champasek
Attapeu	87,229	4,559	5	82,670	95	-
TOTAL	**4,574,848**	**787.753**	**17**	**3,792,095**	**83**	

SOURCE: Laos 1997 Table 2.2.
* Vientiane Municipality, Vientiane Province and Xaysomboon Special Region constitute greater Vientiane.

Urban-Rural Differences

The 1997 publication of census results provides a few sets of data from which we can see urban-rural differences. We summarize these here in five categories: industrial activity, household size and composition, physical living conditions, education, and fertility.

Industrial activity

Laos is still a land of subsistence agriculture, which employed some 83 per cent of the working-age population in 1995. There is, as would be expected, a substantial urban-rural difference in the agricultural proportion, with only 35 per cent in urban areas and 91 per cent in rural areas (Laos 1997, Table 5.7). What is striking here, of course, is that even in the urban areas more than a third of the working-age population is still engaged in subsistence agriculture.

Household size and composition

There is only a very small difference between rural and urban areas in household size: 5.9 for urban areas and 6.1 for rural areas (Laos 1997, Table 3.1). The great majority of households is headed by men, but there is a slight urban-rural difference. In urban areas, 15 per cent are headed by women; in rural areas it is only 10 per cent (Laos 1997, Table 3.2). Rapid urbanization normally produces the opposite; as men migrate to the towns for work, rural households are headed by women. We have no explanation for this difference.

Physical living conditions

Urban areas show substantially more physical amenities than do rural areas. These are summarized in the Table 12.6.

Urban dwellers have a clear advantage. They have better housing, better water supply, more electricity, and better sanitary facilities. The rural areas are still definitely isolated from modern amenities. At the same time, it is striking that even urban areas show substantial "rural" characteristics. The majority of urban houses are made of wood, as they are in rural areas; more than a fifth of urban houses are, like most rural houses, "semi permanent." Protected water supplies are more prevalent in urban areas, but still over 10 per cent of the urbanites take their water from the river; the majority of all people, urban and rural still cook with wood and charcoal; and even as many as one-quarter of urbanites have no toilet. This may be considered characteristic of the very early stages of urbanization in a very poor country.

Education

The report shows the percentage of the population over six by their school condition: no schooling, attending school, and having left school. Data are shown by rural and urban areas and by gender. Table 12.7 reports the figures.

331

TABLE 12.6 Urban and rural physical living conditions

House Constr.	Concrete	Wood + Conc.	Wood	Semi-Prem.
Urban	16%	15%	46%	22%
Rural	1%	2%	41%	55%

Water Source	Piped	Well	River
Urban	44%	42%	12%
Rural	1%	39%	60%

Electricity	Public	Own Gen./Batt.	None
Urban	84%	4%	21%
Rural	10%	5%	86%

Cooking Fuel	Elect	Wood + Charc.	Other
Urban	10%	85%	4%
Rural	0	99%	1%

Toilet Type	Mod./Normal	Dry/Other	None
Urban	56%	19%	25%
Rural	6%	15%	80%

SOURCES: In order of appearance: Laos 1997, Tables 8.2, 8.5, 8.4, 8.6, 8.7.
Totals may not add to 100% due to rounding, and other errors in publication.

TABLE 12.7 Educational activity of people over 6 years by gender and urban rural residence

	No Schooling %	Attending %	Left School %
Total			
Urban	14	35	52
Rural	43	23	34
Males			
Urban	9	38	53
Rural	32	27	41
Females			
Urban	19	32	50
Rural	53	19	27

SOURCE: Laos 1997, Table 4.1.

Urban people again have a clear advantage. Nearly half of all rural people report no schooling; that figure is only 14 per cent in urban areas. Whereas a third of urbanites are now attending school, less than a quarter of rural people now attend. There are also gender differences, with rural females being doubly disadvantaged. Only a tenth of the urban males but a fifth of the females have had no schooling. In rural areas, a third of the males and half of the females have had no schooling. Educational services are increasing, with relatively little gender difference in urban areas: just over a third of urban boys and just under a third of urban girls are now attending school, and for both boys and girls in urban areas about half have had some schooling but have now left school.

Fertility
The census report does not give much information on fertility (though there is more below in the section on projections). Table 6.2 (Laos 1997) provides information on the age of first birth for all women aged 15–49. The census asked of all women 15–49, first, if they had given birth. If the answer was "Yes," three more questions were added: "how many children were with you during the census night;" "how many children were elsewhere during the census night;" and how many children have died?" From the responses, four tables were produced. Table 6.1 (Laos 1997) showed the number of children born alive for each five-year age category by years of schooling. No urban-rural distinction is made. Table 6.2 (Laos 1997) shows the percent distribution of mother's age at first birth, for seven five-year age categories, for the total, urban, and rural populations. Table 6.3 (Laos 1997) shows the number of children currently living by seven five-year age categories of women. Finally, Table 6.4 (Laos 1997) shows the number of children (boys, girls, and total) born in the past 12 months by province, and by urban-rural residence. From these four tables, we can construct two tables, as follows. Table 12.8 shows the total women aged 15–49 and the percent distribution of the age at first birth for the total population, broken by urban and rural residence. Table 12.9 shows the urban-rural distribution of all boys and girls born, from which we can calculate the sex ratio, birth/married women of reproductive age (MWRA) ratio, and the Crude Birth Rate (CBR).

There is a substantial urban-rural difference here. Age of first birth is lower for rural than for urban women. One quarter of all women had their first birth before the age of 20; only 17 per cent of urban women had their first birth at that early age. It is reasonable to expect

TABLE 12.8   Age at first birth for women 15–49 years of age in 1995

All 15–49		Age at first birth %				
	% No Births	<15	15–19	20–24	25–30	>30
Total	1,054,588	34.3	0.2	25.6	29.4	8.3	2.2
Urban	198,874	42.8	0.1	17.2	29.0	9.0	1.9
Rural	855,714	32.3	0.2	27.6	29.5	8.1	2.3

SOURCE: Laos 1997, Table 6.2.

TABLE 12.9   Children born in 1995 by gender and residence, with calculations of various ratios

	Children Born 1995			Calculated Ratios			
	Total	Boys	Girls	Sex Ratio	(Women*)	Br/Woman	CBR
Total	120,300	61,022	59,278	103	(1,054,588)	114.1	25.3
Urban	15,264	7,187	7,447	105	(198,874)	76.8	19.4
Rural	105,036	53,205	51,831	103	(855,714)	122.7	27.7

SOURCE: Cols. 1–4 Table 6.4; other columns calculated; * age 15–49.

that increased education for women, rising age of marriage, and increased use of modern contraception are at work, but we cannot estimate the relative impact of the three. This table does not, of course, give us differences by time, but we can expect that fertility is declining; a higher age of first birth is probably more prevalent among younger than among older women. The UN data indicate that national fertility peaked at 6.69 in 1985–90 and has been declining since then. It is also likely that the increased age of first birth is greater in urban than in rural areas.

Table 12.9 shows us basic data on birth to woman ratios for 1995, from which we can calculate the CBR and sex ratios.

Urban fertility appears substantially lower than rural fertility in these calculations. Urban births per woman aged 15–49 are only 62 per cent of those for rural women. Similarly, the CBR in urban areas is only 70 per cent that in rural areas.

For all the differences, and some similarities in the above analyses of urban and rural conditions, it is clear that fertility is substantially lower in urban areas. It is likely to decline more rapidly in the future in urban areas, and will possibly spread to rural areas as well. The spread to rural areas will depend primarily on the extension of social services, especially education, health, and family planning. Given the deep poverty of Laos and the apparent weakness of government in providing social services, the rural fertility decline is likely to be rather slow.

Projections

The 1983 census report includes two projections to the year 2020. One assumes constant 1995 mortality and fertility levels, a second assumes both will decline. The constant fertility-mortality assumptions imply a Laotian population of 8.7 million in 2020; the declining fertility-mortality assumptions result in a population of only 7.7 million. The projections say nothing about the urban-rural distribution of the population. The report also recalls the 1985 projection, which proposed the 1995 population would be 4.8 million. That turned out to be an overestimate by about 225,000.

It is only in the "Projections" section of the report that we are given data on mortality and fertility. These are shown in Table 12.10.

MYANMAR

Another ancient kingdom, Myanmar is the primary avenue though which Theravada Buddhism entered Southeast Asia. It is also a kingdom with an especially bloody history of succession. This violent nature was exacerbated as Myanmar became the first of the mainland Southeast Asian nations to experience the West's imperial thrust. Abutting on British India, it is not surprising that Myanmar felt the pressure of British expansionism. Early in the 19th century, it lost control of its southern regions in a war with the British. This ended with the humiliating Treaty of Yandabo, 1823, which began a half-century process by which Myanmar would be deprived of its monarchy, and subjected to the influx of Indians who would become money-lenders, landlords, and a hated minority, whom the

TABLE 12.10   Select fertility and mortality assumptions

Measure	1995–2000	2000–2005	2005–2010	2010–2015	2015–2020
TFR	5.0	4.5	4.0	3.5	3.0
GRR	2.4	2.2	2.0	1.7	1.5
NRR	1.9	1.8	1.6	1.5	1.3
Life Expectancy					
Females	55	57	60	62	65
Males	51	54	56	59	61
Infant Mortality					
Girls	85	76	66	57	49
Boys	101	90	79	69	59
Both Sexes	94	83	73	63	54

SOURCE: 1997 report page 80.

Myanmarese would forcibly expel after independence in 1948. Myanmar's subjugation in 1823 also signaled to the Thai the dangers of resisting external incursions, leading King Mongkut to begin the long process of negotiations that would open the country to trade, but guarantee its continuing independence of foreign rule. Since independence, Myanmar has been ruled mostly by a military dictatorship that has despoiled the economy, and brought poverty and repression to the people.

Urban Definition

Neither the 1983 census nor the 1997 Statistical Yearbook, which reports on the 1983 census, provides a definition of urban. The census report does indicate that the census covered 314 townships, 288 towns, and 2,190 wards in what appear to indicate urban areas. In addition, there were 13,756 "Village Tracts," of which 12,814 were completely enumerated, and 112 partially enumerated. This leaves 830 village tracts that were excluded for security reasons. The estimated population of those excluded tracts was estimated at 1,183,005 in 1983. Again, the United Nations provides basic estimates of population and urban growth, see Table 12.11. Data published by Myanmar are shown in bold type.

TABLE 12.11   Population growth and urbanization in Myanmar

Year	Population (million) Total	Urban	Rural	% Urban	Ann Growth Rate (%) Total	Urban	Rural
1950	17.8	2.88	14.92	16.2			
	19.6	3.45	16.15	17.6	2.02	3.96	1.50
60	21.7	4.18	17.52	19.2	2.14	4.23	1.72
	24.2	5.07	19.13	21	2.3	4.26	1.67
70	27.1	6.12	20.98	22.8	2.4	4.14	1.82
1973	**28.9**						
	30.4	7.28	23.12	23.9	2.44	3.79	2.04
80	33.8	8.11	25.69	24	2.24	2.28	2.09
1983	**35.3**	**8.47**	**26.8**	**24**	**2.02**		
	37.5	9.02	28.48	24	2.19	2.24	2.08
90	40.5	9.98	30.52	24.6	1.6	2.13	1.36
	42.9	11.08	31.82	25.8	1.19	2.2	0.81
2000	45.6	12.63	32.97	27.7	1.26	2.8	0.73
	48.3	14.57	33.73	30.2	1.18	3.07	0.42
10	50.9	17.01	33.89	33.4	1.08	3.35	0.12
	53.5	19.66	33.84	36.7	1.02	3.12	−0.01
20	56	22.4	33.6	40	0.93	2.79	−0.19
	58.1	25.19	32.91	43.3	0.75	2.49	−0.38
30	60	27.96	32.04	46.6	0.65	2.2	−0.55

SOURCE: UN 1999; figures in bold are from the 1983 Census of Myanmar (Burma 1987), which excludes the tracts not enumerated.

Urbanization and Population Growth

The population of Myanmar rose from 17.8 million in 1950 to 45.6 million at the turn of the millennium, about a 150 per cent increase. Starting at about 2 per cent in 1950–55, the average annual growth rate rose to almost 2.5 per cent in the 1970s, then began a gradual decline to about 1.25 per cent in 2000. The growth rate is expected to continue its decline in the near future, to considerably less than 1 per cent.

Urbanization has increased steadily from just 16 per cent of the population in 1950 to about 28 per cent in 2000, and is expected to continue increasing for the next three decades. Even in 2030, however, the level of urbanization is not expected to be over 50 per cent. Urban

FIGURE 12.3   Population and urbanization in Myanmar

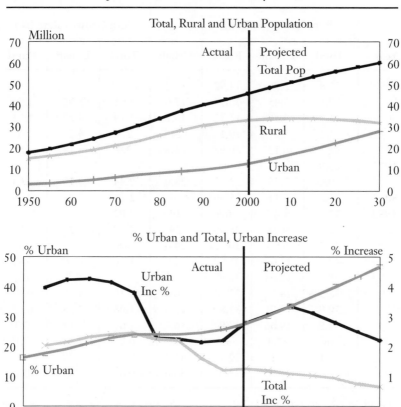

growth rates surpassed rural rates throughout this period and are expected to continue this superiority in the near future. The urban advantage has, however, varied over time. From 1950 to 1965, urban growth rates were about 2.5 percentage points higher than the rural rates. The advantage declined to only 0.19 percentage points in 1975–80, from which point it has grown rapidly to about 2 percentage points today. Moreover, it is expected to continue growing to over 3 percentage points, since the rural population is expected to begin an absolute decline in 2010–15.

This, then, can be called a special type of early urbanization. Urbanization will be slow and gradual, but we shall also see an absolute decline in the rural population in the near future. These patterns can be seen clearly in the following charts

Migration

The 1983 census says nothing about internal migration. The 1997 Statistical Yearbook (Myanmar CSO 1997) does, however, give data on international migration, reported by the Immigration and Population Department (Table 2.07). It lists, however, only international arrivals and departures, by Total, Air, Sea, and Land. The numbers are striking; even more are the sources of movement and their change over time. Most remarkable, however, from our perspective, is that a note in Table 2.07 says that these data refer to all visas except Tourist Visas. In a moment the exceptional character of this note will become clear. The data are given yearly from 1987 to 1996. In 1987, there were 20,920 arrivals and 26,270 departures, all of these by air. In 1988, the numbers were almost the same. In 1989, however, the total arrivals rose to 701,853 and departures to 852,307, the great majority of whom arrived and left by land. The number of arrivals rose in 1990 to 1.02 million, then to 1.5 million by 1994. In 1995, there was a substantial drop to 654,000, but then a rise the next year to 1.3 million. In all years, the great majority of this movement was by land. There is no official explanation for this substantial internal migration by land.

Tourism is another matter. We noted above that it is well known that Myanmar opened to the outside world substantially in the 1990s, promoting tourism and hotel construction especially in Rangoon and Mandalay. The 1997 Statistical Yearbook provides data on the extent of this opening. The basic data are shown in Table 12.12.

In 1988, there were severe disruptions, with mass demonstrations and highly repressive state reactions. This cut the tourist flow from about 40,000 in 1987–88 to less than 10,000 the next year. Tourist flow remained very low through 1991–92, then began a rapid increase to about 250,000 in 1996–97. When the tourist flow began to increase, it came almost equally by air into Rangoon airport and by land, especially over the border with Thailand near Chiang Mai.

This rapid influx of tourists was accompanied by a rapid development of hotels, especially in Rangoon and Mandalay. The 1997 Statistical Yearbook shows this development clearly, as we see in Table 12.13.

TABLE 12.12   Tourist arrivals in Myanmar, 1987–1997

Year	Total	By Air	By Sea and Land
1987–8	41,418	41,418	0
1988–9	9,963	9,963	0
1989–90	7,699	7,699	0
1990–91	8,806	8,406	360
1991–92	7,947	7,779	68
1992–93	22,363	11,510	10,853
1993–94	62,096	26,251	35,845
1994–95	95,616	47,230	48,386
1995–96	120,205	81,428	38,777
1996–97	248,225	110038	138,187

SOURCE: Myanmar 1997, Table 20.01, page 390.

TABLE 12.13   Tourist hotels and rooms, 1992–1996

Type + Location	1992		1996	
	Hotels	Rooms	Hotels	Rooms
Government				
Rangoon	8	497	1	30
Mandalay	15	455	9	313
Other	23	515	18	753
Private				
Rangoon	8	74	140	2,178
Mandalay	10	285	155	3,258
Other	1	85	107	1,519
Total				
Rangoon	16	571	141	2,208
Mandalay	25	740	164	3,571
Other	24	1,255	125	2,272

SOURCE: Myanmar 1997, Table 20.03

It is clear that Myanmar has experienced a boom in hotel building, especially in Rangoon and Mandalay. Moreover, this has been primarily a private boom. The number of government hotels has declined, though the number of rooms has increased slightly outside of Rangoon and Mandalay. The great boom has been in private hotels, which grew from 19 in 1992 to 402 in 1993, increasing their rooms by a factor of 15. The overwhelming majority of this development has been in Rangoon and Mandalay, though other towns, especially in the Shan State, have also seen substantial development. This analysis will provide support for the caveat offered below where we examine urban-rural differences in urbanization.

A System of Cities

The 1983 census provides population numbers for eight cities. These are shown in Table 12.14, with a calculation of their proportion of the total urban population.

This indicates a high degree of primacy, since the first city is about five times the size of the second, and the third city is less than half the size of the second. But there is something else here as well. The fifth through eighth of these "most populous cities" are all just over 100,000 in population. In effect, they are very small cities, or not much more than modest towns. But even the inclusion of these modest towns only includes less than half of the country's total urban population. This

TABLE 12.14   The eight largest cities in Myanmar

City	Population	% of Urban	Cu. % of Urban
Rangoon	2,513,023	29.68	29.68
Mandalay	532,949	6.29	35.97
Moulmein	219,961	2.60	38.57
Pegu	150,528	1.78	40.35
Bassein	144,096	1.70	42.05
Taunggyi	108,231	1.28	43.33
Sittwe	107,621	1.27	44.60
Monywa	106,846	1.26	45.86

SOURCE: Burma 1983, Map.

indicates a large number of very modest-sized urban areas. (This will help explain what we see later in examining urban-rural differences.) In fact, a map provided in the Myanmar Central Statistical Organization's Statistical Yearbook 1997 shows 55 cities and towns located throughout Myanmar, but especially along the main rivers and the coastal area. This is something of a paradox: a low overall level of urbanization is matched by a large number of small towns scattered throughout the countryside. There is urbanization everywhere, but it is low-level urbanization.

Table 12.15 shows the states or divisions with their total and urban populations and the percent urban. This helps to fill out the picture presented above.

What this table shows is a small but important level of urbanization throughout the country. The six least urbanized states or divisions have about 15 per cent of the population in "urban" areas, most of which have a handful of "towns." The rest, except Rangoon Division, are about one-fifth to one-quarter urbanized. There is some measure of urban organization throughout the country. But note that even the most urbanized division, Rangoon (a small area of 3,917 square miles, or only 1.5 per cent of the total area) still has a third of its urban population living in what are classed as rural areas.

We might call this widespread, limited urbanization.

TABLE 12.15   Population and urbanization by state or division

State/Div	Tot Pop (000)	Urb Pop (000)	% Urb	Major City/Towns**
1. Kachin	819.8	181.7	22.2	Myitkyina, Bhamo Putao, Sumpraban
2. Kayah	159.7	41.5	26.0	Loikaw
3. Karen	633.0	104.8	16.6	Pa An, Kwakareik
4. Chin	368.9	54.1	14.7	Haka, Falani, Mindat
5. Sagaing	3,825.2	529.7	13.8	Sagaing, Khamti, Mawlaik, Monywa, Shwebo

TABLE 12.15 (cont'd)

State/Div	Tot Pop (000)	Urb Pop (000)	% Urb	Major City/Towns**
6. Tenasserim	913.9	216.2	23.7	Dawei, Myeik, Tavoy (?)
7. Pegu	3,799.8	740.1	19.5	**Pegu** + (Prome), Letpadan, Pyay, Taungoo, Thayarwady
8. Magwe	3,243.2	493.7	15.2	Magwe, Minba, Pakokku, Thayetmyo, Yenangyoung, Chaulk(?)
9. Mandalay	4,577.8	1,214.4	26.5	**Mandalay + Monywa,** Kyankpadaung, Kyaukse, Meiktila, Myingyan, Ysamethin
10. Mon	1,680.2	473.1	28.2	**Moulmein,** Thaton
11. Rakhine	2,045.6	303.8	14.9	**Akyab (Sittwe)**, Kyaukphyu, Thondue
12. Rangoon	3,965.9	2,705.0	68.2	**Rangoon**, Hamwbi
13. Shan	3,090.3	658.65	21.3	**Taunggyi**, Kanlong, Loilem, Mongmet, Muse, Tachileik, Tengtauny
14. Irrawady	4,994.1	741.8	14.9	**Bassein (Pathein)**, Ma-U-Beo, Myaungmya, Pyapon
Total*	34,125.1	8,458.6	24.8	

* includes 7,710 listed as "Burmese nationals abroad."
** The eight "populous" cities listed in the map provided with the 1983 Census are in bold; other cities shown in the map for this section are in normal type. The division or state capital is underlined.
SOURCE: Burma 1983, Table 1; maps in Burma 1997 and 2001.

Urban-Rural Differences

Caveat

The latest population census from Myanmar is for 1983. As we have seen above, Myanmar has opened more to the world in the past decade, attracting visitors and engaging in a considerable building boom of new luxury hotels, especially in Rangoon and Mandalay. The 1983 census will have missed the impact of this development. As we examine past urban-rural differences, we shall speculate on which of these differences might have been affected by the developments of the past decade.

Housing

In conditions of house type, household structure, and sex ratio, there are only small or no differences between urban and rural areas. House types are shown in Table 12.16.

Myanmar is a poor country. Housing is somewhat better in urban than rural areas, but urban areas still have a majority of simple wood, bamboo, and thatch houses. This accords with the previous picture of widespread but simple urbanization. In the past decade, the urban advantage in "pucca" (or "proper," implying cement or cement block construction) houses may have increased, but it is unlikely that there has been a significant decline in the more modest houses.

In the structure and size of the household, there is little urban-rural difference. Eighty per cent of all households are headed by married males in both urban and rural areas (Census Table 5). The mean size of all households is 5.3 persons; urban 5.6 and rural 5.3 (Census Table 15).

TABLE 12.16 House type in urban and rural areas

	Total	Pucca + Semi P.	Wood	Wood Bamboo	+Other
Total N	6,365,521	206,591	944,402	3,442,159	1,772,369
Total %		3.2	14.8	54.1	27,9
Urban %		10.7	24.2	45.5	19.6
Rural %		1.4	12.5	56.2	29.9

* Pucca implies cement, cement blocks or brick.
SOURCE: Burma 1983, Table 3.

The overall sex ratio is 98.6 males per 100 females; in urban areas it is 99.1 and in rural areas 98.4 (census Table 6). There is little reason to expect changes in this condition over the past decade. With the urban building boom, one might expect a greater sex imbalance as more males leave rural areas to work in the towns. At the same time, Burmese women have always been active in the market place and have few restrictions on their movement. Thus, it is also likely that the rural women have joined the men in whatever movement to the towns there has been.

Reproductive Behavior

In reproductive behavior, there is a mixed pattern. First, the (singulate) age of marriage is increasing. From 1973 to 1983, it increased about one year for males, from 23.8 to 24.5, and changed only slightly for females, from 22.1 to 22.4 years. The urban ages were more than a year greater than the rural ages in both periods (Census Chapter 1, 19).

Fertility has declined as seen in the proportion of the population under 15 years of age, which fell from 42 per cent in 1973 to 39 per cent in 1983. There has also been a greater decline in urban areas (from 41 to 36 per cent) than in rural areas (from 42 to 40 per cent). In 1973, there was no difference between urban and rural areas; by 1983, the difference had increased to 4 percentage points (Census Chapter 1, 14).

The Total Fertility Rate is substantially lower in urban than in rural areas, 3.4 vs. 5.2 (Census Chapter 1, 37). At the same time, the numbers of children born to women aged 15–19 and 20–4 show no real urban (0.56 and 1.33) rural (0.55 and 1.39) difference. After age 25, however, rural numbers are about one-half child greater than in urban areas (Census Table 33). In effect, age of marriage and fertility are declining, especially

TABLE 12.17   Singulate mean age of marriage

	Total		Urban		Rural	
	1973	1983	1973	1983	1973	1983
Males	23.8	24.5	24.9	25.7	23.4	24.1
Females	21.2	22.4	21.9	23.3	21.0	22.1

SOURCE: Burma 1983, p. 2.

in urban areas, but the urban fertility decline appears to affect older women of somewhat higher parity. Urbanization and economic stress may be considered important factors in reducing fertility. Family planning services and contraceptive availability appear to be very weak, and abortion a widely used method of fertility control (PRB 2002).

Education

Although Myanmar has a long history of literacy and expanding educational services, it is striking that in 1983 there were substantial urban-rural differences in school attendance (Census Table 12). Characteristic for Southeast Asia, however, there is little gender difference in educational services. The reported proportion of age 6–11 attending school was 74 per cent for males and 72 per cent for females. For males, the urban-rural difference was 85 to 70 per cent; for females, it was 84 to 68 per cent. Rural areas are obviously not as well served by educational services as are urban areas. This may help explain the somewhat anomalous lack of urban-rural differences in household size. As we have

TABLE 12.18 Urban and rural age distributions

	1973			1983		
	Total	**Urban**	**Rural**	**Total**	**Urban**	**Rural**
<15 (%)	41.5	40.8	41.7	38.6	35.7	39.5
15–59 (%)	52.5	53.7	52.1	55.0	58.1	54.1
60+ (%)	6.0	5.5	6.2	6.4	6.2	6.4

SOURCE: Burma 1983, p. 14.

TABLE 12.19 Proportion (%) of 6–11 year olds attending school

	Total	**Urban**	**Rural**
Total	71	85	69
Males	74	85	70
Females	72	84	68

SOURCE: calculated from Burma 1983, Table 12.

seen in Thailand (Chanawongse 2000), it is common for rural children to live with friends and relatives in urban areas in order to further their education. It is most likely that the urban advantage will have increased in the past decade, as most of the development and, thus, social service expansion is likely to have been concentrated in urban areas, and especially in a few large cities like Rangoon and Mandalay.

Vital Statistics

The 1997 Statistical Yearbook of Myanmar notes that the present vital registration system was introduced to the urban areas in 1962, and, by 1996, it covered 255 towns with a total population of 10.4 million, representing 91 per cent of the urban population. The system was introduced to the rural areas in 1979, and, by 1996, covered 166 townships with a total population of 21.5 million, representing 63 per cent of the rural population. Some of these data are reported by urban and rural areas, which we show here in Table 12.20. For comparison, the UN estimates for the total population in the same year are shown in italics. The data show that Myanmar still has substantially high fertility rates, and a very high level of infant mortality compared with the rest of the region.

The Statistical Yearbook shows no change in urban or rural crude birth rate (CBR) and crude death rate (CDR) from 1977 to 1995 (1987–95 for rural areas). The infant mortality rate (IMR) shows a slight decline from 50.8 to 47.3 in urban areas and a slight increase in rural areas from

TABLE 12.20   Urban and rural vital rates for 1995

	CBR	**CDR**	**IMR**	**MMR***
Urban	28.0	8.6	47.3	1.0
Rural	30.1	9.9	49.7	1.8
UN Total	29.9	12.2	98	–

* Maternal mortality per 1000 live births.
SOURCE: Myanmar, 1997, Tables 4.01 and 4.02, pp. 56–57. The number of towns reporting is given as 170 (of 255 noted above); the number of rural townships reporting is given as 62 (of the 166 noted above). UN, World Population Prospects 2000.

TABLE 12.21 Life expectancy 1991 and 1995 for urban and rural males and females

	1991			1995		
	Total*	Urb	Rur	Total*	Urb	Rur
Myanmar Est.						
Males		59.6	59.1		60.4	59.9
Females		63.5	61.1		64.3	62.0
UN Est.						
Males	51.5			53.3		
Females	55.9			57.6		

* The UN figures are given for five year periods: 1985–90 and 1990-95; UN 2000. Other Data: Myanmar 1997, Tables 4.06 and 4.07, pp. 62–63.

47.1 (1987) to 49.7 (1995), though note that the UN estimates are considerably higher than the Myanmar estimates. With only 67 per cent of towns and 37 per cent of rural townships reporting, these figures can be expected to have large error margins. Moreover, it is most likely that conditions in the non-reporting areas are less healthy than those in the reporting areas, suggesting a substantial underestimate of the crude and infant death rates.

The yearbook also gives estimates of male and female life expectancy for urban and rural areas. As above, we report the national estimates in bold type here along with the UN estimates in italics.

The Myanmar figures show a four-year advantage for women over men in urban areas and a two-year advantage in rural areas. The urban-over-rural advantage for males is only one-half a year and for females it is just over two years. The progress made in five years shows 0.8 year for urban and rural males, and just over two years for both urban and rural females. The urban and gender advantages seem intuitively correct, though it is likely that the overall estimates may be a bit inflated. Again, UN estimates provide a less happy view of this measure of human welfare.

NEPAL

Nepal is another ancient kingdom, like Laos in being landlocked, and like Myanmar in being subjected to a long period of British imperialism. The heartland, around Katmandu, and the northern tier of the country are mountainous, presenting immense difficulties for transportation and resulting in extensive isolation of most parts of the country. The southern tier, the Terai, is less mountainous, sloping gently into the Ganges Plain. The heartland is strongly Buddhist, but the Terai is more influenced by the great Hindu neighbor to the south. Its mountainous geography makes it a poor and isolated country. Although urbanization has begun, it is still only in the very early stages.

Urban Definition

Nepal defines as urban, places of 20,000 or more with at least one million rupees in annual revenue and other urban facilities (Nepal 2000). As we shall see, this implies that some places of less than 20,000 will still be considered urban. Urban areas are further classified by size as: metropolitan (>300,000 population), sub-metropolitan (>100,000), and municipality (>20,000).

The basic data for Nepal are shown in Table 12.22. As before, these data are taken from UN 1999, with official Nepalese figures shown in bold where available. These Nepalese data are taken from the Ministry of Population and Environment (Nepal 2000). Unless otherwise noted, this is the source for Nepalese data presented throughout this section.

Urbanization and Population Growth

The picture is a common one for the less developed regions. The country began the second half of the last century overwhelmingly rural, poor, and with low population growth rates that reflected high mortality and fertility. Mortality began to fall while fertility remained high, giving a period of rising population growth rates, from just over 1 per cent per year to just over 2.5 per cent per year in 1990–95. Population growth rates then began a decline that is expected to continue into the near future. All this time, however, urbanization has been proceeding relatively rapidly. Urban growth rates have been from 2 to 5 percentage points

349

TABLE 12.22 Population growth and urbanization in Nepal

	Population (mill.)			% Urban	Ann Growth Rate (%)		
Year	Total	Urban	Rural		Total	Urban	Rural
1950	7.9	0.18	7.72	2.2			
1952–4	8.2	0.25	7.9	2.9			
1955	8.5	0.22	8.28	2.7	1.52	4.44	1.43
1960	9.3	0.29	9.01	3.1	1.88	6.36	1.68
1961	9.4	0.34	9.1	3.6	1.65	4.53	1.56
1965	10.2	0.36	9.84	3.5	1.94	4.83	1.97
1970	11.3	0.44	10.86	3.9	2.16	4.44	1.99
1971	11.6	0.46	11.13	4.0	2.07	3.23	2.03
1975	12.8	0.64	12.16	5	2.65	9.09	2.22
1980	14.5	0.95	13.55	6.5	2.66	9.69	2.17
1981	15.0	0.96	14.04	6.4	2.66	7.55	2.40
1985	16.5	1.28	15.22	7.8	2.76	6.95	2.33
1990	18.8	1.68	17.12	8.9	2.79	6.25	2.32
1991	18.5	1.70	16.80	9.2	2.10	5.89	1.79
1995	21.3	2.19	19.11	10.3	2.66	6.07	2.2
2000	23.9	2.84	21.06	11.9	2.44	5.94	2
2000	22.9				2.37		
2005	26.8	3.67	23.13	13.7	2.43	5.85	1.82
2010	29.7	4.68	25.02	15.8	2.16	5.50	1.61
2015	32.7	5.91	26.79	18.1	2.02	5.26	1.35
2020	35.5	7.34	28.16	20.7	1.71	4.84	1.02
2025	38	8.9	29.1	23.4	1.41	4.25	0.65
2030	40.3	10.64	29.66	26.4	1.21	3.91	0.41

SOURCE: UN 1999; figures in bold, Nepal 2000.

higher than total growth rates for the past half-century. In 1950, there were less than 200,000 urbanites in the country; by 2000, there were almost three million.

The broad patterns of population growth and urbanization are also seen in the following two figures.

Migration is reported between major regions—mountain, hill, and Terai—but not by urban and rural residence.

FIGURE 12.4   Urban and rural population growth in Nepal

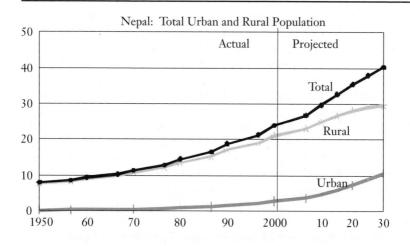

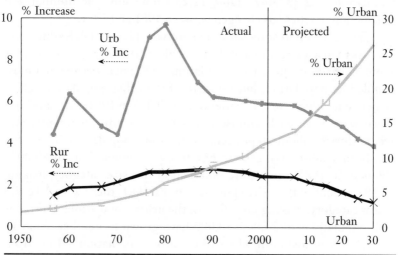

A System of Cities

Data on numbers ands sizes of cities are presented only for the period 1981–91.

TABLE 12.23 Changing distribution of cities in Nepal, 1982–1991

Size	1981				1991			
	No	Pop (000)	% Urb	CU % Urb	No	Pop (000)	% Urb	CU % Urb
Kathmandu	1	235	24.6	24.6	1	421	18.4	18.4
100K +	0	–	–	24.6	2	245	10.7	29.1
50-100K	2	173	18.1	42.6	8	517	22.6	51.7
20-50K	13	458	47.8	90.5	24	720	31.4	83.1
< 20K	7	91	9.5	100	24	386	16.9	100

SOURCE: Computed from Nepal 2000, Table 36 pp. 57–8.

In 1981, there were 23 "municipalities" or urban areas, with a total population of 956,721; by 1991, the number had grown to 58 with a total population of 2,287,487. Table 12.23 shows how the number and distribution of cities has changed between 1981 and 1991.

This is an interesting pattern of growth. The capital, Kathmandu, had less than a quarter of a million people in 1981, and accounted for about a quarter of the urban population. In the next decade, it almost doubled its population, but its share of the urban population fell to 18 per cent. There were no cities over 100,000 in 1981; a decade later there were two, with almost a quarter of a million people, and accounting for about 10 per cent of the urban population. There has also been a substantial growth of cities with populations of 50,000– 100,000. In 1981, there were only two in this size category, making up 18 per cent of the urban population. By 1981, there were 10 cities in this category, making up a third of the urban population. The cities with populations of 20,000–50,000 have grown in number, from 13 to 24, but have lost in the share of the urban population, falling from almost half to just a third. And the very smallest cities, with populations of less than 20,000, have tripled in number, grown four times in population numbers, and almost doubled their share of the urban population. That is, there has been a substantial growth in the medium-sized and very small towns.

Urban-Rural Differences

The 2000 census report provides urban-rural differences only for the total fertility rate. A 1987 (Nepal 1987) publication, however, of the 1986–87 Demographic Sample Survey, provides a wide array of these differentials. We shall begin with vital rates—fertility and mortality—and move on through marital status, age distributions, education, and literacy, and a brief statement on international migrants.

Vital Rates

Mortality has been declining steadily in Nepal since 1954, when the first estimates were made. The crude death rate (CDR) fell from 37 to 10.3 in 2000, while the infant mortality (IMR) rate fell from about 250 to 64 in 1999. Consequently, the life expectancy at birth rose from about 28 to 59 (MOPE 2000, 18–19). Urban-rural differences are reported only for IMR in 1986, and are shown in Table 12.24.

Fertility has also been falling, but only since the mid-1980s. The crude birth rate (CBR) fell from an estimated 46 in 1954 to 34.1 in 1999. The total fertility rate (TFR) is reported as 6.3 from 1971 through 1981. It declined to 6 in 1986 and to 4.6 in 1996. Urban-rural differences are reported for the last two periods, as shown in Table 12.24.

The recent timing of the fertility decline is evident form these data. As late as 1986, the rural-urban difference was only .38 children; by 1991, it was almost two children. The age of marriage is increasing (Table 25) and the national family planning program is spreading contraceptive knowledge and services widely. In 1976, only 21 per cent

TABLE 12.24 Selected vital rates for urban and rural areas

	TFR	**IMR**	
	1986**	**1986****	**1991***
Urban	5.70	2.90	78–80
Rural	6.08	4.80	113–115
Total	6.00	4.60	108

SOURCE: * Nepal 2000, p. 17; ** Nepal 1987, pp. 59 and 73.

of married women knew of some form of contraception; by 1986, it was 56 per cent; and, by 1996, it had risen to 98 per cent. Contraceptive prevalence also rose from 3 per cent in 1976 to 29 per cent in 1996. Urban-rural differences are not reported, but it is obvious that urban women are considerably advantaged, since their fertility dropped by almost three children from 1986–91; even rural women have been affected, however, as their fertility dropped by more than one child in that period.

Marital Status

As might be expected, urban dwellers show slightly higher proportions unmarried and a later age of first marriage than do their rural counterparts. Table 12.25 provides a summary of the extensive data reported from the 1986–87 survey.

Age Distribution and Sex Ratios

There is a surplus of the very young (<15) in the rural areas for both males and females, and a surplus of those of productive age in urban areas, again for both males and females. The differences are slightly larger for males than for females. There is very little difference between urban and rural areas in the proportion of the aged, but here the slight surplus is for males in rural areas and females in urban areas. The overall sex ratio is 106. This male advantage is characteristic of South Asian countries, where female status is exceptionally low. The urban-rural difference is substantial; with a larger male surplus in urban areas, and a much smaller

TABLE 12.25 Marital condition in urban and rural areas

Residence	Never Married %	Married %	Age of First Marriage %			
			<10	10–14	15–19	20–24
Urban	36	56	7.5	28.1	45.2	19.2
Rural	30	62	8.1	32.4	46.3	13.1
Total			8.1	32.2	46.2	13.5

SOURCE: Nepal 1987, pp. 39 and 48–50. Married refers to both males and females; age of first marriage refers to women above the age of 25.

TABLE 12.26 Age distributions and sex ratios

	Age Distribution %				Sex Ratio
	<15	**15–24**	**25–59**	**60+**	
Urban					115
Males	39.5	21.0	34.2	5.2	
Females	38.4	21.5	21.5	5.8	
Rural					104
Males	44.5	17.1	32.4	5.9	
Females	41.9	18.1	34.5	5.5	
Total					106

SOURCE: Nepal 1987, pp. 31 and 33. Sex ratio is from the 1981 census.

male surplus in rural areas. These data suggest a substantial migration to urban areas of people of productive age, with males showing higher rates of migration than females.

Education and Literacy

Urban dwellers are considerably advantaged over rural dwellers in both literacy and education. Two-thirds of urbanites over six are literate; the rural rate is just half that. In both urban and rural areas, males are considerably advantaged, but the gap is lower in urban areas. Urban female literacy is two-thirds that of males; rural female literacy is only one-third that of males. Nepal had obviously made considerable progress by 1986 in promoting education, especially for such a poor country. By 1986, two-thirds of the children were enrolled in primary school, and as many as a third were attending secondary school. Again, the urban and male advantages are clear. There is universal primary school attendance for urban males, and the great majority of urban females are also enrolled. In the rural areas, almost 80 per cent of males are enrolled in primary school, but the rate for girls is just half that. At all levels, the male-female gap is lower in the urban than in the rural areas. Table 12.27 summarizes the extensive data given in the report of the 1986–87 survey.

TABLE 12.27 Literacy and school enrollment in urban and rural areas

Residence	% Literate*	Enrollment Rates**		
		Primary	Low Sec	Sec
Urban	62.7	91.4	77.2	66.4
Males	77.7	101.4	79.2	79.8
Females	47.5	80.7	75.1	53.1
Rural	32.8	60.9	34.6	31.7
Males	49.9	78.5	49.6	49.0
Females	16.1	41.4	18.5	13.2
Total	34.8	62.7	37.2	34.0
Males	51.8	79.8	51.6	51.1
Females	18.0	43.7	21.7	15.9

SOURCE: Nepal 1987, pp 34 and 37. * percentage of population six years and over; ** the enrollment rate is the number enrolled divided by the relevant age category: 6–10 years for primary, 11–2 for lower secondary and 13–15 for secondary.

International Migrants

The survey notes a slight superiority of international migrants in urban over rural areas (Nepal 1987, 75). In 1986, some 2.8 per cent of the population were classed as international migrants. This was 2.6 per cent in the rural areas and 4.7 per cent in the urban areas. In both areas, women show higher proportions than do men. As many as 6 per cent of urban women were migrants; their rural counterparts made up 4 per cent of the population. The great majority of international migrants come from India, and the largest numbers are found in the Terai, the area immediately adjacent to India.

OVERVIEW

Here are four small poor countries in the very early stages of urbanization. Well below regional averages, they are moving rapidly to catch up. It is projected, however, that they will still remain considerably behind the rest of the region for the next three decades. The three Southeast Asian countries have a long history of violence and government repression.

Cambodia and Laos seem to be emerging from this violent past, though their futures are hardly secure. Myanmar remains under a highly repressive government. Nepal has known more peace in the past, though its recent history has taken on a violent nature. It is not sure how the country will emerge from this.

Poor and less urbanized, these countries show some interesting developments. Urban areas often look more like large agrarian villages than true cities. They often have substantial numbers of agriculturalists in the urban boundaries, and urban dwellings often look much like those in the villages. Yet there is change. Urbanization implies better public services, higher levels of health and welfare, and the profound changes in reproductive behavior that have been sweeping the world for the past two centuries. Age of marriage is rising as boys and girls are going to school and extending their years in school. This is associated with the decline of fertility and the rise of smaller families. We have seen, however, that falling fertility does not always bring with it a decline in household size. This comes from the enhanced social services found in urban areas, which often attract young people from the villages, moving for education and jobs, who take up residence with urban families.

Of the four countries, Nepal is the most disadvantaged by geography. The rough mountain terrain isolates much of the country from other parts. It will be useful to watch how this affects both the speed and character of the urbanization process.

Myanmar is the most urbanized of the four, and its pattern is quite striking. Towns are widespread, though of modest dimensions. Were the government to become less repressive and more open to movement and trade, these towns could well act as growth nodes to spread development and urban lifestyles rapidly throughout the country.

13

Urbanization in China: 1959–2000

SHENGJIN WANG AND LIDA FAN

Urbanization in China has proceeded in a unique way since the establishment of the People's Republic of China in 1949. The planned economic system defined the processes and choices of urbanization before the economic reforms initiated in 1978. The economic and urban conditions of the planned economy from 1949 defined the range of policy choices after the economic reforms beginning in 1978 (Fan and Sun 1992). Although the control of rural to urban migration precluded the development of some of the urban problems that other developing countries experienced, urbanization in China lagged behind the process of industrialization. A great change took place in urbanization after the new urban policies of 1984. After 1984, urbanization in China proceeded quickly and reached a satisfactory level. Now, China is experiencing an accelerated pace of urbanization.

This chapter provides data and discussions on urbanization in China between 1959 and 2000, and pays especial attention on the data of the 2000 census.

URBAN GROWTH

Definition of Urban Population

The definition of the urban population in China has caused considerable confusion since the late 1980s. There are two major ways to count the urban population in China: (1) total population in cities and towns (PCT), and (2) the total non-agricultural population in the cities and towns (NPCT). Although there have been some changes in the definition of urban population in the first three People's Republic of China's censuses of 1953, 1964, and 1982 (Bai 1986), it is believed that PCT can be used to measure the urban population before 1984. Owing to the redefinition of city boundaries and the restipulation of criteria for towns after 1984, a large number of rural people statistically belonged to PCT in the statistical yearbook published before the result of the 1990 census became available in 1991. Fortunately, the 1990 census resolved this problem by correcting the PCT data after 1982. According to the "second definition" of the 1990 census, "population of cities and towns" is the population residing in the districts of cities (excluding the population of towns administrated), and residential districts or neighborhood committees of towns (excluding population in the villages). PCT is used as the urban population in this chapter.

There are a few changes in the definition of population of cities and towns in the 2000 census, and these also caused a few more complications. According to the 2000 Census, for cities, if the population density is greater than 1,500 persons per square kilometer, the population of the city includes all the people in all the administrated districts. If the population density is smaller than 1,500 persons per square kilometer, the population of the city includes the people in the location of municipal government and the administrated other neighborhood committees. For towns, the population of the towns includes the location of the county government and the other administrated neighborhood committees (State Office of Census 2000). Only the urban population of the year 2000 in Table 13.1 is under this definition.

Urban Growth

Urban growth in China has gone through three stages since 1959 as shown in Table 13.1. Those three stages reflect three stages of economic conditions and policy changes.

TABLE 13.1 Urbanization and the growth of the urban population, 1959–2000

Year	Population (000)	% Gr.	% Urban	Year	Population (000)	% Gr.	% Urban
1959	123710		18.4	1980	191400	3.5	19.4
1960	130730	5.7	19.7	1981	201710	5.4	20.2
1961	127070	–2.8	19.3	1982	214800	6.5	21.1
1962	116590	–8.2	17.3	1983	222740	3.7	21.6
1963	116460	–0.1	16.8	1984	240170	7.8	23.0
1964	129500	11.2	18.4	1985	250940	4.5	23.7
1965	130450	0.7	18.0	1986	263660	5.1	24.5
1966	133130	2.1	17.9	1987	276740	5.0	25.3
1967	135480	1.8	17.7	1988	286610	3.6	25.8
1968	138380	2.1	17.6	1989	295400	3.1	26.2
1969	141170	2.0	17.5	1990	301910	2.2	26.4
1970	144240	2.2	17.4	1991	305430	1.2	26.4
1971	147110	2.0	17.3	1992	323720	6.0	27.6
1972	149350	1.5	17.1	1993	333510	3.0	28.1
1973	153450	2.7	17.2	1994	343010	2.8	28.6
1974	155950	1.6	17.2	1995	351740	2.5	29.0
1975	160300	2.8	17.3	1996	359500	2.2	29.4
1976	163410	1.9	17.4	1997	369890	2.9	29.9
1977	166690	2.0	17.55	1998	379420	2.6	30.4
1978	172450	3.5	17.9	1999	388920	2.5	30.9
1979	184950	7.2	19.0	2000	458440	17.9	36.2

SOURCES: National Bureau of Statistics of China: *China Statistical Yearbook* (1999), China Statistics Press, Beijing, p.352, (2001): p. 91, and National Bureau of Statistics of China: *China Labour Statistical Yearbook* (1999), China Statistics Press, p. 4.

(1) *1959–77.* We can see that from 1959 to 1977, the percentage of the urban population increased in the first year then declined slightly till 1977, from 19.8 to 17.6 per cent. China experienced severe difficulties after the failure of the so-called "Great Leap Forward." The severe shortage of agricultural products at that time led the government to reduce the number of urban workers. In addition, many urban citizens were sent to the countryside in the late 1960s. High school and middle school graduates, the "educated youths," were sent to the countryside to "be educated" by the peasants. Politically undesirable people and some urban employees were also sent to the countryside. It has been estimated that more than 50 million urban people were sent to the countryside during the 1960s (Guo and Liu 1990). In the beginning of the 1970s, many factories were built in the countryside of the northeast areas. Consequently, many workers and their families migrated from the eastern coastal provinces to the northeastern areas. During this period, the government issued household register regulations to restrict rural people from migrating to the cities and towns. We will discuss this policy later. The restriction of rural-to-urban migration was in line with China's industrial policy, which aimed to realize industrialization with the transfer of agricultural surplus to the urban sectors. The slow growth or even shrinkage of urban population in the early part of this period caused many problems for the periods that followed. It made the population structure more dualistic and hindered the development of urban sectors, especially in the service industries.

(2) *1978–83.* The rural economic reform initiated in 1978 released the peasants from much state control. With the dismissal of the commune system, peasants enjoyed more freedom, and agricultural productivity increased dramatically. At the same time, some people who were sent to the countryside were allowed to go back to the cities and towns. Thus, the percentage of urban population increased rapidly, from 17.92 per cent in 1978 to 21.62 per cent in 1983. (Table 13.1 also shows, however, that a slow growth of urban population and percentages had already begun in 1975.) Although the agricultural technology could not be improved greatly in a short time, the progress in economic reform was sufficient to release the hidden agricultural surplus. The rise of a surplus labor force in

agricultural posed a new demand for industrial transition, as well as a demand for urbanization.

(3) *1984–2000*. The urban reform of 1984 met this demand. On 10 October 1984, the government promulgated the "Instruction on the Issues for Peasants to Migrate to the Towns." This instruction permits those who have useful skills and who will work in the enterprises of towns for a long term to reside in towns. This change of migration policy brought a new era for urbanization. During this period, the percentage of urban population increased from 17.92 per cent to 36.22 per cent, at a rate of 0.83 percentage points annually. Note, however, that, as earlier, the new policy followed a change that was already taking place. The urban percentage point growth from 1978 to 1984 was also 0.83 points per year.

Changes are being made step by step. More and more rural people have found jobs in cities. With the changes in household registration regulations and employment regulations, the cities gradually accepted the rural people as equal employees. More importantly, by the end of this period, the urbanization process was becoming an economic process, that is, urbanization was being driven by economic forces.

Regional Differences in Urbanization

Table 13.2 shows percent urban and rural population by provinces in 2000. The four special districts, Beijing, Shanghai, Tianjin, and Chongqing, are considered as provinces. From Table 13.2, we can see that the percent urban in all the eastern coastal provinces, except Hebei, (Beijing, Tianjin, Liaoning, Shanghai, Jiangsu, Zhejiang, Fujian, Shandong, Guangdong, and Hainan), is greater than the national average (36.22 per cent). This pattern of distribution represents the characteristics of the country's colonial history a century ago. The eastern coastal provinces were more developed and more industrialized. Although the government of China has undertaken strong efforts to balance the regional distribution of population and industries since the beginning of the People's Republic of China in 1949, the general geographical distribution has not changed very much.

TABLE 13.2   Urban and rural proportions by region

Region	% Urban	% Rural	Region	% Urban	% Rural
National Total	36.22	63.78	Henan	23.20	76.80
Beijing	77.54	22.46	Hubei	40.22	59.78
Tianjin	71.99	28.01	Hunan	29.75	70.25
Hebei	26.08	73.92	Guangdong	55.00	45.00
Shanxi	34.91	65.09	Guangxi	28.15	71.85
Inner Mongolia	42.68	57.32	Hainan	40.11	59.89
Liaoning	54.24	45.76	Chongqing	33.09	66.91
Jilin	49.68	50.32	Sichuan	26.69	73.31
Heilongjiang	51.54	48.46	Guizhou	23.87	76.13
Shanghai	88.31	11.69	Yunnan	23.36	76.64
Jiangsu	41.49	58.51	Tibet	18.93	81.07
Zhejiang	48.67	51.33	Shaanxi	32.26	67.74
Anhui	27.81	72.19	Gansu	24.01	75.99
Fujian	41.57	58.43	Qinghai	34.76	65.24
Jiangxi	27.67	72.33	Ningxia	32.43	67.57
Shangdong	38.00	62.00	Xinjiang	33.82	66.18

SOURCES: National Bureau of Statistics of China: *China Statistical Yearbook* (2001), China Statistics Press, Beijing, p. 101.

Sources of Growth

Three sources contribute to urban growth: natural increase, rural-to-urban migration, and changes of city boundaries and registration. These three sources played different roles in different periods. Table 3 shows the increase or decrease in the number of cities, total urban population growth, and its three components. Before 1961, the major source of urban growth was migration (56 per cent). Natural increase contributed about one-third, and administrative changes about 10 per cent. As mentioned earlier, a large number of people were sent to the rural areas in the 1960s after the failure of the "Great Leap Forward." The urban population declined by 5.7 million in the 1960s. The net out-migration was nearly 20 million for that period (calculated from Table 13.3). (Note that the decade 1961–70 was, to say the least, an unusual decade.) In the period between 1971 and 1978, the urban population increased by 12.92

TABLE 13.3   Urban growth and its sources by decade, 1949–1988

Years	Number of new cities	Urban Population Growth		Component of urban growth %		
		0	% Ann. Gw.	Nat. Inc	Mig.	Adm. Ch.
1949-1957	41	26,510	8.5	33.0	56.4	10.5
1958-1960	22	17,210	9.4	19.0	73.4	7.6
1961-1970	-23	-5,720	-0.8	264.5	-346.2	-18.4
1971-1978	15	12,920	2.2	48.8	41.7	9.5
1979-1988	241	60,680	5.8	17.1	45.0	37.9
1949-1988	296	111,600	4.1	39.3	36.5	24.3

SOURCES: Ruojian Li (1991)"An Analysis on the Spatial Pattern of Urbanization in China", *Population Research*, No. 5, p. 34.

million: 49 per cent by natural increase, 41 per cent by in-migration, and only 10 per cent by administrative boundary changes. After the economic reforms initiated in 1978, migration and administrative changes played the most import roles. Natural increase declined dramatically as China's national family planning program produced a rapid decline in fertility. Ma (1990) made an estimate of the three sources of urban growth between 1949 and 1988, based on a survey of 74 cities. This shows both natural increase and in-migration contributing just over a third each and administrative changes contributing about one-quarter of urban growth. Further study on the sources of urban growth for recent years is needed.

Profile of In-migrants and Out-migrants

There is as yet no nationwide study of the details of the urban in-migrants and out-migrants. Some research projects, however, have given partial descriptions of the migrants. Ma (1990) studied the profile of those who moved to the cities and towns during the years 1949–86 based on the survey covering 74 cities. Unfortunately, that study did not indicate whether the in-migrants came from cities or rural areas.

As discussed above, the profile of migrants changed dramatically in different periods. In the 1960s, the main stream was from urban to rural. From 1961 to 1965, most of the out-migrants were the downsized urban workers. During the "Cultural Revolution" of 1966–76, three major components were middle and high school graduates, aged 16–18, politically undesirable, mostly middle-aged intellectuals, and urban workers moving to the newly built factories in the periphery. From 1978 to 2000, the main stream of migration was from rural to urban. In this period, most of the in-migrants were young rural laborers. There were also a large number of educated youths, who were sent to the countryside during the "cultural revolution," who returned to the cities and towns during this period.

National System of Cities

Figure 13.1 shows the changes in the number of cities of different sizes from 1959 to 1999. From Figure 13.1, we can see that the number of cities with a population of more than five million remained unchanged. This reflects the urban policy of "controlling the size of large cities." The number of cities with a population between 0.5 and 1.0 million increased the fastest. It should be noticed that some towns, although large enough, are not considered as cities in the statistical yearbook because they are not officially administrated as cities.

The population proportions of capital cities in the provinces for the period 1994–99 are shown in Table 13.4. In most of the provinces, the proportions in capital cities increased during that period, except Shenyang (the capital of Liaoning) and Guangzhou (the capital of Guangdong). This proportion increased quickly in some hinterland provinces such as Harbin of Heilongjiang Province and Kunming of Yunnan Province.

Changes in the population of the national capital, Beijing, are shown separately in Table 13.5. From 1992 to 1999, the urban population in Beijing increased by 57 million and the proportion urban in the Beijing area increased from 85.06 per cent to 95.01 per cent. Beijing's proportion of the total national population has remained stable at just under 1 per cent.

The population growth in China's 10 largest cities in 1994–2000 is shown in Table 13.6. This shows index numbers with 1994 as 100. Chongqing and Harbin are the two fastest growing cities, increasing 104

FIGURE 13.1   Changes of number of cities of different size

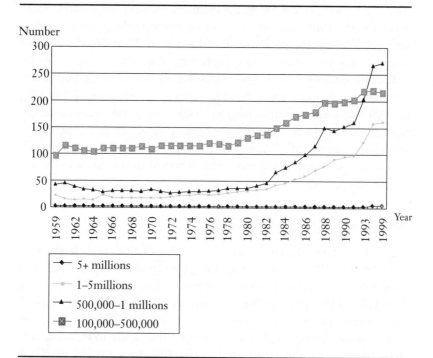

SOURCES: Calculated from National Bureau of Statistics of China: *China Population Statistics Yearbook*, China Statistics Press, (1990): pp. 595–599, (19991): pp. 330–333, (1994): pp. 468–472, (1999): pp. 388–395 (2000): pp. 481–486.

per cent and 76 per cent, respectively. Both are hinterland cities. The other cities have grown much more slowly. Guangzhou and Wuhan are the next, with increases of only 8 per cent and 7 per cent, respectively. The degree of primacy has declined only slightly; it was 1.13, 1.12, and 1.09 for the years 1982, 1990, and 1998, respectively.

Future Projections

Table 13.7 shows the projected future urban population percentages for the next half-century. Ding (1995) projected the proportion of urban population by provinces based on the urban population, urban and rural natural growth rates, rural-to-urban migration rates, and inter-provincial

366

TABLE 13.4 Proportion of population in capital city by region

Region	1994	1996	1997	1998	1999
Beijing	87.9	88.6	91.6	91.9	95.0
Tianjin	74.9	78.7	80.1	80.9	81.5
Shanghai	86.2	97.2	98.4	98.6	98.8
Chongqing	–	–	87.1	77.7	77.6
Shijiazhuang	13.1	13.2	13.2	13.2	13.3
Taiyuan	9.3	9.4	9.5	9.5	9.5
Hohhot	6.5	8.7	8.7	8.9	8.9
Shenyang	16.5	16.5	16.5	16.5	16.5
Changchun	26.2	26.3	26.3	26.4	26.4
Harbin	14.9	25.2	25.2	25.3	25.3
Nanjing	7.6	7.6	7.6	7.6	7.7
Hangzhou	13.7	13.7	13.8	13.8	13.8
Hefei	6.8	6.9	6.9	6.9	6.9
Fuzhou	17.8	17.8	17.8	17.8	17.8
Nanchang	10.0	10.1	10.1	10.2	10.3
Jinan	6.2	6.2	6.2	6.2	6.3
Zhengzhou	6.4	6.4	6.4	6.5	6.5
Wuhan	12.4	12.4	12.4	12.4	12.5
Changsha	8.9	8.9	8.9	8.9	8.9
Guangzhou	9.5	9.5	9.5	9.5	9.4

TABLE 13.4 (cont'd)

Nanning	6.0	6.1	6.1	6.2	6.1
Haikou	6.7	7.0	7.0	7.2	7.3
Chengdu	8.5	8.7	12.0	12.0	12.0
Guiyang	4.9	9.0	8.9	8.9	9.0
Kunming	9.7	9.7	9.7	9.8	11.8
Xi'an	18.8	18.9	19.0	19.1	19.2
Lanzhou	11.3	11.4	11.4	11.4	11.5
Xining	23.7	23.8	23.8	26.4	28.3
Yinchuan	17.5	17.5	17.6	17.6	17.6
Urumqi	8.7	8.8	8.9	8.9	9.0

SOURCES: Calculated from National Bureau of Statistics of China: *China Statistical Yearbook* (1995–1999), *China Population Statistics Yearbook* (2000), China Statistics Press, Beijing, pp. 442–445.

TABLE 13.5 Population of the national capital and its proportion of the total population, 1992–1999

	1992	1993	1994	1995	1996	1997	1998	1999
Population of Capital	1048.7	1056.9	1068.2	1077	1083.2	1092.3	1097.8	1106.2
Population of country	115563	116596.6	117673.7	118787.6	119866	120902.7	121818.1	122811.5
Proportion	0.91	0.91	0.91	0.91	0.90	0.90	0.90	0.90

SOURCES: National Bureau of Statistics of China: *China Population Statistics Yearbook* (2000) China Statistics Press, Beijing, pp. 442–445.

TABLE 13.6   Growth of the 10 largest cities 1994–200 (Index 1994 = 100)

City	1994	1996	1997	1998	1999	2000
Shanghai	100	100.38	100.46	100.58	101.09	101.74
Beijing	100	101.51	114.60	115.20	117.69	104.29
Chongqing	100	101.19	201.26	202.36	203.20	204.44
Tianjin	100	100.34	100.56	101.13	101.69	101.90
Wuhan	100	102.29	103.43	104.54	105.74	107.03
Shenyang	100	101.36	101.81	101.94	102.28	103.49
Guangzhou	100	102.98	104.55	105.83	107.54	110.00
Xi'an	100	102.50	103.60	104.57	105.56	107.67
Chengdu	100	102.19	103.02	103.85	104.54	105.56
Harbin	100	171.00	172.32	173.60	174.59	176.02

SOURCES: National Bureau of Statistics of China: Calculated from *China Urban Statistical Yearbook* (1999) *China Statistical Yearbook* (1995–2000) *China Population Statistics Yearbook* (1999–2000).China Statistics Press, Beijing.

migration rates of the period 1982–90. It should be noted that after 1990, with the changes in urban policy, the rural-to-urban migration became more active. It even showed some acceleration at the end of the 1990s; thus, it can be expected that the actual urbanization process may be faster than the projections in Table 13.7.

URBAN-RURAL DIFFERENCES

Although a dual urban-rural economic situation is seen in most of the developing countries, the case of China is considered more dualistic. This is largely due to the history of China's planned economy. At the beginning of the People's Republic of China, the policy of "giving priority

TABLE 13.7 Projection of Urban Proportions by Provinces 2010-2050

Regions	2010	2020	2030	2040	2050
National Total	38.30	43.40	48.00	52.10	55.90
Beijing	87.10	91.10	93.80	95.70	97.10
Tianjin	71.60	72.60	83.50	74.40	75.30
Hebei	31.90	37.60	42.90	47.80	52.40
Shanxi	45.30	52.20	58.20	63.40	68.00
Inner mongolia	47.00	54.10	60.30	65.70	70.40
Liaoning	67.80	73.40	78.80	82.90	86.10
Jilin	48.50	51.50	54.30	57.00	59.50
Heilongjiang	63.40	69.30	74.30	78.50	82.00
Shanghai	79.70	84.30	87.90	90.70	92.90
Jiangsu	34.70	40.60	46.00	51.10	55.70
Zhejiang	43.50	48.90	53.90	58.50	62.70
Anhui	26.40	30.30	34.10	37.60	41.00
Fujian	21.80	22.00	22.10	22.30	22.50
Jiangxi	22.60	23.70	24.80	25.80	26.90
Shangdong	44.90	52.10	58.50	64.10	68.90
Henan	17.10	18.10	19.00	19.90	20.90
Hubei	50.90	59.30	66.20	72.00	76.80
Hunan	26.80	30.80	34.60	38.20	41.60
Guangdong	67.30	76.70	83.50	88.40	91.80

TABLE 13.7 (cont'd)

Guangxi	22.20	25.70	29.10	32.30	35.40
Hainan	27.10	42.90	48.10	53.00	57.30
Sichuan	33.30	39.10	44.40	49.30	53.70
Guizhou	20.10	20.60	21.00	21.50	22.00
Yunnan	19.50	21.60	23.70	25.70	27.60
Tibet	16.30	18.70	21.00	23.30	25.50
Shaanxi	27.60	30.40	33.20	35.80	38.30
Gansu	36.50	42.60	48.20	53.20	57.80
Qinghai	37.80	42.40	46.60	50.20	53.50
Ningxia	33.90	37.40	40.70	43.70	46.50
Xinjiang	41.40	45.30	48.80	51.90	54.90

SOURCES: Jinhong Ding (1995). "A Projection of Future Levels of China's Urbanization", *Population Research*, No. 4, pp. 24–29.

to the heavy industry" was practised. In the implementation of this policy, the agricultural "surplus" was transferred from the rural sector to the urban sector. Other policies, such as food and housing subsidies to the urban citizens and urban employment policies, were also implemented. Consequently, after those policies were implemented for more than three decades, the urban-rural differences widened. Although these differences have been narrowed following the economic reforms, the differences in living standards, education, and ideology are still substantial.

DEMOGRAPHIC DIFFERENCES

Differences in Birth, Death and Natural Growth Rates

From Table 13.8, we can see that both the birth and death rates for the rural areas are higher than those of the urban areas in every year between 1978 and 1999. The differences in birth rates are declining, however, from over five points to just under three points; while the differences in death rates have remained stable at about one point. Part of these differences reflects the different age structures, which we see below. Both birth and death rates also reflect living standards and reproductive norms. We can expect further declines in rural-urban differences in birth rates. Urban death rates may also rise if the projected increase in the urban aged materializes.

Differences of Age Structure

Table 13.9 shows the recent and projected urban and rural age structures to the year 2050. The projections are based on the natural increase and migration data of the period between 1990 and 1996. As shown in Table 13.9, the proportion of people in the rural area aged 0–14 is significantly higher than that in the urban areas in all the years, both in the period 1990–96 and the projected period. The proportion of the aged (65 years and over) for the rural population is also higher than that of the urban population in the period between 1990 and 2020. After that, however, the urban aged gain over the rural. That means the dependency ratio for rural areas is higher and will continue to be higher than that of the urban population for some years. The urban areas have the benefit of abundant labor supplies and has a lower dependency ratio. This reflects the fact that the migration stream to the urban areas is heavily made up of young working-age people.

Mobility

The migration rate of urban people is much greater than that of the rural people in China. According to the study by Li (1994), gross migration rates for cities with populations of more than 1 million, 0.5 to 1 million, 0.2 to 0.5 million, smaller than 0.2 million, and counties were

TABLE 13.8 Urban and rural birth and death rates and rate of natural increase, 1978–1999

	Urban			Rural			R-U	R-U
Year	CBR	CDR	RNI	CBR	CDR	RNI	CBR	CDR
1978	13.56	5.12	8.44	18.91	6.42	12.49	5.35	1.30
1979	13.67	5.07	8.60	18.43	6.39	12.04	4.76	1.32
1980	14.17	5.48	8.69	18.82	6.47	12.35	4.65	0.99
1981	16.45	5.14	11.31	21.55	6.53	15.02	5.10	1.39
1989	16.73	5.78	10.95	23.27	6.81	16.46	6.54	1.03
1990	16.14	5.71	10.43	22.80	7.01	15.79	6.66	1.30
1991	15.49	5.50	9.99	21.17	7.13	14.04	5.68	1.63
1992	15.47	5.77	9.70	19.09	6.91	12.18	3.62	1.14
1993	15.37	5.99	9.38	19.06	6.89	12.17	3.69	0.90
1994	15.13	5.53	9.60	18.84	6.80	12.04	3.71	1.27
1995	14.76	5.53	9.23	18.08	6.99	11.09	3.32	1.46
1996	14.47	5.65	8.82	18.02	6.94	11.08	3.55	1.29
1997	14.52	5.58	8.94	17.43	6.90	10.53	2.91	1.32
1998	13.67	5.31	8.36	17.05	7.01	10.04	3.38	1.70
1999	13.18	5.51	7.67	16.13	6.88	9.25	2.95	1.37

SOURCE: National Bureau of Statistics of China: *China Statistical Yearbook* (2001), China Statistics Press, Beijing, p. 91.

TABLE 13.9   Urban and rural age structure, 1990–2000 (%)

Years	0-14 years old Urban	15-64 years old Rural	Urban	64 years old and older Rural	Urban	Rural
1990	22.2	29.6	72.6	64.6	5.2	5.8
1996	20.3	29.3	73.8	64.3	5.9	6.5
2000	17.7	28.8	75.5	64.1	6.8	7.1
2010	12.2	25.8	79.9	65.8	7.9	8.4
2020	10.8	25.7	78.3	62.4	10.9	11.9
2030	9.4	25.3	75.6	59.2	15.1	15.6
2040	8.5	25.7	70.8	54.9	20.6	19.4
2050	8.5	27.0	69.2	54.6	22.3	18.3

SOURCES: Ying Hu: "Urban and Rural Population Projections of China", *Population Science of China*, No.6, 1997, pp. 15–22.

6.83 per cent, 9.00 per cent, 6.89 per cent, 3.99 per cent, and 31.18 per cent, respectively.

Fertility Rates

There is a declining, but persistent, difference in fertility rates between rural and urban areas. From Figure 13.2, we can see that the total fertility rate (TFR) in the rural areas was significantly higher than that in the urban areas in most years between 1950 and 1998, except those three years after the "Great Leap Forward" when both urban and rural areas faced severe difficulties. The differences in fertility rates exist due to the differences of reproductive norms, living standards, and education between the two areas.

FIGURE 13.2   Total fertility rates of urban and rural areas in China TFR

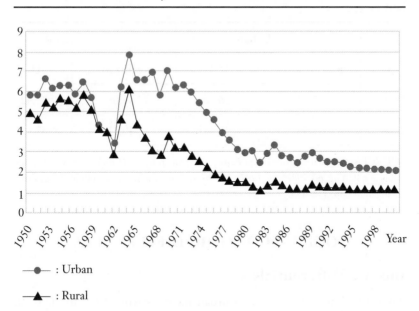

—●— : Urban

—▲— : Rural

SOURCE: Chewei Zhang (2000). "Urban and Rural Differences in Population Transition and Policy Choices in China", *Population Science of China*, No. 4, pp. 46–50.

Contraception

Table 13.10 shows the major methods of contraception for the urban and rural areas in the years 1986 and 1988 (the 1986 percentages are unexpectedly low and we have no explanation for this.) From Table 10, we can see that the combined percentage of the two methods was 77.03 per cent for the urban areas and 78,14 per cent for the rural areas for the year 1988. The IUD is the major method of contraception for the urban areas and sterilization is the major method for the rural areas. The lack of any rural-urban difference in contraceptive use reflects the substantial success of the national family planning program.

TABLE 13.10 Contraceptive use rates of urban and rural women of child bearing age

	Urban		Rural	
Year	Sterilization	IUD	Sterilization	IUD
1986	17.96	26.28	34.08	32.42
1988	31.58	45.45	40.21	37.93

SOURCES: Calculated from *China Family Planning Yearbook* (1987), People's Hygiene Publisher, Beijing, pp. 398–400, (1989), Northern Women and Children Publishing house, Changchun, pp. 332–335.

SOCIAL-ECONOMIC DIFFERENCES

Income Differentials

Table 13.11 lists the rural and urban incomes from 1978 to 2000. In 1978, urban incomes were about 2.5 times rural incomes. Although rural incomes have grown more rapidly, in part due to the economic reforms, the rural-urban ratio does not seem to have declined. In 2000, urban incomes were still about 2.5 times rural incomes.

Education

The urban and rural difference in education has declined in the recent decades, though it still remains substantial. According to the results of the last three censuses, the illiteracy rate for the urban areas was 16.43 per cent, 11.96 per cent, and 4.04 per cent for the years 1982, 1990, and 2000, respectively; The illiteracy rate for the rural areas was 34.98 per cent, 26.23 per cent, and 8.25 per cent for the years 1982, 1990, and 2000, respectively. That is, despite rapid gains in both rural and urban areas, rural illiteracy remains about twice that of urban areas. This may reflect the impact of age differences, since illiteracy is greater among the aged, and the aged form a larger proportion of rural than of urban populations. Thus, we might expect the rural-urban difference to decline with the passing of the older population.

TABLE 13.11   Urban and rural per capita annual income

	Rural		Urban		Ratio
Year	Yuan	index (1978=100)	Yuan	index (1978=100)	U/R
1978	133.6	100	343.4	100	2.57
1979	160.2	119.2	378.0	112.7	2.36
1980	191.3	139.0	477.6	127.0	2.50
1981	223.4	160.4	491.9	127.6	2.20
1982	270.1	192.3	526.6	133.9	1.95
1983	309.8	219.6	564.0	140.6	1.82
1984	355.3	249.5	651.2	158.1	1.83
1985	397.6	268.9	739.1	160.4	1.86
1986	423.8	277.6	899.6	182.5	2.12
1987	462.6	292.0	1002.2	186.9	2.17
1988	544.9	310.7	1181.4	182.5	2.17
1989	601.5	305.7	1375.7	182.8	2.29
1990	686.3	311.2	1510.2	198.1	2.20
1991	708.6	317.4	1700.6	212.4	2.40
1992	784.0	336.2	2026.6	232.9	2.58
1993	921.6	346.9	2577.4	255.1	2.80
1994	1221.0	364.4	3496.2	276.8	2.86
1995	1577.7	383.7	4283.0	290.3	2.71
1996	1926.1	418.2	4838.9	301.6	2.51
1997	2090.1	437.4	5160.3	311.9	2.47
1998	2162.0	456.2	5425.1	329.9	2.51
1999	2210.3	473.5	5854.0	360.6	2.65
2000	2253.4	483.5	6280.0	383.7	2.79

NOTE: According to the official price in 2001, 1 US$ = 8.2 Yuan.
SOURCES: National Bureau of Statistics of China: *China Statistics Yearbook* (2001), p. 304.

Labor Participation

Labor participation rates for urban and rural areas were 72.2 per cent and 85.4 per cent, respectively, in 1990, and 88.8 per cent and 71.3 per cent in 1995. According to Jia and Meng (1996), the labor participation rates for urban and rural areas are not expected to change substantially, 71 per cent and 86.0 per cent, respectively, till the year 2040. But the labor participation rate for the whole country is expected to decline because of urbanization. The reduction of the labor participation rate is due to the increase of education and improved economic conditions.

IMPLICATIONS

Urban Conditions

As mentioned above, the early control of rural-to-urban migration has precluded some of the urban problems that have appeared in other developing countries; at the same time, it has caused urbanization to lag behind industrialization in China. Urbanization is now rapidly catching up, however. The dual urban-rural economic structure that arose from the early planning priorities has changed only slightly after the economic reform initiated in the late 1970s. As in most developing countries, urban conditions in China are still much better than those in rural areas. There are more services available, such as schools, commercial centers, healthcare centers, and cultural and recreational facilities, in urban areas than in rural areas. The major unfavorable conditions in the urban areas are air pollution and the crowded traffic conditions, which we discuss below.

Major Benefits

As elsewhere, urbanization in China as produced some major benefits. These include the following.

Absorption of the Rural Surplus Labor

According to estimates by the Ministry of Agriculture, as a result of the decrease of land for agriculture use and the improvement of technology, some six million rural surplus laborers have been created in the agricultural sector in each year between 1996 and 2000. Most of this surplus is absorbed by the rapidly growing urban sectors.

Control of Population Size

China experienced very rapid population growth in the first two decades after the revolution. Since the mid-1970s, however, the reduction of population growth rates and fertility rates has been a major goal of the government. Urbanization tends to increase the cost and to reduce benefits that children bring; thus, it can help to reduce the rate of natural increase. Some researchers have used multi-regional population projection methods to project the population in China and conclude that urbanization provides a substantial advantage in the effort to reduce population growth (Zeng 1987 and Yang 1994).

Saving the Land

Land use per capita declines with the increase of population density in Chinese cities and towns. It is estimated that in 1995, the land use per person for cities of larger than 2 million, 1–2 million, 0.5–1 million, 0.2–0.5 million and smaller than 20,000 is 63.23 square meters, 83.77 square meters, 96.41 per square meters, 105.05 square meters, and 151.69 square meters, respectively (see Table 13.12). Thus, urbanization may save much land both in residential and industrial use.

TABLE 13.12   Per capita urban land occupied by non-agricultural population, 1990 and 1995

Year	2 million +	1-2 million	0.5-1 million	0.2-0.5 million	< 0.2 million	All cities average
1990	54.84	80.71	93.19	92.42	118.98	87.43
1995	63.23	83.77	96.41	105.05	151.69	102.24

SOURCES: Fang Wang: "The Sustainable Way of Urbanization in China: Limitations of the Current Urban Policy", The Second National Conference on Population, Resources and Environment, December 8–10, 1999, Beijing.

Benefits of Scale Economy

China is still a developing country and is still experiencing industrialization. Concentration increases productivity and the economies of scale, especially for the secondary industries.

Improving the Environmental Conditions in the Rural Areas

Some researches have found that urbanization helps improve the environmental and ecological conditions in the rural areas (Wang 1999 and Zhu 1999). This is because urbanization increases productivity and improves the efficiency of energy and transportation facilities, thus making it easier to control pollution.

Major Problems

As elsewhere, urbanization in China also involves major problems. These include the following.

Unemployment

Hidden unemployment is already very high after the reforms of urban state-run enterprises. These reforms increased efficiency and competition, largely by reducing labor use; the result has been increased unemployment. Moreover, as rural laborers move to the urban areas, this causes some pressure in the employment of the urban sectors.

Education

There is an increasing concern for the education of the children of the rural-to-urban temporary migrants in recent years. Some of them cannot be registered in the schools subsidized by city governments. The government is now issuing regulations to address this problem.

Traffic and Air Pollution

Traffic in most of large cities is crowded, mostly because the mass transportation systems are not efficient. Very few cities have underground or overhead light railways, due to the lack of financial resources. Although there is significant improvement in the construction of roads, the number of vehicles increases more rapidly. Per capita road area increased by 1.4 times from 3.1 square meters to 7.3 square meters from 1985 to 1995, but the number of motor vehicles increased by 5.1 times during the same period (Yang 1999, 229). The roads in the major Chinese cities are far from sufficient. In 1994, the per capita road area for the city of Shanghai, Beijing, and Guangzhou was 3.5 square meters, 4.8 square meters, and 4.7 square meters, respectively, much lower than the level of Tokyo, which has about 10.5 square meters (Yang 1999, 263).

Traffic also creates serious air pollution as well. It is estimated that traffic contributes about 60 per cent to the air pollution in large cities. The number of motor vehicles in Shanghai and Guangzhou was 0.37 million and 0.42 million, respectively, in 1994, much lower than that of Tokyo, which is 2.9 million in 1989. Considering that, for the time being, the number of motor vehicles in the Chinese cities is still very low compared with those of the cities of developed countries, the potential increase in the number of motor vehicles will create more problems and will be a big challenge in the near future.

Pollution

The major sources of air pollution are heating and transportation. In 1996, the average density of polluted particulate matter (SPM) was 309 microgram/m^3. Air pollution is more serious in the cities of Northern China than in Southern China. SO$_2$ is becoming the prime pollution substance in some cities. This has become a serious source of acid rain in Guangzhou, Changsha, and other cities. The average density of SO$_2$ is 83 milligram/m^3 for the cities of Northern China and 76 milligram/m^3 for the cities of Southern China. With urbanization, industrial and residential waste has increased rapidly. In 1995, only 45 per cent of the solid polluted industrial substances were dealt with for recycling. It is estimated that more than 30 cities stored solid industrial substances of more than 10 million tons (Yang 1999, 227). Those polluted substances cause other problems such as water pollution. In recent years, the Chinese government has issued policies and standards to deal with urban pollution problems.

The Government's Role in Addressing the Urban Issues

The central government has played an important role, both in the planning of rural-to-urban migration and in urban planning. In the period between 1959 and 1984, the government had policies to control urban population growth by greatly limiting rural-to-urban migration. This policy intended that the agricultural surplus was to be transferred to the urban industrial sectors in order to realize the aims of rapid industrialization. It was believed that the peasants should stay in rural areas to provide the needed agricultural surplus. In January of 1958, the government issued the regulations for household registration based on the registration regulation of 1955. Under this regulation, all the citizens are registered by their place of residence, either as urban people or as rural people. In general, rural people could not change their registered status to become non-agricultural urban people. In 1964, the government issued more restrictive regulations to further limit the migration from rural areas to cities and towns. As mentioned earlier, after the economic reforms initiated in the late 1970s, the government has gradually allowed the rural people to migrate to the cities.

In the 1960s, the government issued a policy to "Control the scale of large cities and develop small cities and towns." In 1980, the government changed the policy a little to "Control the scale of large cities, reasonably develop medium-sized cities, and develop small cities and towns." After 1993, more attention has been given to the development of major cities, such as Pudong Special District of Shanghai, which implies a further change in the urban policy. The Pudong District will add a population of two million when the construction is completed.

The government's role in addressing the urban issues in China also includes urban planning. Within the framework of the planned economy, all the urban projects were initiated by the government before the economic reforms of the late of 1970s. The government had regulations on household registration, providing subsidized housing for the urban residents, and health care for the urban employees. The government was also responsible for all the major construction projects, such as roads and major buildings, although those projects were conducted in an inefficient way. Although after the economic reform, more and more urban facilities and construction projects have been conducted by private and foreign companies, and organizations, the government still plays the most important role in the urban issues.

After the 1980s, the government began to pay more attention to improving the urban environment. The Ministry of Construction issued some regulations and standards for the principle of urban planning that "economic development, urban construction and environment construction are planned simultaneously, conducted and developed simultaneously" as stated in the world environment and development conference in 1992.

CHAPTER 14

Urban Scenario in Japan in the New Millennium

TOSHIO KURODA

GENERAL TREND OF URBANIZATION IN JAPAN

Urbanization is not simply a post-war phenomenon in Japan. As Table 14.1 shows, it was a process already underway early in the 20th century. By 1920, Japan was already 18 per cent urban. This was greater than the figure of almost all Asian states (except Singapore) in 1950. From 18 per cent in 1920, the urban proportion grew steadily until the Second World War. During the war, a large-scale evacuation was undertaken to move families and children out of the cities that were the targets of devastating air attacks. The urban proportion of the population doubled from 1920 to 1940 to 38 per cent, then dropped to 28 per cent in 1945, but returned quickly to pre-war levels by 1950. From that point, it has continued without reservation. Table 14.1 and Figure 14.1 provide the data and their graphic representation.

The post-war urbanization process in Japan has been quite remarkable. Since 1945, rapid reconstruction and economic growth brought about a rapid rise in urbanization. This was due at first to the tremendous shift of the young population from rural to urban areas, essentially returning to the cities from which they had been evacuated. The percent urban doubled in just 10 years, from 28 per cent in 1945 to 56 in 1955, 72 in 1970 and 79 in 2000. During about half a century, 1945–2000, the urban percentage increased by almost three times, and the actual number of urban areas of 20 to 100 million inhabitants increased

TABLE 14.1 Population growth and urbanization in Japan, 1920–2000

Year	Total	Urban	Rural	% Urban
1920	55,963	10,097	45,866	18.0
1925	59,745	12,897	46,848	21.6
1930	64,450	15,444	49,006	24.0
1935	69,254	22,666	46,588	32.7
1940	73,115	27,578	45,537	37.7
1945	71,998	20,022	51,976	27.8
1947	78,102	25,858	52,244	33.1
1950	84,115	31,366	52,749	37.3
1955	90,076	50,532	39,544	56.1
1960	94,300	59,678	34,622	63.3
1965	99,209	67,356	31,853	67.9
1970	104,666	75,429	29,237	72.1
1975	111,939	84,967	26,972	75.9
1980	117,060	89,187	27,873	76.2
1985	121,049	92,889	28,160	76.7
1990	123,612	95,644	27,968	77.4
1995	125,570	98,009	27,561	78.1
2000	126,926	99,865	27,061	78.7

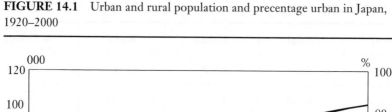

FIGURE 14.1   Urban and rural population and precentage urban in Japan, 1920–2000

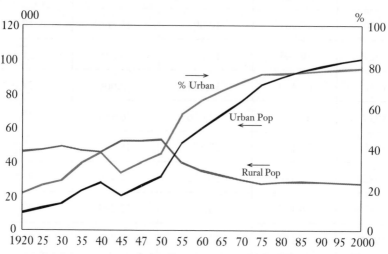

five times. The urban population during this time rose from 20 to 100 milllion, or a five-fold increase.

Since 1970, however, a steady decline of the rate of urbanization can be seen, suggesting a trend approaching a plateau, which is generally found in all the more developed regions, where the urbanization level is estimated at around 80 per cent or more. From 1950 to 1970, the urban proportion doubled again from 37 to 72 per cent. After 1970, urban growth added only 8 percentage points to the level of urbanization. This is something of a plateau, which suggests our perception reflected in the title, the end of urbanization.

Table 14.2 shows urban and rural population growth in terms of size of population, and percent growth rates. It is interesting to note that the year 1955 is the critical time at which the urban proportion exceeded the rural population, followed by a continuing increasing urban population and decreasing rural population. The rise of the urbanization trend corresponds with very rapid economic growth during the latter half of the 1950s and 1960s when many migrants moved into urban areas from rural areas. It also coincides with an absolute decline in the rural population, which has continued to the present, and projected into the

TABLE 14.2 Population growth and urbanization in Japan, 1950–2000.

Year	Population (000) %				Average Annual Growth Rates		
	Total	Urban	Rural	Urban	Total	Urban	Rural
1950	84115	31366	52749	37.3			
1960	94302	59678	34622	63.3	1.15	6.64	–4.12%
1970	104665	75429	29237	72.1	1.05	2.37	–1.68%
1980	117060	89187	27873	76.2	1.13	1.69	–0.48%
1990	123611	95644	27968	77.4	0.55	0.70	0.03%
2000	126926	99865	27061	78.7	0.26	0.43	–0.33%
2010	128220	103211	25009	80.5	0.04	0.27	–0.89
2020	125985	104039	21920	82.6	–0.25	0.02	–1.46
2030	121285	102819	18466	84.8	–0.41	–0.16	–1.74

SOURCE: 1950–2000: National Population Censuses of Japan; 2010–2030: UN 2001.

foreseeable future as well. The urban population is expected to continue growing until 2020, then begin an absolute decline. With its low fertility rate, Japan is expected to show a decline in population growth after 2010. With the rural population in absolute decline since 1960, it is the urbanization process that accounts for Japan's total population growth

TWO DEFINITIONS OF URBANIZATION IN JAPAN

Conventionally, urbanization is based on a count of the population residing in cities, known as *shi* in Japanese. Officially, the following requirements should be met for an area to be promoted to "city" status (Local Government Autonomy Law):

(1)   Population should be more than 50,000 persons.

(2) Number of houses located in central established area of the city should be more than 60 per cent of the total number of houses.
(3) People who are occupied in urban business including industries, commerce, trade and so on, and their family members should be more than 60 per cent of the total population.
(4) In addition, certain urban infrastructure stipulated by the prefectural authorities concerned should be provided.

Another, and more recent, definition of urbanization is based on the idea of the Densely Inhabited Districts (DID)

For the statistical presentation of urban and rural areas, "all *shi*" and "all *gun*" (that is, *machi* and *mura*) have generally been included in Japan. However, after the Town and Village Merger Acceleration Law was established in 1953, there was considerable enlargement of *shi* areas through absorption of neighboring *machi* and *mura* As a consequence, many *shi* came to encompass the sparsely inhabited agricultural areas under their jurisdiction. In this sense, "all *shi*" can hardly represent pure urban areas nowadays. Under these circumstances, the concept of DID was developed by the Statistics Bureau. It has been applied in and after the 1960 population census. It is defined as an area within a *shi*, *gun*, *machi*, or *mura* that is composed of a group of contiguous enumeration districts, each of which has a population density of about 4,000 inhabitants or more per square kilometer and whose total population exceeds 5,000 as of 1 October each census year.

The DIDs are shown in Table 14.3. However, DID statistics are only available after 1960, and, consequently, they are not sufficient for longer term analysis, even though they can provide more accurate information about urban population. In 1960, about 45 per cent of Japan's population resided in the DIDs. This included 65 per cent of the urban population and 6 per cent of the rural population. By 2000, 65 per cent of the country's population resided in the DIDs, including almost 80 per cent of the urban population and as much as 16 per cent of the population still classified as rural.

THE SYSTEM OF CITIES

The distribution of localities by size of population is quite diversified country by country. However, Japan is typically characterized by a hierarchical structure that is rather smooth and regular. Table 14.4 shows

TABLE 14.3 Densely Inhabited district (DID) population by urban and rural (Percentage)

Year	National	Urban	Rural
1960	43.7	65.1	6.4
1965	48.1	66.7	8.5
1970	53.5	69.9	11.3
1975	57.0	71.8	10.6
1980	59.7	74.4	12.8
1985	60.6	74.9	13.3
1990	63.2	77.2	15.4
1995	64.7	78.3	16.3
2000	65.2	78.6	15.9

SOURCE: National Population Census

the changing distribution of localities by size. This uses five size categories: over 1 million, 0.3 to 1 million, 0.1 to 0.3 million, under 0.1 million, and rural areas.

We first see the great decline in rural areas, especially between 1950 and 1970. The decline in the rural population brought rapid increases in all categories except the 0.3 to 1 million sized cities. By 1980, the current pattern of roughly hierarchical balance was established and continues today with roughly one-fifth of the population in all categories, including the rural areas.

Particular attention should be paid to the fact that there is a strong convergence, with each category of city size (plus the rural area) now accounting for about 20 per cent of the total population. (see Table 14.4).

One thing this table shows is that the largest urban centers, especially Tokyo, Osaka, and Nagoya, attracted many migrants in the period up to 1970. This migration stream was not directed towards the second tier of cities, from 0.3 to 1 million. It was, however, directed as well towards the smaller towns. By 1980, however, the second tier of cities had caught up with the rest in both size and proportion of population.

TABLE 14.4 Distributional change by different localities by their sizes of population in Japan, 1950–2000

Class of Localities	1950	1960	1970	1980	1990	2000
(A) Population (million)						
1. Cities 1 Million +	9.5	16.7	20.9	23.3	25.3	26.8
2. Cities 0.3 to 1.0 million	3.1	6.1	12.5	19.5	23.2	23.5
3. Cities 0.1 to 0.3 million	8.8	15.3	20.5	23.3	23.8	26.6
4. Cities under 0.1 million	10.0	21.7	21.6	23.1	23.3	22.9
5. Rural	52.8	34.6	29.2	27.9	28.0	27.1
6. Total	84.1	94.3	104.7	123.6	123.6	126.9
(B) Percentage (%)						
1. Cities 1 Million +	11.3	17.7	19.9	19.9	20.5	21.1
2. Cities 0.3 to 1.0 million	3.6	6.4	11.9	16.6	18.8	18.5
3. Cities 0.1 to 0.3 million	10.4	16.2	19.6	19.9	19.3	21.0
4. Cities under 0.1 million	11.9	23.0	20.7	19.8	18.8	18.0
5. Rural	62.7	36.7	27.9	23.8	22.6	21.3
6. Total	100.0	100.0	100.0	100.0	100.0	100.0

Another view of this distribution is found in Table 14.5, which shows the population of the largest eight cities from 1950 to 2000. This shows the dominance of the two largest cities, Tokyo and Osaka, and to a lesser extent Nagoya, which are considered in greater detail below. Not only have they remained the largest, their share of the total urban population has continued to grow. Tokyo had 15 per cent of the urban population in

TABLE 14.5 Japan's eight largest cities, 1950–2000

	1950 Pop (000)	% of Urb.	Cu %	1975 Pop (000)	% Urb.	Cu%	2000 Pop (000)	% of Urb.	Cu %
Tokyo	6920	15.4		19771	23.4		26444	26.5	
Osaka	4147	9.2	24.6	9844	11.7	35.1	11013	11.0	37.5
Nagoya	992	2.2	26.8	2293	2.7	37.8	3225	3.2	40.7
Kitakyushu	954	2.1	28.9	1853	2.2	40.0	2750	2.8	43.5
Kobe	805	1.8	30.7	1361	1.6	41.6	1450	1.5	44.9
Sapporo	254	0.6	31.2	978	1.2	42.8	1813	1.8	46.8
Hiroshima	200	0.4	31.7	505	0.6	43.4	866	0.9	47.6
Sendai	324	0.7	32.4	635	0.8	44.1	953	1.0	48.6
Tot. Urban	45067			84409			99,865		
Rank									
Size Index	1.136			1.413			1.557		
(1/2+3+4)									

1950; this rose to 23 per cent in 1975 and to almost 27 per cent in 2000. Together, the eight largest cities had only a third of the country's urban population in 1950; today they have nearly half. The table also shows the Rank Order Index (the ratio of the largest city to the sum of the next three cities). This, too, suggests an increasing concentration of the urban population in the top one or two cities.

Thus, on the one hand, urbanized Japan has large urban centers throughout the island, with a fairly balanced distribution of cities of various sizes. At the same time, there is a high and apparently growing concentration in the two largest cities, Tokyo and Osaka.

MAJOR PATTERNS OF MIGRATION STREAMS

Factors of Urbanization

Factors directly affecting urbanization change are: (1) natural increase due to the difference between fertility and mortality, (2) net in-migration in the urban areas from rural areas and the demographic behavior of fertility and mortality, and (3) merger of local communities (cities, towns, and villages) into a major city or cities.

In Japan, the migratory movement due to rapid economic and social development has been really influential and effective in contributing to a successful distribution of the population. Secondly, in the Town and Village Merger Acceleration Law in 1953, the national government has provided assistance to meet the financial difficulties facing towns and villages due to serious ageing and depopulation.

Then, there was considerable enlargement of *"shi"* areas through the absorption of neighboring *"machi"* and *"mura"* as well as an increase in the number of *"shi"* due to the new incorporation of former *"machi"* or *"mura"* into *"shi."* Very recently, the government is also recommending an administrative policy to incorporate financially distressed small *"machi"* or *"mura"* due to heavy depopulation.

Thirdly, the demographically noticeable point should be emphasized; this is the effect on vital rates in both urban and rural areas of the dominant selective propensity of young people to migrate. Young migrants are very likely to get married soon after moving into urban areas. This contributes to raising the birth rates and also reducing the mortality rates due to lower mortality of young migrants. In this way, vital rates in urban areas introduce a higher population increase rate through higher fertility rate and lower death rate; this is quite a different trend than expected so far. In turn, the rural population is suffering from a serious shortage of young labor force, and a very rapid unexpected ageing process, which has the opposite effect on vital rates.

Data Availability

Basically, two kinds of migration data are available. One is annual reports on internal migration, which have been compiled since 1954 from residence registration records called the "Basic Residence Registers." Another source is the national population censuses, which are quinquennial population censuses since 1920. In particular, the national censuses included questions on the place of residence one year before or five years before. The population registration of births and deaths includes vital statistics available annually since the turn of the 20th century.

Detailed analyses of migration can still be hampered at times, however, due to lack of such basic demographic data as the age of migrants. Only a limited number of prefectures collected the information on age of migrants and the reasons for changing residences; and this was only from the standpoint of the prefectural level. It should be pointed out, however, that we can estimate age-sex-specific net migration rates for the five-year intercensal periods, applying the census survival method to the quinquennial census data.

Trends of Internal Migration

The migration stream in terms of number of internal migrants in the post-war period is characterized by two stages. The first stage saw the rapid increase of internal migrants, from five to eight million a year, or from 6 to 8 per cent of the total population, extending from the latter half of the 1950s to the first half of the 1970s. The second stage saw migration slowing down but maintaining the level of six million migrants per year in the whole period, 1975–2000, which amounted to about 5 per cent of the total population. (See Table 14.6 and Figures 14.2 and 14.3.)

It may be interesting to note that the first stage was characterized slightly more by within-prefectural migration for a few years until 1960. From that point on, within-prefecture and inter-prefectural migration have been quite similar.

Another interesting point is a quite different sex-ratio of migrants. Males are strongly dominant in inter-prefectural migration, giving us sex ratios about 130 males per 100 females. Within-prefectural migration, however, has a sex ratio lower than the total for all migrants, indicating

FIGURE 14.2 Internal migration in Japan, 1954–2000

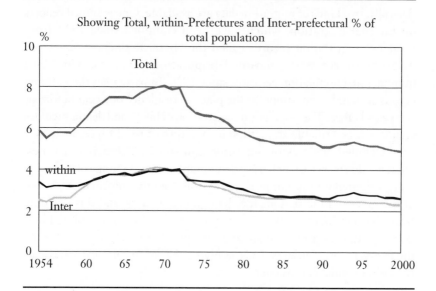

Showing Total, within-Prefectures and Inter-prefectural % of total population

FIGURE 14.3 Internal migration in Japan, 1954–2000

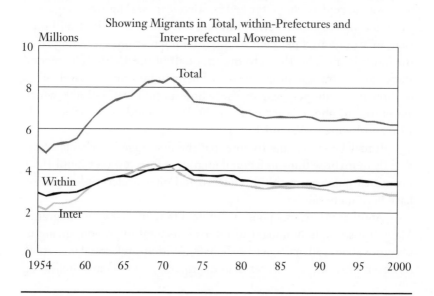

Showing Migrants in Total, within-Prefectures and Inter-prefectural Movement

TABLE 14.6   Trends of internal migrants by total, within-prefecture and inter-prefectural

	Persons (000)			Rates (%)			Sex Ratio of Migrants		
	Total Pref.	W/in Pref.	Intr	Total	W/in	Inter	Total	W/in	Inter
1954	5150	2900	2250	5.9	3.4	2.5	109	100	120
1955	4850	2750	2100	5.5	3.1	2.4	108	100	118
1956	5250	2850	2400	5.8	3.2	2.6	111	101	126
1957	5300	2900	2400	5.8	3.2	2.6	115	102	131
1958	5350	2900	2450	5.77	3.17	2.6	116	104	132
1959	5550	2950	2600	6.1	3.2	2.9	115	104	129
1960	6050	3100	2950	6.5	3.3	3.2	116	105	128
1961	6500	3250	3250	6.97	3.47	3.5	116	105	129
1962	6900	3450	3450	7.2	3.6	3.6	114	104	126
1963	7190	3600	3590	7.5	3.75	3.75	114	104	127
1964	7400	3700	3700	7.5	3.75	3.75	115	105	127
1965	7520	3750	3770	7.5	3.8	3.7	114	104	126
1966	7600	3700	3900	7.45	3.7	3.75	114	104	128
1967	7950	3850	4100	7.7	3.8	3.9	113	103	127
1968	8250	4000	4250	7.9	3.9	4	112	103	125
1969	8350	4050	4300	8	3.9	4.1	113	103	126
1970	8250	4150	4100	8.05	4	4.05	112	103	125
1971	8450	4200	4250	7.9	3.95	3.95	111	102	124
1972	8200	4300	3900	7.95	4	3.95	110	102	121
1973	7800	4100	3700	7.08	3.48	3.6	111	102	124
1974	7330	3800	3530	6.75	3.45	3.3	111	102	125
1975	7300	3780	3520	6.63	3.43	3.2	111	102	125

TABLE 14.6 (cont'd)

1976	7260	3770	3490	6.6	3.4	3.2	112	102	127
1977	7230	3750	3480	6.5	3.4	3.1	113	102	129
1978	7200	3800	3400	6.25	3.25	3	114	102	130
1979	7100	3750	3350	5.9	3.1	2.8	114	102	130
1980	6850	3550	3300	5.8	3.05	2.75	114	102	131
1981	6790	3540	3250	5.6	2.9	2.7	115	102	133
1982	6650	3450	3200	5.45	2.8	2.65	116	103	136
1983	6570	3420	3150	5.4	2.8	2.6	118	104	138
1984	6600	3400	3200	5.3	2.7	2.6	119	105	138
1985	6620	3380	3240	5.3	2.7	2.6	119	105	138
1986	6600	3400	3200	5.3	2.65	2.65	119	105	139
1987	6610	3380	3230	5.3	2.7	2.6	120	105	140
1988	6630	3400	3230	5.3	2.7	2.6	121	106	141
1989	6590	3390	3200	5.3	2.7	2.6	121	106	142
1990	6450	3300	3150	5.1	2.6	2.5	120	105	140
1991	6450	3350	3100	5.1	2.6	2.5	117	103	138
1992	6450	3450	3000	5.23	2.75	2.48	115	103	136
1993	6498	3448	3050	5.25	2.8	2.45	115	102	136
1994	6490	3500	2990	5.35	2.9	2.45	115	102	136
1995	6530	3550	2980	5.23	2.8	2.43	115	102	135
1996	6410	3510	2900	5.15	2.75	2.4	115	102	136
1997	6400	3500	2900	5.15	2.75	2.4	115	102	136
1998	6330	3380	2950	5.05	2.65	2.4	116	103	135
1999	6250	3400	2850	4.95	2.65	2.3	115	103	133
2000	6250	3400	2850	4.9	2.6	2.3	114	103	133

SOURCE: Basic Residence Registers, Japan Statistics Bureau.

that women are more prominent in the short distance, within-prefecture migration.

Migration and Urbanization in Major Metropolitan Regions

A major part of the urbanization in Japan is characterized by a heavy concentration of population in the three large metropolitan regions of Japan. In Japan, there are 47 prefectures *(ken)*, and these prefectures in turn constitute 12 larger regions. Among the 12 regions, we can consider *Minami-kanto* (Tokyo metropolitan), *Nishi-kinki* (Osaka metropolitan), and *Tokai* (Chukyo metropolitan) as the three main metropolitan areas, which include11 prefectures. The remaining nine regions are non-metropolitan regions.

These three metropolitan regions, located along the *Tokaido* line, facing the Pacific Ocean, have been developed economically, socially, politically, and also in culture, remarkably contrasting with all other parts of Japan. For example, the area of the three metropolitan regions together is only 15 per cent of the total land, but the population of the three regions is more than 50 per cent of the total population of Japan in 2000, 64 million out of 125 million.

Consequently, it can be said that urbanization in Japan is greatly affected by migratory movement between these metropolitan regions and non-metropolitan regions, including all remaining nine regions composed of 36 prefectures.

CONCENTRATION INTO METROPOLITAN JAPAN

The rapid urbanization during the late 1950s and the early 1960s was remarkable. In particular, during the early 1960s, net immigrants in the three metropolitan regions together exceeded 600,000 per year. The figures can be seen in Table 14.7.

In the 1970s, two noticeable changes were recognized. First is the so-called sub-urbanization. Large numbers of migrants into large cities within the three metropolitan regions during the 1950s and 1960s started to find new residential areas just outside the metropolitan regions in order to enjoy a new healthy life, free from environmental deterioration. This was most pronounced in Osaka, next in Nagoya, and least in the Tokyo metropolitan region.

TABLE 14.7   Migration to the three main metropolitan areas, 1954–2000

	Net In-Migration			% of Migrants			
Year	Total	Tokyo M.	Nagoya M.	Osaka M.	Total	Tokyo M.	Nagoya M.	Osaka M.
1954	384680	257756	23872	103052	100	67	6	27
1955	352833	234658	23067	95108	100	67	7	27
1956	401956	247117	41725	113114	100	62	10	28
1957	507195	294637	44017	168541	100	58	9	33
1958	421652	272818	26082	122752	100	65	6	29
1959	490864	300883	44621	145360	100	61	9	30
1960	593820	333208	71777	188835	100	56	12	32
1961	654698	359237	74612	220849	100	55	11	34
1962	647453	364360	72072	211021	100	56	11	33
1963	620184	354349	81292	184543	100	57	13	30
1964	577742	327361	76320	174061	100	57	13	30
1965	480606	297582	52364	130660	100	62	11	27
1966	405876	265908	37145	102823	100	66	9	25
1967	403908	255107	41577	107224	100	63	10	27
1968	418145	258747	47523	111875	100	62	11	27
1969	425699	249951	54784	120964	100	59	13	28
1970	393044	248046	53551	91447	100	63	14	23
1971	287900	205500	36543	45857	100	71	13	16
1972	206908	158881	23726	24301	100	77	12	12
1973	114124	96985	22063	-4924	100	85	19	-4
1974	38836	52950	6879	-20993	100	136	18	-54
1975	10572	44513	-3782	-30159	100	421	-36	-285
1976	-22508	25571	-6903	-41176	-100	114	-31	-183

TABLE 14.7 (cont'd)

1977	-9447	35368	-298	-44517	-100	374	-3	-471
1978	7310	44500	421	-37611	100	609	6	-515
1979	-14629	29583	-2752	-41460	-100	202	-19	-283
1980	-5819	30578	-232	-36165	-100	526	-4	-622
1981	30682	52712	1746	-23776	100	172	6	-78
1982	54896	64927	3719	-13750	100	118	7	-25
1983	82660	82889	4330	-4559	100	100	5	-6
1984	89576	85863	5868	-2155	100	96	7	-2
1985	102452	94782	11807	-4137	100	93	12	-4
1986	149805	124777	16820	8208	100	83	11	6
1987	147076	129165	15341	2570	100	88	10	2
1988	103789	98451	11479	-6143	100	95	11	-6
1989	92011	89335	14180	-11504	100	97	15	-13
1990	63583	67012	14293	-17722	100	105	23	-28
1991	52819	50590	12037	-9808	100	96	23	-19
1992	16398	24372	6921	-14895	100	149	42	-91
1993	-27909	-11751	3714	-19872	-100	-42	13	-71
1994	-45371	-26772	1069	-19668	-100	-59	2	-43
1995	-48961	-17878	1270	-32353	-100	-37	3	-66
1996	-2652	5360	1345	-9357	-100	202	51	-353
1997	20010	22556	4403	-6949	100	113	22	-35
1998	47060	42953	6177	-2070	100	91	13	-4
1999	45172	45517	4354	-4699	100	101	10	-10
2000	56507	57811	3673	-4977	100	102	7	-9

SOURCE: Same for Table 14.6.

Secondly, non-metropolitan regions experienced a significant population recovery, slowing the concentration the into three metropolitan regions. Net migrants from non-metropolitan regions into the three metropolitan regions since 1961 up to 1976 dropped from over 600,000 to *negative* 5,000 or 10,000 through 1980.

After 1980, net migration into the metropolitan regions rose again, reaching over one million in the years 1985–88. In this period, it was mostly the Tokyo and Nagoya regions that participated in this surge. Following this, net migration again declined to negative numbers in 1993–96. As in the mid-1970, it was Osaka that lost the largest proportion to what is presumably the sub-urbanization trend. For the past few years, net migration has been rising again in Tokyo and Nagoya, but not in Osaka, which has shown net out-migration continuously from 1988 to 2000.

It should be noted that remarkable out-migration from the established urbanized metropolitan regions into non- metropolitan regions has become a common feature of some industrialized countries It presents an extremely interesting subject for social scientists. Is this a new stage of urbanization never experienced before? Is it a transitional change not affecting the urbanization process? American scholars called it Rural Renaissance. British experts named it Counter-Urbanization.

In Japan, based on detailed statistical analysis of migrants by age and sex, using quinquennial census data of each prefecture, we found that relatively large numbers of young workers who moved into metropolitan regions during 1960s and early 1970s started to go back to their home towns in non-metropolitan regions where new employment opportunities came to be available due to regional development policies. In view of such a strong home-town oriented movement, we noted that it may be called the "U-Turn" movement, because they are going back to the home-towns which they left to move to metropolitan regions several years ago.

In particular, net out-migration in the late 1970s and repeated in the early 1990s, in the metropolitan regions, produced an impression that urbanization may be essentially changing, by taking a different direction.

However, it is found that the late 1970s are characterized by a stationary situation of urbanization in terms of balancing in-and out-migration. On the other hand, remarkable urbanization seems to have been achieved by rapidly increasing migrants within metropolitan regions. In particular, the number of migrants within the metropolitan regions reached was largest compared with other patterns of migrants from 1966 to the present. This suggests another aspect of urbanization; it is expanding into less urbanized, or even rural areas within metropolitan regions.

THE END OF URBANIZATION?

Post-World War urbanization in Japan is characterized by several stages. The most important factors promoting urbanization were the remarkable baby-boom of the immediate post-war years, followed by rapid fertility decline, and, after 1960, an exceptionally rapid economic development. The development was fueled in part by the post-war baby boom, which greatly increased the young labor force in the 1960s.

The first stage was characterized by a process of population concentration in the three major metropolitan regions. During the late 1950s and the 1960s, the rate of concentration was especially high due mainly to a large population influx from rural agricultural regions. They were more than one million per year, continuing from the 1960s to early 1970s when urban concentration slowed down and there was even net out-migration in the late 1970s.

The second stage was a multi-directional urbanization process. First, there was the urbanization within metropolitan regions in terms of sub-urbanization. Second, there was the so-called counter-urbanization in terms of an increase in the rural population due to out-migration from metropolitan to non-metropolitan regions, which was an interesting topic for social scientists. This kind of deconcentration raised the question of whether it is a temporary anomaly, a long-term trend, or a transitional phase.

The second stage is quite complicated because it consisted of contradictory movements. However, a third stage may be characterized by reconcentration in the 1980s. It is clear that the net inflow in the metropolitan regions from non-metropolitan regions continued in the 1980s up to the early 1990s. It should be noted that the majority of the net inflow in the metropolitan regions depended on the Tokyo and, to a lesser extent, the Nagoya metropolitan regions, in spite of net outflow in the Osaka metropolitan region. Rapid change in the 1990s should be

401

considered seriously, however, because the net outflow occurred in the metropolitan regions, including Tokyo and Osaka metropolitan regions, in the early 1990s; after that Tokyo recovered its net inflow.

Maturity of Urbanization

Urbanization is necessary process of economic, social, and cultural development. Japan's case should be carefully examined from the standpoint of topography. For example, Japan is one of the most populous countries in terms of population density per square meter of inhabitable land, more than 2000 persons.

Now, the percent urban is about 80 per cent of the total population, approaching a plateau in what might be the final stage. We experienced several stages of urbanization after World War Two. First was the rapid concentration of the national population into three major metropolitan regions, Tokyo, Osaka, and Nagoya, from all the remaining non-metropolitan regions. This was followed by net outflow from the metropolitan regions to non-metropolitan regions, which is called counter-urbanization or rural renaissance process, which contributed to the acceleration of the urbanization process in rural areas. Another interesting point is the drastic change of the people's way of life and value system. People living in major metropolitan regions or even non-metropolitan regions have come to enjoy the same pattern of living and also way of thinking.

We are now entering the final stage of balanced urbanization as a way of human life. It may be expressed as a society of "ecumenopolis."

CHAPTER 15

Rapid Urbanization and Structural Change in the Republic of Korea

JUNG-DUK LIM

RAPID URBANIZATION IN A SHORT TIME PERIOD

The Republic of Korea was basically an agricultural society, heavily devastated by war, before she started her first five-year economic development plan in 1962. Since then, Korea experienced one of the world's most rapid transitions to an urban industrial society. As shown in Tables 15.1–15.3, Korea became an urban industrial country within 30 years. All the socio-economic variables dramatically changed in a short period of time.

Table 15.1 shows the dramatic movement in urbanization. Urban dwellers increased from less than a fifth of the population to almost four-fifths of the population in the span of only half a century. Throughout this period, three things can be seen. First, the total population grew rapidly then declined basically to replacement level. This represents a rapid demographic transition. Second, throughout this period, urban growth was substantially greater than rural growth, often more than 5 percentage points. Indeed, from the 1970s the rural population began an absolute decline in numbers. Third, all rates of growth have slowed as the Republic of Korea has become an urban industrial society with a low and declining rate of population growth.

In 1965, 58 per cent of the employed workers were engaged in the primary sector, basically agriculture; and almost half of the country's added value came from this sector (Table 15.2). As is common in the process of industrialization, the manufacturing, or secondary, sector grew, then leveled off, while the tertiary sector came to dominate the economy. By 1995, two-thirds of the workers and two-thirds of the value added in production came from the tertiary or services sector. Agriculture was

TABLE 15.1 Urbanization of Korea (1,000 persons,%)

| Year | Nation | | Urban | | Rural | | % |
	Pop.	Growth rate	Pop.	Growth rate	Pop.	Growth rate	Urban
1949	20,188	–	3,472	–	16,716	–	17.2
1960	24,989	2.13	6,996	7.01	17,993	0.74	28.0
1970	30,882	2.12	12,709	5.97	18,172	0.10	41.1
1980	37,436	1.92	21,434	5.23	16,002	–1.27	57.3
1990	43,410	1.48	32,308	4.10	11,101	–3.66	74.4
2000	46,136	0.61	36,755	1.29	9,381	–1.68	79.7
2000/1949	2.29		10.59		0.56		–

SOURCE: National Statistics Office.

TABLE 15.2 Industrial structure of Korea (%)

| Year | Employment | | | Value added | | |
	Primary	Secondary	Tertiary	Primary	Secondary	Tertiary
1965	58.0	10.3	31.0	42.9	13.1	44.0
1970	50.4	14.3	35.3	28.7	16.3	54.9
1975	45.9	19.1	35.0	24.2	23.5	52.3
1980	34.0	22.6	43.4	15.1	22.0	52.9
1985	24.9	24.5	50.6	12.2	30.8	57.0
1990	18.3	27.3	54.4	8.4	31.6	60.0
1995	12.4	23.6	64.0	6.4	30.6	63.0
1999	11.6	19.9	68.6	5.3	33.8	60.9

SOURCE: National Statistic Office.

TABLE 15.3   Social and economic changes in Korea

	Unit	1960	1980	2000	2000/1960
Total Population		24,989	37,436	46,136	1.8
Male	1,000 persons	12,544	18,767	23,159	1.8
Female		12,445	18,669	22,977	1.8
Urban Pop.		6,996	21,434	36,755	5.3
Exports		32.8	17,504.9	172,267.5	5252.1
Imports	Million US $	343.5	22,291.7	160,481.0	467.2
Per capita income	US $	79	1,598	9,628	121.9
Average years of Educational attainment	Year	5.0	7.6	10.6	2.1
Number of households	1,000	–	7,470	11,928	–
Housing units	1,000	–	5,450	11,472	–
Housing supply rate	%	82.2	71.2	96.2	–
Motor vehicles	1,000 cars	31	528	12,059	389.0
Persons per car	Persons	806.1	72.2	3.9	–
Length of road	Km	27,169	46,951	88,775	3.3
Cars per km	Cars	1.1	11.3	135.8	–
Telephone subscribers	Per 100 persons	–	7.1	46.7	–
Mobile telephone subscribers	Per 10,000 persons	–	0.7	5,704.6	–
Medical facilities	Number	4,013	6,666	38,668	9.6
Physicians	Persons	7,765	22,564	72,503	9.3

* The statistics of 1960 may represent other years in 1960s.
SOURCE: National Statistics Office.

reduced to just over a tenth of the labor force and agriculture's value added accounted for less than a tenth of the country's productive wealth.

This chapter tries to explain the overall picture of the change, especially from the standpoint of urbanization above, and to identify characteristics related to that change.

Definition of Urban in the Census

By Korean administrative definitions, a county (*Gu* or *Goon*) with more than 50,000 residents becomes a "City (*Si*)" and a rural area (*Myun*) with more than 20,000 residents becomes a populated area called an "*Uhp*." Those administrative units of city level and above are defined as urban areas in Korean statistics.

Urban Population in Korea

As shown in Table 15.1, above, the Korean population doubled during half a century, but the urban population increased by more than 10 times. In terms of annual growth rate, that of the total population began to decline after the 1970s, but the growth rate of the urban population maintained a very high level until the 1990s. Therefore, the urbanization process proceeded at a high speed up to the 1990s.

Sources of Growth

The major source of Korean urban growth has been migration to cities from rural areas. Changes in administrative boundaries and natural increase contribute to urban population growth to a certain extent but the lion's share comes from urban migration. Table 15.1, above, shows the population change in urban and rural areas in Korea. While the urban population increased from the early 1960s, the rural population decreased at an accelerating speed. In the past, younger generations left the rural areas for the purpose of employment, education, and urban amenities. Therefore, the average age of the population in rural areas tends to be higher and the average education attainment lower than urban areas. The Korean case is almost the same as Japan's in experiencing industrialization after World War II. This model will be applied in other countries in the future.

Since Korea is a homogeneous society there are no significant differences between regions in demographic characteristics such as the sex ratio. The overall demographic dynamics are shown in Table 15.4. The crude birth (CBR), crude death (CDR), total fertility (TFR), and natural increase rates are not much different between urban and rural areas these days.

TABLE 15.4 Demographic change in Korea

Year	Natural Increase Rate	Crude Birth Rate	Crude Death Rate	Total Fertility Rate	Life expectancy (Age)		
					Male	Female	All
1960	30.0	42.1	12.1	6.0	51.1	53.7	52.4
1966	23.3	31.9	8.6	4.8	59.7	64.1	61.9
1970	23.2	31.2	8.0	4.5	59.8	66.7	63.2
1975	17.1	24.8	7.7	3.4	60.2	67.4	63.8
1980	15.4	22.7	7.3	2.8	62.3	70.5	66.2
1985	10.2	16.2	6.0	1.7	64.9	73.3	69.0
1990	9.6	15.4	5.8	1.6	67.7	75.9	71.7
1995	10.6	16.0	5.4	1.6	69.6	77.4	73.5
2000	8.2	13.4	5.2	1.4	72.1	79.5	75.9

* NIR (per 1,000 persons)
* CBR=(Births per year/Mid-year Pop.)´1,000 (per 1,000 persons)
* CDR=(Deaths per year/Mid-year Pop.)´1,000 (per 1,000 persons)
* TFR (per woman)
SOURCE: National Statistics Office.

Although available data cannot give us precise percentages, it can be roughly indicated by the population change of the six largest cities in Korea. As shown in Table 15.5, the growth rate of the six largest cities was higher than that of the national population. While the national population increased by 2.3 times during the last half-century, the population of the six largest cities increased by an average 8.4 times. In the past, the larger the city, the faster was its growth rate. From the 1990s, the two largest cities began to lose population within their administrative boundary.

Characteristics of Urban Migration

Migration in Korea increased rapidly after the beginning of urbanization as shown in Tables 15.6 and 15.7. Throughout the 1970s and 1980s, the migration rate stayed at a higher level than the 1960s. In 1975, the migration rate reached 26.7 per cent, which is two times higher than that of 1967. In the 1990s and 2000s, the rate appears to have stabilized at a slightly lower level than the previous periods. Among migrants, about

TABLE 15.5 Six largest cities of Korea (1,000 persons,%)

Year	National Growth rate	Seoul Pop.	Growth rate	Busan Pop.	Growth rate	Daegu pop.	Growth rate
1949	–	1,446	0	633	–	313	
1960	4.27	2,445	10.51	1,163	12.16	676	15.38
1966	3.09	3,793	8.78	1,426	4.07	845	4.45
1970	1.15	5,433	7.19	1,842	5.12	1,063	4.60
1975	2.33	6,889	4.75	2,453	5.73	1,310	4.18
1980	1.51	8,364	3.88	3,159	5.06	1,604	4.05
1985	1.55	9,639	2.84	3,514	2.13	2,029	4.70
1990	1.41	10,612	1.92	3,798	1.55	2,229	1.87
1995	0.54	10,231	–0.73	3,814	0.09	2,449	1.89
2000	0.67	9,895	–0.67	3,662	–0.81	2,480	0.25
2000/1949	–	6.84	–	5.78	–	7.92	–

Year	National growth rate	Incheon Pop.	Growth rate	Gwangju Pop.	Growth rate	Daejeon Pop.	Growth rate
1949	–	265	–	138		126	–
1960	4.27	401	8.25	314	16.34	228	11.84
1966	3.09	525	5.40	403	4.99	314	6.38
1970	1.15	634	3.74	493	4.03	406	5.12
1975	2.33	800	4.65	607	4.14	506	4.39
1980	1.51	1,083	6.07	727	3.62	651	5.04
1985	1.55	1,386	4.93	906	4.39	866	5.70
1990	1.41	1,817	5.41	1,139	4.57	1,049	3.83
1995	0.54	2,308	4.78	1,257	1.98	1,272	3.85
2000	0.67	2,475	1.40	1,352	1.46	1,368	1.46
2000/1949	–	9.34	–	9.79	–	10.86	–

SOURCE: National Statistics Office.

two-thirds moved within the boundary of provinces and metropolitan cities, while one-third moved between provinces or metropolitan cities. The first characteristic of Korean migration is massive outflow of the labor force from rural to urban areas at the first stage of industrialization

TABLE 15.6   Migrants by province (1,000 persons, %)

Year	Total Migrants			Intra-province		Inter-province	
	Number	Rate	Sex ratio (per 100 females)	Number	Rate	Number	Rate
1967	3,762	12.8	–	2,831	9.6	929	3.2
1970	4,046	13.1	113.5	2,780	9.0	1,264	4.1
1975	9,011	26.7	100.0	6,143	18.2	2,867	8.5
1980	8,258	21.9	107.3	5,652	15.0	2,605	6.9
1985	8,679	21.4	104.7	5,753	14.2	2,925	7.2
1990	9,459	22.0	103.3	6,228	14.5	3,231	7.5
1995	9,073	19.9	100.1	6,208	13.6	2,864	6.3
2000	9,009	19.0	98.7	6,164	13.0	2,845	6.0

SOURCE: National Statistics Office.

TABLE 15.7   Migrants between urban and rural (1,000 persons, %)

Year	Total (000)	Rural to Urban %	Urban to Urban %	Urban to Rural %	Rural to Rural %
1965–1970	4,395	41.6	34.8	8.8	14.8
1970–1975	5,151	34.1	44.2	10.8	10.9
1975–1980	7,618	33.1	50.7	8.9	7.3
1980–1985	8,366	29.0	54.8	10.6	5.6
1985–1990	9,816	23.7	65.0	7.6	3.7
1990–1995	10,087	11.6	76.6	9.7	2.1

SOURCE: National Statistics Office.

(1967–75). Most of the out-migrants were young males seeking job opportunities in urban areas. This produced a sex ratio of 113 males to 100 females in the migrant stream.

Table 15.7 shows an interesting pattern. Throughout this period, rural-to-urban and urban-to-urban movements dominated the migration pattern. But also throughout the period, rural-to-urban migration declined, while urban-to-urban migration increased. Basically, the rural-to-urban transition had been completed by the 1980s. However, as the rural-to-urban migration was completed, the concentration of the urban population in the Seoul metropolitan area (Capital City, Inchon City, and Gyeonggi Province) produced another dominant pattern of migration. That is, in addition to the continuation of rural-to-urban migration, urban-to-urban migration (especially to the Seoul metropolitan area) became another characteristic (Table 15.8).

For instance, Seoul has been absorbing migrants from all regions in Korea, except the surrounding regions, Gyeonggi Province and Inchon City. Therefore, the Seoul metropolitan area itself has been consistently expanding. On the other hand, Busan, the second largest city, began to lose its population to all regions in the nation since the 1990s. Gyeongnam

TABLE 15.8   Net migration rate

Year	1970–75	1975–80	1980–85	1985–90	1990–95	1995–00
Seoul	2.16	2.15	0.97	0.23	–1.58	–1.51
Busan	3.43	2.92	0.22	–0.17	–0.83	–1.34
Daegu	1.97	2.68	1.04	0.46	0.38	–0.48
Incheon	2.14	3.31	2.42	2.80	2.56	0.46
Gwangju	1.30	1.61	2.29	0.39	1.16	0.50
Daejeon	1.92	3.21	1.63	0.67	3.06	0.58
Ulsan	4.03	5.51	1.95	1.49	2.34	–0.21
Gyeonggi	1.49	2.32	2.79	3.41	3.66	2.14
Gangwon	–2.22	–2.16	–2.06	–2.77	–1.57	–0.08
Chungbuk	–1.52	–2.66	–1.65	–0.96	–0.14	0.46
Chungnam	–2.90	–2.85	–2.06	–1.21	–2.55	0.58
Jeonbuk	–2.23	–2.79	–1.95	–2.07	–1.77	–0.50
Jeonnam	–3.66	–3.53	–2.64	–2.14	–3.67	–0.87
Gyeongbuk	–2.28	–2.85	–2.30	–2.00	–0.75	0.04
Gyeongnam	–2.04	–2.12	–0.88	–0.80	0.10	0.10
Jeju	–0.20	0.90	–0.33	–0.11	–0.98	–0.54
Nation	–0.32	0.02	–0.01	0.04	–0.06	–0.05
Capital area	1.97	2.30	1.63	1.48	0.72	0.18
Major cities	2.36	2.56	1.08	0.47	–0.29	–0.86

SOURCE: National Statistics Office.

Province, which is the hinterland to Busan, is losing its population to other areas in the nation but gaining from Busan; the sum of two areas is therefore declining.[1]

While the Seoul metropolitan area expanded its boundary by absorbing population from other areas, Busan began to lose its population from the 1990s, showing a net out-migration to other areas. In the early periods, the major cause of migration was job opportunity. As the economy grew, good education for children became another major cause of migration. It is shown that 40.9 per cent (2000) of higher education institutions are concentrated in the Seoul metropolitan area, attracting more immigrants for educational purposes (Table 15.9).

TABLE 15.9   University location (number)

Year	1985	1990	1995	2000
Seoul	36	34	35	39
Busan	10	10	11	11
Daegu	5	4	2	2
Incheon	2	2	2	4
Gwangju	0	5	5	7
Daejeon	0	6	6	7
Ulsan	–	–	–	1
Gyeonggi	9	13	18	23
Gangwon	5	5	5	8
Chungbuk	4	4	6	8
Chungnam	9	3	10	11
Jeonbuk	5	5	7	8
Jeonnam	6	4	6	10
Gyeongbuk	4	7	12	16
Gyeongnam	4	4	5	4
Jeju	1	1	1	2
Nation	100	107	131	161
% in Capital area	47.0	45.8	41.9	40.9
% in Major cities	53.0	57.0	46.5	44.1

* Capital area : Seoul, Incheon, Gyeonggi.
* Major cities : Seoul, Busan, Daegu, Incheon, Gwangju, Daejeon, Ulsan.
SOURCE: Ministry of Education and Human Resources.

National System of Cities

From 1945 to 1962, there were nine provinces and one special city (Seoul) in South Korea. Because of industrialization and migration to cities, Busan was elevated to a province level city (*Jikhal-Si*) from a city in Gyeongnam Province in 1963. The population size of Busan in 1963 was 1,360,630. As the growth of other large cities continued, the Korean government designated three other large cities (Daegu, Incheon, and Gwangju) having a population of more than one million as Jikhal-Si in 1985.

The two next largest cities (Daejeon and Ulsan) became Jikhal-Si in the 1990s. In the past, the criterion for reclassification was population size. But for the last two cities, political pressure also came into operation, and the one million rule was ignored. The name Jikhal-Si was changed to *Gwangyuk-Si* meaning "a metropolitan city" in 1995. That means a metropolitan city can have a Goon instead of a Gu as a sub-region (see above). Since the 1990s, there has been one special city (Seoul) with six metropolitan cities and nine provinces in Korea.

In 1949, four years after the liberation from Japanese colonialism, there were 14 cities in Korea and only one had more than 500,000 people. During the height of urbanization in Korea, the number of cities increased and the proportion of the population in the larger cities, especially the cities with populations of more than one million, increased rapidly up to the late 1980s.

Even though the urbanization process stabilized after the 1990s, the redistribution of population among cities continued actively afterwards. For example, Table 15.10 shows that the proportion of the urban population in cities of 500,000 persons or less has continually declined (except for a slight rise in 2000 in the proportion of cities of 250,000–500,000 persons). Cities with population of over one million continued to gain a larger proportion of urban residents until 1980, when they began to lose their proportions. On the other hand, cities with populations between 500,000 and one million have continued to gain a greater proportion of urban residents throughout the period. In summary, there are two points to be made. One is the increasing concentration of urban dwellers in large cities, and second is the more recent shift from the largest cities to their slightly smaller neighbors.

Another characteristic is the increased concentration in the capital region (Seoul metropolitan areas). By 2000, Seoul was

TABLE 15.10   Cities by sizes (1,000 pop.) and percentage of urban population (number, %)

Size> Year	<100 No.	<100 % of Urb.	100–250 No.	100–250 % of Urb.	250–500 No.	250–500 % of Urb.	500–1,000 No.	500–1,000 % of Urb.	1,000+ No.	1,000+ % of Urb.	Total No.	Total % of Urb.
1949	6	12.0	5	21.9	2	23.0	–	–	1	43.1	14	100
1960	18	18.5	4	10.1	2	10.2	1	9.7	2	51.6	27	100
1970	14	9.7	11	10.6	2	5.2	2	8.9	3	65.6	32	100
1980	6	2.1	21	14.2	7	11.0	2	6.4	4	66.3	40	100
1990	33	6.9	21	10.7	8	7.3	5	10.7	6	64.4	73	100
2000	10	2.0	31	11.0	21	16.3	10	16.5	7	54.2	79	100

SOURCE: National Statistics Office.

surrounded by numerous satellite cities that were basically rural areas in the past. Other metropolitan areas show similar trends, though with less intensity than the Seoul metropolitan area. Therefore, the share of the population living in metropolitan cities, including Seoul City, decreased from 64.4 per cent in 1990 to 54.2 per cent in 2000, even though the overall urbanization ratio in Korea increased during the same period.

The Korean urbanization process has almost reached the state of saturation. The Korean land policy regulates the transformation of green areas into sites for other purposes such as housing and factory sites. As economic growth continues, people begin to prefer rural or suburban life to a pure urban setting. Therefore, further urbanization is not likely to occur in the future, except in the Seoul metropolitan area. Instead, rural areas are being developed to have convenient facilities and social overhead capital such as paved roads, hospitals and markets, and better transportation to other urban centers.

However, the primacy problem remains to be solved in the future. The greater Seoul metropolitan area, including Seoul City, Inchon City, and Gyeonggi Province, accounted for 46.3 per cent of the total population by 2000. A serious point here is that the concentration has continued for half a century against the general expectation of decentralization as the congestion cost and diseconomy of scale increased.

413

The capital area had less than a fifth of the total national population in 1955, today it has almost half (Table 15.11).

The headquarters function of government and private firms is concentrated in the capital, and the opportunities for better education and more employment are also centered around the capital area. So far, the central government has failed to alleviate this concentration problem by various policies. Better and stronger policies are needed in the future. Otherwise, the Korean urbanization process could end up in unbalanced regional/urban development.

Table 15.12 shows that the concentration in the capital area is expected to increase, from its current 42 per cent of the total population to nearly 51 per cent in 2030. The concentration in other major cities is expected to decline slightly from 48 to 45 per cent.

Future Projections

Korean family planning is one of the most successful programs in the world. In fact, it was too successful to be sustained! Both the family planning program and improved standards of living led the Korean

TABLE 15.11 Population concentration (1,000 persons, %)

Year	Population of Capital Area				Migration		
	Seoul	Gyeonggi-do	Inchon	C. A./ Nation %	In	Out	Net
1955	1,568	2,359	–	18.3	–	–	–
1960	2,445	2,748	–	20.8	–	–	–
1966	3,793	3,102	–	23.6	–	–	–
1970	5,433	3,296	–	28.3	524	131	392
1975	6,889	4,039	–	31.5	1,047	405	641
1980	8,364	4,933	–	35.5	771	469	302
1985	9,639	4,794	1,386	39.1	765	458	307
1990	10,612	6,155	1,817	42.8	748	472	276
1995	10,231	7,649	2,308	45.2	515	447	68
2000	9,895	8,984	2,475	46.3	586	436	150

SOURCE: National Statistics Office.

TABLE 15.12   Projections of distribution of Korean population

Year	2000	2010	2020	2030
Seoul	21.4	19.9	18.8	17.9
Busan	7.9	7.2	6.7	6.3
Daegu	5.4	5.2	5.0	4.9
Incheon	5.4	5.6	5.8	6.0
Gwangju	2.9	3.1	3.2	3.3
Daejeon	3.0	3.2	3.5	3.7
Ulsan	2.2	2.3	2.3	2.4
Gyeonggi	19.5	22.8	25.1	26.8
Gangwon	3.2	3.1	2.9	2.8
Chungbuk	3.2	3.1	3.1	3.1
Chungnam	4.0	3.9	3.8	3.7
Jeonbuk	4.1	3.8	3.6	3.4
Jeonnam	4.3	3.8	3.4	3.2
Gyeongbuk	5.9	5.6	5.3	5.1
Gyeongnam	6.5	6.3	6.2	6.2
Jeju	1.1	1.1	1.1	1.1
Nation	100.0	100.0	100.0	50,294
Capital area(%)	46.3	48.3	49.8	50.8
Major cities(%)	48.2	46.5	45.4	44.6

SOURCE: National Statistics Office.

fertility rate to drop below replacement level. It is now even lower than France and Japan. This will lead to serious problems of ageing and even to population decline. Therefore, the Korean government changed its policy to encourage people to have more children. The tax laws favoring two or less children and other benefits were abolished in the 1990s.

It is estimated that the Korean population will begin to decline after 2020 (Table 15.13). If the two Koreas are unified before 2020, the total population may not decrease because of the North Korean situation. For a time, the North Korean fertility rate may be higher than the South after reunification.

As rapid urbanization is under control, the single most important policy issue for the future will be the ageing problem (Table 15.13). Korea is rapidly becoming an aged society and there is no difference between

TABLE 15.13   Projections of demographic changes in Korea

Year		2000	2010	2020	2030	2040	2050
Total Pop. (1,000 persons)		47,008	49,594	50,650	50,294	48,204	44,337
Sex Ratio (per 100 females)		101.4	101.1	100.4	99.2	97.8	96.3
Total Fertility Rate (per woman)		1.47	1.37	1.36	1.39	–	–
Life Expectancy (age) 75.9		78.8	80.7	81.5	–	–	
Pop. by age	0–14	21.1	17.2	13.9	12.4	–	–
group	15-64	71.7	72.1	71.0	64.6	–	–
(%)	65+	7.2	10.7	15.1	23.1	–	–

SOURCE: National Statistics Office.

the urban and rural areas. The Korean government is trying to put allocate more available resources for the aged. Since Korea is not much experienced in, nor ready for, this kind of change, the aged society may affect industry, consumption, housing, and many other sectors. As of today, a fiscal problem due to pension and medical insurance in the near future is anticipated. Korea is likely to follow the way of advanced countries in this respect.

URBAN-RURAL DIFFERENCES

Demographic Changes

Comparing urban-rural differences in demographic changes, the urban areas gained population constantly while the rural areas lost it by out-migration, as shown in Table 15.14. The CBR of the rural areas was higher than that of the urban up to the 1980s. However, the urban CBR superseded the rural after the 1980s because of structural changes in rural demography. The out-migration of younger people to the urban areas left the rural areas with older people and fewer in the reproductive

TABLE 15.14 Demographic differences between urban and rural area

Year		1970–75	1975–80	1980–85	1985–90	1990–95	1995–00
Total increase rate	Urban	4.09	4.66	3.36	2.43	2.79	1.07
	Rural	0.22	–0.81	–0.68	–0.99	–0.81	0.50
Crude birth rate	Urban	2.20	2.06	2.09	1.66	1.82	1.48
	Rural	3.23	2.32	1.91	1.32	1.37	1.37
Crude death rate	Urban	0.52	0.50	0.46	0.44	0.43	0.43
	Rural	0.88	0.89	0.86	0.81	0.78	0.77
Natural increase rate	Urban	1.68	1.56	1.63	1.22	1.38	1.05
	Rural	2.35	1.44	1.05	0.51	0.59	0.60
Diff(TIR–NIR)	Urban	2.41	3.10	1.73	1.20	1.41	0.02
	Rural	–2.13	–2.25	–1.73	–1.50	–1.41	–0.10

SOURCE: National Statistics Office.

ages. In the same context, the CDR of the rural areas is constantly higher than that of the urban.

There is no significant difference between urban and rural areas in life expectancy. Since younger people tend to leave the rural areas for the urban, the age structure in the rural areas is different from the national average. In Table 15.15, the characteristics of the farming population, representing rural areas, are compared with those of the population of Seoul, representing all urban areas in Korea.[2] The rural population was relatively younger up to the mid-1980s, but have turned into an aging society with one-third (32.2 per cent) of the people aged 60 years or more in 2000, while the proportion of younger people (less than 19 years old) declined from 53.9 per cent in 1970 to 19.5 per cent in 2000.

Table 15.15 shows some basic urban-rural demographic characteristics. The farming population is used to represent the rural, and Seoul is used to represent the country's urban population. Both show the same general trends, though some are at considerably different rates. Both saw a substantial decline in the average household size. Both have seen the same general changes in the age distribution: decline of the

TABLE 15.15 Population by age group and sex

Year	Rural: Farm population 000			House Holds (N)	Pers. per hh	Population by age group %		
	Male	Female				<19	20-59	60>
1960	14,559	7,154	7,405	2,350	6.2	-	-	-
1970	14,422	7,164	7,258	2,483	5.8	53.9	38.2	7.9
1980	10,827	5,415	5,412	2,155	5	45.4	44.1	10.5
1990	6,661	3,279	3,383	1,767	3.7	31.6	50.6	17.8
2000	4,032	1,972	2,060	1,384	2.9	19.5	48.3	32.2

Year	Urban (Seoul population)			House Holds	Per per hh	Population by age group		
	Male	Female				<19	20-59	60>
1960	2,445	1,222	1,223	446	5.48	48.2	48.2	3.6
1970	5,525	2,762	2,763	1,096	5.04	48.2	48.5	3.3
1980	8,350	4,160	4,190	1,849	4.51	42.5	53.4	4.1
1990	10,603	5,321	5,282	2,820	3.75	35.0	59.6	5.4
2000	9,853	4,943	4,910	3,540	2.78	26.4	64.7	8.9

SOURCE: National Statistics Office.

young, and increase of the productive aged and the aged. The first and third, however, were much more pronounced in the farming population than in Seoul's population. In effect, the ageing of the population is overwhelmingly a farm or rural phenomenon. As we saw above, however, ageing will also become very much an urban phenomenon in the near future.

The above change is contrasted with the change in Seoul. Even though Seoul also follows the general pattern of change, the speed is much slower than the rural change. For instance, the aged group (60 years old and over) made up 8.9 per cent of total population in 2000, which is only about 2.2 times more than in 1960; contrasted to the rural increase of just over 4 times. The younger group (19 years old or less) shows a similar trend, such that their percentage decreased relatively slowly from 48.2 per cent in 1960 to 26.4 per cent in 2000, compared to a decline from 54 to 20 per cent in the rural areas..

Demographic and Socio-economic Differentials

In terms of persons per household, there were more families in a household in rural areas up to 1990 (Table 15.16). However, the average number has become smaller than in urban areas, showing the consequence of continuing out-migration.

Reasons for living in the urban areas are quite different from those for living in the rural (Table 15.17). In the urban areas, education, employment, transportation, and financial reasons have been important but, in the case of the rural areas, the attraction of the old hometown has been the single most important reason.

In terms of income distribution, the gap between urban and rural is complex (Table 15.18). At the lower levels of income, the urban areas become wealthier than the rural areas. That is, the ratio of urban to rural rose. At the upper end, however, the gap is narrowing. In the 1980s, the upper tiers of urban income were four to five times the proportion found in the rural areas. In the 1990s, those proportions dropped to two to three.

Table 15.19 shows an interesting contrast of consumption expenditure between urban and rural areas. Residents in rural areas have spent less on food, clothing and footwear, transportation, and recreation and culture. On the other hand, they generally spend a little more on

TABLE 15.16   Composition of households (thousand, person)

Year	By number of household members (%)										Average persons of household members	
	One person		two persons		three persons		four persons		fiver and over			
	Urban	Rural	Urban	Rural	Urban	Rural	Urban	Rural	Urban	Rural	Urban	Rural
1975	4.5	3.9	9.1	7.6	13.5	11.0	17.9	14.4	55.0	62.9	4.8	5.3
1980	4.7	4.9	10.7	10.3	15.3	13.3	22.3	17.5	46.9	54.0	4.4	4.7
1985	6.8	7.2	11.6	13.7	16.8	15.9	27.4	21.2	37.4	42.0	4.0	4.2
1990	8.6	10.3	12.2	18.3	19.5	17.6	31.9	22.4	27.7	31.4	3.7	3.7
1995	11.8	15.6	14.5	24.9	20.8	18.7	34.5	22.3	18.4	18.5	3.4	3.1
2000	14.6	18.9	16.8	27.3	21.5	18.4	33.7	21.7	13.4	13.7	3.2	2.9

SOURCE: National Statistic Office.

TABLE 15.17 Reasons for living in current residential area   (%)

	1987		1992		1997	
	Urban	Rural	Urban	Rural	Urban	Rural
Children's education	9.1	2.5	8.5	2.3	8.1	1.5
Childcare	–	–	–	–	1.7	0.5
Employment	30.8	26.2	24.1	22.3	23.1	20.6
Transportation	12.2	2.2	9.4	2.0	14.5	2.7
Financial	30.7	13.6	39.5	14.7	33.7	17.4
Environment	2.8	1.9	3.7	2.6	4.4	5.5
Lived there for a long time	9.9	50.2	12.4	53.6	11.9	49.2
Others	4.5	3.4	2.4	2.5	2.6	2.6
Total	100.0	100.0	100.0	100.0	100.0	100.0

SOURCE: National Statistic Office

TABLE 15.18   Household distribution by monthly income (1,000 Won) (%)

	1985		1988		1993		1996	
	Urban	Rural	Urban	Rural	Urban	Rural	Urban	Rural
Less than 200	12.8	14.6	2.6	4.9	0.4	1.6	0.5	1.8
200–400	35.1	35.3	16.6	21.5	2.1	4.5	0.8	2.8
400–600	25.2	28.0	26.3	29.0	5.1	8.0	1.9	4.3
600–800	12.1	11.9	20.1	20.7	7.2	10.9	3.4	6.1
800–1,000	6.4	5.5	12.5	11.9	10.1	13.6	4.2	6.6
1,000–1,200	3.4	2.8	7.8	5.3	12.1	12.7	6.6	8.4
1,200–1,500	2.3	1.0	5.8	4.1	16.7	15.9	11.5	15.3
1,500–2,000	1.4	0.6	4.4	1.9	20.5	16.2	21.8	21.9
2,000–2,500	1.3	0.3	3.9	0.7	11.6	8.8	18.6	13.9
2,500–3,000	–	–	–	–	6.1	4.2	11.4	8.1
3,000–4,000	–	–	–	–	8.1	3.6	11.6	7.2
4,000 or More	–	–	–	–	–	–	7.7	3.6
Total	100.0	100.0	100.0	100.0	100.0	100.0	100.0	100.0

SOURCE: National Statistic Office

TABLE 15.19 Composition of monthly consumption expenditures

Year	Urban							Rural						
	F	H	C	E	T	R	M	F	H	C	E	T	R	M
1978	45.5	3.8	10.4	5.8	5.1	1.8	27.6	38.3	8.6	7.0	8.0	2.9	1.2	34.0
1980	43.0	4.7	9.9	5.9	5.8	1.9	28.8	36.8	6.7	6.1	9.4	3.4	1.7	35.9
1985	37.7	4.7	7.8	6.8	6.6	3.6	32.8	28.4	7.6	4.0	11.8	4.1	1.2	42.9
1990	32.7	4.6	8.3	7.5	8.6	4.6	33.7	23.5	7.8	4.6	10.5	5.1	0.9	47.6
1995	29.0	3.7	7.7	9.3	11.8	5.3	33.2	21.2	8.0	4.2	10.5	5.4	1.0	49.7
2000	27.5	3.3	5.7	10.9	16.4	5.3	30.9	20.2	6.8	2.8	10.2	7.4	0.8	51.8

F: Food; H: Housing; C: Clothing & Footwear; E: Education; T: Trans. & Communication;
R: Recreation & Culture; M: Misc. expenses.
SOURCE: Family income & Expenditure survey, National Statistic Office.

TABLE 15.20 Composition of housing in urban and rural areas

Year	1975	1980	1985	1990	1995	2000
Total of Nation	100	100	100	100	100	100
Owned	63.6	58.6	53.6	49.9	53.3	54.2
Leased	17.5	23.9	23.0	27.8	29.7	28.2
Monthly rent	15.7	15.5	19.8	19.1	14.5	14.8
Free rent or others	3.3	2.0	3.7	3.1	2.5	2.8
Total of Urban	100	100	100	100	100	100
Owned	44.8	43.0	41.3	40.5	46.3	49.0
Leased	31.1	35.5	31.1	34.6	35.3	32.6
Monthly rent	21.9	20.0	24.6	22.5	16.6	16.2
Free rent or others	2.1	1.6	3.0	2.4	1.9	2.1
Total of Rural	100	100	100	100	100	100
Owned	82.5	80.8	77.5	77.4	77.5	72.8
Leased	3.7	7.5	7.1	7.9	10.5	12.3
Monthly rent	9.3	9.1	10.4	9.4	7.1	9.5
Free rent or others	4.5	2.7	5.0	5.3	4.8	5.4

SOURCE: National Statistic Office.

education. The cost of communication, medical expenses, and others are also consistently higher in rural areas.

In the case of housing, there is a distinctive difference between urban and rural areas. In rural areas, ownership is much higher than in urban areas. Therefore, rent and tenement is more prevalent in urban areas. Up to the early 1980s, the most popular type of dwelling in Korea was detached housing (Table 15.21).

In order to meet the explosive demand for new housing, collective dwelling (condominiums and apartments) became very popular, mainly in urban areas. Within 20 years, the proportion of apartments in urban areas changed from 8 to 41.9 per cent. Even in the rural areas, apartment-type living is becoming popular, rising from 0.6 per cent to 18.3 per cent in 20 years. Since Korea is short of housing sites, this trend seems likely to continue in the future (Table 15.21).

Another difference between urban and rural areas is the type of fuel used for the home. Up to the mid-1980s, coal briquettes were the most important fuel for cooking and heating in both urban and rural homes (Table 15.22). By 1985, gas and oil were also used in urban homes but firewood was as important as the coal briquettes in the rural. By 1995, the urban fuel use was almost completely transformed to gas; the rural areas followed but still lag behind the urban areas. It is predicted that most homes in both urban and rural areas will use gas as a main fuel in the 2000s. In 2000 (Lim 2000), we saw the relation of this change in fuel types to the decline of urban air pollution. The shift from coal-dust pressed briquettes to gas and oil has made Korean urban areas much more healthy.

Table 15.23 shows some additional indicators of urban-rural differences. In the case of road length, which is a representative transportation indicator in the country, urban areas have greatly increased their advantage in the period 1990–95, but they also have far greater vehicle density than the rural areas. This is not surprising. Traffic jams are common in urban areas, not in the countryside. In health services, however, there is a real rural advantage. Both persons per doctor and persons per facility are lower in rural than urban areas.

TABLE 15.21 Composition of housing type

Year	1975	1980	1985	1990	1995	2000
Total of Nation	100	100	100	100	100	100
Detached dwelling	91.9	89.7	82.2	75.3	59.8	49.9
Apartment	1.4	4.9	9.0	14.8	26.9	36.8
Town house, apartment unit						
In a private house	4.4	2.3	4.6	6.4	8.8	9.1
Housing unit						
In non-residential building	2.2	2.8	4.1	3.4	4.5	4.2
Total of Urban	**100**	**100**	**100**	**100**	**100**	**100**
Detached dwelling	87.5	84.4	76.3	69.4	53.5	44.0
Apartment	2.7	8.0	12.8	18.9	31.9	41.9
Town house, apartment unit						
In a private house	6.5	3.7	6.0	7.8	10.1	10.2
Housing unit						
In non-residential building	3.3	3.8	4.9	3.9	4.5	3.9
Total of Rural	**100**	**100**	**100**	**100**	**100**	**100**
Detached dwelling	96.5	97.0	93.6	92.4	81.4	71.5
Apartment	0.2	0.6	1.8	3.0	10.0	18.3
Town house, apartment unit						
In a private house	2.3	0.9	1.9	2.6	4.4	5.1
Housing unit						
In non-residential building	1.0	1.5	2.6	2.0	4.2	5.1

SOURCE: National Statistic Office.

TABLE 15.22 Type of fuel used in urban and rural areas (%)

	1985		1990	
	Urban	Rural	Urban	Rural
Coal Briquettes	51.5	41.8	8.9	14.2
Gas	35.0	9.5	86.8	67.5
Fire Wood	0.9	41.7	0.2	9.2
Oil	11.1	2.5	2.3	2.0
Electricity	1.2	1.9	1.4	6.7
Others	0.3	2.6	0.4	0.4
Total	100.0	100.0	100.0	100.0

SOURCE: National Statistic Office.

TABLE 15.23   Socio-economic urban-rural differences

2000		Urban	Rural
No. of students(%)	Primary school	68.77	31.23
	Middle school	67.75	32.25
	High school	66.66	33.34
	Univ.	63.07	36.93
No. of schools(%)	Primary school	43.47	56.53
	Middle school	46.46	53.54
	High school	51.14	48.86
	Univ.	65.22	34.78
		1990	**1995**
Total length of road	Urban	24,269	46,003
(Km)	Rural	32,446	28,234
Total motor vehicles	Urban	2,907	7,215
(000)	Rural	488	1,254
Motor vehicles per km	Urban	119.8	156.9
	Rural	15	44.4
Persons per motor vehicle	Urban	11.1	4.8
	Rural	22.7	7.6
		1990	**1995**
Medical facilities	Urban	10,117	13,310
	Rural	1,374	1,697
Doctors	Urban	26,956	38,141
	Rural	3,114	3,587
persons per medical facility	Urban	3,193	2,632
	Rural	8,079	5,641
persons per doctor	Urban	1,198	918
	Rural	3,564	2,668

SOURCE: National Statistic Office.

IMPLICATIONS

Highlights of the Urban Condition

During the past 40 years (1962–2002), a rapid industrialization in Korea was accompanied by an even more rapid urbanization. Consequences of urbanization and the subsequent problems can be summarized as follows.

(1) A dramatic rise in the quality of life, including better health, better education, better housing, better jobs, higher income, and greater opportunities for all to develop their own talents.

(2) Shortage of infrastructure. A very rapid increase in population and expansion of the city size resulted in a chronic shortage of infrastructure such as roads, transportation, housing, water, and sewage systems.

(3) Mismatch by the unplanned expansion. The very rapid expansion in the early period and the following slower speed of expansion brought about a mismatch of problems in both urban and rural areas. Most of the infrastructure should be increased and decreased discretely, not continuously. Therefore, a marginal change in demand results in a larger change in supply at an accelerating rate.

For example, a changing population by sub-regions and changing age structure affect classroom demand and supply. The population-gaining regions needs more classrooms but the losing regions have idle classrooms.

Since the 1990s, many schools of various levels in rural areas began to close because of reduced enrollment, while new schools and more classrooms are still in urgent demand in expanding areas. Migration and population change and other factors also affect the SOCs.

(4) Impact on the labor market. The same logic as in the above applies to the labor market. The average number of urban employment changes slowly but the industry in an urban area may change fast and thus cause a structural problem. For example, the footwear industry in Busan declined rapidly in the 1990s but a substitute which can absorb surplus labor from the footwear industry can hardly be developed quickly. Here, the speed of adjustment becomes a critical factor.

(5)   Quality of the environment. Rapid urbanization has been realized at the cost of the environment. It is an irony that if a country like Korea had paid sufficient attention to the environmental problem, the rapid economic growth may not have been possible at all. Nevertheless, as income rises, people tend to want better environmental quality. From the standpoint of the entire economy, the cost of a cleaner environment rises as industrialization progresses. For example, Korea used to be a country with clean and fine drinking water. These days, most urban dwellers in Korea buy bottled water even though municipal governments invest heavily in the production of clean piped water.

Major Benefits

As shown by indicators in Table 15.1, above, the urban population increased by 5.3 times in the past 40 years. Most of the urban-related variables increased much more than the population increase rate. That means quality of life in terms of urban amenities or social overhead capital is improved, except transportation.

An average urban dweller in Korea has experienced a better life in that he or she acquired more and better housing, piped water, sewage service, telephone and mobile phone service, and medical services. Education opportunities were expanded and extended, including continuing education for adults and the aged. One or more passenger cars per household have been reported. Increasing income level naturally demands more parks and green areas, and other sports and leisure facilities.

Needless to say, the above scene applies in rural areas as well to a certain degree and with some differences. However, the inequality between urban and rural areas is apparent in certain aspects. Hospitals, doctors, lawyers, and specialists are concentrated in the urban areas which causes serious problems for rural dwellers.

Major Problems

Rapid urbanization results in problems and expenses too. Representative problems are congestion, and a deterioration in the quality of life, such as air and water quality. First of all, the congestion problem comes mainly from the transportation sector. Over the past 40 years, the Korean road length has increased more than three times. However, the number of motor vehicles increased by 389 times. These extended roads have not been able to accommodate the explosive increase in motor vehicles. Another vehicle-related problem is parking. As the provision of parking spaces for vehicle owners is not enforced, illegally parked vehicles occupy parts of roads, which makes the flow of cars slower and more difficult.

Polluted air, water, and soil are other by-products of rapid urbanization. The main cause of air pollution today is motor vehicle exhaust. Since the control of automotive exhausts is not strictly regulated, air quality improvement is very slow. The ozone-related air quality is another recent serious problem.

The water quality is other important problem. As the river is polluted by factories, live stock industry, and home sewage, the purifying and cleaning process of the original water costs more with less desired quality. The solid waste management, terminal waste water control, and other environment-related problems can be cited too.

Central Government Policy

As the movement towards local autonomy progresses, urban management and related matters have been delegated to the local governments. The construction of national highways and some social overhead capital such as rivers, dams, and ports are planned and financed by the central government, but many other matters are under the control and management of the local governments. The central government does set policy and standards for urban planning and management. Thus, the division of execution is quite obvious. For the investment and financing of the local projects, the central government adopts the policy of matching funds in most cases.

The most important policy of the central government is balanced regional development of the nation. The topic covers the balanced development between urban and rural areas, small and medium-sized cities and large cities, and the problem of population concentration in the Seoul metropolitan area (the capital region). The central government has been trying to correct this imbalance by legal, institutional, and political instruments, but it has not been successful so far. A stronger policy and more effective measures may be required to solve the problem. A lesson from the Korean case is that a policy goal for balanced development is necessary from the beginning.

In conclusion, there is no free lunch in the world. Rapid industrialization and urbanization require more expense and pose difficulties to be addressed in the future.

ENDNOTES

1   Busan is limited by its "Metropolitan boundary;" as its population growth is spilling into the surrounding suburbs (Lim 2000).

2   The farming population does not represent all the rural population; in 2000, for example, there were 9.4 million rural people, but only 4 million in the farming population, or 43 per cent of the rural population. That proportion has declined steadily from 81 per cent in 1960.

16

Urbanization in Taiwan in the New Millenium

TOM T. H. SUN AND PAUL K. C. LIU

URBAN GROWTH

Taiwan is an island of 36,000 square kilometers, situated in a sub-tropical area, 100 miles east of the China Mainland. The central range of high mountains (above 3,500 meters) runs from north to south, occupying about half of the island, leaving a relatively large plain area in the west coast but only a little strip of plain in the east.

The Proto-Malay aborigines migrated to Taiwan many centuries ago, occupying mostly the east coast and the mountain area. Chinese settlement in Taiwan dates as far back as the 12th century, but not until the 17th century did large numbers of Chinese begin to cross the Taiwan Strait. By 1624, when the Dutch invaded the southwestern part of the island, the Chinese settlers were estimated at around 30,000. At that time, Taiwan had already become an exporter of deer meet, sugar, and rice. In 1661, Koxinga captured Taiwan from the Dutch and chose Tainan as his capital. The Manchus (Ching Dynasty) conquered the island in 1683. For the next 200 years, the island was a home for the landless from South Eastern China, but Taipei was chosen to be the provincial capital by Governor Liu in 1875. So, there were three major cities in Taiwan at that time, including Tainan in the south, Taipei in the north, and Lu-kang, a port, in the middle part of the west coast.

Definition of Urban Areas

The official classification of "urban population" in the population censuses of Taiwan is based on all persons living in the civil divisions, which have been classified by the government as cities and urban townships. Taiwan is administratively divided into seven municipalities (cities) and 16 prefectures (counties). The municipality is sub-divided into districts, and the prefecture is sub-divided into small cities, urban towns, and rural towns. The boundaries of these administrative areas have remained almost unchanged over time, although some townships have been reclassified as small cities as they meet the criteria set for municipalities, and a few of the townships have been incorporated into municipalities. The changes include: in 1932, Taipei City was expanded to cover its surrounding areas; in 1968, Taipei City incorporated six adjacent townships; in 1971, Kaohsiung City incorporated one township; and in 1984, Hsinchu City incorporated one township into its administrative area.

With a considerable time lag, urban townships have been promoted to the status of cities as they meet the requirement of a minimum of 100,000 inhabitants. Only a few of the urban and rural townships in the vicinity of large cities have been merged into large cities. All the others, in spite of the differential socio-economic development, have never had their designation changed since the beginning of the 20th century. With few exceptions, the boundaries of the townships and city districts have remained unchanged over time. At the time of designation, cities were clearly characterized as large and densely settled urban concentrations, and the urban townships generally had market centers of urban character, but the boundaries of cities and urban townships tended to be over bounded to include large rural areas.[1] As the process of urbanization gained momentum, especially in recent years, most of the cities and urban townships have overgrown their fixed boundaries. Only a few of them have lost their urban character, but some of the rural townships became as urban as cities. As a consequence of the rigid civil status of local areas, the official classification can be used only as a rough measurement of urbanization. To obtain a more precise urban definition for Taiwan, this paper adopts an urban definition of cities, and urban and rural townships with 100,000 inhabitants, as recommended by the United Nations for international comparison, and also uses the definition of cities and towns of 50,000 or more inhabitants, as used by the Urban and Housing Development Department of the Council for Economic Planning and

Development for the purpose of urban planning, to show specific urban characters of Taiwan. Due to the limitation of data, some tables used administrative cities and prefectures. The map on p. 429 shows the location of major cities in the four regions of Taiwan in 2000.

The Historical Development of Cities

The development of cities and urban places in Taiwan may be roughly divided into four phases: (1) a rural settlement phase (1600–1894), (2) a colonial development phase (1895–1944), (3) a rapid urban growth phase (1945–1979), and (4) a transition towards metropolitan society (1980–present). In each period, the social-economic conditions were distinctly different and, consequently, the urban development process was also different. The existing pattern of urban system is the cumulative result of the socio-economic evolution. It is most likely that, in contrast to many developing countries, the prospective urban patterns in Taiwan will develop along the lines in the west as Taiwan reaches a knowledge-based economy.

(1)   Prior to 1600, Chinese fishermen and merchants only occasionally visited Taiwan. Thereafter, a large inflow of farmers from the southern provinces of Fukien and Kwangtung settled on the western plain of Taiwan, entering first through the ports along the southern coast and then gradually moving northward. In this phase, small towns along the western coast plain, east of the central range grew and prospered. The traditional Chinese rural market system also took form.

(2)   Japanese occupation of the island in 1895 stopped the stream of Chinese migrants and resulted in the building of two modern ports—Keelung in the northeast quadrant of Taiwan near the capital city Taipei, and Kaohsiung in the southwest—to function as the main entrances to the island. This caused the deterioration of the other small coastal ports. At the same time, foothill towns lost their importance due to the decline in trading with the aborigines. Only the capital city Taipei grew rapidly to match expanding economic relations with Japan. Cities and towns on the west plain, and later on the eastern-strip plain, continued to grow uniformly in pace

431

with the growth of population and agricultural development. As a result, a typical colonial pattern of primacy developed, as shown in Table 16.1, with a rise in the four city index[2] from 1.01 in 1920 to 1.09 in 1930, but declined to 0.88 in 1940 due to dispersion of the urban population in preparation for the Second World War.

(3) Since the restoration of Taiwan to the Republic of China in 1945, the rapid population growth, due to a persistently high fertility rate with falling mortality rate and limited arable land, had constituted the crucial factor in the rapid rate of urbanization. One of the major factors of the rapid urbanization, as experienced in many developing countries, has been the extremely high rate of unemployment and underemployment in both urban and rural areas. Taiwan has, however, successfully alleviated this ill effect, mainly through a success in fertility control and dispersion of labor-intensive industrial development. Universal decline in fertility has not only lowered the population growth in urban areas directly, but also reduced the migratory flow from rural to urban areas. Successful dispersion of labor-intensive industrial development was mainly attributable to the construction of 88 "industrial zones" by the government, occupying a total area of 11,850 hectares all over the island since 1950, to help private industries get access to land and infrastructures, and the establishment of three "export processing zones" in the outskirts of core cities in the southern and central regions. This not only reinforced the expansion of core cities in the regions along the west coast, but also helped the rapid growth of medium-sized cities. In addition, population growth and the rising living standards of rural populations are likely to bolster the growth of small towns. As a consequence, the urban system of Taiwan in this period has been transformed from a primate to a normal ranking of cities by

TABLE 16.1 Four city index of primacy for Taiwan, 1920–2000

Year	1920	1930	1940	1956	1966	1970	1980	1990	2000
Four city index	1.01	1.09	0.88	0.82	0.81	1.02	0.94	0.98	0.81

SOURCE: Census of respective years.

size. This point is supported by the evidence, as shown in Table 16.1, above, that the temporary drop in the four city index during the war continued to 0.81 in 1966, but when Taiwan achieved full employment in the late 1960s, the ratio reverted back to 1.02 in 1970, indicating a trend towards primacy.

(4) In the 1980s, Taiwan's economy had encountered the rising protectionism of the industrialized world and fierce competition of low-wage laborers from the developing countries. To cope with these adverse conditions, the enterprises and government strived to restructure the economy by switching industrial development from low-skilled, labor-intensive manufacturing to energy-saving, capital- and knowledge-intensive industries. The most important and direct measures taken by the government were the creation of the Institutes for Information Industry to promote the development of computer-related technologies and their use in industries and business in 1979, and the creation of several Science-based Parks to solicit the creation and development of new, science- (technology) based firms since 1980. All these Parks are located in the proximity of research facilities and technology-oriented universities in Hsin-Chu city and Taipei city. The plan for establishing the third Science-based Park is underway. All the efforts of technology upgrading caused the four city index to increase somewhat from 0.94 in 1980 to 0.98 in 1990; it then dropped to the previous lowest level of 0.81 by 2000. This reversed trend of polarization indicates that Taiwan is currently in the process of rapid metropolitanization.

The number of urban areas with populations of 100,000 or more increased from one in 1920 to four in 1940 during the colonial period, and then from seven in 1950 to 36 in 2000 (Table 12.2). In 1920 and 1930, Taipei was the only city with a population over 100,000. It had a growth rate of 3.5 per cent per year during the 1920s, compared to the 2.3 per cent average growth rate for the total population.

During the 1930s, Japan was preparing for the war and started to develop primary industries in urban centers in Taiwan. By 1940, Tainan, Keelung, and Kaohsiung joined Taipei as cities of over 100,000. The growth of the urban population accelerated to an average annual growth rate of 11.1 per cent, and its share in the total population more than doubled from about 5 per cent to 12 per cent.

TABLE 16.2 Growth of population of Taiwan and of cities over 100,000, 1920–2000

Year	Total Population (in 1000s)	Average Annual Growth in Previous Period	Number of Cities 100,000+	Population in Cities over 100,000	Average Growth in Preceding Overall (Percentage)	1956 Const. Bound (Percentage)	Percent Total Population Iin Cities 100,000+
1920	3,655		1	163		4.46	
1930	4,593	2.28	1	231	3.49		5.03
1940	5,872	2.46	4	701	11.10		11.94
1950	7,554	2.52	7	1,560	8.00		20.65
1956	9,311	3.49	9	2,353	6.85		25.27
1966	13,318	3.58	12	3,941	5.16	3.77	29.59
1970	14,676	2.43	14	5,081	6.35	3.11	34.62
1980	17,969	2.02	22	8,548	5.20	2.68	47.57
1990	20,286	1.21	32	11,806	3.23	2.12	58.20
2000	22,167	0.89	36	13,086	1.03	0.71	59.03

SOURCES: 1920–1950: Speare, Jr. Alden, Paul K. C. Liu, and Ching-lung Tsay, 1988, *Urbanization and Development: The Rural-Urban Transition in Taiwan*. Westview Press, Boulder: 1956, 1966, 1980, 1990, 2000: Population Censuses of Taiwan 1970: *1970 Taiwan-Fukien Demographic Fact Book*.

During the decade of 1940 to 1950, the exodus of the Japanese and the influx of Mainland Chinese resulted in an 8 per cent average annual growth of the urban population and its share in the total population doubled again to 21 per cent.

In 1956, the number of cities with over 100,000 inhabitants increased to nine and the proportion of the population living in these cities exceeded 25 per cent of the total population. From 1956 to 1980, urban population grew at an average rate of over 5 per cent per year when city expansion was included but only about 3 per cent when the growth rate was calculated within 1956 constant boundaries. By 1980, there were 22 cities containing almost a half of Taiwan's population.

In the 1980s, the average growth rate for all cities was reduced to 3.2 per cent per year, and only 2.1 per cent if limited within the constant boundaries (mostly in the old city center). This trend continued in the 1990s, averaging 1 per cent for current and 0.7 per cent for cities within per cent in the 1990s, while that to cities within the constant boundaries declined from 0.9 percent to –0.2 per cent, indicating a transition from the rapid urban growth period towards the metropolitan development period.

Columns 6 and 7 in Table 16.2 show an interesting phenomenon. The "overall" growth in column 6 includes the greater urban "built-up" area. That these growth rates are considerably greater than those in column 7, showing growth within the original administrative area, indicates a very high rate of sub-urbanization in the 1960s to 1980s. The sub-urbanization continues after that, but at a slower rate as Taiwan has become almost completely urbanized.

In the post-war period, as shown in the map on p. 429, above, urban growth has occurred mostly in the western plain stretching from north to south. This growth path tends to stretch simultaneously downward from the Taipei metropolitan area in the northern region and upward from the Koahsiung metropolitan area in the southern region. At the same time, a new path that follows the north-south corridor stretching outwards from the Taichung metropolitan area in the central region is emerging. Evidently, a large metropolitan region centering at the urban cores of Taipei, Taichung, and Kaohsiung has been formed as the urbanization process continues. On the other hand, the urban population in a little strip of plain in the eastern region has grown slowly at the two ends of the plain area.

Growth of Urban Population by Size and Region

The number and population of all cities with populations over 50,000 in Taiwan for 1956–2000 are presented in Table 16.3 by size and region. There were 22 cities (100,000 and above) and urban towns (50,000–100,000) with a total of 3.14 million urban population in 1956. The number increased to 74 with a population of 12 million in 1980. By 2000, the number increased to 91 with a population of 17 million.

Between 1956 and 1980, the proportion of urban population in the total population of Taiwan was raised from 33.3 per cent rapidly to 66.8 per cent and then moderately to 78.1 per cent by 2000. The proportion of urbanization was highest in the northern region, rising from 54 per cent in 1956 to 92.2 per cent in 2000, followed by the southern and central regions, from 28.7 per cent to 67.9 per cent and from 20.7 per cent to 67.4 per cent, respectively. For the eastern region, the proportion rose from 14 per cent to 50.7 per cent.

In terms of geographic distribution, Table 16.3 shows that, of the 28 new cities between 1956 and 1966, the central region gained the largest number (11), followed by the southern region (eight), and the northern region (seven). The eastern region gained only two. In 2000, 52 per cent of the urban population was concentrated in the northern region, followed by 25.1 per cent in the southern region, 21.3 per cent in the central region, and 1.6 per cent in the eastern region. This proportion did not change much since 1956 (Table 16.3).

Components of Urban Growth

The growth of urban population in a specific urban place is attributable to three processes: (1) natural increase (excess of births over deaths); (2) net gain of migrants from other urban or rural areas and from abroad; and (3) reclassification (change of townships into cities as their populations exceed 50,000, or the extension of the boundaries of existing cities). Table 16.4 shows the total growth rates, and growth from natural increase and net migration for the country as a whole for the period 1956 to 2000.

It is evident that in each census year, the natural increase rate contributed substantially more than net migration to the growth of cities and towns of all sizes in the four regions. There was a steady decline of increase rates in each size category over time. Large cities tended to have lower natural increase rates than small cities but the variations among different sizes were insignificant. This implies that the large cities were leading the fertility and mortality decline, but this trend had spread to the small cities and towns quickly. We also find that after 1980 some of the larger cities had net out-migration rates, indicating the sub-urbanization that we saw in Table 16.2. This pattern holds for all regions of the country (not shown in Table 16.4).

TABLE 16.3 Number and population of cities by size and region, 1956–2000

Population Size (in 000)	Taiwan Area No.	Population in 000s Persons	%	North No.	Population in 000s Persons	%	Center No.	Population in 000s Persons	%	South No.	Population in 000s Persons	%	East No.	Population in 000s Persons	%
1956															
1,000+	0	0	0.0	0	0	0.0	0	0	0.0	0	0	0.0	0	0	0.0
500–1,000	1	736	7.9	1	736	25.9	0	0	0.0	0	0	0.0	0	0	0.0
100–500	8	1,617	17.4	3	467	16.4	1	247	8.4	4	903	28.7	0	0	0.0
50–100	12	702	7.5	5	287	10.1	6	360	12.3	0	0	0.0	1	55	14.0
All Cities	21	3,055	32.8	9	1,490	52.5	7	607	20.7	4	903	28.7	1	55	14.0
Rural area	302	6,256	67.2	68	1,349	47.5	92	2,328	79.3	114	2,244	71.3	28	335	86.0
Total Pop.	323	9,311	100.0	77	2,839	100.0	99	2,935	100.0	118	3,147	100.0	29	390	100.0
1966															
1,000+	1	1,203	9.0	1	1,203	27.7	0	0	0.0	0	0	0.0	0	0	0.0
500–1,000	1	672	5.0	0	0	0.0	0	0	0.0	1	672	14.8	0	0	0.0
100–500	10	2,066	15.5	4	770	18.9	2	504	13.1	3	792	17.4	0	0	0.0
50–100	38	2,446	18.4	11	711	17.4	16	1,001	26.0	8	527	11.6	3	207	34.9
All Cities	49	6,387	48.0	16	2,684	65.8	18	1,505	39.1	12	1,991	43.8	3	207	34.9
Rural area	274	6,932	52.0	61	1,651	34.2	81	2,341	60.9	106	2,555	56.2	26	385	65.1
Total Pop.	323	13,319	100.0	77	4,335	100.0	99	3,846	100.0	118	4,546	100.0	29	592	100.0

437

TABLE 16.3 (cont'd)

1970

1,000+	1	1,741	11.9	1	1,741	33.5	0	0	0.0	0	0	0.0	0	0	0.0
500–1,000	1	806	5.5	0	0	0.0	0	0	0.0	1	806	16.9	0	0	0.0
100–500	11	2,534	17.3	6	1,092	21.0	2	574	14.0	3	868	18.2	0	0	0.0
50–100	43	2,804	19.1	12	783	15.1	18	1,181	28.9	10	614	12.9	3	227	36.2
All Cities	56	7,886	53.7	19	3,616	69.7	20	1,754	42.9	14	2,289	48.0	3	227	36.2
Rural area	267	6,790	46.3	58	1,574	30.3	79	2,334	57.1	104	2,483	52.0	26	399	63.8
Total Pop.	323	14,676	100.0	77	5,190	100.0	99	4,088	100.0	118	4,772	100.0	29	626	100.0

1980

1,000+	2	3,475	19.3	1	2,257	31.6	0	0	0.0	1	1,218	21.9	0	0	0.0
500–1,000	2	1,187	6.6	0	0	0.0	1	605	13.0	1	582	10.4	0	0	0.0
100–500	18	3,886	21.6	10	2,600	36.5	3	413	8.9	3	662	11.9	2	212	33.4
50–100	52	3,447	19.2	18	1,236	17.3	21	1,422	30.7	12	738	13.3	1	50	7.9
All Cities	74	11,994	66.7	29	6,093	85.4	25	2,440	52.6	17	3,199	57.5	3	262	41.3
Rural area	244	5,975	33.3	43	1,039	14.6	74	2,196	47.4	101	2,368	42.5	26	372	58.7
Total	318	17,969	100.0	72	7,132	100.0	99	4,636	100.0	118	5,567	100.0	29	634	100.0

TABLE 16.3 (cont'd)

1990

1,000+	2	4,141	20.4	1	2,760	31.7	0	0	0.0	1	1,380	23.1	0	0	0.0
500-1,000	3	1,979	9.8	1	533	6.1	1	773	15.4	1	673	11.3	0	0	0.0
100-500	27	5,686	28.0	17	3,947	45.3	5	728	14.5	4	901	15.1	1	111	19.0
50-100	52	3,582	17.7	16	1,100	12.6	22	1,550	30.9	12	774	12.9	2	158	27.1
All Cities	84	15,388	75.9	35	8,341	95.8	28	3,051	60.8	18	3,727	62.4	3	269	46.0
Rural area	233	4,898	24.1	36	364	4.2	71	1,971	39.2	100	2,248	37.6	26	315	54.0
Total Pop.	317	20,286	100.0	71	8,705	100.0	99	5,022	100.0	118	5,976	100.0	29	584	100.0

2000

1,000+	2	4,028	18.2	1	2,559	25.6	0	0	0.0	1	1,470	23.4	0	0	0.0
500-1,000	3	2,210	10.0	1	522	5.2	1	970	18.1	1	718	11.4	0	0	0.0
100-500	31	6,848	30.9	20	4,787	47.9	6	933	17.4	5	1,128	18.0	0	0	0.0
50-100	55	3,900	17.6	13	963	9.6	24	1,719	32.0	15	951	15.1	3	266	50.7
All Cities	91	16,986	76.6	35	8,831	88.4	31	3,622	67.4	22	4,267	67.9	3	266	50.7
Rural area	225	5,181	23.4	35	1,157	11.6	68	1,749	32.6	96	2,016	32.1	26	259	49.3
Total Pop.	316	22,167	100.0	70	9,988	100.0	99	5,371	100.0	118	6,283	100.0	29	525	100.0

SOURCE: Tabulated from various census years.

TABLE 16.4 Components of urban growth

Size (in 000)	Total %	Nat. Inc %	Net. Mig. %
1956			
1,000+			
500–1,000	5.93	3.43	2.50
100–500	4.24	3.71	0.53
50–100	3.84	3.63	0.21
0–50	2.74	3.62	–0.88
Total Pop.	3.33	3.62	–0.29
1966			
1,000+	3.79	2.34	1.45
500–1,000	5.29	2.69	2.60
100–500	3.94	2.50	1.44
50–100	2.55	2.53	0.03
0–50	2.16	2.69	–0.52
Total Pop.	2.82	2.60	0.22
1980			
1,000+	1.57	1.70	–0.14
500–1,000	1.66	1.82	–0.16
100–500	3.74	1.96	1.78
50–100	1.80	1.23	0.57
0–50	0.76	2.25	–1.48
Total Pop.	1.82	1.86	–0.03
1990			
1,000+	0.88	1.07	–0.19
500–1,000	1.55	1.19	0.36
100–500	2.28	1.15	1.12
50–100	1.63	1.15	0.48
0–50	-0.03	1.08	–1.11
Total Pop.	1.23	1.12	0.11
2000			
1,000+	0.49	0.76	–0.27
500–1,000	1.69	0.82	0.87
100–500	1.68	0.88	0.79
50–100	0.07	0.86	–0.79
10–50	0.15	0.74	–0.59
Total Pop.	0.84	0.82	0.02

The rapid industrialization and subsequent development of a knowledge-intensive economy have introduced a considerable shift in the composition of Taiwan's labor force. The proportion of labor force employed in agriculture declined steadily from 56 per cent in 1952 to 8 per cent in 2000, while the proportion employed in industry increased from 17 per cent to the top of 43 per cent in late 1980s and then decreased to 37 per cent in 2000. The proportion employed in the service sector increased from 27 per cent to 55 per cent in 2000. The proportion of population living in cities and urban towns with a population of more than 50,000 as shown in Table 16.3, however, increased at a relatively slow pace, from 33.3 per cent in 1956 to 66.8 per cent in 1980, and then to 78.1 per cent in 2000. The rapid inter-sector labor transfer with less physical movement of populations was largely the result of government emphasis on agricultural development and industrial decentralization policies. A major precondition for this success was the provision of high-quality infrastructure—good transportation and communication networks, universal electrification, and efficient local public administration. The completion of land reforms in the early 1950s also created employment opportunities in rural areas and absorbed a large amount of agricultural surplus labor. The construction of "industrial areas" and labor intensive "export processing zones" in the vicinity of core cities in the southern and central regions' rural areas in the 1960s provided non-agricultural jobs for numbers of farmers. All these efforts worked to avoid overurbanization as experienced in most developing countries, and saved much of the costs of urbanization.

The net migration rate of Taipei, the capital city located in the northern region, registered the highest net in-migration rate of 2.5 per cent in 1956, but shrank to 1.5 per cent in 1966. It turned to a net out-migration rate of 0.53, 0.4, and 0.59 per cent in 1980, 1990, and 2000, respectively. However, the satellite cities of Taipei with a populations of 100,000–500,000 in the Taipei Basin started to have a high net migration rate in the 1960s, indicating that the whole Taipei Basin was developing as a metropolitan area. The gains in Taipei's urban population were largely from small cities and rural towns in the central region.

In 1966, Kaohsiung, the second largest industrial city in the southern region, experienced a high net migration rate of 2.6 per cent by attracting migrants from nearby small cities and rural towns. The opening of two "export processing zones", and the induced development of labor-intensive industries in the zones played an important role. The subsequent

441

development of capital-intensive heavy industries, such as steel, shipbuilding, and petroleum industries, however, invoked a declining net migration rate from 0.59, 0.31, to 0.29 percent in 1980, 1990, and 2000 respectively.

Taichung and Changhwa, two cities of agricultural market centers ranging from 100,000–500,000 people in the central region, had a moderately high net in-migration rate of 1.66 in 1966 and 2000. Construction and opening of Taichung Harbor in the 1960s and later development of machinery industries were the major reasons for high urban growth rates in these years.

In 1956, only Hualien, a fishing harbor city in the northern region of the east coast, had grown with 4.3 per cent of net migration. By 1966, Taitung, another fishing harbor city in the southern tip, and a nearby town grew to the rank of cities with only 0.5 per cent of net migration rate. As a result of the geographical barriers separating the east coast from the rest of the island, the growth of cities through migration has primarily been restricted to the western plain area and the Taipei Basin in the northern area.

The increase of urban population by reclassification of towns into urban during the years 1956–66, a period of historically high fertility, constituted more than 25 per cent of the total urban population in 1966 (Table 16.5). Evidently, it was the result of success in rural development. Owing to a substantial decline in fertility since 1966, its contribution dropped drastically, with little variation, to a low level of only 2 per cent in 2000 (See Table 16.5).

TABLE 16.5 Intercensal growth of urban population of reclassified towns with population in excess of 50,000

	Reclassified No. of Towns	Increased Urban Population in 1000s	% of Total Urban Pop. in End Year
1956–1966	28	1,650	25.22
1966–1970	6	304	3.85
1970–1980	18	544	4.54
1980–1990	10	966	6.28
1990–2000	7	359	2.12

SOURCE: Calculated from censuses of respective years.

The extension of city boundaries has not been very significant. Taichung city was extended to include three adjacent townships with some 65,000 persons in 1947. Taipei city amalgamated five townships with about 295,000 persons in 1968. Kaohsiung city amalgamated one township with 40,000 persons in 1979. As Table 16.5 shows, there was a major expansion of urban boundaries in 1956–66, adding about 1.6 million people, or a quarter of the urban population. After that, however, there were few adjustments, and they involved only small proportions of the total urban population.

DISTRIBUTION OF CITIES

It has long been established that if socio-economic development is spread throughout the country, the natural distribution of cities fits a rank-size rule (Browing and Gibbs 1961 and Cheshire 1999). According to this rule, a graph of logarithm of city population against logarithm of city ranks will form an approximate straight line with a slope of –1. If the slope becomes steeper, greater than 1, it means that the population growth rate of upper ranked cities was larger than that of lower-ranked cities, and vice versa. A parallel up-shift of the straight line means that there was a population increase proportionate to the population size of each city from upper-rank to lower-rank during the period.

Rank-size distribution diagrams for Taiwan from 1956 to 2000 and the intercept and gradient of the estimated regressions are prepared by using administrative cities (Table 16.6). A decline in absolute value of gradient from 0.932 in 1956 to 0.790 in 1966 suggests that many medium

TABLE 16.6 Estimates of rank-size rule of Taiwan, 1956–2000

	No. of Cities	Intercept	Gradient	R-squire
1956	22	5.89	–0.932	0.98
1966	56	5.97	–0.790	0.96
1970	56	6.03	–0.808	0.96
1980	74	6.23	–0.849	0.98
1990	84	6.36	–0.874	0.99
2000	91	6.40	–0.867	0.99

SOURCE: Calculated from censuses of various years.

and small cities had developed in this decade. Followed by continuous increase of gradient to 0.808 in 1970, and then to 0.874 in 1990, suggests the growth of medium-sized cities was prevailing during this period. The gradient's slight decline to 0.867 in 2000 represents the slower growth of the large core cities. Since urban growth has gradually expanded beyond the boundaries of some of the large cities, the values of estimates tend to be lower than that calculated on the base of the functionally defined metropolitan areas. If data had been available on the larger urban conurbations, the absolute value of gradients over the census years would be progressively greater, suggesting the movement towards metropolitanization. For example, the population of Metropolitan Taipei (including satellite cities in the Taipei Basin) in 2000 would have been 5.3 million instead of 2.6 million (within the administrative area).

Projections of Urban Growth

According to the Urban and Housing Development Department of the Council for Economic Planning and Development, there were 122 urban planned districts in Taiwan in 2000, amounting to a population of 17.3 million, which stands for 77.9 per cent of the total population. It is planned to accommodate 24 million people in these planned districts by 2025, i.e., more than 90 per cent of the total population would be living in the urban planned areas. Of this urban population, 5.8 million or 24 per cent would be living in Taipei Metropolitan Area (i.e., Taipei Basin) in the north. Another metropolitan center would be Kaohsiung Metropolitan Area in the south, with a population of about 3.8 million, or 15.7 per cent of the total population. The third metropolitan area would be Taichung Metropolitan Area in the central region, with a population of about 2.9 million, or 12 per cent of the total population. Tainan city in the south would have a population of 1.1 million. Actually, Kaohsiung and Tainan could be joined together to form a bigger metropolitan area. This would create a metropolitan area with a population of 4.9 million, or 20 per cent of the total population. These three metropolitan areas together would have a population of 13.6 million, or 56.6 per cent of the total population. The rest of the population (about 10 million) would be scattered in the western plain area, and only about 0.8 million in the east coast. However, it should be pointed out that the population of some small towns (about 20) has already reached or

444

exceeded their planned population, yet many have already passed their target year without achieving the size planned, especially in the western area of the central region.

URBAN-RURAL DIFFERENCES

Demographic Characteristics

Age and Sex Composition

The age composition of the population of Taiwan right after the Second World War was very young due to the high fertility rate during the after-war baby-boom. In 1956, 42.2 per cent of the population was under 15 years of age, and only 2.4 per cent was over 65 years of age. These proportions changed drastically as fertility fell quickly due largely to promotion of family planning and unprecedented social-economic development. By 2000, these two proportions changed to 21.6 and 7.7 per cent respectively. As to the urban-rural differentials, Table 16.7 shows that, in 2000, there were more elderly people in the rural areas (12.1 per cent) than in the cities and towns (7.7 per cent), as a result of migration of young people from rural areas to cities and towns. The population of ages 40–64 is especially high in the cities of more than one million, indicating the ageing of earlier migrants to these cities. On the contrary, the proportion of the population aged 15–39 is higher among medium-sized cities, indicating that these cities are still absorbing young workers and college students. The population of ages 0–14 reflects both fertility level and the number of women in child-bearing age in that area. The age composition of the whole of Taiwan reflects the fact that, with rapidly declining fertility and mortality, it already belongs to an aged population.

The high sex ratio among people of 0–14 years old in the year 2000 reflects the traditional notion of "son preference" in Taiwan. There is not much difference among areas of different sizes. The sex ratio of ages 15–64 in cities with population of more than 500,000 is especially low, reflecting the in-migration of young female workers to these large cities to work in labor-intensive industries. The high sex ratios in the rural areas and among the elderly people are partly a result of the large number of migrants after the War from Mainland China, who were mostly men. They have reached those ages and most of them are living in small cities or towns.

TABLE 16.7 Age and sex composition of cities and towns by size and rural area, 2000

Population size (in 1,000)	Total		Age composition (%)				Sex ratio by age groups				
	Population (in 1,000)	%	0–14	15–39	40–64	65+	Total	0–14	15–39	40–64	65+
1,000+	4,030	100.0	19.0	41.8	30.4	8.8	98	108	94	92	115
500–1,000	2,210	100.0	21.3	44.0	27.9	6.8	98	108	93	96	111
100–500	6,849	100.0	21.8	44.3	27.0	6.9	103	109	101	97	125
50–100	3,900	100.0	22.2	42.9	26.4	8.5	108	109	111	104	109
City total	16,989	100.0	21.2	43.3	27.8	7.7	102	109	100	97	117
Rural area	4,773	100.0	20.2	39.9	27.8	12.1	112	108	119	112	96
Total	21,762	100.0	20.9	42.6	27.8	8.7	104	109	104	100	110

SOURCE: Census of 2000.

Marital Composition

The marital composition of the population of post-war Taiwan has been changing remarkably in response to the rising level of education, rapid urbanization, and industrialization. Traditionally, men and women got married quite early and marriage was universal. The 1935 census results show that 64 per cent of men and 67 per cent of women aged 15 and above were currently married, while only 30 per cent of men and 16 per cent of women remained single. By 1956, these proportions changed to 51 and 45 per cent for men, and 65 and 22 per cent for women. The large increase of single men was due to a large influx of single military service men from Mainland China in the early 1950s. These proportions changed slightly to 57 and 38 per cent for men, and 59 and 30 per cent for women. Another disturbing factor is the increase in the proportion divorced; it increased from 0.9 per cent for both sexes in 1956 to 2.7 per cent for men and 3 per cent for women. As for urban-rural differentials, the proportions of single and divorced are higher in the large cities than in the towns and rural areas. This is related strongly to industrialization and urbanization, also the concentration of universities in large cities.

Mortality, Fertility and Contraceptive Use

Although the mortality rate has been very low (about six per 1,000) in Taiwan in general since the 1960s, there still are some differences between urban and rural areas due to differences in socio-economic level, public health, and access to medical facilities (see Table 16.8). A study by Wen et al.(1989) pointed out that the mortality rate (1981–86) was lower in cities and more urbanized counties, and higher in less urbanized prefectures. For example, the mortality rate of Taipei city is 25 per cent below the average, and that of the two prefectures in the eastern region is 33–7 per cent above the average.

Because of the post-war baby boom, the total fertility rate (TFR) in Taiwan went up to more than 7 in 1951. It then started to decline as socio-economic development progressed, especially in the urban areas where educational levels and levels of living are higher. Since Taiwan started to promote family planning in 1964, the emphasis has been put on the rural high fertility areas. Therefore, by about 1985, the contraceptive prevalence rate both in the cities and rural areas all went up to about 80 per cent of the eligible couples (Sun 2001). Along with this was a dramatic decline in the TFR. However, the TFR is still

TABLE 16.8 Changes in Crude Birth Rate (CBR), Total Fertility Rate (TFR), Contraceptive Prevalence Rate (CPR) and Infant Mortality Rate (IMR) for urban and rural areas, 1963–2001

Rate and type of area	1963	1965	1970	1975	1980	1985	1990	1995	2000	2001
Crude Birth Rate	35.6	32.1	27.2	22.4	23.4	17.9	16.6	15.4	13.9	11.5
Cities	33.3	30.0	26.8	21.3	22.3	16.7	15.6	14.3	13.0	10.7
Urban townships	35.4	32.0	26.8	22.2	23.6	18.9	17.2	16.0	14.4	12.3
Rural townships	37.4	33.7	27.7	23.7	24.7	19.3	18.0	17.2	15.5	13.1
Total Fertility Rate	5.35	4.83	4.00	2.77	2.52	1.88	1.81	1.78	1.68	1.40
Cities	4.69	4.19	3.63	2.42	2.25	1.69	1.65	1.60	1.52	1.25
Urban townships	5.32	4.80	3.98	2.84	2.67	2.05	1.92	1.91	1.81	1.55
Rural townships	5.88	5.36	4.41	3.16	2.85	2.09	2.00	2.04	1.94	1.65
CPR	-	24.1	43.3	62.7	70.1	79.1				
Cities: Natl		37.2	55.1	69.5	73.5	80.3				
Cities Other	-	26.6	43.7	66.2	73.7	79.5				
Urban townships	-	22.2	41.7	58.6	66.8	77.7				
Rural townships	-	18.6	38.3	57.9	67.3	78.5				
IMR	26.4	22.2	15.7	12.7	10.1	7.0	5.4	6.8	6.4	6.6
Cities	20.7	18.0	11.3	10.2	8.3	5.9	5.0	6.5	6.2	6.3
Urban townships	26.5	22.4	16.4	12.6	10.7	7.6	6.3	6.7	6.5	6.5
Rural townships	29.7	24.7	19.0	15.3	12.0	8.2	5.7	7.3	6.8	7.3

SOURCES: CBR, TFR, and IMR are from the Household Registration; data for CPR are from The Institute of Family Planning KAP surveys.

somewhat higher in the rural areas than in the cities, due largely to the difference in the ideal family size in the two types of areas. The ideal number of children is about 2.2 in the urban areas, compared to about 2.6 in the rural areas. This is also reflected in the actual fertility, i.e., TFR in the urban areas is about 1.5, compared to 1.9 in the rural areas. The decline in fertility has also been accompanied by a dramatic decline in infant mortality; it is well established that the two are closely related. These changes can be seen readily in Table 16.8.

Socio-economic Status Differentials

Income and Employment
Following the rapid economic development of the last four decades, the average family income for the year 2000 was about four-fold that in 1975, increasing from NT$287,093 to NT$1,139,336, all at 2000 constant price. As shown in Table 16.9, the average family income is much higher in the cities than in the prefectures. That in Taipei city was about 49 per cent higher than the country average in 1975, and this was maintained until 2000; it declined to 43 per cent higher than the country average. The growth rates of family income for cities and prefectures are almost the same indicating that the rapid economic growth was island wide, more or less evenly spread out. Table 16.9 shows the data.

The rapid economic development is also reflected in household amenities, which indicate the rise of living standards. Color television had become almost universal by 2000, although the proportion having a color television was somewhat higher in the cities than in the prefectures. The ownership of air conditioners had also gone up to around 80 per cent by 2000, from only about 15 per cent in 1980, again with a slightly higher rate in the cities. The stereo set is somewhat lower, but it has increased to about 50 per cent by 2000 from 25 per cent in 1980. There is also a small difference between cities and prefectures (See Table 10).

As for communication and transportation facilities, the telephone has become a necessity, especially in the large cities. Automobiles are also getting more popular than ever, increasing from about 40 per 1,000 population in 1980 to 250 per 1,000 in 2000. The difference between cities and prefectures is quite small, due to better public transportation facilities and lack of parking space in the cities. However, the motorcycle is more popular in the prefectures than in the cities, due to different traffic situations in these two types of areas. It is astonishing to see that

449

TABLE 16.9 Average family income by region, city, and prefecture (NT$, at 2000 constant prices)

Region, City and Prefecture	1975	1980	1990	2000	2000/1975
Northern Region	331,512	497,907	875,027	1,314,380	4.0
Taipei City	430,396	535,595	1,026,019	1,630,330	3.8
Keelung City	286,550	482,139	762,272	1,094,019	3.8
Hsinchu City	} 278,279	} 476,357	885,562	1,448,624	} 4.4
Prefectures			788,619	1,171,029	
Central Region	258,841	386,814	711,134	988,387	3.8
Taichung City	289,911	493,977	882,121	1,162,161	4.0
Prefectures	254,456	367,643	675,406	944,588	3.7
Southern Region	249,127	378,014	713,387	1,008,498	4.0
Kaohsiung C.	306,722	430,589	885,201	1,200,691	3.9
Tainan City	293,175	443,714	783,681	1,057,802	3.6
Chiayi City	} 227,513	} 347,787	781,395	1,046,789	} 4.2
Prefectures			621,166	911,895	
Eastern Region	228,437	371,024	608,187	896,930	3.9
Prefectures	228,437	371,024	608,187	896,930	3.9
Total	287,093	430,639	782,083	1,139,336	4.0

SOURCE: Council for Economic Planning and Development, *Urban and Regional Development Statistics, Republic of China*, respective years.

more than half of the population possess motorcycles, especially in the southern region.

A little more than half of the population aged 15 and over were employed in 2000. This proportion has not changed much in the past. The difference between cities and prefectures is also not significant. The industrial distribution of employed persons, however, is quite different between the two types of area. The proportion engaged in tertiary industry is especially high in several cities such as Taipei and Keelung in the northern region, Taichung in the central region, and Kaohsiung and Chiayi in the southern region. The proportion engaged in primary industry (mostly agriculture) is higher in the prefectures in the central, southern, and eastern regions. The proportion of secondary industry is higher in several prefectures where industrial areas are located.

TABLE 16.10 Percentage of household having modern durables and utilities by region, city, and prefecture, 1980 and 2000

Region, City and Prefecture	Percentage of household having modern durables						Communication and transportation facilities					
	Color TV set		Air Conditioner		Stereo set		Telephone subscriber per 100 people		Automobiles per 1,000 population		Motorcycles per 1,000 population	
	1980	2000	1980	2000	1980	2000	1980	2000	1980	2000	1980	2000
Northern R.	76.4	99.6	22.2	87.1	30.7	57.4	17.9	67.3	50.4	243.3	177.1	445.8
Taipei City	81.9	99.8	33.1	92.3	34.1	62.8	27.7	87.5	81.1	249.1	158.9	362.7
Keelung C.	71.4	98.7	9.4	84.8	22.1	52.5	16.4	54.1	24.4	187.8	106.8	391.1
Hsinchu C.	}73.4	98.3	}16.5	87.3	}29.3	52.4	}13.0	72.0	}36.7	285.7	}192.0	566.3
Prefectures		99.7		84.8		55.5		50.1		241.9		477.8
Central R.	64.1	99.5	7.4	68.6	21.5	45.6	10.0	50.0	34.2	274.8	246.6	530.1
Taichung C.	77.5	99.8	18.8	82.1	29.6	53.4	22.6	85.7	78.6	301.7	275.2	496.1
Prefectures	61.7	99.4	5.4	65.2	20.0	43.6	8.2	42.6	27.7	269.3	242.4	537.1
Southern R.	64.2	99.3	10.0	78.0	21.6	44.3	10.6	49.3	29.9	240.3	264.7	600.6
Kaohsiung C.	74.7	99.5	14.8	86.8	22.0	49.4	19.5	63.6	53.6	247.1	280.2	646.1
Tainan C.	73.4	99.8	22.9	83.2	30.0	48.1	19.0	85.4	44.6	244.3	277.6	602.3
Chiayi C.	}58.9	99.0	}6.2	79.6	}20.0	47.1	}6.5	77.2	}20.2	253.7	257.9	620.4
Eastern R.	64.0	98.0	7.1	58.7	26.9	40.2	6.9	42.0	17.4	235.0	233.8	566.7
Prefectures	64.0	98.0	7.1	58.7	26.9	40.2	6.9	42.0	17.4	235.0	233.8	566.7
Total	69.6	99.5	14.8	79.5	25.7	50.4	13.6	57.0	39.6	250.2	220.3	515.1

SOURCE: Same as Table 16.9.

451

TABLE 16.11 Employment rate and industrial distribution of employed persons by region, city, and prefecture, 2000 (population 15 and older) (%)

Region, City and Prefecture	% employed among pop. of ages 15 & over	Industrial distribution of employed persons		
		Primary Industry	Secondary Industry	Tertiary Industry
Northern Region	56.2	1.9	37.1	61.0
Taipei City	54.8	0.3	20.8	78.9
Keelung City	54.0	1.2	28.4	70.4
Hsinchu City	60.5	1.8	44.3	53.9
Prefectures	56.8	2.7	44.2	53.1
Central Region	56.4	12.4	40.5	47.1
Taichung City	56.5	1.2	27.6	71.1
Prefectures	56.4	14.6	43.1	42.3
Southern Region	55.2	11.5	35.6	53.0
Kaohsiung C.	52.7	1.5	32.0	66.5
Tainan City	56.4	2.2	38.4	59.4
Chiayi City	52.5	2.8	26.4	70.8
Prefectures	55.4	17.3	36.9	45.8
Eastern Region	55.2	19.5	26.2	54.3
Prefectures	55.2	19.5	26.2	54.3
Total	56.0	7.8	37.2	55.0

SOURCE: Same as Table 16.9.

Literacy and Education

The literacy rate is very high in Taiwan; education is compulsory up through junior high school level. It is being planned to raise it to senior high school level. Thus, there is very little rural-urban or regional difference in education level up to junior high school. However, there still is a significant difference in the education level of senior high school or higher education between cities and prefectures. It was so in 1980, and is still true in 2000. For example, the proportion with senior high school or higher education in Taipei city was 51 per cent and 75 per cent for 1980 and 2000, respectively, compared to 23 per cent and 48 per cent in the prefectures of the central region. The gap has narrowed, however.

In 1980, the central region prefecture's level was only 46 per cent of Taipei's level; by 2000, it had risen to 64 per cent. The same narrowing has taken place throughout the country. Table 16.12 provides the details.

IMPLICATIONS

Highlights of Urbanization in Taiwan

Although urban settlement in Taiwan started about a century ago, it was not until the 1920s that a relatively large-scale city developed. However, the urban growth was quite fast after that. The average annual growth rate was maintained at above 2 per cent, and it was especially high after the Second World War, about 3.5 per cent per annum from 1950 to 1970, due largely to fast economic development. Then, it slowed down from 2.4 per cent in 1970 to 0.9 per cent in 2000, and entered the stage of metropolitanization and the development of medium to small size cities. At the same time, there was a fast development of rural areas, including the creation of many towns and the modernization of farming villages.

Because of the special topography, urban development was concentrated in the plain stretching from north to south on the west side of the island. Three urban centers developed along this plain: one in the north, around Taipei city, one in the south, centered at Kaohsiung and Tainan, and the third in the central part, centered at Taichung (see Figure 16.1).

The development of cities in Taiwan follows very closely to the rank-size rule, i.e., the four city index never got too high. It went up to 1.09 in 1930, but came down to 0.81 in 2000. The urban development pattern was quite similar to that of the Western countries. The largest city, Taipei, only had a population of 2.64 million in 2000, followed by Kaohsiung city with a population of 1.48 million, and the third Taichung City with a population of 0.95 million. There are two more cities with populations of 500,000–1,000,000, 31 cities with populations in the range of 100,000–500,000, and 55 cities and towns with populations of 50,000–100,000.

The growth of large cities in Taiwan before 1966 depended largely on net migration, especially for those with populations of 100,000–500,000. During the last several decades, however, the growth has been mainly due to natural increase, and there are even net migration losses in

TABLE 16.12 Level of education by region, city, and prefecture, 2000 and 1980 (%)

Region, City and Prefecture	Educational level of pop. aged 15 & over (2000)						Senior high and above	
	Grand total	Illiterate & self-educated	Primary school	Junior high school	Sr. high & vocationed	Jr. college & above	2000	1980
Northern R.	100.0	4.9	16.9	16.0	34.4	27.8	62.2	38.2
Taipei City	100.0	3.2	10.3	11.6	32.7	42.3	75.0	51.0
Keelung C.	100.0	5.7	19.7	17.4	37.1	20.1	57.2	36.1
Hsinchu C.	100.0	6.2	18.2	14.9	32.7	28.0	60.7	}31.4
Prefectures	100.0	5.5	19.7	18.0	35.0	21.8	56.8	
Central R.	100.0	8.0	22.0	18.2	32.6	19.2	51.8	25.6
Taichung C.	100.0	3.2	12.8	13.7	36.2	34.1	70.3	41.2
Prefectures	100.0	8.9	23.8	19.1	31.9	16.3	48.2	23.3
Southern R.	100.0	7.8	20.7	17.1	33.4	21.0	54.4	28.9
Kaohsiung C.	100.0	4.8	14.5	14.7	37.7	28.2	65.9	36.9
Tainan C.	100.0	4.6	18.4	14.7	33.1	29.2	62.3	34.6
Chiayi C.	100.0	4.5	139	13.4	36.1	32.1	68.2	}25.6
Prefectures	100.0	9.8	24.0	18.7	31.5	16.0	47.5	
Eastern R.	100.0	8.2	28.9	19.9	30.5	12.5	43.0	25.8
Prefectures	100.0	8.2	28.9	19.9	30.5	12.5	43.0	25.8
Total	100.0	6.6	19.6	17.0	33.5	23.3	56.8	31.6

SOURCE: Same as Table 16.8.

some of the large cities. This is due mainly to the more even development of the plain area in Taiwan

ADVANTAGES AND DISADVANTAGES
OF URBANIZATION

It is natural that modern businesses and infrastructures have a tendency to be concentrated in the large cities, and Taiwan is no exception. The large cities are usually the political and business centers, and there are also more universities and cultural organizations. Therefore, inhabitants in the large cities can enjoy a higher standard of living, with higher income and more modern facilities. The medical services are also better in the cities than in the rural areas. As Table 16.13 shows, the government spends more money (per capita) in the cities than in the prefectures, and there are more hospital beds, physicians, and dentists (per 10,000 persons) in the cities than in the prefectures. The life expectancy is also longer in the cities than in the prefectures, even though air pollution tends to be more serious in the cities because of too many automobiles, air conditioners, and factories in an area of limited size.

The first impression of large cities in Taiwan is their traffic problem, especially in recent years. The construction of roads cannot keep up with the increase of automobiles. As Table 16.14 shows, the average area of road per automobile decreased from 214.5 square meters to 32.6 between 1980 and 2000. It is only 3.1 square meters per automobile in Taipei city. Housing is another problem. The housing expenditure in 2000 was 2.6 times that in 1980 on the average, and was 2.8 times in Taipei city. In the northern region, housing expenditure in the cities was about 1.6 times of that in the prefectures. City dwellers consume more water than rural dwellers: more than 600 liters per person in the cities compared to about 400 liters in the prefectures. Therefore, water supply becomes a problem during the dry season.

The collection and treatment of refuse is another problem for city governments. Every city dweller produces more than 1 kilogram of refuse per day. How to collect and treat this refuse is a headache to the municipal governments. There are usually not enough landfills to bury the refuse and therefore the government has to spend more money in building more incinerators. The problem is that people welcome the collection of refuse but are against construction of landfill sites or incinerators in their neighboring areas.

TABLE 16.13   Government expenditure per capita (2000), and availability of medical facilities by region, city, and prefecture, 1980 and 2000

Region, City And Prefecture	Government Expenditure Per Capita (NT$)	No. of hospital beds per 10,000 pop.		No. of physicians per 10,000 pop.		No. of dentists per 10,000 pop.	
		1980	2000	1980	2000	1980	2000
Northern R.	48,014	26.3	54.7	8.6	14.6		4.58
Taipei City	93,386	38.7	79.8	14.6	26.3		7.89
Keelung C.	47,432	25.8	55.2	7.8	12.6		3.18
Hsinchu C.	41,695	} 19.9	50.1	} 5.6	12.3		4.60
Prefectures	24,064		44.2		9.8		3.24
Central R.	32,386	16.4	52.6	5.0	11.5		3.54
Taichung C.	34,520	47.6	85.0	10.6	24.2		8.03
Prefectures	26,124	11.8	45.9	4.2	8.9		2.62
Southern R.	39,346	20.2	61.2	5.7	13.1		3.28
Kaohsiung C.	61,077	41.2	70.1	8.9	17.8		5.26
Tainan C.	37,681	26.8	70.7	8.9	17.4		5.06
Chiayi C.	39,451	} 12.6	132.2	} 3.3	23.0		5.50
Prefectures	25,796		51.2		9.8		2.03
Eastern R.	45,229	43.0	91.8	6.0	13.9		2.36
Prefectures	45,229	43.0	91.8	6.0	13.9		2.36
Total	41,478	22.4	57.0	6.7	13.3	1.06	3.88

SOURCE: Same as Table 16.8.

Effort of the Government in Taiwan

The planning and development of urbanization is mainly the responsibility of the Urban and Housing Development Department of the Council for Economic Planning and Development of Executive Yuan (Cabinet), and the local municipal governments.

The basic idea is to develop the whole island by regions with a metropolitan center in each region. It is emphasized, however, that the population should not be overly concentrated in urban areas, i.e., the aim is to disperse population distribution by developing rural areas. For example, industrial parks, new communities, universities, and large companies are encouraged to move to the rural areas. In this sense,

TABLE 16.14 Automobile density, housing expenditure, and water consumption, by region, city, and prefecture, 1980 and 2000

Region, City and Prefecture	Average area of road per automobile (m²)		Housing expenditure per household (NT$) (At 2000 constant prices)		Per capita daily water consumption (liters)	
	1980	2000	1980	2000	1980	2000
Northern R.	94.2	17.5	69,038	181,313	321.6	507.8
Taipei City	10.4	3.1	90,755	254,338	376.7	754.5
Keelung C.	83.7	11.3	53,626	129,544	283.6	602.7
Hsinchu C.	} 189.5	16.8	} 57,136	158,319	} 249.4	706.9
Prefectures		8.2		151,448		377.2
Central R.	308.2	40.2	42,057	118,799	185.2	431.7
Taichung C.	49.5	9.1	66,201	159,325	236.6	651.1
Prefectures	455.0	47.2	37,737	108,585	173.8	379.2
Southern R.	513.2	41.1	43,742	111,823	169.4	512.6
Kaohsiung C.	...	...	61,754	139,472	189.3	686.7
Tainan C.	59.8	11.4	63,315	137,011	176.5	377.7
Chiayi C.	} 666.8	15.6	} 33,584	123,056	} 157.6	367.1
Prefectures		65.1		93,870		475.0
Eastern R.	1,125.4	12.9	36,419	98,494	185.3	408.6
Prefectures	1,125.4	12.9	36,419	98,494	185.3	408.6
Total	214.5	32.6	54,631	144,508	233.6	488.5

SOURCE: Same as Table 16.8.

improvement of transportation becomes an important issue, both inside the cities and between these different centers. Taipei city has already completed an MTR system, and another one in Kaohsiung city is in progress. Other cities also have plans to improve their traffic situation. An express railway is under construction to connect Taipei in the northern area and Kaohsiung in the southern area. The improvement of the highway network in the plain area is also being carried out extensively.

Each city has its own development plans, which are being implemented as long as financial conditions permit. These plans include improvement of transportation, city renewal, park and recreational area construction, control and treatment of environmental pollution, improvement of sanitary and health conditions, and building of houses for the poor, etc. The purpose is to make city life more convenient, comfortable, healthy, and safe.

ENDNOTES

1   Based on a study by C. S. Chen (1959) who limited urban population only to those who live in an urbanized area, i.e., a place with 2,500–25,000 population, a street of more than 100 meters and 50 per cent or more of the dwelling units are shops, and has a marketing function for neighboring areas, was classified as "town." Such a locality with 25,000–100,000 population was classified as "small city," with 100,00–500,000 population or more population as "medium city," with 500,000–to one million population as "large city." Based on this definition, the urban population stands for about 14 per cent of the total population in 1900, 18 per cent in 1920, 25 per cent in 1940, and 34 per cent in 1958. There were 112 towns, 17 small cities, four medium-sized cities and one large city in Taiwan in 1958.

2   The four city index indicates the ratio between the top ranked city and the sum of the second to fourth ranked cities' populations. If the city followed the rank size rule, this ratio would be "1/(1/2+1/3+1/4)" or approximately 0.92.

CHAPTER 17

Urbanization in Asia: Summary and Implications

GAYL D. NESS AND PREM P. TALWAR

This overview gives us an opportunity to engage in some comparative analysis. There is probably no better region than Asia for this type of analysis. In one sense, the region is one, roughly homogeneous, ecosystem. It is well watered, either by major rivers or the great monsoon system. It also has a long history of state-like systems with major urban centers supported by rich agricultural hinterlands. This has made Asia one of the world's most densely settled regions for the past two to four millennia. Asia shares this high density with Europe, which is also a well-watered land mass. But as we saw in the introductory chapter, Asian urbanization, and density as well, has led that of Europe from antiquity up until the 19th century. It also lies on a somewhat different base. Europe's high density is supported by a worldwide trading system in which global resources have produced high population density. Asia's high density rests on effective political control of a rich and productive hinterland.

At the same time, Asia is quite diverse. It consists of three substantially different cultural regions associated with major ecosystems. South Asia is a massive arid plain watered by large rivers and the great monsoon system. The arid plain that is Southern Asia actually extends from Bangladesh west to Morocco. For millennia, it has been traversed by horses and camels and their drivers, largely men. It has also known central governments with relatively limited and declining control over hinterlands of power centers. Southeast Asia, the southern extension of the great Asian land mass, is well watered by monsoon and rivers. Its impenetrable jungles have for millennia turned populations from land

459

to river and sea routes, navigable as well to women as to men. The famous tourist attraction in Bangkok, the floating market, almost exclusively a market of women sellers, is merely a modern and highly commercialized version of what has gone on for centuries. East Asia has been the focus of one of the world's great civilizations for more than 2,000 years. It is a land mass traversed by two major rivers, around which highly centralized governments have grown up and survived, for centuries. This land mass has also been buffeted from the north and west by militant nomadic peoples who have helped to shape East Asian history and its memory.

This is, indeed, a rich land for comparative analysis.

We begin this overview with a brief summary of the major findings of previous chapters. Following the brief summary, we provide more detail on each of the points, with tables and charts that tell the story of the countries included in this volume. Next, we consider the implications and what lies ahead with special attention to needed research and policy considerations. Finally, we step back to consider the process of urbanization on an historical and global scale. Here we are especially interested in asking what next? What should scholars examine in the future? More importantly, what should national governments do to address the seemingly inexorable process of urbanization? How can they best reap the benefits and avert the disasters that lurk in the near future?

BRIEF SUMMARY:
DIFFERENCES AND SIMILARITIES

Urban Growth

(1)   The countries of Asia define urban areas in different ways, making a strict comparison difficult. Some use simple numeric definitions, all places of 5,000 or more. Others include functional conditions, such as a minimum proportion of the population in non-agricultural pursuits, or a select number of urban services. Nonetheless, there is a relatively common feature that makes rough comparisons useful and accurate. Towns and cities are relatively easy to identify by their size, population density, and behavioral characteristics. Census procedures tend to identify towns and cities roughly by size, and this gives us considerable strength in comparative analysis.

(2) The countries of Asia vary immensely in the level of urbanization. A few (Singapore, Japan, South Korea, and Taiwan) are fully urbanized, while another few have less than a quarter of their populations in urban areas. All, however, with the exception of Singapore, are becoming more urbanized. Everywhere urban populations are growing more rapidly than rural populations. Moreover, for an increasing number of countries the rural populations are, or will soon be, in absolute decline; everywhere, however, the urban population continues to grow.

(3) Although urbanization continues, the pace is slowing everywhere. This follows the general trend of population growth.

(4) Urbanization derives from both net in-migration and natural increase. In some cases, there is information on both. In most cases, natural increase was the major source of urban growth from 1950 to about 1970–75. Since then net migration has been the major source of growth. A third source of urban growth, however, is the expansion of urban administrative boundaries. There is very little systematic information on this source of growth, which identifies an important area for future research.

(5) Relatively little is known about migration streams. Some census data collection and some national sample surveys provide limited views of who is moving in what direction for what reasons. It is most common for young males to move to urban areas, but there are many differences as well. This, too, represents another important area for future research.

(6) Where data exist on the national system of cities, we typically find growth of all sizes of cities: the largest and the smaller sized cities as well. Asia varies greatly in the degree of primacy. Bangkok stands at one extreme, while countries as different as India, Indonesia, Japan, and Pakistan show a more balanced distribution of city sizes.

(7)   All countries, again with the exception of Singapore, project a continued increase of urbanization. Even the least urbanized, Nepal, is expected to have 26 per cent of its population in urban areas by 2030. By that time, seven countries will have more than half their populations in urban areas; and another six will have a percentage at 40 or above. For the two giants, China is expected to be 60 per cent urban and India 41 per cent.

Urban-Rural Differences

(1)   Demographic differences between urban and rural populations are found in all countries. There is typically an excess of young males in urban areas, matched by a deficit in rural areas. Fertility and mortality are typically lower in urban areas.

(2)   Socio-economic differences are also found, but here the picture is more complex. In virtually all countries, urban dwellers are advantaged in social infrastructure and services, which comes as no surprise. On the other hand, we find that in the poorest and least urbanized countries, urban areas look like large villages, with much agricultural occupation and village style houses quite common. At later stages of urbanization, the rural-urban differences decline, as the entire population takes on an urban lifestyle. This produces something like an inverted U-shaped pattern of rural-urban differences, somewhat lower at both early and later stages of urbanization, and greatest at the middle stages.

(3)   A paradox emerges in most of the poorer or developing countries of Asia. Great cities also imply great slums. These are highly visible and show sometimes appalling conditions of poverty with poor housing, poor or non-existent utilities and social services. Yet everywhere the data show a higher quality of life in urban than rural areas.

DETAILED SUMMARY:
SIMILARITIES AND DIFFERENCES

Urban Growth

As the previous chapters show, Asian urbanization has many faces. A few countries (Singapore, Japan, Taiwan, and South Korea) are what can be called "fully" urbanized. Others have less than a quarter of their populations in urban areas. A few are wealthy urban, industrial societies. One of these, the Republic of Korea, has made the transition from a poor, rural, agrarian society to a wealthy urban industrial society in less than the past half century. Many other countries remain poor and largely rural. Some show a high degree of urban primacy, such as Thailand with the overwhelming proportion of its urban population in just one city, Bangkok. We expand on the issue of Primacy below.

All countries have in common, however, a surge of urbanization. All are involved in what appears to be the relentless and irreversible process of urbanization, which began in Europe just three centuries ago. In all countries, the urban population has grown more rapidly, often many times as rapidly, as the rural population. This is expected to continue for the foreseeable future.

At the same time, the pace of urbanization is slowing. This follows the pattern of population growth as a whole. World population growth rates peaked at 2.01 per cent in 1965–70. Asian annual population growth also peaked in 1965–70, though at a higher level, 2.40 per cent; the rate of growth has been declining since then. Rates of urban growth for the world as a whole peaked somewhat earlier at 3.07 per cent in 1955–60. The Asian urban growth rate has two peaks: in 1955–60 it stood at 3.76 per cent per year, and then declined to 3.27 per cent in 1965–70. It rose again to another peak of 3.72 per cent in 1985–90, and has declined steadily since then. The sub-regions of Asia have followed slightly different trajectories, but all rates have been declining since 1990 (UN 2001).

Rural population growth is another matter. For the world as a whole, rural population growth peaked in 1965–70, along with total population growth, but at a lower level, 1.65 per cent. It has been declining since then and is projected to show negative growth in 2020. Asia has followed the same trajectory, but some of the countries are moving much more rapidly. In five of the countries (China, Japan, Republic of Korea, Indonesia, and the Philippines), the rural population has already (2000) begun to decline in absolute numbers, showing negative growth rates. By 2030, that group will be joined by nine more: Bangladesh, India, Indonesia, Malaysia, Myanmar, Malaysia, Sri Lanka, Thailand, and Vietnam. The great surge of total population growth may be declining, but the process of urban population growth continues. Thus, in the majority of countries, and in the great majority of the Asian populations, rural populations will decline while urban populations continue to increase.

Tables 17.1 and 17.2 lay out the basic data on urbanization, and Figures 17.1 and 17.2 provide a graphic representation. A table on urban

TABLE 17.1 Asian urbanization; % of total population, 1950–2000

Country	1950	1960	1970	1980	1990	2000
South Asia						
Bangladesh	4	5	8	15	20	22
India	17	18	20	23	26	28
Nepal	2	3	4	7	9	12
Pakistan	17	22	25	28	31	33
Sri Lanka	14	18	22	22	21	23
Southeast Asia						
Cambodia	10	10	12	12	13	17
Indonesia	12	15	17	22	31	42
Laos	7	8	10	12	15	19
Malaysia	20	27	34	42	50	57
Myanmar	16	19	23	24	25	28
Philippines	27	30	33	38	49	59
Singapore	100	100	100	100	100	100
Thailand	10	13	13	17	19	20
Vietnam	12	15	18	19	20	24
East Asia						
China	13	16	17	20	27	36
Japan	50	62	71	76	77	79
Republic of Korea	21	28	41	57	74	82
Taiwan	25	30	35	48	58	59

SOURCE: Country chapters and UN 2001.

TABLE 17.2 Projected asian urbanization (%), 2000–2030

Country	2000	2010	2020	2030
South Asia				
Bangladesh	25	31	38	44
India	29	32	35	41
Nepal	12	16	20	26
Pakistan	33	37	42	48
Sri Lanka	23	27	33	40
Southeast Asia				
Cambodia	17	23	30	36
Indonesia	42	50	55	64
Laos	19	24	30	37
Malaysia	57	64	69	73
Myanmar	28	33	40	47
Philippines	59	66	71	75
Singapore	100	100	100	100
Thailand	20	22	27	33
Vietnam	24	29	35	41
East Asia				
China*	36	45	53	60
Japan	79	81	83	85
Republic of Korea	82	87	89	91
Taiwan	59			90

* Chinese official data show lower rates: 48% for 2030 (see Chapter 3).

and rural growth rates is relegated to an appendix due to its size. In the main charts of Figure 17.1, we have used the same vertical scale to make the three charts more readily comparable. Singapore has been omitted to make the charts more accessible. The four smaller countries are shown in a separate chart in Figure 17.2. For that chart, we have used a smaller vertical scale, otherwise all four would be very closely arrayed near the bottom and would not be clearly visible.

It is notable that the four small countries are projected to have an increased rate of urban growth after 2000. All four have, of course, experienced considerable turmoil and violence in the past few decades,

FIGURE 17.1

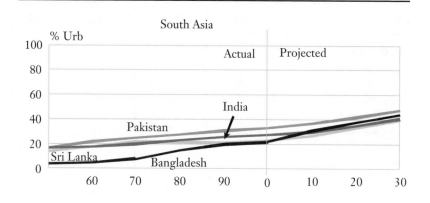

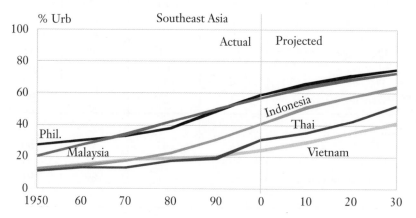

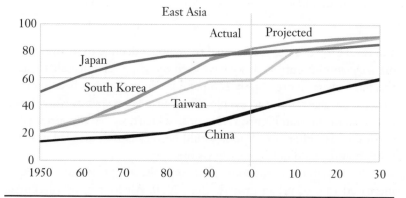

FIGURE 17.2

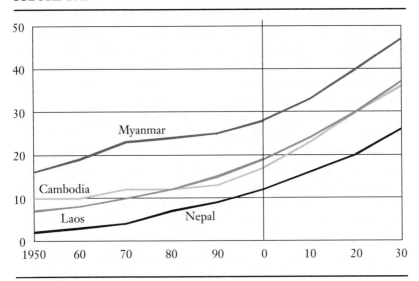

which probably reduced the rate of urbanization. The projections obviously assume no such turmoil for the future; they appear to assume continuation of the most recent urban growth rates.

The two Asian giants, China and India, are no exception. In 1950, both were at very low levels of urbanization (13 and 17 per cent respectively). By 2000, China had a third of its population in urban areas; India was close with 28 per cent. By 2030, it is projected that 60 per cent of China's population will live in urban areas; India will lag somewhat with only 41 per cent. But, together, their urban populations will number some 1.459 billion, or about 29 per cent of the world's urban population. In both countries, the rural populations are expected to be in absolute decline by 2030.

Sources of Growth: Natural Increase, Migration and Administrative Changes

As we have said before (AUICK 1997), urban growth has three major sources. It is easy to understand both natural increase (the excess of births over deaths) and net in-migration (the excess of in- over out-migration). But cities also grow by administrative changes as well. Governments redraw boundaries, often to include urbanized areas that have grown up as a sprawl from the urban center. At times, these administrative expansions include rural areas as well, previously outside of the administrative boundaries of the cities. A variant of administrative changes is reclassification when small villages grow sufficiently to be classified as urban areas. This reclassification, however, comes about primarily from natural increase and net in-migration.

We have also argued that these three sources of urbanization have very different implications for urban administration. Growth by natural increase implies increased demands for maternal and child health care and for primary education in the city. Growth by net migration usually implies demands on housing for young male workers, and for many services—including entertainment—for those young male workers. Growth by administrative expansion, on the other hand, usually increases the revenue base of the city, as well as the demand to take over infrastructure and social services from smaller administrative units. The implication of growth by reclassification from rural to urban depends on whether that growth comes from natural increase or net migration. What do these Asian countries show in the varying sources of urban growth?

First, there is relatively little systematic data to tell us how much urban growth comes from these different sources. Many countries provide no data at all. When data are provided, however, we find a number of different trends.

One of the common findings is that growth by administrative expansion or reclassification tends to come in spurts, highly concentrated in time. Sri Lanka, for example, reclassified towns in 1951–71, when 40–50 per cent of urban growth came from this administrative redefinition. From 1979–88, China redefined urban boundaries to include large tracts of rural areas, so that almost 40 per cent of its urban growth came from this administrative expansion. In Indonesia, administrative changes were made in 1961–71, when they increased urbanization by some 10 percentage points. Taiwan had a reclassification in 1951–61, which contributed 25 per cent to the urban growth. In this case, however, most of the growth still came from natural increase. Vietnam's major reclassification came in 1989–99, which contributed 27 per cent. This reflected growth by both natural increase and migration, but the former was declining while the latter was increasing.

Thus, we can see major spurts of reclassification that can contribute 10 to 50 per cent or more to urban growth. This is clearly an area that needs more research, especially since such changes have immediate consequences for urban administration, even if we do not know exactly what those implications are.

The relative impact of natural increase and net migration varies considerably in the region and over time. The dominant pattern is for natural increase to be dominant early in the half-century (1950–70) and then to decline and net migration becomes the major source of urban growth. The spread of modern health techniques and services brought a rapid mortality decline and equally rapid population increase just after 1950. This is what drove urbanization early in the half decade. From the mid-1960s, new anti-natalist policies and programs brought rapid declines in fertility to most countries of the region. Urban areas have usually seen the earliest and most rapid fertility declines, but in many cases the rural areas have followed close behind. Thus, it is common for natural increase to play a large role in urban growth early in the period and then to decline as the major source of both total and urban growth. From roughly the 1970s or 1980s in most countries, net migration has thus become the major source of increase. The implications for urban administrators are clear and should be carefully considered by national governments.

But there are also interesting differences that defy explanation. Both Sri Lanka and Thailand remain far less urbanized than other countries at the same levels of economic and social development. Both have relatively low levels of migration into the urban areas. And both have had very successful programs of fertility limitation, so that cities are also growing slowly from natural increase. Recently, Sri Lankan cities have had the notable experience of a net decline from urban out-migration, leaving natural increase to account for as much as 125 per cent of urban growth.

Migration

Many countries conduct surveys and pose questions in the decennial censuses about migration. Yet the data remain sparse, and the difficulties of both data collection and analysis are imposing. For the most part, however, we find young males dominating the rural-to-urban migration stream, and the search for jobs is a major motivation. Where data do exist we find strong regional differences. In South Asia, males migrate for jobs and education; females migrate more for family reasons, usually to follow a husband. Southeast Asia, and Sri Lanka, show much greater freedom for females, who also migrate for employment. Vietnam shows a pattern that might be more common if better data were available. There, males dominate the longer distance, inter-provincial migration stream while females dominate the shorter distance, intra-provincial stream. East Asia resembles Southeast more than South Asia, with females joining males in the migration for better jobs.

The System of Cities

If there is a dominant pattern here, it is that all cities throughout all countries are growing. In the two giants, China and India, there is a relatively balanced growth of cities of all sizes throughout most of the country. This pattern is characteristic for most of Asia. Even where there is a more unbalanced growth, with high concentrations of the population in a major city, as in Thailand and South Korea, we find substantial growth in smaller and medium-sized cities as well. Even the smaller cities, with populations of less than 20,000, typically show a substantial growth in size as they move from small towns to medium-sized cities. In effect, Asia is becoming urbanized, and the process is widespread.

In the smaller and poorer countries, the process of urbanization is more led by one or a few major cities, which come to hold the majority of the urban population. In Laos, half the urban population resides in the capitol, Vientiane. That city has been three to ten times the size of the next two cities. Rangoon has a third (29 per cent) of all Myanmar's urban population; adding the next eight towns increases the proportion to half of the urban population. Moreover, Rangoon is about five times the size of the next city, Mandalay.

At the same time, Myanmar shows a most interesting pattern, which we call widespread low-level urbanization. There are major towns throughout the country, in all states and provinces. Nepal has shown an interesting distribution of cities. Katmandu has gone from holding 25 per cent to 18 per cent of the country's urban population. Medium-sized cities have grown more rapidly there, taking a greater share of the country's urban population.

In effect, Asia is becoming urbanized in every way we can imagine. Large cities are growing rapidly and attracting more and more of the population. But medium and smaller-sized cities throughout all of the countries are also growing rapidly, drawing more and more people from the rural areas into the villages, towns, and cities. Urbanization is widespread.

Urban-Rural Differences

Since urbanization began, scholars and observers have seen major differences in the conditions of life and in behavior between urban and rural areas.[1] Urban dwellers typically have advantages in housing, utilities, health, and education. This is associated with lower mortality and fertility rates in urban areas, smaller household size, later age of marriage, and greater use of contraception. We see all of these differentials in the countries of Asia.

Asian cities typically have higher sex ratios and smaller under-15-year-old populations than rural areas. This results from young working-age males migrating to cities for employment. These differentials are greater in South than in Southeast or East Asia. Japan now faces a new serious problem of age structure differences in rural and urban areas, which may well portend patterns in the rest of Asia. Rural areas are losing people, especially younger people, leaving the rural areas increasingly dominated by an aged population. South Korea is following Japan closely in this process.

The cities of Asia also typically have better housing, more health and education services, and higher levels of employment than rural areas. As expected, this means lower fertility, later age of marriage, greater contraceptive use, lower levels of mortality, and higher school enrollment and literacy rates in urban areas. It also means higher living standards in urban areas. There is little doubt that urban living carries with it a substantial advantage over rural living. In effect, the urban areas are at the forefront of major changes in reproductive behavior, and in the broad range of indicators that point to higher standards of living. Note that this represents a major change from the history of European urbanization, when cities were far less healthy and had higher death rates than the rural areas until well into the 19th century.

Despite the statistical evidence of urban advantages in the quality of life, the cities of Asia also show signs of extreme poverty. Virtually all cities in the less developed regions have large and highly visible slums. Houses built of scrap material, little or no public water or sanitation facilities, little or no social services like schools or health centers, all characterize these slums. Some emerge beside, or atop, the cities' garbage dumps, providing slum dwellers with a source of livelihood scavenging from the refuse of the city. Conditions are often appalling and call, usually in vain, for amelioration. Here then is a paradox: statistical evidence of a higher quality of urban life alongside scenes of the most abject poverty.

There is also substantial change in these urban-rural differentials in many parts of Asia. National health and education services and national family planning services have often carried urban advantages to rural areas. In most cases, the fertility and mortality differentials are declining. In some cases, as in South Korea, Sri Lanka, Taiwan, and Thailand, urban-rural fertility differentials have virtually disappeared. Where they have not disappeared, they have declined dramatically. Urban living styles and urban cultures are spreading inexorably to rural areas.

On some dimensions, however, we see something that resembles an inverted U-shaped curve. At the earliest stages of urbanization, especially among the very poor countries like Cambodia, Laos, Myanmar, and Nepal, cities and towns often have the air of little more than large villages. Roughly half the population of Vientiane, for example, is still engaged in agriculture. Urban areas in Myanmar still have many houses constructed of natural (jungle) materials. While schools expand rapidly, there is still a large, often older, population that is illiterate in the urban areas. Thus, here we have relatively lower and less dramatic levels of urban-rural differences.

As urbanization and economic development proceed, the differences in infrastructure, utilities and social services, like education and health, become more pronounced. With independence, almost all Asian countries have made great progress in increasing educational and health facilities and services. These come first to the cities and towns, however, and only later and more slowly to the rural areas. This brings an increased urban-rural differential in infrastructure and services that leads to a different lifestyle. At this middle level of urbanization and development, urban lifestyles and urban culture are more typically "urban" and not rural.

With continuing urbanization and development, however, urban services and urban life styles spread to rural areas. Japan's levels of health and education, for example, are national phenomena, with very little urban-rural differences. Food, communication, work, and entertainment become more homogenized; the national culture becomes an urban culture. One difference may remain, however; rural areas appear to be getting older more rapidly than urban areas, largely due to the out-migration of the young from the rural areas.

IMPLICATIONS

Most governments of the region recognize the benefits of urbanization, but they also recognize the problems and are ambivalent about the process. Most note that urbanization brings economies of scale. This also implies that cities are major centers of development, innovation, and trade. These are welcome, primarily as they represent the growth of centers of wealth, and nodal points through which the country can become an increasing part of the global community. In this respect, urbanization is welcomed and promoted, occasionally explicitly, more often implicitly. Governments typically allocate more resources to the urban centers than to the rural areas, even when they actively espouse rural development programs.

There is also, however, much ambivalence about urbanization. For most governments, urban areas are centers of power and wealth, but they are also centers of opposition and dissent, of popular pressure against government for a variety of reasons. Thus, urbanization is also distrusted. It must be noted that this is an almost universal phenomenon, through both time and space. At the onset of urbanization in Europe, governments were also distrustful of the new "unwashed" and "unchurched" urban masses. Marx saw the revolutionary potential of these new urban masses, whose close proximity to one another led them to develop a revolutionary "class consciousness." The current ambivalence over urbanization is not new.

All governments appear to have attempted in some ways to slow urbanization. There have been rural development programs that have attempted to stem urbanization by making rural areas more attractive. India attempted to develop "new towns" that would relieve the congestion of major urban centers in the early stages of development. There have also been more draconian attempts, as in Maoist China, to forbid rural-to-urban movement through strong government registration policies. None of these has been successful. Developing rural areas, especially with better infrastructure, including schools and roads, has simply facilitated rural-to-urban migration. New towns have either failed to attract people or become another major urban center with all the problems of the older ones. China's anti-urban policies under Mao only succeeded in producing a large "floating population" that was unregistered and unrecognized by government.

Somewhat greater success has been achieved where governments invest heavily in growth centers outside the main city. Taiwan has been especially successful in developing urban growth centers outside of Taipei, giving the country an overall urban character of development. Thailand has also been relatively successful in developing growth centers in Khon Kaen, Chieng Mai, and Songkala. Nonetheless, Bangkok continues to grow and to attract the mass of rural-to-urban and urban-to-urban migration. Still, the low level of Thai urbanization presents a problem for analysts. How has the country managed to make so much progress in social and economic development while remaining so rural? This is a major question to which systematic research should be turned. But that research must be basically comparative. The next paragraph suggests another link in the strategy.

Sri Lanka also remains an anomaly. It is less urbanized than its wealth and social development would predict, and urbanization may be slowing and giving way to a more balanced development of urban and rural areas. Here let us hazard an explanation. By almost any measure, Sri Lanka is the oldest and most democratic state in Asia. It achieved universal suffrage in 1932, only 10 years after the United States. Since then, it has had two major political parties, one representing more urban interests, the other representing more rural interests. Since independence in 1948 and until more drastic changes in 1983, those two have shared power. One gained power in one election to be overturned and followed by the other in the next election. Under these conditions, political parties appealed to what was most important to voters: education and health services, for the entire country. The outcome was precisely that: a substantial development of basic health and education services throughout the country. In Sri Lanka, urban areas may well have an attraction for rural youth, but rural areas have their attractions as well.

Theses two cases, Sri Lanka and Thailand, raise basic questions because they differ from the common process of urbanization throughout Asia. All countries are urbanizing. Urbanization, modernization, and economic development appear to be interlocked processes. It is not difficult to understand this process: more investment in social infrastructure, economies of scale, etc. Why then do Sri Lanka and Thailand appear as deviant cases? This should surely be a major question for scholars concerned with economic and social development.

Primacy and the Primate City

Before turning to the next steps, let us examine briefly one of the critical issues of urban life today: that of primacy and the primate city. The primate city is the dominant city of a country, and primacy is an issue of the extent to which one city dominates all urban life. Both conditions vary from country to country.

Views of urban centers in the developing countries of Asia often refer to the immense size of the new and rapidly growing metropolises, which they see as set in an extensive poor, rural landscape. The great mega cities of Mumbai, Kalcut, Bangkok, Jakarta, Manila, or Seoul are often cast as lonely giants towering over a countryside of backward small towns and rural areas. Is this an accurate picture? The question has been raised before.

There is immense literature on the primate city and primacy. A dominant idea in this area is credited to Mark Jefferson (1939), who proposed that the dominant city in a country may be four to ten times as large as the second city. It would be a city that dominated all urban life of the country. George Henry Zipf (1941) took strong exception to Jefferson and proposed his "natural" law of rank size distribution. This stated that the largest city in a natural community, or nation, would be twice the size of the second, three times the size of the third and so on to N times the size of the nth city. This is proposed as a "natural" law of social organization. It is also recognized that not all countries follow this natural law. Indeed, much literature (Linsky 1969) suggests that one of the problems with the less developed regions is precisely their diversion, marking a high degree of primacy, which may be one of the causes of their low levels of social and economic development.

This issue has spawned a large literature in geography, sociology, and more recently in economics (Krugman 1993 and Henderson 2002). A fine University of Michigan website, titled "A Geography of A Systems of Cities" (http://164.76.128.51/gsc/), and another at Eastern Michigan University (http://ceita.emich.edu/gsc/), where Mark Jefferson (1863–1949) was a professor, trace the developments of these ideas. One extensive review of literature and data (Alprovich 1993) finds two universals: (1) the rank size rule does provide a good description of most countries, but (2) there is also considerable variance among countries in the rank size distribution. Another (Henderson 2002) asks if there is really a natural order of cities and, more important, does it matter for economic development.

Our Asian countries provide an opportunity to examine both the fit of the rank size rule, or the character of urban primacy, and some of the consequences. Is Thailand with Bangkok as the dominant urban system representative of Asia? Or are there other urban systems that are more common? The issue has not been discussed by most of our authors; only in Japan, Malaysia, Pakistan, and Taiwan do we find some discussion of the degree of primacy. Nonetheless, we can find data to speak to the issue for all the countries we cover.

Demographers typically use two common and easily constructed measures of primacy: the ratio of the first city to the sum of the next three cities; or the ratio of the first city to the second city (Browning 1963 and Cheshire 1993). We shall call these R1 and R2 respectively. Economists (Henderson 2002) have used such things as the Hirschmann-Herfindahl Index,[2] Zipf's law,[3] a Pareto distribution, or the more simple proportion of the total urban population in the largest city. For this brief analysis, we shall confine ourselves to R1 and R2

It is also useful to compare Asia with the rest of the world. For this comparison we use the UN data (UN 2001) showing city size for the capital and for all cities that had over 750,000 inhabitants in the year 2000 for the period 1950–2030. This is an impressive and very useful data set covering 113 countries. It is not, however, without limitations. First is the data limitation. There are only 32 countries for which we can calculate R1; and only 49 for which we can calculate R2. The rest (64 countries) have no second city, and sometimes not even the capital, over 750,000. Second, it relies on country data for most cases. This introduces an error bar whose dimensions are unknown. Third, the measures rely on national definitions of urbanization, thus for the most part they do not speak of the greater urban built-up areas, but only of the administrative boundaries of the central cities themselves. These are all serious limitations, but the data can still be used to give us a preliminary sense of the degree and distribution of urban primacy in Asia, and how this compares with the rest of the world.

From the data we can make the following five observations.

(1)   There is a high correlation between the two primacy ratios. The correlation coefficient for R1 and R2 is +.932 for Asia and +.944 for the 33 countries for which the UN provides data for computing R1. This is especially useful since we have more cases of R2 (49) than of R1 (33).

(2)   The mean value of R1 for Asia is 1.25 with a standard deviation of 0.67. For the 33 UN data countries, the mean is 1.19 with a standard deviation of 0.70. R2 has a mean in Asia of 4.05 with a standard deviation of 5.78. It is highly skewed to the right due to the extreme outlier of Thailand, where Bangkok is about 24 times the size of the second largest city. Comparable figures for the 49 countries of the world are 3.00 and 3.51. Skewness and Kurtosis measures are very high for this measure. But the histograms show a high concentration around the 2.0 levels indicating that Alprovich's judgment is correct: the rank order rule does provide a good description for most countries.

(3)   The R1 and R2 measures for both Asia and the world are skewed to the right. For R1 Myanmar (2.78) and Thailand (9.00) are the two extreme outliers in Asia; Argentina (3.41) and France (2.58) are the two extremes in the rest of the world.

(4)   For Asia and all countries together there is *no significant relationship* between the R1 and R2 measures of primacy and measures of demographic conditions (population size, urban size, urban percent, population growth rate), social conditions (IMR, Eo, TFR),[4] or economic conditions (GDP, per capita GDP in 1995 US dollars or per capita output expressed in 1995 PPP).[5] This suggests that whatever primacy or "balanced" distribution exists, it does not make much difference to social and economic development.[6]

(5)   Some Asian countries have increased their primacy measures since 1960 (Bangladesh, Indonesia, and Japan). Some have decreased the measure (China, India, North Korea, and the Philippines). One, Pakistan, remained roughly stable. And three varied over time: Myanmar, South Korea, and Taiwan first increased then decreased

their measures. Table 17.3 shows the measures for these countries. *Neither increasing nor decreasing the measure of primacy appears to be associated with either progress or stagnation in social and economic development.*

The two extremes of primacy, Myanmar and Thailand might also be considered near extremes of failure and success in promoting economic and social development. Taiwan's national policies to redistribute industrial development obviously paid off in reduced primacy. Japan's policies, such as they were, did not. Nonetheless, both have continued to advance human well being. Whatever the condition of primacy in Asia, it does not appear to be associated with any particular success or failure in promoting social and economic development.

ASIAN URBANIZATION FOR THE NEW MILLENNIUM: NEXT STEPS

What is next? What do these studies tell us about what should be done next? What more do we need to know, and what do we need to do to improve the quality of urban life? And it is not just the quality of urban life that is at stake. Cities have for long been the major centers of human advancement, but their effectiveness in promoting progress varies. Thus, the question becomes a broader one. How do we make cities more effective centers of human advancement? To answer these questions we need both better information on the urban condition and its dynamics, and a better understanding of how to act on that knowledge. That is, three are both research and policy or action issues.

TABLE 17.3 Changing measures of primacy in Asia: 1960, 1980 and 2000

Country	1960	1980	2000
Bangladesh			
R1	1.00	1.49	2.04
R2	1.50	2.46	3.43
China			
R1	0.60	0.61	0.51
R2	1.41	1.37	1.19

TABLE 17.3 (cont'd)

North Korea			
R1	–	–	–
R2	7.35	6.16	3.06
India			
R1	0.67	0.49	0.46
R2	1.32	1.04	1.05
Indonesia			
R1	1.14	1.26	1.37
R2	2.78	3.37	3.23
Japan			
R1	1.20	1.50	1.56
R2	1.76	2.19	2.40
Myanmar			
R1	–	–	–
R2	3.78	4.95	4.71
Pakistan			
R1	1.10	1.06	1.10
R2	1.89	1.75	1.84
Philippines			
R1	–	–	–
R2	9.84	9.70	8.68
South Korea			
R1	1.07	1.39	1.06
R2	2.05	2.74	2.58
Taiwan			
R1	0.81	0.94	0.81
R2	–	–	–
Thailand			
R1			8.17
R2			21.44

Research Issues

(1)   First, we surely need more scientific research and data gathering that will tell us more about the processes of urbanization, their causes, and consequences. We use the word processes advisedly. Although urbanization appears ubiquitous, and more and more driven by migration, it is still a process with much variation from country to country. We have already alluded to the need for better information on migration. Governments typically include questions relevant to migration in regular censuses. But we have also seen, especially in the Vietnam chapter, how effective and useful a national sample survey on migration can be. Thus, one can suggest three types of migration studies.

   (a)   Include migration relevant questions in regular censuses. Here it would be most useful if the United Nations Population Commission could assist in developing a standard set of migration questions for national censuses. This would facilitate both cross-national and time-series analyses that can tell urban planners and administrators more about the streams of humans that add to their cities.

   (b)   Make census data available in a timely fashion. We have often seen in these country studies that recent census data, usually for the year 2000 or 2001, are not yet available. Thus, the rich human resource of scholars and social scientists available in all countries are unable to examine census results to advance understanding of the migration process.

   (c)   Promote national sample surveys on migration-related topics. The technology of national sample surveying is well developed and is one of the most powerful research tools in the social sciences.

(2)   We have also noted the three sources of urban growth: natural increase, net in-migration, and expanding administrative boundaries.[7] There is substantial information about the first two, but very little on the third. We have seen the extensive Chinese

480

expansion of administrative boundaries (UNFPA 1987) or the boundary expansion of Singapore or Kobe during their modern development (Nihon 1985). We have also seen that cities in Java tend to be "under bounded," with extensive built-up areas spreading beyond the city boundaries; those in the Outer Islands tend to be over bounded, including large rural areas in the administrative boundaries. This is a variance that calls for explanation. What are its sources and consequences? The expansions of Kobe and Singapore were found to be dictated by the need to construct a more effective base for urban planning. A Philippines analyst (Fleiger 2000) noted that Mayors strive to include larger areas in their administrative boundaries since that increases their official status. Are there, then, financial advantages to urban officials arising from boundary expansion? We have suggested above that boundary expansion may be primarily a mechanism to increase the revenue base of a city. In any event, it is clear that boundary expansion as a mechanism of urban growth deserves greater study. To what extent has it contributed, along with natural increase and migration, to urban growth?

(3) Ageing. It is in some sense remarkable how quickly the major population problem has turned from growth to ageing. The world came to recognize the high cost of rapid population growth in the two decades following the end of the Second World War, led largely by Asia, it should be noted (Ness and Ando 1984). This led to major policy changes, from pro-natalism to fertility limitation, and the rapid growth of programs to limit fertility. For three decades, massive amounts of time, energy, and human and financial resources were mobilized and directed at reducing fertility. That movement spread to a more general attention to the wider problem of reproductive health and the status of girls and women.

While the problems of growth and reproductive health remain important, especially in the poorest countries, the problem of ageing has now gained considerable attention (Hermalin 2003 and UNFPA 2003). In some countries, the change in emphasis has been radical and has come very rapidly. In the 1950s, Singapore was severely pressed by rapid population growth and developed an extremely effective national family planning program. Fertility fell from high "traditional" levels to below replacement in less than one generation.

Now, Singapore is concerned with ageing and the potential for population decline. The proportion of the population 65 and over rose slowly from 2.1 per cent in 1960 to 7.2 per cent in 2000; it is projected to reach 25.6 per cent by 2030. South Korea shows a similar trajectory of rapid change. It, too, went from traditional to below replacement fertility in less than a generation. Its proportion 65 and older grew slowly from 3 to 7 per cent between 1950 and 2000; by 2030, the proportion is projected to reach 20 per cent.

A number of countries made similar, if slightly slower, transitions. China, India, Indonesia, Malaysia, Sri Lanka, Thailand, and Vietnam saw their proportion 65 and over grow slowly but remain below 5 per cent to 2000; all will have proportions reaching 9 (India and Indonesia) to 16 per cent (China), and growing rapidly, by 2030.

Japan made this transition much earlier, but it provides a dramatic vision of what is in store for the other countries. Its proportion 65 and over was already at 5 per cent in 1950; it grew to 17 per cent in 2000, and is projected to rise to 30 per cent by 2030.

These projections clearly demonstrate what can be done with the tools of demographic analysis. For social scientists, it now remains to assess how the aged will be distributed between rural and urban areas. We have already seen in most countries a kind of rural age bias. Is that likely to last? How will governments respond and what will be the most effective ways to deal with the ageing population?

Action Issues

To close this chapter and the book, we turn briefly to policies and programs. Here we wish to address something AUICK and its loose association of Asian Urban Administrators has been confronting since AUICK was born: how can urban administrators improve the quality of life and make their cities more effective places in which to live, work and play?

Much depends, of course, on the extent of the authority and responsibility urban administrators have. For the most part, this is not extensive. Everywhere, power, authority, and responsibility have been heavily concentrated in the central government. In its biannual surveys of urban administrators, AUICK has found that the urban administrators would prefer greater authority and responsibility, and feel that their personnel resources are capable of exercising greater initiative and control. This heavy centralization is now changing in quite important ways. Throughout Asia, there is a move toward decentralization and devolution of authority to lower administrative levels, including to cities. AUICK has encountered this movement for more than a decade, and recently recorded it in its study of five cities (Ness and Low 2000). The new Thai constitution mandates decentralization. The Philippines government has been undertaking devolution programs for some decades. These are only brief illustrations of a movement that is quite general in the region.

In some cases, this devolution has been no more than an out for the central government, allowing it to abdicate responsibility for human welfare without providing lower level units with the resources to carry that responsibility. But in many cases, there is now a new set of opportunities for urban administrators to take the initiative. The question AUICK continues to address is how to help those administrators work out more effective means to take advantage of those opportunities.

Kobe has been training small groups of urban administrators in integrated urban management for more than a decade. It has now designated a set of 13 cities as AUICK Associate Cities. These will be the focus of both training and research in the near future. It is hoped that this will build a critical mass of trained personnel in these Associate Cities and that those cities themselves can act as nodes of initiative, illustrating effective policies and procedures to other cities in each country.

One of the specific techniques AUICK has been promoting is dynamic modeling for urban systems. This was illustrated in a recent publication, *Five Cities: Modelling Asian Urban Population Environment Dynamics* (Ness and Low 2000). The modeling requires a collaborative effort between the city administration and local university natural and social scientists. A specific proposal was made in the *Five Cities* publication to create City-University Partnerships to collect the needed data and carry out the modeling exercises.

Dynamic modeling allows urban administrators to look into the future. This is done first by examining the recent past to chart critical movements and their sources. Then the model permits administrators to run scenarios that suggest possible futures. If these appear undesirable, administrators can then search for ways to alter processes to produce a more desirable outcome.

The major advantage of this kind of deliberate dynamic modeling is that assumptions are stated clearly and become highly visible. This means they can be challenged and changed. It is often noted that all planning requires assumptions about how different actions are connected: what causes certain things to happen, and what are the consequences of those happenings. We typically carry those assumptions in our heads and do not make them explicit. Deliberate dynamic modeling makes those assumptions visible. They can then be assessed, their validity determined, and they can be changed when necessary.

This kind of dynamic modeling also requires extensive cooperation across specializations. Different scientific disciplines and different administrative specializations are needed to determine, for example, what vehicle growth to expect in the future, how this will be related to road construction, traffic patterns and speed of movement, and what impact this will have on such things as human health. One could as well illustrate this need for inter-disciplinary cooperation with problems of water and sewage, electrical power, food production and movement, housing, education, health services, economic production, or parks and recreational facilities. The list is endless, but it also can be seen to coincide with specific areas of urban administrative responsibility.

ENDNOTES

1   Indeed, the origins of Sociology lie in the 18th–19th centuries, when scholars began to observe great differences between urban and rural people.

2   This is the sum of the squared shares of every city in a country in the national urban population.

3   Zipf 's law proposes that the log of city size regressed on the log of rank order produces a slope coefficient of -1.0. Krugman (1995) prefers to refer to this as Zipf's proposition rather than law.

4   IMR is the Infant Mortality Rate; Eo is life expectancy at birth; and TFR is the Total Fertility Rate.

5   GDP is Gross Domestic Product; PPP is the Parity Purchasing Power measure of per capita GDP.

6   It should be noted that Henderson (2002) found that a deviation from the rank size rule did in fact reduce productivity in most countries, though it enhanced productivity in the less developed countries. He used a somewhat different measure for primacy, however, the percent of the entire urban population that resides in the largest city. This is fairly closely associated with R1 and R2, but it has a different distribution. For the world as a whole and for various regions, it is not skewed to the right, but has a more normal distribution. Moreover, this measure is more closely associated with the conditions of the less developed regions.

7   There is another source in administrative changes that should not be confused with boundary expansion. This is reclassification. That is, as villages grow they may meet the minimum standard to be classed as an urban area and thus add to the number and population of urban places in a country. The growth from village to town still may have three sources.

APPENDIX
Asian Urban and Rural Population Growth Rates (%) 1950–2030

Country	1950–55	1975–80	2000–05	2025–30
South Asia				
Bangladesh				
Urban	3.89	10.68	4.33	2.63
Rural	1.88	1.30	1.28	**–0.06**
India				
Urban	2.39	3.66	2.29	2.52
Rural	1.91	1.63	1.22	**–0.26**
Nepal				
Urban	4.46	6.87	5.11	3.88
Rural	1.31	1.72	1.92	0.72
Pakistan				
Urba	4.31	4.12	3.54	3.01
Rural	1.42	2.44	2.02	0.44
Sri Lanka				
Urban	4.66	1.12	2.36	2.06
Rural	2.06	1.67	0.51	**–0.76**
Southeast Asia				
Cambodia				
Urban	2.24	2.25	5.54	3.22
Rural	2.14	**–1.88**	1.74	0.31
Indonesia				
Urban	3.30	4.96	3.59	1.53
Rural	1.43	1.50	**–0.63**	**–0.64**
Laos				
Urban	2.98	3.37	4.59	3.16
Rural	1.97	0.87	1.71	0.26
Malaysia				
Urban	5.52	4.52	2.86	1.56
Rural	1.94	0.86	0.07	**–0.36**

APPENDIX (cont'd)

Myanmar				
Urban	3.52	2.27	2.90	2.20
Rural	1.44	2.21	0.45	**−0.44**
Philippines				
Urban	4.11	3.73	3.19	1.48
Rural	2.56	2.07	**−0.19**	**−0.37**
Singapore (total)	4.90	1.30	1.74	0.24
Thailand				
Urban	4.77	4.70	2.12	2.57
Rural	2.74	1.81	0.90	**−0.42**
Vietnam				
Urban	4.23	2.48	3.06	2.53
Rural	1.54	1.88	0.71	**−0.25**
East Asia				
China				
Urban	4.34	3.90	3.22	1.14
Rural	1.49	0.93	**−0.83**	**−1.14**
Japan				
Urban	3.40	1.06	0.35	−0.16
Rural	**−0.78**	0.51	**−0.64**	**−1.74**
Republic of Korea				
Urban	3.68	4.92	1.32	0.31
Rural	0.23	**−2.17**	**−2.66**	**−1.11**
Taiwan				
Urban				
Rural				

References

Abeykoon, A. T. P. L. 1998. *Population and Manpower Resources of Sri Lanka, Natural Resources of Sri Lanka*. Colombo, Sri Lanka: Natural Resources, Energy and Science Authority of Sri Lanka.

Afsar, R. 2000. *Rural-Urban Migration in Bangladesh: Causes, Consequences and Challenges*. Dhaka, Bangladesh: The University Press Limited.

Alatas, Secha. 1993. Issues of Migration and Urbanization. Paper presented at the Meeting on Urban Population Distribution Pattern organized by the State Ministry for Population/National Family Planning Coordinating Board (NFPCB), 27 December, in Bandung.

Alprovich, G. A. 1993. An Exploratory Note of City Size Distribution: Evidence from Cross-Country Data, Urban Studies 30: 591–601.

Ananta, Aris Turro Wongkaren, and Evi N. Anwar. 1994. *Projection of Indonesian Population and Labor Force: 1995–2020*. Jakarta: Demographic Institute, Faculty of Economics, University of Indonesia.

Arif, G. M. and Sabiha Ibrahim. 1998. The Process of Urbanization in Pakistan, 1951–98. *The Pakistan Development Review* 37:4, Part II: 507–22.

Asian Development Bank (ADB)—Government of Bangladesh (GOB). 1996. *Study of Urban Poverty in Bangladesh, Final Report*. Dhaka, Bangladesh: Asian Development Bank.

AUICK. 1997. *AUICK: The First Decade: Lessons Learned and Views of the Future*. Kobe: AUICK.

Bai, Jianhua. 1986. The Situation of China's Urban Population. *Population Research*, Beijing, No. 2: 11–14.

Bangladesh Bureau of Statistics. 1977. *Bangladesh Population Census 1974*. Dhaka, Bangladesh: Ministry of Planning.

———. 1984. *Bangladesh Population Census 1981*. Dhaka, Bangladesh: Ministry of Planning.

———. 1988. *Report on Labour Force Survey 1984–85*. Dhaka, Bangladesh: Ministry of Planning.

———. 1992. *Report on Labour Force Survey 1990–91*. Dhaka, Bangladesh: Ministry of Planning.

———. 1994. *Bangladesh Population Census 1991*. Vol. 1. Dhaka, Bangladesh: Ministry of Planning.

———. 1995. *Report on Labour Force Survey 1995*. Dhaka, Bangladesh: Ministry of Planning

———. 1997. *Bangladesh Population Census 1991*. Vol. 3. Dhaka, Bangladesh: Ministry of Planning.

———. 1998. *Household Expenditure Survey 1995–96*. Dhaka, Bangladesh: Ministry of Planning.

———. 1999. *Bangladesh Population 1991*. Vol. 4. Dhaka, Bangladesh: Ministry of Planning.

————. 2000. *Report of Sample Vital Registration System 1997–98*. Dhaka, Bangladesh: Ministry Planning.

————. 2001a. 1999. *Statistical Yearbook of Bangladesh*. Dhaka, Bangladesh: Ministry of Planning.

————. 2001b. *Population Census 2001 Preliminary Report*. Dhaka, Bangladesh: Ministry of Planning.

————. 2001c. *Report of the Health and Demographic Survey 2000*. Dhaka, Bangladesh: Ministry Planning.

Barkley, Andrew P. 1991. The Determinants of Inter-district Labor In-migration in Pakistan, 1971–80. *The Pakistan Development Review* 30(3): 275–96.

Begum, A. 1999. *Destination Dhaka, Urban Migration: Expectations and Reality*. Dhaka, Bangladesh: The University Press Limited.

Broeze, Frank, ed. 1989. *Brides of the Sea: Port Cities of East Asia from the 16th–20th Centuries*. Honolulu: University of Hawaii Press.

Browning, H.L. and J.P. Gibbs. 1961. Some Measures of Demographic and Spatial Relationships among Cities. *Urban Research Method*. Edited by J. P. Gibbs. Princeton, N.J.: D. Von Norstrand Co.

Browning, Harley, and Jack P. Gibbs. 1961. Systems of Cities. *Urban research Methods*. Edited by Jack P. Gibbs. Princeton: Van Norstrand Co.

Buckley, Robert M., and Fredricio Mini. 2002. *From Commissions to Mayors: Cities in the Transition Economies*. Infrastructure Sector Unit, Europe and Central Asia Region. New York: The World Bank.

Burma. 1983. *Burma 1983 Population Census*. Rangoon: Census Division.

————. 1997. *Statistical Yearbook, 1997*. Rangoon: Central Statistical Organization.

————. 2001. *Statistical Yearbook 2001*. Rangoon: Central Statistical Organization.

CBS, NFPCB, MOH, DHS. 1988. *1987 Indonesia Demographic and Health Survey*. Jakarta.

————. 1992. *1991 Indonesia Demographic and Health Survey*. Jakarta.

————. 1995. *1994 Indonesia Demographic and Health Survey*. Jakarta.

————. 1998. *1997 Indonesia Demographic and Health Survey*. Jakarta.

CCSC (Central Census Steering Committee). 1991. *Completed Census Results*,

————. 2000. *Population and Housing*

Census Vietnam 1999. Sample Results. Hanoi: The Gioi Publishers.

Central Bureau of Statistics. 1966. *1961 Population Census*. Jakarta.

————. 1975. *1971 Population Census*. Jakarta.

————. 1983. *1980 Population Census*. Jakarta.

————. 1992. *1990 Population Census*. Jakarta.

————. 1997. *Population Migration and Urbanization in Indonesia: Result of 1995 Intercensal*. Jakarta.

————. 1997a. *Profile of In-Migration in Six Big Cities, Result of 1995 Survey of Urbanization*. Jakarta.

————. 2002. *2000 Population Census*. Jakarta.

Chandler, Titus, and Gerald Fox. 1974. *3000 Years of Urban Growth*. New York: Academic Press.

Chen, C. S. 1959. *A Geography of Taiwan*, Chapter 7, Vol. 1, Research Report No. 94. Taipei, Taiwan: Fu-Ming Geographical Institute of Economic Development.

Cherunilam, Francis. 1984. *Urbanization in Developing Countries*. Bombay: Himalaya Publishing House.

Cheshire, Paul. 1999. Trends in Size and Distribution of Urban Areas. Volume 3, Applied Urban Economics. *Handbook of Regional and Urban Economics*. Edited by Paul Cheshire and Edwin S. Mils. Amsterdam: North-Holland.

Chonawongse, Krasae, Peerasit Kamnuansilpa, Supawatanakorn Wongthanavasu, and Yupin Techamanee. 2000, Khon Kaen: Heart of the Northeast. *Five Cities: Modelling Asian Urban Population Environment Dynamics*. Edited by Gayl D. Ness and Michael Low. Singapore: Oxford University Press.

Chowdhury, Hamidul Haq. 1989. *Memoirs*. Kajla, Dhaka: Associated Printers Ltd. for the Hamid Halima Trust.

Chowdhury, R. H. 1980. *Urbanization in Bangladesh*. Dhaka, Bangladesh: Center for Urban Studies. Dhaka University.

Connell, John. 2000. Urbanization and Settlement in the Pacific. *Resettlement Policy and Practice in Asia and the Pacific*. Manila: Asian Development Bank.

CPDF. 2004. *Fact Sheet on Population*. Manila: Philippines Legislators Committee on Population and Development Foundation.

Davis, J., and J. V. Henderson. 2002. Evidence of the Political Economy of the Urbanization Process. *Journal of Urban Economics* vol. 53, no. 1: 98–125.

Department of Census and Statistics. 1995. *Sri Lanka Demographic and Health Survey 1993*. Colombo, Sri Lanka.

———. 2001. *Census of Population and Housing 2001: Preliminary Release*. Colombo, Sri Lanka.

———. 2001. *Sri Lanka Demographic and Health Survey 2000: Preliminary Report*. Colombo, Sri Lanka.

Department of Statistics. 1993. *General Report of the Population Census, 1991*. Malaysia.

———. 1996. *Internal Migration in Malaysia. Population Census Monograph Series, No. 2*. Malaysia.

———. 2001. *Population and Housing Census of Malaysia—Population Distribution and Basic Characteristics*. Malaysia.

———. 2001. *Preliminary Count Report for Urban and Rural Areas, Population and Housing Census of Malaysia, 2000*. Malaysia.

———. 2002. *Population and Housing Census of Malaysia—Education and Social Characteristics of the Population*. Malaysia.

———. 2003. *Population and Housing Census of Malaysia—Economic Characteristics of the Population*. Malaysia.

———. Various Years. *Vital Statistics, Peninsular Malaysia*.

DHS. 2004. *DHS Dimensions* Vol. 6, No. 1. Washington, D.C.: Demographic and Health Surveys Project.

Eberhard, Wolfram. 1977. *A History of China*. Berkeley: University of California Press.

Economic and Social Commission for Asia and Pacific (ESCAP). 1993. *The State of Urbanization in Asia and the Pacific*. Bangkok, Thailand: ESCAP.

———. 1976. *Population of Sri Lanka: Country Monograph Series No. 4*. Bangkok, Thailand.

———. 1980. *Migration, Urbanization and Development in Sri Lanka*. Bangkok, Thailand.

ESCAP-UN. 1993. *State of Urbanization in Asia and the Pacific*. New York.

Fan, Lida and Shaoyan Sun. 1992. Economic System, Agriculture Surplus and Urbanization in China. *Population Journal*, Changchun: 11–19.

Firman, Tommy. 1996. Urbanization Pattern in Indonesia: Analysis of 1980 and 1990 Population Censuses. *Population Mobility in Indonesia*. Jakarta: Demography Institute, Faculty of Economics, University of Indonesia and State Ministry for Population/NFPCB.

Fleiger, Wilhelm. 2000. Cebu City: Heart of the Central Philippines. *Five Cities: Modeling Asian Urban population Environment Dynamics*. Edited by Gayl D. Ness and Michael Low. Singapore: Oxford University Press of Singapore.

General Statistical Office (GSO). 1991. *Detailed Analysis of Sample Results*. Hanoi: Vietnam Population Census 1989.

———. 2000. *Report of Vietnam Population Projection Results, 1999–2024*.

Government of Pakistan. 1995. *Multiple Indicators Clusters Survey of Pakistan*. Ministry of Health.

———. 1998. District Census Reports. Population Census Organization.

———. 1998. Provincial Census Report of Punjab. Population Census Organization.

———. 1998. Provincial Census Reports. Population Census Organization.

———. 1998–99. *Pakistan Integrated Household Survey (PIHS)*, Round 3. Islamabad: Federal Bureau of Statistics.

———. 2001a. *Economic Survey 2000–2001*. Islamabad: Ministry of Finance, Economic Adviser's Wing.

———. 2001b. *Ten-Year Perspective Development Plan 2001–11 and Three-Year Development Program 2001–04*. Islamabad: Planning Commission.

———. 2002. *Interim population sector perspective plan 2012*. Islamabad: Ministry of Population Welfare.

Government of Thailand. 2001. *The Ninth National Economic and Social Development Plan (2002–6)*. Bangkok: Office of the National Economic and Social Development Board.

Gunatilleke, Godfrey. 1973. Rural Urban Balance and Development. The Experience in Sri Lanka. *Marga* Vol. 2. No. 1. Colombo.

Guo, S., and Chuenbin Liu. 1990. *Unbalanced China: the Past, Present and Future of Urbanization*. Hebei People's Publishing House.

Hassan, Syed Fayyaz, and Hafiz A. Pasha. 1986. Land Densities in Karachi.' *Pakistan Journal of Applied Economics* V: 2: 143–62.

491

Henderson, V. 2002. Urbanization in Developing Countries. *The World Bank Research Observer* 17(1): 89–112. Washington DC, USA: The World Bank.

Hugo, Graeme, Terence H. Hull, Valerie J. Hull, and Gavin W. Jones. 1986. *The Demographic Dimension in Indonesia Development.* Singapore, Oxford, New York: Oxford University Press.

Hugo, Graeme. 1981. Levels, Trends, and Patterns of Urbanization, Migration, and Development in Indonesia. *Comparative Study on Migration, Urbanization and Development in the ESCAP Region.* New York: United Nations.

Huq, M. N., and J. Cleland. 1990. *Bangladesh Fertility Survey 1989. Main Report.* Dhaka, Bangladesh: National Institute of Population Research and Training (NIPORT).

ICOMP. 2003. Reproductive Health Challenges I the Philippines. *Newsletter on Management of Population Programmes* Vol. XXVIII, Nos. 3 & 4: 1.

Ingram, Gregory K. 1998. Patterns of Metropolitan Development: What Have We Learned? *Urban Studies* 35 (7): 1019–35.

IOS (Institute of Sociology). 1999. *Migration and Health Survey Vietnam 1997*, Survey Report. Hanoi: Institute of Sociology and Population Studies and Training Center.

Irfan, Mohammad. 1986. Migration and Development in Pakistan: Some Selected Issues. *The Pakistan Development Review* 25:4, Part II: 743–55.

Islam, N. 1994. *Urban Research in Bangladesh.* Dhaka, Bangladesh: Center for Urban Studies, Dhaka University.

———. 1996. *The Urban Poor in Bangladesh.* Dhaka, Bangladesh: Center for Urban Studies, Dhaka University.

———. *Urbanization Migration and Development in Bangladesh: Recent Trends and Emerging Issues.* Dhaka, Bangladesh: Center for Policy Dialogue.

Islam, N., N. Huda, Francis B. Narayan and Pradumna B. Rana. 1997. *Addressing the Urban Poverty Agenda in Bangladesh: Critical Issues and the 1995 Survey Findings.* Dhaka, Bangladesh: The University Press Limited.

Jia, Shaofeng and Xiangjing Meng. 1996. Analysis and Projections on Population and Employment in China. *Population Science of China*, Beijing, No. 6: 26–30.

Kartasasmita, Ginanjar. 1995. Land Management in Development Growth and Equality. Paper presented at the Land Management in Development Growth and Equality Workshop organized by CIDES and National Development Plan Bureau, 10 October 1995, in Bandung.

Karyoedi, Mochtarram, Ibnu Sabri, and Iwan P. Kusumantoro. 1993. Study of Urban Population Distribution in Indonesia. Paper presented at the Meeting on Urban Population Distribution Pattern organized by the State Ministry for Population/National Family Planning Coordinating Board, 27 December, in Bandung.

Khan, Amir Nawaz and Atta-ur-Rahman. 1999/2000. Urbanization: Trends and Prospects in Pakistan. *Pakistan Journal of Geography* 9 & 10: 1 & 2: 31–44.

Khan, Asmatullah. 1996. Urbanization and its Impact on Rural-Urban Economic Integration in TWCs: The Case Study of Peshawar, NWFP, Pakistan. *Journal of Rural Development & Administration* 28:1: 130–58.

Kitisin, Praphan . 2003. Environmental Health and Air Quality in the City of Bangkok. Paper presented at the WHO meeting, in Mississauga, Canada.

Kiyani, M. Framurz and H. B. Siyal. 1991. Dimensions of Urban Growth in Pakistan. *The Pakistan Development Review* 30:4, Part II: 681–91.

Kok Kim Lian and Chan Kok Eng. 1988. *Urbanization in Malaysia: Patterns, Determinants and Consequences*. Malaysia: National Population and Family Development Board.

Krugman, Paul. 1995. *Development, Geography and Economic Theory*. Cambridge, MA: The MIT Press.

Laos. 1997. *Results from the Population Census 1995*. Vientiane: State Planning Commission, National Statistical Office.

Leete, R. 1996. *Malaysia's Demographic Transition—Rapid Development, Culture, and Politics*. Kuala Lumpur: Oxford University Press.

Li, Ruojian. 1994. Study of Population Migration. *Population Research*, Beijing, Vol. 18, No. 4: 23–8.

Lim Jung Duk. 2000. Promises and Challenges of Rapid Growth.–*Five Cities: Modeling Asian Urban population Environment Dynamics*. Edited by Gayl D. Ness and Michael Low. Singapore: Oxford University Press of Singapore.

Linsky, Arnold. 1969. *Urbanization in Newly Developed Countries*. Edited by Gerald Breeze. New York: Prentice Hall.

Liu, Paul K. C., and H. H. Tsai. 1991. Urban Growth and Employment Restructuring in Taiwan. *The Extended Metropolis Settlement Transition in Asia*. Edited by Norton Ginsburg, Bruce Koppel, and T. G. McGee. Honolulu: University of Hawaii Press.

Local City Government of Jakarta. 1994. *City of Jakarta in Data and Information*. Jakarta.

Ma, Xia. 1990. Migration Pattern and Its Transit in China. *Social Science of China*, Beijing, No. 5: 141–53.

Malaysia. 2000. *Eighth Malaysia Plan*. Kuala Lumpur: Government of Malaysia.

McEvedy, Colin, and Richard Jones. 1978. *Atlas of World Population History*. Middlesex, England: Penguin Books.

McGee, Terry G. 1991, The Emergence of Desakota Regions in Asia: Expanding a Hypothesis. *The Extended Metropolis: Settlement Transition in Asia*. Edited by Norton Ginsburg, Bruce Koppel, and Terry G. McGee. Honolulu: University of Hawaii Press.

Ministry of Construction (MOC). 1992. *Data Book National Urban*. Hanoi: National Institute for Urban and Rural Planning.

Ministry of Construction (MOC). 1999. *Guidelines on master planning of urban development in Vietnam toward 2020*. Hanoi: Ministry of Construction.

Ministry of Health and Indigenous Medicine. 1998. *Population and Reproductive Health Policy*. Colombo, Sri Lanka.

Ministry of Housing and Local Government and Universiti Sains Malaysia. 1999. *A Study on the Policy and Strategies for the Elimination of Squatters in Malaysia*. Malaysia.

Mitra et al. 1997. *Bangladesh Demographic Health Survey, 1996–97*. Dhaka, Bangladesh: National Institute of Population Research and Training (NIPORT), Mitra and Associates and ORC Macro.

Mitra, S. N., and G. M. Kamal. 1985. *Bangladesh Contraceptive Prevalence Survey 1983: Final Report*. Dhaka, Bangladesh: Mitra and Associates.

Mitra, S. N., A. Larson, G. Foo, and S. Islam. 1990. *Bangladesh Contraceptive Prevalence Survey 1989: Final Report*. Dhaka, Bangladesh: Mitra and Associates.

Mitra, S. N., C. Lerman, and S. Islam. 1993. *Bangladesh Contraceptive Prevalence Survey 1991: Final Report*. Dhaka, Bangladesh: Mitra and Associates.

Mitra, S. N., M. N. Ali, S. Islam, A. R. Cross, and T. Saha. 1994. *Bangladesh Demographic and Health Survey 1993–94*. Calverton, Maryland: National Institute of Population Research and Training (NIPORT), Mitra and Associates and Macro International Inc.

Mumford, Louis. 1961. *The City in History*. Middlesex, England: Penguin Books.

Murphey, Rhodes. 1989. On the evolution of the port city. *Brides of the Sea: Port Cities of East Asia from the 16th–20th Centuries*. Edited by Frank Broeze. Honolulu: University of Hawaii Press. 223–45.

Myanmar, Central Statistical Office. 1997. *Statistical Yearbook 1997*. Yangon, Myanmar: Central Statistical Office.

National Physical Planning Department. 2002. *National Physical Planning Policy*. Bataramulla, Sri Lanka.

National Population and Family Development Board. 1994. *Malaysian Population and Family Survey*. Malaysia.

Nepal, Ministry of Population and Environment. 2000. *Nepal Population Report 2000*. Kathmandu: Singh Durbar.

Nepal. 1987. *Demographic Sample Survey, 1986/87*. Kathmandu: Ramshah Path.

Ness, Gayl D. 1962. Asian Overurbanization and the Industrial Distribution of the Labor Force. *Proceedings of the 2nd Bi-annual Conference of the 2nd International Association of Asia*, Taipei, September. 657–75.

———. 1967. *Bureaucracy and Rural Development in Malaysia*. Berkeley, CA: University of California Press.

———. 1993. The Long View: Population-Environment Dynamics in Historical Perspective. *Population-Environment Dynamics: Ideas and Observations*. Edited by Gayl D. Ness, William D. Drake, and Steven R. Brechin. Ann Arbor: University of Michigan Press. 33–56.

Ness, Gayl D., and Hirofumi Ando. 1984. *The Land is Shrinking: Population Planning in Asia*. Baltimore: Johns Hopkins University Press.

Ness, Gayl D., and Michael M. Low, eds. 2000. *Five Cities: Modelling Asian Urban Population Environment Dynamics*. Singapore: Oxford University Press.

Ness, Gayl D., William D. Drake, and Steven R. Brechin, eds. 1993. *Population-Environment Dynamics: Ideas and Observations*. Ann Arbor: University of Michigan Press.

Nihon University Population Research Institute. 1986. *Population Redistribution in Planned Port Cities*. Tokyo: Nihon University Population Research Institute.

NIPORT and ORC Macro. 2002. *Bangladesh Maternal Health Services and Maternal Mortality Survey 2001. Preliminary Report*. Dhaka, Bangladesh: National Institute of Population Research and Training (NIPORT) and ORC Macro.

NIPORT, Mitra and Associates, and ORC Macro. 2001. *Bangladesh Demographic and Health Survey 1999–2000*. Dhaka, Bangladesh: National Institute of

Population Research and Training (NIPORT), Mitra and Associates, and ORC Macro.

Parry, J. H. 1974. *The Discovery of the Sea*. New York: The Dial Press.

Parveen, Azra. 1993. Inter-Provincial Migration in Pakistan: 1971–81. *The Pakistan Development Review* 32:4, Part II: 725–35.

Pasha, Hafiz A. and Tariq Hassan. 1982. Development ranking of districts of Pakistan. *Pakistan Journal of Applied Economics* I: 2: 157–92.

Pasha, Hafiz A., Salman Malik, and Haroon Jamal. 1990. The Changing Profile of Regional Development in Pakistan.–*Pakistan Journal of Applied Economics* 10:1: 1–26.

Pirenne, Henri. 1952. *Medieval Cities: Their Origins and the Revival of Trade*, trans Frank D. Halsey. Princeton: Princeton University Press.

PRB Population Reference Bureau 2002. *Women of Our World*. (Washington, DC: Population Reference Bureau.)

Prijono, Tjiptoherijanto. 1997. Poverty Alleviation (Pengentasan Kemiskinan). Paper presented at the Seminar on the Role of Private University on Poverty Alleviation in Indonesia, 26 September, in Bandar Lampung.

Reddy, A. Geeta. 1994. *The Indian Ocean Countries: Comparisons in Urbanization and Primate City Growth*. New Delhi: Sterling Publishers, Private Limited.

Reeves, Peter, Frank Broeze, and Kenneth McPherson. 1989. Studying the Asian Port City. *Brides of the Sea: Port Cities of East Asia from the 16th–20th Centuries*. Edited by Frank Broeze. Honolulu: University of Hawaii Press. 29–53.

Reid, Anthony. 1989. The organization of production in the pre-colonial Southeast Asian port city. *Brides of the Sea: Port Cities of East Asia from the 16th–20th Centuries*. Edited by Frank Broeze. Honolulu: University of Hawaii Press. 54–74.

Rukanuddin, Abdul Razzaque and M. Naseem Iqbal Farooqui. 1988. *The State of Population in Pakistan, 1987*. Islamabad: National Institute of Population Studies (NIPS).

Siddiqui, K., J. Ahmed, A. Awal and M. Ahmed. 2000. *Overcoming the Governance Crisis in Dhaka City*. Dhaka, Bangladesh: University Press Limited.

Speare, Jr. Alden, Paul K. C. Liu, and Ching-lung Tsay. 1988. *Urbanization and Development: The Rural-Urban Transition in Taiwan*. Boulder & London: Westview Press.

State Ministry for Population and Environment. 1992. *Population of Indonesia During the First Long Term Development Plan*. Jakarta

State Office of Census. 2000. *Handbook of the Fifth Census of China*. Statistics Publishing House of China.

Sun, T. H. 2001. The Impacts of a Family Planning Program on Contraceptive/Fertility Behavior in Taiwan. *Journal of Population Studies'* No.33: 45–92. Taipei, Taiwan: Population and Gender Studies Center, National Taiwan University.

Tey Nai Peng, Pazim Othman, Tan Poo Chang, and Ng Sor Tho. 2000. *Consequences of Rural Depopulation in Peninsular Malaysia*. Malaysia: University of Malaya.

Tey Nai Peng. 1988. Migration, Job Mobility and Income Differentials in the Klang Valley, Melaka and Johor Bahru. *Current Issues in Labour Migration in Malaysia—A Collection of Seminar Papers.* Kuala Lumpur: National Union of Plantation Workers and the University of Malaya.

Thwin, A. A., M. A. Islam, A. H. Baqui, W. A. Reinke, and R. E. Black. 1996. *Health and Demographic Profile of the Urban Population of Bangladesh: An Analysis of Selected Indicators. Special Report No. 47.* Dhaka, Bangladesh: ICDDR,B.

Tjiptoherijanto, Prijono. 1995. Problems of a Large Cities: with Reference City of Jakarta. Paper presented at the Sixteenth General Assembly and Conference of the Eastern Regional Organization for Public Administration (EROPA), 10–16 September, in Tokyo, Japan.

Todaro, M. P. 1969. A Model for Labor, Migration and Urban Unemployment in Less Developed Countries. *American Economic Review* 59: 138–48.

Todaro, M. P. 1997. Urbanization and Rural-Urban Migration: Theory and Policy. *Economic Development.* 6th ed. Addison-Wesley Publishing Company.

Turner, Billy L. et al. 1990. *The Earth as Transformed by Human Action.* Cambridge, England: Cambridge University Press.

Ullah, A. K. M. A, A. Rahman, and M. Murshed. 1999. *Poverty and Migration: Slums of Dhaka City the Realities.* Dhaka, Bangladesh: Association for Rural Development Studies.

UNDP. 2003. *Thailand Human Development Report 2003.* Bangkok: United Nations Development Program.

UNESCO. 1957. Urbanization in Asia and the Far East: proceedings of a joint UN/ UNESCO Seminar (in cooperation with The International Labor Office) on urbanization in the ECAFE Region, Bangkok, 8–18 August 1956. Calcutta: UNESCO.

United Nations. 1999. *World Urbanization Prosepects 1999.* New York: United Nations

———. 2000. *World Population Prospects: The 2000 Revision.* New York: United Nations.

———. 2001. *World Urbanization Prospects: The 1999 Revision.* New York: United Nations.

Urban and Housing Development Department. *Urban and Regional Development Statistics.* Council for Economic Planning and Development, Executive Yuan Taipei, Taiwan, respective years.

Volume I. Hanoi: Vietnam Population Census 1989.

Wang, Fang. 1999. The Sustainable Way of Urbanization in China: Limitations of the Current Urban Policy. Paper presented at The Second National Conference on Population, Resources and Environment, 8–10 December, in Beijing.

Wen, C. P., S. F. Tsai, and J. P. Guo. 1989. Mortality Analysis in Taiwan: Geographic Differences. *Mortality Analysis in Taiwan.* (1989 IBMS Yearbook, Vol. One). Edited by C. P. Wen and C. J. Chen. Taipei: Institute of Biomedical Sciences, Academia Sinica.

Whitmore, Thomas M. et al. 1990 Long Term Population Changes. *The Earth as Transformed by Human Action.* Edited by Billy Turner et al. Cambridge, England: Cambridge University Press. 25–39.

Williamson, Jeffrey G. 1988. Migration and Urbanization.*Handbook of Development of Economics*. Vol. 1. Edited by Hollis Chenery and T. N. Srinivasan. Elsevier Publishers.

World Bank. 1984. *Economic and Social Development: An Overview of Regional Differential and Related Processes*, main report from Indonesia: *Selected Aspect of Spatial Development, Report No. 4776-IND*. Country Program Department, East Asia and Pacific Regional Office, World Bank.

———. 1994. *Indonesia: Sustaining Development*. Washington D.C.

———. 1998/99. *World Development Report*. Washington, DC: World Bank.

———. 2004. Online statistics from the World Bank.

Xie, Wenhui. 1987. *China's Medium-Sized Cities the Urban Hierarchy and in the National Political-Administrative Structure*. UNFPA,'*Report of the Conference on Population and Development in Medium-Sized Cities*, Kobe, Japan, 11–14 August. New York: UNFPA.

Yang, Chunzhi and Wenxuan Gu. 2000. Summary of the Panel Discussion on the Research of Object and Strategy of Urbanization. *Urban Studies*, Beijing, No. 1: 6–11.

Yang, Lixun. 1999. *Strategies of Urbanization and Urban Development*. Guangzhou: Guangdong Publisher for Advanced Education.

Yang, Yunyan. 1994. *Migration and Long Term Strategies of Development of China*. Wuhan Publishing House.

Yap, Lorene Y.L. 1977. The Attraction of Cities: A Review of the Migration Literature. *Journal of Development Economics* 4: 239–64.

Zeng, Yi. 1987. Exploring the Impact of Population Urbanization on Population Control in China. *Population and Economics*, Beijing, No. 6: 30–6.

Zhu, Baoshu. 1999. Urbanization in China: From the Controlled Development to the Control in the Development. Paper presented at The Second National Conference on Population, Resources and Environment, 8–10 December, in Beijing.

Zipf, George Kingsley. 1941. *National Unity and Disunity: The Nation as a Bio-Social Organism*. Bloomington, Indiana: The Principia Press.

Index

Titles on Geography and Environmental Research

3075   92